Burton Anderson's

BEST ITALIAN WINES

Burton Anderson's

BEST ITALIAN WINES

WEBSTERS

LITTLE, BROWN AND COMPANY

LONDON

A LITTLE,BROWN/WEBSTERS BOOK

This edition first published in 2001 by
Little,Brown and Company (U.K.)
Brettenham House,
Lancaster Place,
London WC2 7EN, U.K.

Distributed in the U.S.A and Canada by
Antique Collectors' Club, Ltd
Market Street Industrial Park
Wappingers' Falls
N.Y. 12590
U.S.A.

First published as:
101 Grandi Vini Rossi d'Italia and
101 Grandi Vini Bianchi d'Italia
Copyright © 2000 and 2001
Colophon srl
San Polo 1978 Venezia (Italy)
Created and designed by Andrea Grandese

CORPORATE SALES
Companies, institutions and other organizations wishing to make bulk purchases of
this title should contact the Little,Brown (U.K.) Special Sales Department on +44(0)20-7911 8089;
in the U.S., contact Antique Collectors' Club on (845) 297 0003.

Page 2: photograph shows Felsina's Rancia vineyards in the
commune of Castelnuovo Berardenga in southern Chianti Classico (see page 284)

CONVERSIONS

Length	Weight
1 meter = 1.0936 yd	1 kilogram = 2.2046 lb
1 kilometer = 0.6214 miles	
Area	**Temperature**
1 hectare = 2.4711 acres	Celsius (or Centigrade): Under standard
Volume	conditions, water boils at 100°C and freezes at
1 liter = 2.2 pints (U.S.)	0°C. To convert Celsius into Fahrenheit,
1.76 pint (U.K.)	multiply by 1.8 and add 32.

Contents

The Northwest

The Northeast

Central Italy

The South

The Islands

Red wine producers

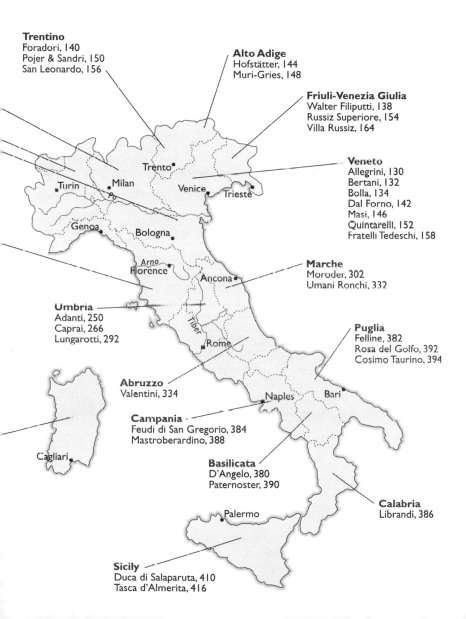

Trentino
Foradori, 140
Pojer & Sandri, 150
San Leonardo, 156

Alto Adige
Hofstätter, 144
Muri-Gries, 148

Friuli-Venezia Giulia
Walter Filiputti, 138
Russiz Superiore, 154
Villa Russiz, 164

Veneto
Allegrini, 130
Bertani, 132
Bolla, 134
Dal Forno, 142
Masi, 146
Quintarelli, 152
Fratelli Tedeschi, 158

Marche
Moroder, 302
Umani Ronchi, 332

Umbria
Adanti, 250
Caprai, 266
Lungarotti, 292

Puglia
Felline, 382
Rosa del Golfo, 392
Cosimo Taurino, 394

Abruzzo
Valentini, 334

Campania
Feudi di San Gregorio, 384
Mastroberardino, 388

Basilicata
D'Angelo, 380
Paternoster, 390

Calabria
Librandi, 386

Sicily
Duca di Salaparuta, 410
Tasca d'Almerita, 416

Trento
Turin   Milan
Venice   Trieste
Genoa   Bologna
Arno
Florence   Ancona
Tiber
Rome
Naples   Bari
Cagliari
Palermo

White wine producers

Alto Adige
Abbazia di Novacella, 166
Arunda Vivaldi, 170
Produttori Colterenzio, 182
Peter Dipoli, 188
Hofstätter, 200
Alois Lageder, 206
Cantina Produttori San Michele Appiano, 230
Cantina Produttori di Termeno, 234
Tiefenbrunner, 236
Elena Walch, 244

Friuli-Venezia Giulia
Bastianich, 172
Borgo del Tiglio, 174
La Castellada, 178
Cantina Produttori Cormons, 186
Girolamo Dorigo, 190
Livio Felluga, 192
Gravner, 198
Vinnaioli Jermann, 204
Lis Neris, 208
Livon, 210
Miani, 216
Pierpaolo Pecorari, 218
Rocca Bernarda, 224
Ronco del Gelso, 226
Schiopetto, 232
Venica, 238
Vie di Romans, 240
Villa Russiz, 242

Veneto
Anselmi, 168
La Cappuccina, 176
Col Vetoraz, 184
Gini, 196
Inama, 202
Maculan, 212
Pieropan, 220
Ruggeri, 228

Emilia-Romagna
Fattoria Zerbina, 246

Umbria
Castello della Sala, 342
Palazzone, 360

Marche
Bucci, 338
Coroncino, 344
Fazi Battaglia, 350
Garofoli, 354
Fattoria la Monacesca, 358
Santa Barbara, 368
Sartarelli, 370
Umani Ronchi, 374

Abruzzo
Masciarelli, 356
Valentini, 376

Campania
D'Ambra, 396
Feudi di San Gregorio, 398
Mastroberardino, 400
Terredora Di Paolo, 402
Villa Matilde, 404

Sicily
Marco De Bartoli, 424
Florio, 426
Hauner, 430
Murana, 432
Pellegrino, 434
Planeta, 436
Tasca d'Almerita, 438

Introduction

I taly might well be envisioned as a young wine country were it not for a culture of grapes and vines that dates back beyond the Romans, Greeks and Etruscans. Rejuvenated, or perhaps reborn, would aptly describe the ancient land of vineyards that over the last quarter of a century has recorded the most sweeping changes in the history of wine.

Witnessing this revolution has been an inspiration and a challenge. When I arrived in the 1960s, Italy was known for tasty if rustic local wines and mass-market versions of cheap and cheerful Soave, Valpolicella, Frascati and above all Chianti in straw-covered flasks. Admirable winemaking traditions existed here and there. But foreign critics, myself included, would not have seriously compared even the most esteemed of Italian wines with a ranking cru of Burgundy, Bordeaux or Champagne.

Since then, techniques have evolved from antiquated to avant-garde with stunning rapidity in the country that regularly produces more types of wine from more grape varieties than any other. The challenge has been to keep abreast of the relentless changes during an era that has been characterized as Italy's modern renaissance of wine.

Agonizing decisions

The advent of the new millennium seemed an appropriate time to reflect on my experiences with a tribute to wines that have inspired me over the decades. My selections are collected in this volume, though I admit that the choices involved agonizing decisions, for there were many worthy candidates.

The wines were picked on the basis of proven class and style backed by the reputations of their producers, though the indispensable requirement was that they have provided me with thoroughly enjoyable drinking. I do not pretend that my personal selections constitute a definitive list of Italy's finest wines. The choices were purposely limited to one red and one white wine per cellar, even though certain producers might have had more types that qualify.

A major share of my selection comes from northern and central regions, exemplified by the prominence of reds from Piedmont and Tuscany and white and sparkling wines from Friuli-Venezia Giulia, Trentino-Alto Adige, Veneto and Lombardy. Still, the field does represent a reasonable cross-section of current premium production in Italy with wines from a wide range of grape varieties, both native and foreign, from all parts of the country.

Italy on average is the world's largest producer of wine, though only about 20 percent of production is classified under denominations of controlled origin (see Labels and laws, page 19). Yet all but a few of my choices qualify as DOCG, DOC or IGT (a general category for typical wines), indicating that the long-criticized system of controls has taken effect in the premium field.

Each wine is presented in a profile with details about vineyards and winemaking techniques along with background information about the estates and producers. Comments on the style and maturity of the wine are followed by guidelines to ideal serving temperatures, preferred glasses and matches with foods, emphasizing regional and local dishes.

In an era when tastes in wine have become increasingly standardized, Italy has asserted its role as the world champion of diversity. The country is a treasure trove of local grape varieties. Some are well known, though the merits of many are only gradually being discovered.

My selections reveal a bias for wines from native vines, Sangiovese and Nebbiolo chief among them. Nor would I deny a special feeling for the wines of Tuscany, where I make my home and do most of my tasting (preferably with food). It is no coincidence that Chianti, Brunello di Montalcino and the so-called Super-Tuscans based on Sangiovese are so prominent in the field.

Covering the country

In the northwest, Piedmont is amply represented by the aristocratic Barolo and Barbaresco, along with Barbera, the once common red now triumphantly on the rise, and Dolcetto, the prince of wines for every day. Piedmont is also the source of lightly bubbly white Moscato d'Asti and fully sparkling Asti from the same grape. Liguria's gems are white Pigato and Vermentino.

In northeastern Italy, I've admired the renewed stature of Verona's Soave, Valpolicella and, especially, Amarone, as well as the Prosecco that makes bubbly wines in the hills north of Venice. Friuli-Venezia Giulia is amply represented by the whites of Collio, Colli Orientali del Friuli and Isonzo from a range of varieties, notably the native Tocai. Trentino-Alto Adige excels with still whites from a range of varieties, including the partly native Gewürztraminer, though red wines from the local vines of Teroldego and Lagrein can also be outstanding.

Moving to the center, I've reserved special praise for the rising star of Verdicchio in Marche, as well as Abruzzo's Montepulciano and Umbria's Sagrantino. The ancient varieties of Malvasia and Trebbiano have regained some of their former luster in Tuscany's Vin Santo and the remarkably improved dry whites of the Roman hills.

In the deep south, I've noted the venerable class of Aglianico in Basilicata and Campania, a region that also produces distinguished whites from the ancient Fiano, Greco and Falanghina varieties. Puglia is making strides with Negroamaro and Primitivo, the latter related to California's Zinfandel.

Among the islands' wealth of native varieties, Sardinia has made an impact with DOCG Vermentino di Gallura and the antique Vernaccia di Oristano, while showing unexpected style with red Cannonau and Carignano. In Sicily, the traditional sipping wines of Marsala and Malvasia delle Lipari hold their own amid the rise of modern dry whites. The island's native Nero d'Avola has gained stature as one of the south's noblest red wine varieties.

Still, it must be acknowledged that foreign varieties have played an important role in elevating Italian wines to international status, in particular those from Chardonnay, Cabernet Sauvignon, Merlot, the Pinots and Sauvignon Blanc. Italy's unrivaled inventory of native vines permits producers to play the options with foreign varieties to create a greater range of distinctive wines than any other country.

Merlot and Cabernet had made ordinary reds in northeastern Italy for the better part of a century, though some producers there now fashion wines that are opulent and elegant. Tuscany's Sassicaia proved decades ago that Italy could make reds of consummate class from Cabernet Sauvignon. That variety is blended with Sangiovese in Tignanello, the prototype for the proudly independent Super-Tuscans that ushered Italian wine into the modern era.

Myths and misconceptions

The pace of change has been astonishing in places, yet in the not so distant past the technology of cold fermentation in stainless steel tanks resulted in alarming uniformity of style and lack of character in Italian whites. Distinguished wines from Friuli-Venezia Giulia and Trentino-Alto Adige broke that pattern, yet the myth persists that Italian whites are invariably best from the latest vintage. More and more wines of depth and personality have come forth to dispel the misconception that Italy can't produce dry whites of world class.

Producers increasingly ferment and mature white wines in barrels, mainly barriques from France, though large casks of Slavonian oak are also used to round out aromas and flavors. The use of barriques in the hands of novices has resulted in too many wines—white and red—that are blatantly oaky (some detractors call them "carpenter's wines"). But skilled practitioners are using small barrels to achieve greater concentration in wines with subtle background notes of oak that enhance style and complexity.

The rapid rise in quality of bottle-fermented sparkling wines based on Chardonnay and the Pinots is exemplified by the DOCG of Franciacorta and the DOC of Trento. Still, despite admirable improvements in the class and style of whites, Italy is still perceived primarily as a red wine country.

In Piedmont, long noted as a bastion of tradition, producers of Barolo and Barbaresco decades ago split into factions sometimes noted as the old school of winemaking and the new. The division is not as clear cut as it used to be, since winemakers have access to the tools of modern enology and tend to use them in increasingly similar ways.

Barrels remain a point of contention. Most traditionalists use large casks of oak from Slavonia to round out red wines as their hard tannins mellow slowly. Progressives prefer smaller barrels of new or relatively new oak mainly from France to lend their wines soft tannins.

At the risk of sounding equivocal, I appreciate the best of both schools, as is clear in my selections of Barolo and Barbaresco, as well as Chianti, Brunello and Amarone. Yet, to those of us who believe that great wines are made in the vineyard, cellar techniques are a secondary consideration.

It's not always easy to explain why certain wines combine richness and depth of bouquet and flavor in a harmony that seems to give them extra dimensions. If there's a secret, it surely lies in the vineyards: grape varieties, soil composition, microclimate, lay of the land, the rapport of a grower with a special plot, or what the French call a terroir. I have always admired the decisive personalities of wines that are true to their origins. That's why most of those selected for this book come from a specific and privileged place.

Many wine drinkers rely on the point ratings and notes of expert tasters to guide them in their purchases. But perhaps too much attention is paid to temporary assessments these days and not enough to the enduring factors that determine a wine's value over time: the natural and human elements that lie behind its evolution.

This book has no rating system—points, stars, or other. Most of the wines have been familiar to me for years, and in some cases for decades. So, rather than relying on summary judgments, I preferred to assess them in the light of how they have stood the test of time. Wines that have debuted recently come from producers whose previous performances merit my complete trust.

Had I made the selection five years ago, the list would have been somewhat different, as I'm sure it would be five years from now. Whatever their achievements to date, the winemakers of Italy seem certain to realize even more dramatic progress in the future as they continue to rejuvenate their ancient land of vines.

Italian wine today

Italy's growing ranks of skilled winemakers have brought about unprecedented improvements in the class of wines from all parts of the country. Critical raves and lofty point ratings confirm that certain Italian wines now stand with the world's finest. Yet optimists insist that even better things will be coming as the most prolific of wine nations begins to realize the eternal quality potential of its vineyards.

In an area smaller than the state of California, Italy produces nearly a fifth of the world's wine. The annual average of 5.9 billion liters through the 1990s was a shade higher than that of France, which, however, in some recent vintages has surpassed Italy's volumes. Yet, after the record crop of 8.6 billion liters in 1980, Italian wine production has diminished steadily. So has wine drinking among a people whose per capita consumption has decreased over the last 30 years from 110 liters to less than 60.

The cheerful conclusion is that Italians are drinking less but decidedly better. Improvements have been impressive everywhere, though certain regions and sectors of the country have achieved more than others. The leaders are northern and central regions: Piedmont and Tuscany, which excel with red wines, and the Veneto, Friuli-Venezia Giulia and Trentino-Alto Adige, where whites also stand out. But by now it's clear that all 20 regions have the potential to make first-rate wines from both native and international varieties. In coming decades the most significant gains seem destined to be realized in the south and the islands of Sicily and Sardinia.

Complete array of vines

Vines thrive from the Alps to southerly Mediterranean shores in a country whose surface consists of roughly 80 percent hills or mountains. Well over 1,000 vine varieties grow in Italy, though the numbers were drastically reduced a century ago when the vine louse called phylloxera devastated the nation's vineyards. Today the nearly 400 varieties in regular use for Italian wines are predominately indigenous, complemented by a virtually complete array of Europe's major vines.

Much recent planting has been in red wine varieties, which cover nearly two-thirds of Italy's vineyards. Prominent native vines are Sangiovese, Barbera, Montepulciano d'Abruzzo, Dolcetto, Cannonau, Nebbiolo, Negroamaro and Nero d'Avola. Certain white wine varieties are also on the rise, notably Verdicchio, Vermentino, Moscato, Prosecco and Gewürztraminer. Also prominent are vines of French origin—Cabernet Sauvignon, Merlot, Chardonnay, Sauvignon Blanc, Pinot Grigio and Pinot Bianco—though most have been grown in Italy for over a century.

Not long ago it appeared that the so-called international varieties would continue to gain vineyard space at the expense of native vines. But instead planting has tended to level off, so that today wines from foreign varieties represent only about 10 percent of Italian production.

Unrivaled diversity

The unrivaled diversity of Italian wines is due not only to the wealth of grape varieties but also to the infinite variations in contours, soils and microclimates of vineyards along the extended boot-shaped peninsula. Italy's generally sunny weather favors ripe grapes nearly everywhere, and that may explain why viticulture was often practiced with a certain nonchalance in the past. But today, with the growing emphasis on quality, vineyard maintenance is essential.

Dedicated growers have been planting vines in greater density, using studied training methods and sharp pruning to reduce grape yields. In abundant years, they practice green pruning, the thinning out of bunches to limit production to superior grapes. Harvesting is invariably done by hand to select perfectly ripe grapes placed in crates and taken immediately to the cellars, where subsequent culling of the best bunches is carried out.

Still, for all the recent advancement in viticulture, Italians lag behind the French, who have been fussing over their vineyards for the last couple of centuries. That explains why prime French varieties—Cabernet Sauvignon, Chardonnay, Merlot, the Pinots, Sauvignon Blanc and Syrah—set international standards. Italy boasts far more varieties, some no doubt as worthy as the French elite, though their full merits may not be known until current research is completed.

Only recently have Italians conducted systematic selections of superior clones of native varieties analyzed over time in relation to the soils and microclimates of individual estates and vineyards. An exception could be made for Piedmont in the Barolo and Barbaresco zones, where more than a century ago the value of individual vineyards was well documented. Yet there, as elsewhere, the French terms cru and terroir are used colloquially to describe special vineyards and terrains as there are no Italian equivalents.

A shift to premium quality

Considerable credit for the revolution in quality is due to the laws of controlled origin introduced in the 1960s when Italy was known around the world mainly for cheap wines of questionable authenticity. The advent of *denominazione di origine controllata* (DOC) forced a wayward industry to change, gradually shifting the emphasis to premium quality even in wines without a denomination.

DOC applies to wines from more than 300 geographical zones, including 21 that qualify for the highest status of DOCG. Recently introduced was a broader category of *indicazione geografica tipica* (IGT) for "typical" wines from specific territories. (See Labels and laws, page 19.)

DOC, DOCG and IGT now cover a fair share of premium production, though Italians still sell vast quantities of ordinary wine outside certified channels as *vino da tavola*. Italy is the world's leading exporter of wine in volume, though much of that has been in bulk for blending.

Diminishing markets for blending wines have prompted wineries in prolific southern regions to shift the emphasis to premium quality. Still, discrepancies remain in patterns of production around the country.

The regions today

The eight northern regions (Valle d'Aosta, Piedmont, Lombardy, Trentino-Alto Adige, Veneto, Friuli-Venezia Giulia, Emilia-Romagna and Liguria) produce about 40 percent of Italy's total volume of wine and about two-thirds of the DOC/DOCG. Piedmont is renowned for its noble reds, though it is also the home of Asti, the most popular of sweet sparkling wines. The Veneto leads all regions in volume of wine produced as well as in amounts of DOC, bolstered by Verona's familiar Soave, Valpolicella and Bardolino and by bubbly Prosecco from Conegliano and Valdobiaddene. Trentino-Alto Adige and Friuli-Venezia Giulia produce much less than the Veneto, but boast higher percentages of DOC among wines largely from international varieties.

The six central regions (Tuscany, Marche, Umbria, Lazio, Abruzzo and Molise) produce about 20 percent of Italian wine and 20 percent of the DOC/DOCG. Tuscany ranks only eighth among the regions in volume, but has a giant reputation for its DOCG reds, as well as for the Super-Tuscans that are now often covered by IGT. Marche, Lazio and Umbria are noted respectively for white Verdicchio, Frascati and Orvieto, though red wines are on the rise, led by the increasingly admired Montepulciano d'Abruzzo.

The six southern regions (Campania, Puglia, Basilicata, Calabria, Sardinia and Sicily) produce nearly 40 percent of Italy's wine but a scant 14 percent of the DOC/DOCG. Sicily and Puglia had been Italy's most prodigious regions for decades, though the decline in bulk exports has favored a quest for quality in bottled wines. Major wineries from elsewhere have been investing in the south, where the climate permits consistent quality and production costs are lower. Their aim is to offer premium wines at reasonable prices, a sure formula for increasing success.

Labels and laws

The extraordinary diversity of Italian wines is graphically conveyed by their labels. Variations in concept and design also reflect the sense of creativity among wine producers who until recently often regarded the use of an official appellation as an undesirable option.

That spirit of individuality partly explains why only about 20 percent of Italian wine comes under the auspices of *denominazione di origine controllata* (DOC) *e garantita* (DOCG). Until recently, many winemakers preferred to sell their most inspired creations as *vino da tavola* (table wine), a category that also covered the lowest levels of production. But a growing share of premium quality now qualifies under *indicazione geografica tipica* (IGT) appellations for "typical" table wines from specified territories.

In the year 2000, the number of DOC appellations surpassed 300 with another 22 designated for the maximum rank of DOCG, which "guarantees" the authenticity of wines of particular esteem. To qualify as DOCG, wines must meet standards of typology (and, in theory, quality) imposed by commissions of experts before being labeled and sold with the official pink strip seal at the top of the bottle.

Each DOC and DOCG applies to a geographical zone, which may range in size from the entire vineyard area of a region (Trebbiano d'Abruzzo, for instance) down to the confines of a community (Brunello di Montalcino). Classico identifies the historic core zone of a subsequently expanded appellation (Chianti Classico and Soave Classico are examples).

DOC/DOCG wines are always identified by a place name, sometimes together with the lone or dominant grape variety (Collio Tocai Friulano, Aglianico del Vulture) or the color (Collio Bianco, Langhe Rosso). Some wines are further identified by type—*secco* (dry), *amabile* (medium sweet), *dolce* (sweet), *frizzante* or *vivace* (lightly bubbly), *spumante* (sparkling), *liquoroso* (fortified or naturally strong). Some may be qualified by age (young as *novello*, aged as *riserva*, *vecchio*, *stravecchio* or, for vintage sparkling wine, *millesimato*). The term *superiore* may apply to wine with a higher degree of alcohol than the norm or a longer period of aging. Wine produced from grapes dried after the harvest may be referred to as *passito*. Examples are Recioto di Soave and Vin Santo.

A denomination may cover a basic type of wine (Valpolicella, Cinque Terre, for instance) or a multiplicity (Alto Adige DOC takes in 25 varietal wines directly plus six subdenominations with another 24 types). All the DOC/DOCG appellations combined cover more than 2,000 variations in types and styles of wine. Each wine covered must come from specific vine varieties (whether alone or in blends) grown in limited grape yields and processed and aged following set methods to meet prescribed standards of color, aroma and flavor and precise measures of such

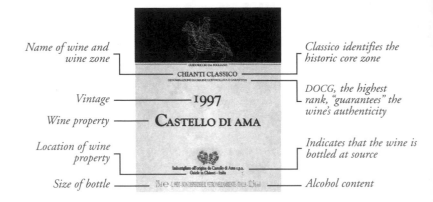

Name of wine and wine zone

Classico identifies the historic core zone

CHIANTI CLASSICO

DOCG, the highest rank, "guarantees" the wine's authenticity

Vintage — 1997

Wine property — CASTELLO DI AMA

Location of wine property

Indicates that the wine is bottled at source

Size of bottle

Alcohol content

components as alcohol, acids and residual sugars.

Bubbly wines may be dry or sweet in varying degrees and produced by tank fermentation methods or refermentation in bottle. *Spumante* refers to wines of more than 3.5 atmospheres of pressure, *frizzante* to those between 1 and 2.5 atmospheres. Asti DOCG applies to Asti or Asti Spumante, fully sparkling, and Moscato d'Asti, usually *frizzante*. Prosecco di Conegliano or Valdobbiadene DOC may be *spumante* or *frizzante*, as may the select versions known as Cartizze or Superiore di Cartizze.

Sparkling wines made by the classic method of refermentation in the bottle in which they are sold are often identified by the description *metodo classico*. (The term *champenoise* is reserved by law for Champagne.) A consortium of producers, including those of Trento DOC, uses the trademark Talento and the description "Metodo Classico" on labels but pointedly avoids the term *spumante*. The leading appellation for classic sparkling wine, Franciacorta DOCG, forbids the term *spumante* and any reference to the production method.

IGT identifies wines from specific regions, provinces or general areas by grape variety, color or typology, though controls are not as strict as for DOC wines. Many wines described in this volume have come under IGT categories. A few labels still carry *vino da tavola* with a geographical indication, though that category is being replaced by IGT. A wine sold as simply *vino da tavola* may not state the origin, grape variety or vintage on the label.

Revisions of Italy's wine laws have broadened the DOC/DOCG system while making controls more flexible, realistic and in tune with the times. Provisions have been made for official recognition of subzones, towns and villages and individual estates and vineyards. The naming of vineyards on labels, as practiced in Italy for decades, is in the process of verification. It is worth remembering that the first guarantee of a wine's quality and authenticity is the integrity of its producer.

Vineyards and winemaking techniques

E ach wine entry in this book includes information on grapes, vineyards and methods of winemaking.

Data under **Grapes** names the variety or varieties used in the featured wine and the normal time and method of harvesting (usually hand picked). There are also notes on the drying of grapes for certain types of wine.

Data under **Vineyards** indicates the size of the plot or plots from which grapes for each wine derive, along with the types of soil, lay of the land, altitude and place of origin. Soil types may be of interest mainly to experts, though even casual readers may note analogies between certain terrains and types of wine.

The data on age of vines and density of planting is also of a technical nature. Vines generally reach full production in 6–10 years and continue to render quality grapes for a couple of decades or, in some cases, much longer. Density of planting is a key quality factor, following trends in Italy to increase vines per hectare with fewer bunches per plant. Densities of 4,000–10,000 vines per hectare are now normal for premium wines, double to quadruple the ratio of earlier days.

Methods of training (pruning and shaping of vines) vary in Italy, depending on grape varieties, soils, climatic conditions and local traditions. Only 25 years ago about half of Italy's vines were grown in mixed culture (interspersed with other crops or olive or fruit trees). The following training systems are prominent in Italy today.

Alberello The low bush, whether free standing or supported by stakes or wires, is planted in much of southern Italy as well as in France, where it is called Gobelet. Spur-pruned or head-trained vines are often planted in high density

Alberello

and, because shoots are severely cut back, produce few bunches per plant. *Alberello* has gained limited favor in central and northern Italy today.

Pergola

Pergola The vines trained onto wires strung between tilted single or double pole arms form a high canopy under a system historically dominant in Veneto, Trentino-Alto Adige and the Po Valley. A shorter, lower version called *pergoletta* is also seen. Pergola, which favors prolific yields, is fading in some of the premium wine areas of the north.

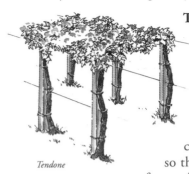
Tendone

Tendone A high trellis supported by crossed wires is popular in the south and south-central regions, but since it favors big yields it must be used discreetly for quality wines.

Spurred cordon Cane pruning of vines trained onto wires strung along rows of poles is generally known as cordon or espalier (*cordone* or *spalliera* in Italian). Spurred cordon means that the mature vine is shaped so that one or two canes that extend horizontally from the trunk are pruned sharply in the winter so that usually only two spurs emit the annual new growth that is trained vertically onto

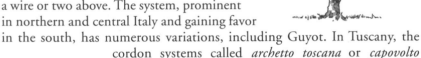
Spurred cordon

a wire or two above. The system, prominent in northern and central Italy and gaining favor in the south, has numerous variations, including Guyot. In Tuscany, the cordon systems called *archetto toscana* or *capovolto toscano* consist of arching the shoots over wires. *Doppio capovolto* is a double arched cordon system used in various regions.

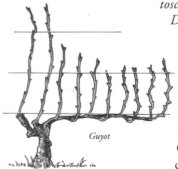
Guyot

Guyot Devised by Frenchman Jules Guyot in the 19th century, the basic system comprises a single cane of six to ten buds, each of which is pruned in winter to a two-bud spur from which new growth is trained vertically onto wires. There is also a double Guyot of two canes. The Guyot system of cordon training, prominent in Piedmont, Tuscany and other premium wine regions, has several variations, including the arching of fruiting shoots over wires.

Vinification and aging describes in basic terminology the steps involved in converting grapes to the featured wine. It begins with the method of crushing grapes, the temperatures and duration of the alcoholic fermentation and type of container used. Notes may indicate if the fermentation occurs with natural grape yeasts or is induced with select yeast cultures.

Fundamental differences in methods are applied to dry red and white wines to drink young and those for aging, as well as to sweet and sparkling wines. Grapes for most modern dry wines are processed immediately after picking in apparatuses that remove stems and apply enough pressure to break the skins gently to release the juice, though exceptions are noted. Musts for red wines invariably remain in contact with the grape skins to macerate for most or all of the alcoholic fermentation and sometimes beyond. White wines may be made from juice that is separated immediately from the skins or from musts that are left in contact with them at cold temperature for a brief time to impart components of color, aroma and flavor.

Malolactic fermentation, the conversion of malic acid to lactic acid, has a mellowing effect by lowering the total acidity of the wine. It may occur naturally when a wine reaches a certain temperature or may be induced by adding yeasts and raising the heat of the cellar or individual tank. Red wines for aging undergo malolactic fermentation, though producers often avoid it for white wines to drink young or induce it only in part to maintain vital acidity.

Many white wines—and some red—to drink young are matured for a time in stainless steel tanks to maintain freshness before bottling. Whites of a certain stature may be fermented and/or matured in wooden barrels—often small barriques of French oak, where they may remain on the lees (the fermentation sediment) to add character to the wine.

Red wines may be matured in small barrels or large casks, usually of oak, though wood aging methods differ according to regional or local traditions or individual concepts applied by winemakers to achieve a certain style or personality. Also noted are the average alcoholic content of each wine (as well as residual sugar for sweet types) and the length of time it remains in bottle before release.

The following notes about production techniques and terminology for sparkling wines fermented in bottle are intended to avoid repetition through the text. The terms Champagne method or *méthode champenoise* may now be used only by the French, so Italians often refer to the process as *metodo classico* or *metodo tradizionale*.

The cuvée is the blend of base wines that have undergone alcoholic fermentation. This blend receives a *liqueur de tirage*, a solution of sugar and active yeasts that induces a second fermentation in the bottle sealed with a crown cap. The yeasts that convert the sugar into alcohol and create carbon dioxide bubbles settle in the bottle and must be removed by techniques known in French as *remuage* (riddling) and *dégorgement* (disgorging). Bottles are inserted neck down into slots in A-frame racks called *pupitres*. Riddlers daily twist and agitate each bottle to coax the sediment down until it settles against the cap, which is frozen into a plug of ice removed by a mild explosion of carbon dioxide. This disgorging (*sboccatura* in Italian) results in a slight loss of wine from the bottle which must be topped up before cork sealing. If topped up with the same wine, it may be called *non dosato, pas dosé, dosage zéro, pas opéré* or *nature* and will be *brut* or *extra brut* (dry to very dry). Wine that receives a dose of so-called *liqueur d'expédition* (usually a solution of sugar and aged wine) may range from *brut* to sweet depending on house formulas.

Glossary

Abboccato Wine with a hint of sweetness, mellow, off dry

Amabile Medium-sweet wine

Amaro Bitter

Amarone della Valpolicella Strong red wine made from grapes partly dried after the harvest in the Valpolicella zone near Verona

Annata Year of vintage

Appassimento The practice of drying grapes before crushing to concentrate sugar and extract for *passito* wines such as Amarone and Vin Santo

Azienda agricola/agraria/ vitivinicola Farm or estate growing all or most of its grapes for wine

Barrique The Bordeaux term for a barrel holding 225 liters is used loosely in Italy to describe a small barrel, not necessarily of French origin. Types may include the 228-liter Burgundy *pièce* and barrels up to about 500-liter capacity. See also *botte, carato,* tonneau

Bâtonnage French term for periodic stirring of the lees of a wine with a wooden stick as it matures in barrels to inhibit formation of malodorous hydrogen sulfide and excessive extraction of wood tannins

Bentonite Clay used as part of a fining process

Blanc de blancs French term for white wine (sparkling as a rule) made from white grapes

Blanc de noirs White wine made from black grapes

Botrytis cinerea The 'noble rot' (*muffa nobile* in Italian) fungus that develops on shriveled grapes (whether late harvested or dried) and enables them to produce luscious sweet wines. Botrytized refers to grapes subject to the phenomenon

Botte Cask or relatively large barrel, usually of oak but sometimes chestnut, of varying dimensions. The traditional *botte di rovere di Slavonia* (oak from northern Yugoslavia) is still used prominently for such classic red wines as Barolo, Brunello and Amarone. Smaller barrels are often preferred for modern wines

Cantina Cellar or winery. *Cantina sociale, cantina cooperativa* and *cantina produttori* are terms for cooperative wineries

Carato Small barrel often used as a synonym for the 225-liter barrique. *Caratello* is a general term for a smaller barrel, synonymous with *botticello,* though sizes vary

Casa vinicola Winery that acquires grapes for wine

Cascina Farmhouse and small estate

Consorzio Consortium of producers that sets standards and promotes wines of a certain appellation or region

Cru French term for a choice vineyard

Dolce Sweet, technically in reference to wines with 5-10% residual sugar

Enoteca Wine library (shops and publicly or privately financed collections or displays)

Fattoria Farm or estate

Frizzante Lightly bubbly wine (from 1–2.5 atmospheres of pressure), not fully sparkling or *spumante*

Governo Tuscan practice (full term *governo all'uso toscano*) of drying late-harvested grapes to add to the fermented wine, setting off a secondary fermentation to enrich body, flavor and color

Hyperoxygenation Process of saturating the must with oxygen during fermentation to minimize use of sulfites

Imbottigliato da... Bottled by...

Liqueur d'expédition French term for a syrupy solution, usually consisting of sugar and aged wine, to top up sparkling wine after disgorging (see page 23)

Liquoroso Wines fortified with (or naturally rich in) alcohol

Madre Mother or matrix, residue from earlier vintages left in barrels to guide the transformation of musts into wine, such as Vin Santo

Metodo classico Italians often refer to the 'classic method' of making sparkling wine by a second fermentation in bottle to avoid *méthode champenoise*, a term legally reserved for Champagne

Millesimato Sparkling wine from a stated vintage, equivalent to French *millesimé*

Noble rot See *Botrytis cinerea*

Passito Wine made from dried grapes, usually sweet with intense, raisin-like fruit

Perlage French term for fine bubbles of sparkling wines, likened to beads of pearls

Podere Small farm or estate

Pomace The grape skins, seeds and pulp left after the must or fermented wine has been extracted is called *vinacce* by Italians; it may be used as a base to distill grappa

Pumping over Fermenting red wines form a cap of grape skins which may be submerged by pumping juice over it and breaking the mass. This circulation hastens extraction of elements from the skins

Recioto Sweet red (Valpolicella) or white (Soave) wine made from grapes that have been dried after the harvest (see also page 158)

Residual sugars The sugars (fructose, glucose and other) that remain unfermented in a finished wine and account for its relative sweetness are usually measured in percent of volume or grams per liter

Ripasso Technique used to enrich red wine in the Valpolicella zone by 'passing' it over the pomace left from newly fermented Amarone or Recioto

Riserva Reserve or special selection officially applied only to DOC or DOCG wines that meet specified aging requirements

Ronco (ronchi) Term for vineyard(s), often terraced, usually in Friuli-Venezia Giulia

Rosato Rosé wine sometimes also called *chiaretto* or *cerasuolo*

Souplesse French for 'suppleness,' typical of a smooth, easy to drink wine

Spumante Literally 'foaming,' in reference to sparkling wine, whether dry or sweet

Superiore Denotes DOC wine of standards superior to the norm (greater alcohol, longer aging, etc.), though conditions vary

Super-Tuscan Term for new styles of red wine that emerged in Tuscany in the 1970s. Originally made outside the official classification system, they were so successful that they prompted a revolution in winemaking standards and rules governing denominations

Tenuta Farm or estate

Terroir French term for every aspect of a vineyard site (soil, climate, etc.)

Tirage Term used in Champagne for the bottling of the base wine with a yeast and sugar solution called *liqueur de tirage* (see page 23)

Tonneau Traditional Bordeaux barrel of 900-liter capacity. The term has been borrowed in Italy for oak containers of other sizes, including those of 550-liter capacity

Vecchio Old, to describe certain aged DOC wines. *Invecchiato* means aged. *Stravecchio*, very old, describes the longest-aged Marsala

Vendemmia Grape harvest. *Vendemmia tardiva*, late harvested, applies to grapes left to ripen fully on the vine and the wine made from them

Vigna, vigneto Terms for vineyard

Vignaiolo, viticoltore, viticultore Terms for grape grower, generally one who makes wine

Vino da tavola 'Table wine' covers the lowest category of the Italian classification system. Though it is used for some fine wines, most come under the category of IGT (see page 20)

Vin Santo Literally 'holy wine' made from grapes dried after the harvest and kept in small barrels in a room known in Tuscany as a *vinsantaia*, where seasonal heat and cold are essential to the extended fermentation-aging process

Using the guide

The information accompanying the wine profiles should be self-explanatory. The left hand column gives details of the **Producers** and **Owners**, **Winemakers** and **Vineyard managers**.

Production refers to the average number of bottles of the featured wine released from favorable vintages. Wine is often not made in unfavorable years.

Vintages refer to years of good to excellent quality, as determined by the author with recommendations from winemakers. Good wines may also be available from vintages not cited.

Price refers to the average retail cost of the wine with a scale to indicate relative expense: • Moderate •• Medium
••• Expensive •••• Very expensive

Information in the column to the right of the photograph of the bottle of wine identifies the **Grape** variety or varieties used in each wine and includes facts about **Vineyards** and methods of **Vinification and aging**. These details are intended to inform experts about origins and production techniques, though they should prove enlightening to anyone interested in understanding the factors that account for the special style and personality of a wine.

The **Style and maturity** section at the bottom of the page contains information on each wine's characteristic color, aroma and flavor with indications of its prime drinking period and aging capacity. Allow for vintage variations.

The **Serving** symbols apply to recommended temperatures, and to types of glasses and food combinations that bring out the best in each wine.

Recommended **temperatures** for red wines range from 12–20°C (54–68°F) to cover various types, including sweet and relatively young reds, which are often served fairly cool. I generally prefer to drink aged dry reds of depth and character at about 18°C (64°F), rarely under 16°C (61°F) and never over 20°C

Bordeaux   Burgundy   Chianti   Syrah   Port   Dessert wine

(68°F). For white wines the range is from 8–18°C (46–64°F) to cover various types, including dry, sweet, young, aged, still and bubbly. I generally prefer to drink fruity young dry whites and rosé at about 10°C (50°F) and mature whites at 12–14°C (54–57°F), sparkling wines, dry or sweet, at 8–10°C (46–50°F) and sweet or dry fortified wines at 15–20°C (59–68°F). In most cases, I have respected serving temperatures recommended by producers, and noted where they have also suggested opening bottles ahead of time and decanting.

Recommended **glasses** refer primarily to sizes and shapes (see below). Most aged reds, and certain mature whites, require an ample glass with plenty of breathing space to bring out the scope and intensity of aromas and harmony of flavors. Younger wines, red and white, usually require glasses of medium to small measure. Fine wines show their best in fine-tuned glass, preferably crystal, with a long, slender stem and a bowl in the shape of a chalice designed to enhance a particular style or character. To simplify matters I refer to basic types of glasses for red wine as Bordeaux (with an ample oval-shaped bowl), Burgundy (with a tall open bowl or *ballon*), Chianti (like Bordeaux but smaller), Syrah (tall, slender oval-shaped bowl somewhat closed in at the top). For white wines, basic types are Chardonnay (medium-large oval bowl), Sauvignon (medium oval bowl), Alsatian or Riesling (medium-wide oval bowl). Sparkling wines made by the classic method are best in a fairly ample flute, tank- fermented types in a normal flute, sweet types in an ample flute or classic Champagne *coupe*. Dessert and fortified wines have individual requirements according to type and age.

Recommended **dishes** usually emphasize regional or local foods matched traditionally with the wine, though suggestions also range into national and international cuisine. The dishes recommended are intended to inspire readers to use their imaginations in combining wines with the foods of other countries.

All measurements are given according to local use. See page 4 for conversion table. ⚕ denotes red and rosé wines; ♀ denotes white wines.

Chardonnay   *Sauvignon*   *Riesling*   *Ample flute*   *Flute*   *Champagne* coupe

The Northwest

Valle d'Aosta, Piedmont, Liguria, Lombardy

The Alps along the borders of Switzerland and France link with the Apennines overlooking the Ligurian Sea to form a great arc of hills whose vineyards render some of Italy's most vaunted wines.

The leader in the northwest is Piedmont, whose southerly hills produce robust red wines, as well as fragrant whites, both still and sparkling. The Langhe hills around the town of Alba are the realm of the aristocratic Barolo and Barbaresco from the Nebbiolo grape, as well as buoyant Dolcetto and the resurgent Barbera, whose ancestral home is the Monferrato hills around Asti. That town lends its name to sweet white wines, lightly bubbly Moscato d'Asti and fully sparkling Asti Spumante.

Northern Piedmont is noted for the red Ghemme and Gattinara from Nebbiolo, which is also the variety of the Alpine Valtellina in Lombardy. Milan's region is also renowned for sparkling wines from Chardonnay and Pinots, led by Franciacorta DOCG.

Valle d'Aosta and Liguria produce the smallest volumes of wine among Italy's 20 regions, but each boasts gems of enology. Valle d'Aosta excels with whites of Alpine fragrance. Liguria's seaside terraces are known for white Cinque Terre, Pigato and Vermentino.

PRODUCERS

Valle d'Aosta ♀ Les Crêtes 100, La Crotta di Vegneron 102 **Piedmont** ♥ Elio Altare 30, La Barbatella 32, Braida 34, Bricco Asili Ceretto 36, Cantalupo 40, Chionetti 42, Cisa Asinari 44, Clerico 46, Aldo Conterno 48, Giacomo Conterno 50, Matteo Correggia 52, Gaja 54, Bruno Giacosa 56, Martinetti 58, Giuseppe Mascarello 60, Prunotto 64, Rabajà 66, Albino Rocca 68, Rocche dei Manzoni 70, Luciano Sandrone 72, Paolo Scavino 74, G.D. Vajra 76, Vietti 78, Roberto Voerzio 80; ♀ A. Bertelli 84, Caudrina 92, Aldo Conterno 96, Contratto 98, Forteto della Luja 106, Gaja 108, Marco Negri 114, Orsolani 116, Rocche dei Manzoni 118, Saracco 120, La Scolca 122, La Spinetta 124 **Liguria** ♀ Bruna 86, Walter De Battè 104, Ottaviano Lambruschi 110 **Lombardy** ♥ Ca' del Bosco 38, Nino Negri 62; ♀ Bellavista 82, Ca' dei Frati 88, Ca' del Bosco 90, Cavalleri 94, Monte Rossa 112, Uberti 126

Oak barrels aging Angelo Gaja's Barbaresco

Elio Altare

Arborina
Langhe DOC

Producer
Azienda Agricola
Altare Elio
Cascina Nuova
Frazione
Annunziata 51
12064 La Morra
(Cuneo)
Tel. 0173 508 35
Fax 0173 508 35
www.italywines.com

**Owner and
winemaker**
Elio Altare

Founded
1948

Production
2,000–2,600
bottles in fine years

Vintages
1999 1998 1997 1996
1995 1993 1990 1989
1988 1985

Price
● ● ●

Elio Altare, a philosophical winemaker who refers to himself proudly as a *viticultore* (grape grower), enjoys celebrity status in Piedmont for wines made by methods that are as avant-garde as any of Europe. It may seem curious to an outsider that the wine that best represents his ideology is Arborina, classified under the common Langhe DOC, instead of the Barolo from the same Arborina vineyard and the same Nebbiolo grapes that qualifies under the highest official category of DOCG.

"They're the same wine, just aged differently," he explains. "Arborina is vinified and matured entirely in new barrels of French oak, Barolo in barrels that are one-fifth new and the rest used once or twice." Which is best? "That's for critics to decide," says Elio, who is known to be mercilessly self-critical. "I'll let you know in a decade or two."

Elio attributes his wines' virtues to grapes grown in low yields due to fastidious pruning and thinning of old vines. He's equally meticulous in the cellars, treating each batch of grapes as a chance to experiment with fermentation temperatures, length of maceration on the skins (which are stirred by a rotary system for rapid extraction of components of color, aroma, flavor and body) and the influence of wood on the final product.

"Most of the world's great wines are matured in small oak barrels, but in Piedmont barriques are still controversial," he says with an ironic grin. "Some of us went ahead with them anyway and by now we have the results of nearly two decades of experience. Tastings of early vintages of Arborina are positive, but I'm willing to wait. If, after ten or twenty years, it appears that barriques were a mistake, well, I'll apologize to the world and start over."

Altare's production of about 50,000 bottles a year includes DOCG Barolo (regular and Vigna Arborina), DOC Barbera d'Alba and Dolcetto d'Alba and DOC Langhe Larigi (Barbera) and La Villa (Barbera and Nebbiolo).

Grapes
Nebbiolo 100%, hand
picked in early October.

Vineyard
The Arborina plot of
1.5 hectares in sandy
calcareous clays with
tufaceous marl on slopes
facing southeast at 280
meters of altitude in the
Annunziata area of the
commune of La Morra.
The vines, of an average
age of 51 years, are
planted at a density of
5,500 per hectare and
trained in the Guyot
cordon method.

Vinification and aging
Grapes are stemmed and
soft crushed and the juice
begins fermenting for
3–4 days in a stainless
steel rotomaceration tank
at temperatures of 22°C
and up. Then it is
transferred to small oak
barrels, entirely new,
where it completes
alcoholic and malolactic
fermentation as
temperatures rise to
34°C. After maturing in
the same barrels for about
18 months, the wine, of
at least 13.5% alcohol, is
bottled and cellared for
about a year before
release.

Style and maturity
Arborina's rich ruby-mulberry
color takes on hints of garnet
with age. The bouquet reveals
the essence of modern
Nebbiolo with enduring scents
of violets and berries and hints
of vanilla and tobacco. Flavors
are rich and vital with fruit
sensations in great
concentration offset by wood
tannins that bring complexity
to a wine that delivers
optimum impact between 5
and 8 years. Aging beyond a
decade brings out inherent
breed and finesse with
smooth, soft textures and
lingering harmony on the
palate.

Serving
🍷 16–18°C.
♀ Tall, ample *ballon*
(Burgundy type).
🍽 Roast and braised beef,
lamb, kid, poultry and
game, as well as aged
Piedmontese mountain
cheeses.

La Vigna dell'Angelo Barbera d'Asti Superiore DOC ❢

Producer
Azienda Agricola
Cascina La
Barbatella
Strada Annunziata 55
14049 Nizza
Monferrato (Asti)
Tel. 0141 701 434
Fax 0141 721 550

Owners
Angelo and Emiliana
Martini Sonvico

Founded
1983

Winemakers
Giuliano and Elena Noè

Vineyard manager
Piero Roseo

Production
About 6,000 bottles
from choice vintages

Vintages
1999 1998 1997 1996
1991 1990 1989

Price
● ●

Angelo Sonvico, originally from Como but a long-time resident of Milan, acquired Cascina La Barbatella in Piedmont's Monferrato hills in the early 1980s to pursue a hobby that soon became a passion. Working with his wife Emiliana and the father-daughter enology team of Giuliano and Elena Noè, he produces minute quantities of a Barbera that is roundly considered to be among the finest of the breed. La Vigna dell'Angelo represents a pure expression of the grandeur of Barbera, the popular but perennially underrated variety that is rapidly emerging as the rediscovered glory of Piedmont.

Barbera as a vine has long been appreciated by growers for its adaptability to diverse conditions of soil and microclimate, a reason why it covers more than half of the vineyards of Piedmont and why its wines have been exceedingly popular on the everyday level, even when light and fizzy. It's curious to note that Piedmontese ofen refer to *la Barbera* in the feminine gender, one of the few wines of Italy to rate that distinction, though the wine at its robust best would seem to be more masculine in character.

Cascina La Barbatella overlooks the town of Nizza Monferrato and the Belbo river valley from a sun-drenched crest long noted for Barbera. Vines that are now half a century old are given meticulous care, including thinning of bunches 40 days before the harvest so that remaining grapes ripen fully and evenly.

La Vigna dell'Angelo proves that Barbera, when treated as a noble, responds accordingly with wines of authoritative structure and warm, rich flavors dignified by maturing in small oak barrels. Perhaps it's not surprising that some critics prefer the estate's Barbera-Cabernet Sauvignon blend known as Sonvico, a Monferrato Rosso DOC that might be considered more appealing to the so-called "international" palate. Fair enough. Admirers of Barbera may assert that possessors of "international" palates still have a lot to learn.

Piedmont

Grapes
Barbera 100%, hand picked in early October.

Vineyard
A plot of 1.1 hectares on a crest of sandy calcareous clay soils oriented south-southwest at 220 meters of altitude near Nizza Monferrato in the Monferrato hills 25 kilometers southeast of Asti. The vines, of an average age of 51 years, are planted at a density of about 4,500 per hectare and trained in the Guyot cordon method.

Vinification and aging
Grapes are stemmed and soft crushed and the must fermented in stainless steel tanks at 28–30°C for 8–10 days. Malolactic fermentation is induced in tanks before the wine is matured for a year in barriques of French oak. The wine, of 13–13.5% alcohol, is bottled and cellared for about 6 months before release.

Style and maturity
La Vigna dell'Angelo shows the intensely deep ruby hue that typifies fine Barbera, with scents of berries and fruit (notably morello cherries) and vanilla in its clean, fresh bouquet. When young (3–5 years), flavors are marked by rich berry sensations and a robust vibrancy due to a healthy measure of acidity, though with time (6–10 years or more) the wine fleshes out and mellows while maintaining essential fruit that is fresh and cleansing on the palate.

Serving
🌡 18°C.
🍷 Ample *ballon* (Burgundy type).
🍴 Piedmontese pasta dishes, such as *agnolotti* or *tajarin* with meat sauce; *bollito misto* (mixed boiled meats) and roast kid.

Braida

Bricco dell'Uccellone
Barbera d'Asti DOC ☙

Producer
Braida di Bologna
Giacomo
Via Roma 94
14030 Rocchetta
Tanaro (Asti)
Tel. 0141 644 113
Fax 0141 644 584
info@braida.it
www.braida.it

Owners
Anna, Raffaella and
Giuseppe Bologna

Founded
1961

Winemakers
Raffaella and Giuseppe
Bologna

Vineyard manager
Giuseppe Bologna

Production
About 38,000 bottles
from choice vintages

Vintages
1999 1998 1997 1996
1991 1990 1989 1988
1985 1982

Price
● ●

Note
Bricco dell'Uccellone,
originally an unclassified
table wine, is now
qualified as Barbera
d'Asti DOC

A decade after his passing, Giacomo Bologna lingers large in memory for the genius and joy he brought to the world of wine. Among his accomplishments was the creation in 1982 of Bricco dell'Uccellone, a grandiose red that heralded the era of what is sometimes known as "Super Barbera." That wine, from hillcrest vineyards at Rocchetta Tanaro near Asti, was matured in small oak barrels, or barriques, to help give it richness and depth of bouquet and flavor with mellow harmony. In short, a revelation.

Other producers followed suit, finding that Barbera with its naturally high acidity and moderate grape tannins took well to new oak barrels. For the record, Giacomo Bologna wasn't the first Piedmontese winemaker to mature Barbera in barriques (a practice apparently initiated by the intrepid Angelo Gaja). But nobody did more than Giacomo to uplift the image of Barbera from its perennial role as a commoner to its newfound status as a noble.

As Bricco dell'Uccellone reached new levels of prestige and price, its success inspired further feats with Barbera. Giacomo, aided by his wife Anna and children Raffaella and Beppe, followed in 1985 with Bricco della Bigotta and in 1989 with Ai Suma, enriched by late-harvested grapes. That triumvirate stands as a monument to the new Barbera and Giacomo Bologna's lasting tribute to his beloved Piedmont.

The estate called Braida, the nickname of Giacomo's father Giuseppe, originated as an outlet for bulk wines in the 1960s when it was connected to the family trattoria. Today, with modern cellars and 32 hectares of vines, the Bologna family produces about 350,000 bottles a year of wines led by the three versions of Barbera d'Asti DOC, as well as a fizzy Barbera del Monferrato DOC, and ranging through Grignolino d'Asti DOC, Monferrato DOC il Bacialè (Barbera with Pinot Nero), Brachetto d'Acqui DOCG and a fine Moscato d'Asti DOCG called Vigna Senza Nome (Vineyard Without Name).

Piedmont

Grapes
Barbera 100%, hand picked in early October.

Vineyards
Plots totaling 7 hectares in clay soils oriented south-southeast at 250 meters of altitude on a crest above the town of Rocchetta Tanaro 15 kilometers east of Asti. The vines, of an average age of 23 years, are planted at a density of 4,000 per hectare and trained in the Guyot cordon method.

Vinification and aging
Grape bunches are selected in vineyards and cellars before being stemmed and soft crushed and the must fermented in stainless steel tanks at 28°C for 12–15 days. Malolactic fermentation occurs naturally before the wine is matured for about a year in small oak barrels. The wine, of about 14% alcohol, is bottled and cellared for a year before release.

Style and maturity
Bricco dell'Uccellone has a dark ruby-garnet color when young and generous bouquet with scents of fruit and berries mingling with hints of spices, vanilla and licorice. The wine is extraordinarily voluptuous in body, yet smoothly dry with solid structure and full fruit sensations balanced against oak tannins that mingle in the soft, long flavors. It reaches an appealing prime after 5–6 years but will maintain style for well over a decade.

Serving
🍷 18°C.
🍷 Ample, tulip-shaped.
🍽 Piedmontese meat dishes, such as braised beef, grilled lamb cutlets, *finanziera* (a stew including veal brain and sweetbreads, chicken livers and cockscombs).

Bricco Asili
Barbaresco DOCG 🍷

Producer
Azienda Agricola Bricco
Asili Ceretto
Ceretto Aziende
Vitivinicole
Località San Cassiano 34
12051 Alba (Cuneo)
Tel. 0173 282 582
Fax 0173 282 383
ceretto@ceretto.com
www.ceretto.com

Owners
Bruno and Marcello
Ceretto

Founded
1973

Chief winemaker
Marcello Ceretto, with
consultant Donato
Lanati

Vineyard manager
Gianluigi Marenco, with
consultant Albino
Morando

Production
7,000 bottles in fine
years

Vintages
1999 1998 1997 1996
1995 1990 1989 1985
1982 1978 1974

Price
● ● ● ●

The Ceretto brothers—Bruno, manager, and Marcello, chief winemaker—are among the most enterprising producers of Piedmont, as their sterling international reputation shows. Over the decades they phased out their old family winery in Alba to focus on production at three estates with headquarters at the splendid La Bernardina villa on the edge of town.

The loquacious Bruno Ceretto explains how the company philosophy evolved from thinking big to thinking small. "When we were a patriarchal wine house and bought all our grapes from growers, we had little control over quality," he recalls. "So we began buying or leasing vineyards in the best areas, because it's clear that to make great wine you have to grow your own grapes."

Their first acquisition was Bricco Asili, a jewel of a domain on the edge of a knoll with some of the most privileged vineyards of Barbaresco. Bricco Asili has its own cellars and 8 hectares of vines for Barbaresco called Bricco Asili (from the choicest plot), Faset and Bernardot.

Next came Bricco Rocche, source of a Barolo of the name, which is among the most esteemed and expensive wines of the appellation. Each property is operated independently with winemakers supervised by Marcello Ceretto and advised by Donato Lanati, but encouraged to bring out the individual nature of each terrain. Although Barolo Bricco Rocche is the showcase wine, some prefer Barbaresco Bricco Asili as an exquisite example of the Ceretto touch that accents the inherent grace of Nebbiolo over sheer power.

Ceretto produces single-vineyard versions of the Alba DOCs of Barbera, Dolcetto and Nebbiolo, as well as Langhe Arneis. But the brothers' main focus seems to be on wines from international varieties grown at the creative center of La Bernardina: Langhe DOC Chardonnay and Monsordo Rosso, from Cabernet Sauvignon, Pinot Noir and Merlot with enough Nebbiolo to give it Piedmontese roots.

Piedmont

Grapes
Nebbiolo 100%, hand picked in early October.

Vineyard
A plot of 1.3 hectares in calcareous rich marl at 290–320 meters of altitude along the crest of a slope facing south-southwest in the Asili area of the commune of Barbaresco. The vines, of an average age of 29 years, are planted at a density of 3,500 per hectare and trained in the Guyot cordon method.

Vinification and aging
Grapes are stemmed and soft crushed and the musts fermented on the skins for 7–10 days starting at 30°C and ending at 26°C in stainless steel tanks that automatically pump the liquid over the cap. After malolactic fermentation at 20°C in stainless steel containers, the wine, of about 13% alcohol, is matured for about 2 years in oak, part in 2,500-liter casks and part in 300-liter barrels, then bottled and cellared for at least 8 months before release.

Style and maturity
Bricco Asili has bright ruby-garnet color tending toward brick red with age. The bouquet is complex and refined with hints of berries, flowers, spices and licorice. On the palate, the wine shows solid structure and strength of components in flavors that begin to show harmony after about 4 years, though the velvety elegance that characterizes this Barbaresco comes to the fore with 10 to 15 years of age.

Serving
🍷 18°C, decanting old vintages before pouring.
🍷 Ample (Burgundy type).
🍽️ Meats and poultry, such as duck braised in white wine *alla favorita*, rabbit stewed in Barbaresco, spring lamb roasted with herbs.

Maurizio Zanella
Rosso del Sebino IGT 🍷

Producer
Ca' del Bosco
Azienda Agricola
Via Case Sparse 20
25030 Erbusco
(Brescia)
Tel. 030 776 6111
Fax 030 726 8425
cadelbosco@
cadelbosco.com

Owner
Ca' del Bosco
directed by
Maurizio Zanella

Founded
1968

Winemaker
Stefano Capelli

Vineyard manager
Luigi Reghenzi

Production
18,000–30,000
bottles in choice years

Vintages
1999 1998 1997 1996
1995 1991 1990 1988
1985

Price
● ● ●

Franciacorta, a sanctuary of vines in Lombardy's lake country, has metamorphosed over three decades from a modest supplier of *vino rosso* into Italy's premier source of sparkling wine by the Champagne method. The first Franciacorta estate to gain international attention was Ca' del Bosco in the 1970s, when a wealthy young man called Maurizio Zanella hired a veteran cellarmaster from Epernay and showed the world that Italy could make sparkling wine to rival Champagne.

Being recognized as the wizard of bubbly wasn't enough for Maurizio, who soon set his aim on world-class still wines from Chardonnay, Pinot Noir and Cabernet-Merlot—succeeding with amazing rapidity in all three categories. The blend of Cabernet Sauvignon, Merlot and Cabernet Franc from 1981 inspired the *enfant prodige* to attach his name to the label as a personal commitment to Ca' del Bosco's growing ranks of admirers.

Maurizio Zanella has aged as impressively as his signature wine. Ca' del Bosco has gradually built production, becoming a corporation bolstered by capital from Santa Margherita, the firm widely known for Pinot Grigio. Maurizio Zanella remains in command with his customary pursuit of excellence in vineyards and cellars.

From 125 hectares of vines, Ca' del Bosco makes 650,000–850,000 bottles a year of wines about evenly split between sparkling and still. Franciacorta DOCG sparkling wines, based on Chardonnay with the possible inclusion of Pinot Noir and Pinot Bianco, come in versions known as Brut, Extra Brut Dosage Zero, Satèn (entirely Chardonnay) and the outstanding Cuvée Annamaria Clementi (see page 90), from base wines matured in oak barrels. Still wines take in the stylish DOC Terre di Franciacorta Chardonnay and Pinot Bianco and the Burgundy-like Pinero (Pinot Noir), which, like Maurizio Zanella, is classified under the IGT of Sebino (the Latin name of nearby Lake Iseo).

Lombardy

Grapes
Cabernet Sauvignon
45%, Merlot 30%,
Cabernet Franc 25%,
hand picked in mid-
October.

Vineyards
Three plots totaling 8
hectares—Poligono at
Erbusco, Formica
between Adro and
Cazzago, Brognolo at
Passirano—in glacial
moraine on slopes
between 160–230 meters
of altitude in the
Franciacorta area west of
Brescia. The vines, of an
average age of 16 years,
are planted at densities
varying from 4,000–
10,000 per hectare and
trained in the Guyot or
high Sylvoz cordon
methods.

Vinification and aging
Grape bunches are
meticulously selected in
the cellars before being
stemmed and soft
crushed and the must
fermented in 2,000-liter
cylindrical tanks at
20–25°C for 10 days.
Malolactic fermentation
occurs naturally before
the wine is matured for
15–18 months in 225-
liter oak barrels. The
wine, of about 13%
alcohol, is bottled and
cellared for 10–12
months before release.

Style and maturity
Maurizio Zanella has deep
ruby-garnet color with vaguely
violet tones and potent
bouquet, rich, concentrated
and complex, revealing distinct
notes of jam and ripe cherries,
raspberries and plums. These
sensations carry over to the
palate in flavors that are
agreeably balanced between
dry and sweet with hints of
spices and herbs, licorice and
vanilla in an elegant long finish.
The wine, attractive after 4 or
5 years, achieves splendor
between 8 and 15.

Serving
🌡 17°C.
🍷 Ample crystal glass.
🍽 Lamb roast with thyme,
duck with green peppers,
manzo all'olio (filet of beef
braised in olive oil with
onion, carrot, celery and
anchovies).

Cantalupo

Collis Breclemae
Ghemme DOCG ❢

Producer
Antichi Vigneti di
Cantalupo
Via Michelangelo
Buonarotti 5
28074 Ghemme
(Novara)
Tel. 0163 840 041
Fax 0163 841 595
cantalupovigneti@
tiscalinet.it

Owner
Arlunno family

Founded
1977

Winemakers
Alberto Arlunno, with
consultant Donato
Lanati

Production
8,000–10,000 bottles in
fine years

Vintages
1999 1998 1997 1990
1989 1988 1985 1982

Price
● ●

Note
Collis Breclemae labels
will carry Ghemme
DOCG from the 1996
vintage on

Few wines speak so poignantly of the past as the Ghemme of Antichi Vigneti di Cantalupo, named for the ancient vineyards of the "howling wolf" that symbolizes the Arlunno family estate. The scholarly Alberto Arlunno, whose family has been in the town of Ghemme since at least 1550, couples his vocation of winemaking with a penchant for ancient history that explains his habit of naming vineyards in Latin.

Collis Breclemae is the acknowledged premier cru of Ghemme, a red wine named for the town founded by the Romans on the banks of the Sesia river in the Alpine foothills north of Novara. Ghemme, made from Nebbiolo (known locally as Spanna), gained DOCG status with the 1996 vintage, five years after the elevation of its more prominent neighbor Gattinara.

In recent times, the Ghemme of Cantalupo has seemed to me to show the most consistent class of all the Nebbiolo wines of northern Piedmont, in an era when producers of Gattinara, Carema, Lessona and other appellations seem to be struggling to develop a modern image. Alberto Arlunno gives top priority to his vineyards, while relying on the aid of eminent consulting enologist Donato Lanati to retain the traditional character of Ghemme. Collis Breclemae is vigorous and austere, yet balanced and full in bouquet and flavor. Cantalupo's other crus of Ghemme, Collis Carellae and Signore di Bayard show similar style, though Collis Breclemae seems to have an extra measure of finesse.

Vespolina and Uva Rara are permitted in Ghemme but Alberto keeps the lineage noble with pure Nebbiolo. He notes that Ghemme wines were praised by Pliny the Elder, the Emperor Frederick I (Barbarossa) and by Italy's first prime minister, Camillo Benso di Cavour, who himself produced Barolo but allowed that Ghemme had superior bouquet.

The estate, with 25 hectares of vines, produces about 150,000 bottles a year, including varietal Nebbiolo, Uva Rara and Vespolina under the DOC of Colline Novaresi, as well as a pure Nebbiolo IGT called Agamium (Latin for Ghemme).

Piedmont

Grapes
Nebbiolo (known locally as Spanna) 100%, hand picked in mid- to late October.

Vineyard
The ripest, healthiest grapes are selected in the Breclemae vineyard of about 10 hectares in mineral-rich alluvial glacial moraine on slopes facing south-southwest at 280–310 meters of altitude in the Pelizzana area of the communes of Ghemme and Romagnano Sesia. The vines, ranging in age from 11–31 years, are planted at densities of 1,900–3,700 per hectare and trained in the Guyot cordon method.

Vinification and aging
Grapes are stemmed and soft crushed and the musts fermented for 8–10 days in stainless steel tanks at temperatures of 30–32°C. After malolactic fermentation, the wine is matured for 27 months in 3,000-liter casks of Slavonian oak. The wine, of about 13% alcohol, is bottled and cellared for 15 months before release.

1990
Collis Breclemæ
GHEMME
DENOMINAZIONE DI ORIGINE CONTROLLATA

Style and maturity
Collis Breclemae has bright ruby-garnet color taking on hints of brick red with age. The bouquet is full and complex, with notes of wild berries, violets and licorice. Flavors are vibrant yet austere, with fruit sensations tempered by tannins that soften as the wine gains in length and elegance on the palate for 10–15 years and sometimes more.

Serving
🌡 18–20°C.
🍷 Tall, ample glass (Burgundy type).
🍽 Roast and braised meats, notably *tapulon,* minced donkey meat, as well as game and aged cheeses, such as Cravariola, from the Ossola valley in the Alps.

Briccolero
Dolcetto di Dogliani DOC ▮

Producer
Azienda Agricola
Chionetti Quinto
& Figlio
San Luigi 44
12063 Dogliani
(Cuneo)
Tel. 0173 711 79
Fax 0173 711 79

Owner
Quinto Chionetti

Founded
1920

Winemaker
Quinto Chionetti

Production
25,000 bottles annually

Vintages
1999 1998 1997 1992
1990

Price
●

Dogliani, a quiet town south of Barolo in Piedmont's Langhe hills, claims to be the birthplace and capital of Dolcetto. Documents verify that the vine was grown there in the sixteenth century, though legend has it that in 1303 the tyrannical Marchese di Clavesana ordered that Dolcetto alone be planted in his lands, warning that violators would be decapitated.

Over the ages, cooler heads prevailed and by 1974 Dolcetto di Dogliani had become a DOC. Yet, somehow, in the 1970s, despite the billboard proclaiming its primacy with Dolcetto, Dogliani as a wine town seemed but a ghost of its former self. The estate of Luigi Einaudi, the native son who became first president of the Italian Republic after World War II, sold respectable Dolcetto in bottle, but most producers peddled their rustic wines in bulk.

Then, in the early 1980s, the Quinto Chionetti estate came forth with Briccolero, the first single-vineyard Dolcetto di Dogliani. Briccolero was the creation of Quinto Chionetti's son Andrea, a gifted young man who demonstrated that lower yields in the vineyards and new techniques in the cellars (including the use of temperature-controlled tanks instead of old oak casks) could bring out unexpected virtues in Dolcetto.

Briccolero quickly became the paragon of Dolcetto in Piedmont in the 1980s and the inspiration for the revival of premium winemaking in Dogliani. Today at least a dozen estates make first-rate wines in what is once again recognized as the capital of Dolcetto.

Andrea Chionetti perished in a car accident in 1989, a tragedy that stunned his many friends and admirers, some of whom remember him as a sort of patron saint of modern Dolcetto. Now in his mid-seventies, Quinto Chionetti carries on gallantly, working his 14 hectares of vines to produce about 70,000 bottles a year of Dolcetto only, led by Briccolero, widely acclaimed as Dogliani's premier cru.

Piedmont

CHIONETTI

DOLCETTO DI DOGLIANI
DENOMINAZIONE DI ORIGINE CONTROLLATA

BRICCOLERO
1998

IMBOTTIGLIATO DA QUINTO E ANDREA CHIONETTI
VITICOLTORI A DOGLIANI - ITALIA

ITALIA   e 75 cl.

Grapes
Dolcetto 100%, hand
picked in September.

Vineyard
Briccolero of 7 hectares
in calcareous soils at the
crest of a hill sloping
southeast at about 400
meters of altitude in the
San Luigi area of the
commune of Dogliani.
The vines, of an average
age of 36 years, are
trained in the Guyot
cordon method.

Vinification and aging
Grapes are crushed
following traditional
methods and the musts
fermented on the skins
for as long as 30 days in
stainless steel tanks at
20–30°C. After
malolactic fermentation
at natural temperatures,
the wine, of about 14%
alcohol, is racked and
settled, then bottled and
cellared for 4 or 5
months before release.

Style and maturity
Dolcetto di Dogliani
Briccolero has a deep
mulberry-purple color and full
fragrance of ripe berries with
a hint of fermenting grapes on
the nose. Rich and round on
the palate, its mellow fruit
flavors are reminiscent of
black cherries with an almost
chocolate-like sweetness offset
by a mouth-tingling bitter
undertone. The wine is
delicious after a year, holding
its buoyant fruit flavors for a
year or two beyond, though, if
necessary, it will maintain
dignity longer.

Serving
🌡 18°C.
🍷 Medium-sized glass.
🍽 Piedmontese antipasti, such
as *carne cruda* (marinated
raw beef) and *fonduta*
(cheese fondue) with white
truffles; *cisrà* (tripe and
chickpea soup); grilled pork
and poultry.

Camp Gros Martinenga
Barbaresco DOCG ▼

Producer
Tenuta Cisa Asinari dei
Marchesi di Gresy
Via Rabajà 43
12050 Barbaresco
(Cuneo)
Tel. 0173 635 221
Fax 0173 635 187
wine@
marchesidigresy.com
www.marchesidigresy.
com

Owner
Alberto Cisa Asinari di
Gresy

Founded
1798

Winemakers
Piero Ballario and
Marco Dotta

Production
7,000–10,000 bottles in
fine years

Vintages
1999 1998 1997 1996
1995 1990 1989 1986
1985 1983 1982 1979
1978

Price
● ● ●

Alberto di Gresy in 1973 decided to start producing wine under his own label rather than selling grapes to merchants who knew perhaps better than did the young marquis that his Martinenga vineyards were among the foremost of Barbaresco. Alberto, whose family had owned the property since the late 18th century, admits that the decision was inspired by his dynamic neighbor Angelo Gaja, who was busy building Barbaresco's international fame.

It took Alberto a while to establish a reputation, perhaps because the full name of his estate—Tenuta Cisa Asinari dei Marchesi di Gresy—spread across two lines of small print under the family crest on labels lacked the visual impact of "GAJA" in bold white letters on black. Or, more likely, the amiable Alberto was content to let his wines express their inherent virtues without being pushed.

Still, by the 1980s, the single-vineyard Barbarescos of Camp Gros Martinenga and Gaiun Martinenga, first produced in 1978, were regularly ranked among the elite of Nebbiolo.

Gaiun, matured in part in small barrels of French oak, has a polish that might be described as modern, while Camp Gros, aged in casks of Slavonian oak, reveals somewhat greater size and authority in a more traditional vein. Critics and admirers seem to be about evenly split in their preferences, though to my taste Camp Gros better expresses the aristocratic yet warm and convivial character that Alberto di Gresy brings to his domain.

From 29 hectares of vines at Martinenga, at the Monte Aribaldo property at nearby Treiso and at Cassine in the hills of Asti, the estate produces about 180,000 bottles of wine a year. Beyond Barbaresco DOCG, these include Nebbiolo d'Alba DOC Martinenga, Dolcetto d'Alba DOC Monte Aribaldo and Langhe DOC Chardonnay, Sauvignon, Virtus (Cabernet/Barbera) and Villa Martis (Nebbiolo/Barbera), as well as Moscato d'Asti DOCG La Serra.

Piedmont

Grapes
Nebbiolo 100%, hand picked in October.

Vineyard
Camp Gros is a plot of 2.4 hectares in calcareous marls on a slope facing south at 280 meters of altitude in the Martinenga area of the commune of Barbaresco. The vines, of an average age of 31 years, are planted at a density of 4,000 per hectare and trained in the Guyot cordon method.

Vinification and aging
Grapes are stemmed and soft crushed and the musts fermented on the skins for 8–10 days at 28–30°C in stainless steel tanks with the cap submerged for about 5 days. After malolactic fermentation at controlled temperatures, the wine, of about 13.5% alcohol, is matured for a year in 2,500-liter casks of Slavonian oak, then bottled and cellared for another year before release.

Style and maturity
Barbaresco Camp Gros Martinenga has bright ruby-garnet color tending toward brick red with age. The bouquet is rich and flowery, with scents reminiscent of blackberries, spices and violets. On the palate, the wine shows solid weight and fine balance with impressive depth of flavors that fill out and lengthen over a decade or more as aristocratic breed comes to the fore.

Serving
🍷 18–20°C, opening the bottle an hour earlier.
🍷 Ample glass (Burgundy type).
🍽 *Agnolotti* pasta envelopes with meat sauce and truffles; stewed pigeon and duck; English-style roast beef.

Pajana
Barolo DOCG ♟

Producer
Azienda Agricola
Domenico Clerico
Località Manzoni-
Cucchi 67
12065 Monforte d'Alba
(Cuneo)
Tel. 0173 781 71
Fax 0173 789 800

Owner
Domenico Clerico

Founded
1976

**Winemaker and
vineyard manager**
Domenico Clerico

Production
6,500 bottles in fine
years

Vintages
1999 1998 1997 1996
1995 1994 1993 1991
1990

Price
● ● ●

D omenico Clerico grew up on a farm, but he didn't consider a career in wine until 1976, when he gave up his job selling olive oil to follow his father's path as a *vignaiolo*. In those days, growing grapes didn't always coincide with making good wine and he admits that he still had a lot to learn when he bottled his first Barolo from 1979. But he soon acquired the knack to become a leader among Piedmont's new wave winemakers, whose innovative cellar techniques include maturing Barolo and other wines in small barrels of French oak.

Clerico and colleagues have been accused of flouting the grand tradition of aristocratically austere Barolo, a frequently voiced charge that the amiable winemaker greets with a patient smile and shrug. "I'm interested in making the best wines possible from native varieties," he says. "New oak used judiciously rounds out Barolo and enhances color and depth of flavors, but the main thing I've learned in these years is that the secret of fine wine is all in the grapes."

Domenico, a wiry man with bushy hair and a prominent mustache, has a jovial nature that can make him hard to take seriously until you taste his wines. His prime Barolos come from Pajana and Ciabot Mentin Ginestra, adjacent vineyards in the Ginestra area of Monforte. Equally admired is his Langhe DOC called Arte (Nebbiolo with 10% Barbera), his first wine to be aged in barriques. Pajana combines smooth opulence with vital fruit sensations and splendid harmony in a style that exalts the so-called new Barolo, though in a blind tasting it would be hard to distinguish from Ciabot Mentin Ginestra.

Astute acquisitions have expanded vineyards to 15 hectares, primarily in the Ginestra area, enabling Domenico and wife Giuliana to gradually build total production to about 75,000 bottles a year. The list includes DOC Barbera and Dolcetto d'Alba and Langhe DOC Freisa La Ginestrina.

Piedmont

Grapes
Nebbiolo 100%, hand picked in October.

Vineyard
Pajana, a plot of 1.8 hectares in tufaceous marl mixed with sand and clay on a slope facing south at 300 meters of altitude in the Ginestra area of the commune of Monforte in the southeastern part of the Barolo zone. The vines, planted between 1965 and 1970 at a density of 3,800–4,200 per hectare, are trained in the Guyot cordon method.

Vinification and aging
Grapes are stemmed and soft crushed and the musts are fermented using indigenous yeasts for 5–10 days in a stainless steel rotomaceration tank at temperatures of 28–30°C. After malolactic fermentation, the wine is matured for 18–24 months in small oak barrels, 90% of which are new. The wine, of about 13.5% alcohol, is bottled without filtering and cellared before release.

Style and maturity
Barolo Pajana has deep ruby color, taking on garnet tones over time. The bouquet is full and vital with scents reminiscent of violets and berries and hints of vanilla and tobacco. On the palate, it has impressive weight and balance, with fruit sensations in great concentration and smooth, round, opulent flavors that linger on the tongue. The wine approaches peaks in 4–5 years after the harvest, but promises to retain rich complexity well beyond.

Serving
- 18°C.
- Ample glass (Burgundy type).
- Piedmontese meat and game dishes, such as beef braised in Barolo or hare stewed with red wine and herbs, as well as aged cheeses, in particular the pungent Castelmagno.

Granbussia
Barolo Riserva DOCG 🍷

Producer
Poderi Aldo Conterno
Località Bussia 48
12065 Monforte d'Alba
(Cuneo)
Tel. 0173 781 50
Fax 0173 787 240
il-vino@il-vino.com
www.il-vino.com

Owner
Aldo Conterno

Founded
1969

Winemakers
Stefano and Franco
Conterno

Vineyard manager
Stefano Conterno

Production
6,500–8,000 bottles in
choice years

Vintages
1999 1998 1997 1996
1995 1990 1989 1988
1985 1982 1978 1974
1971

Price
● ● ●

Aldo Conterno is a contemporary legend in Barolo, thanks to his integrity as a winemaker and the wisdom which he readily shares with other producers in his engaging gravelly voice. After emigrating to America in the 1950s (and serving in the U.S. Army in Korea), Aldo returned to Monforte to resume a career in wine at the estate run by his father Giacomo and older brother Giovanni (see page 50). But in 1969 he split to establish his own domain amid the family vineyards of Bussia.

Poderi Aldo Conterno is truly a family operation, with wife Gemma handling administration and sons Franco and Stefano in charge of cellars and vineyards. Aldo talks of retiring, but remains the driving spirit behind a winery whose Barolo invariably ranks among the most regal: the single-vineyard Bricco Bussia Cicala, Colonnello and Bussia Soprana and, above all, *riserva* Granbussia, made in outstanding vintages from grapes selected in three vineyards and matured for six years before being sold.

Aldo describes himself as a moderate traditionalist, though he admits with undisguised satisfaction that his sons have brought out a progressive streak in his nature. "Today we can make cleaner, fresher wines of greater color, richer fruit and softer tannins than before, without losing that noble stature that is unique to Barolo," he says. They mature Barolo religiously in large casks of Slavonian oak, but other wines, including the fine Barbera d'Alba DOC Conca Tre Pile and Langhe DOC Nebbiolo Il Favot, are finished in barriques.

Total production from 31 hectares of vineyards ranges from 160,000–190,000 bottles a year, including DOC Dolcetto d'Alba Bussia Soprana, Langhe Freisa Bussianella and two types of Chardonnay, one oak fermented, one not (see page 96). Aldo also makes Barolo Chinato, a tonic produced by steeping the bark of the chinchona tree in the wine until it takes on an enticingly bitter flavor. That prized *amaro* is served mainly in the Conterno home.

Grapes
Nebbiolo 100%, hand
picked in October.

Vineyards
Grapes for Granbussia
come from parts of three
plots—Romirasco 70%,
Colonnello 15%, Cicala
15%—covering 1.5
hectares in calcareous
marl with layers of sand
on slopes facing south at
420 meters of altitude in
the Bussia area of the
commune of Monforte in
the heart of the Barolo
zone. The vines, of an
average age of 31 years,
are planted at a density of
4,000 per hectare and
trained in the Guyot
cordon method.

Vinification and aging
Grapes are stemmed and
soft crushed and the
musts are fermented for
8–10 days in stainless
steel vats at 28°C. After
malolactic fermentation
at natural temperatures,
the wine is matured for
2–3 years in casks of
2,500- and 5,000-liter
capacity of Slavonian oak
and then in stainless steel
tanks for 2 years. Barolo
Granbussia, of about
14% alcohol, is bottled
and cellared for a year
before release.

Style and maturity
Barolo Granbussia when
released 6 years after the
harvest has warm ruby-garnet
color showing brick red on the
rim. The bouquet is generous
with scents reminiscent of ripe
berries and faded roses, spices
and tobacco. On the palate, it
has great weight and fine
balance, with concentrated
fruit sensations in richly varied
flavors that gain in length with
time as the wine reveals its
inherent breed. Granbussia is
approachable soon after
release, but peaks of depth and
harmony are reached at 10–15
years after the harvest.

Serving
- 18°C, decanting the wine
  30 minutes earlier.
- Ample glass (Burgundy
  type).
- Piedmontese meat and
  game dishes, such as
  carbonnade of beef stewed
  in red wine with onions, kid
  roast with herbs, venison
  braised in Barolo.

Giacomo Conterno

Monfortino Barolo Riserva DOCG

Producer
Azienda Vitivinicola
Giacomo Conterno
di Giovanni Conterno
Località Ornati 2
12065 Monforte d'Alba
(Cuneo)
Tel. 0173 782 21
Fax 0173 787 190

Owner
Giovanni Conterno

Founded
Late 18th century

Winemakers
Giovanni and Roberto Conterno

Vineyard manager
Albino Morando

Production
5,000–7,000 bottles in choice years

Vintages
1999 1998 1997 1996
1995 1993 1990 1988
1987 1985 1982 1979
1978 1974 1971 1970

Price
●●●●

The spacious cellars of the ultramodern winery that carries his father Giacomo's name seem out of character with Giovanni Conterno's philosophy of making wine. For if brother Aldo (see page 48) follows techniques that qualify as traditional, certain of Giovanni's methods might be considered antediluvian. He vinifies his Barolo for some 35 days on the skins (the current norm is less than 2 weeks) and ages the reserve Monfortino for at least 7 years in old casks (DOCG requires 2 years). Yet even admirers of new-style Nebbiolo concede that Monfortino is a monument to Barolo, a wine of massive structure, soaring bouquet and rich, ripe flavors that manage to be both bold and elegant.

Monfortino was named for the family's home town of Monforte d'Alba when Giovanni's grandfather first produced it in 1912 from acquired grapes. Today it originates in the neighboring village of Serralunga d'Alba, in a privileged plot amid the 14 hectares of vineyards of Cascina Francia. There Giovanni Conterno and son Roberto produce a second Barolo, as well as DOC Barbera and Dolcetto d'Alba, that carry the name Cascina Francia. In all, they produce from 60,000–80,000 bottles a year.

Towering over all is Monfortino, a wine which from the latest available vintage, 1990, was greeted with unprecedented critical praise. Giovanni, courtly and taciturn is modest about his accomplishments. "I make Barolo by the old method because that's the only way I know," he says. "I keep things simple: no clarifying, no filtering. I wouldn't be capable of learning new techniques or using barriques."

Yet, no doubt influenced by son Roberto, he installed stainless steel vats with computerized temperature control. "They are convenient," Giovanni admits. "You know, before we built here, I did everything by intuition, even staying in the old cellars all night to be sure I didn't miss those vital moments. Well, I'm getting on in years and I guess I need m sleep."

Piedmont

Grapes
Nebbiolo 100%, hand picked in mid-October.

Vineyard
Grapes for Monfortino come from Vigneto Francia covering 2 hectares in calcareous soils on slopes facing west-southwest at about 500 meters of altitude in the Francia area of the commune of Serralunga at the southeastern part of the Barolo zone. The vines, of an average age of 21 years, are planted at a density of about 3,000 per hectare and trained in the Guyot cordon method.

Vinification and aging
Grapes are stemmed and soft crushed and the musts are fermented in stainless steel vats at temperatures ranging from 24–30°C, remaining on the skins for 32–35 days. After malolactic fermentation at natural temperatures, the wine is matured for at least 7 years in casks of Slavonian oak of 2,000–10,000-liter capacity. Barolo Monfortino, of about 14% alcohol, is bottled and cellared for a time before release.

Style and maturity
Barolo Monfortino when released at least 8 years after the harvest has medium ruby-garnet color with brick red tones on the rim. The bouquet is intense with floral aspects and ripe fruit and berry sensations mingling with hints of licorice and tobacco. The wine has massive structure with robust fruit flavors offset by ample tannins that give it great depth, complexity and length on the palate. Monfortino may be approached within a decade, but it hits its stride at about 15 years and from great vintages holds virtues for 30 years or more.

Serving
- 18–19°C, opening the bottle 30 minutes earlier.
- Ample glass (Burgundy type).
- Roast and braised Piedmontese beef, saddle of veal, rabbit or hare *in civet* (marinated in red wine), aged cheeses.

La Val dei Preti
Nebbiolo d'Alba DOC ♥

Producer
Azienda Agricola
Matteo Correggia
Case Sparse
Garbinetto 124
12043 Canale
d'Alba (Cuneo)
Tel. 0173 978 009
Fax 0173 959 849
www.italywines.com

Owner
Matteo Correggia

Founded
1985

**Winemaker and
vineyard manager**
Matteo Correggia

Production
About 8,000 bottles

Vintages
1999 1998 1997 1996
1995 1993 1990 1989

Price
●●

The sandy soils of the Roero hills north of the Tanaro river and the town of Alba produce wines from Nebbiolo noted historically as being more delicate than those of the Langhe hills to the south, where calcareous terrains underlie the power and glory of Barolo. In Piedmont's hierarchy, Nebbiolo d'Alba ranks as a common cousin of the "king of wines" though a modest young man named Matteo Correggia provides proof of nobility with his single-vineyard La Val dei Preti.

Matteo had had no formal training as a winemaker when his father died in 1985, leaving him suddenly in charge of an estate that habitually sold its grapes to local cellars. With help from enologist friends, he produced his first bottles from 1987 and in a remarkably short time found himself in the vanguard of the progressive school of Piedmontese winemaking. His mastery of Nebbiolo d'Alba from the hills of Roero is confirmed in La Val dei Preti, a wine that manages to be both majestic and eminently appetizing even in its youth. His Roero Ròche d'Ampsèj (also from Nebbiolo) and Barbera d'Alba from the vineyard of Marun have earned similar acclaim. Those wines have been hailed as models of the new style reds of Piedmont that place the virtues of fragrance, fruity freshness, harmony and grace before the time-honored traits of sovereign might and longevity.

In 1999, a popular guide praised Matteo as among the very best small-scale winemakers of Italy, but he remains as unassuming as ever, quietly dedicating himself to his vines that have the advantage of being extremely old (30–60 years in the case of Nebbiolo), meaning that they render minimal quantities of grapes of exceptional quality.

From 15 hectares of vines, plus 3 hectares leased, Matteo and wife Ornella produce about 60,000 bottles of wine a year. These include DOC Roero Arneis, a regular Barbera d'Alba (as well as Marun) and a *vino da tavola* called Anthos, a rare dry version of the red Brachetto.

Piedmont

NEBBIOLO D'ALBA

Denominazione di Origine Controllata

1996

LA VAL DEI PRETI

Imbottigliato all'origine dal viticultore

Estate Bottled by Matteo Correggia

Canale · Italia

alc 14% by vol.   Net. cont. **750** ML ℮

Grapes
Nebbiolo 100%, hand
picked in mid-October.

Vineyard
La Val dei Preti covers
2.5 hectares in light
sandy soils with layers of
marl on a slope facing
south at 250 meters of
altitude in the Preti valley
in the Roero hills west of
the town of Canale. The
vines, of an average age of
41 years, are planted at a
density of 5,000 per
hectare and trained in the
Guyot cordon method.

Vinification and aging
Grapes are stemmed and
soft crushed and the
musts fermented for
10–15 days in stainless
steel maceration tanks
starting at 30°C and
ending at 20–25°C.
Malolactic fermentation
is done in small oak
barrels in a heated room,
after which the wine, of
about 14% alcohol, is
matured for 18 months
in barriques (80% new)
and 6 months in bottle
before release.

Style and maturity
Nebbiolo La Val dei Preti is
ready to enjoy after 3 years
when it shows deep ruby-
garnet color and exhilarating
bouquet with scents of violets,
plums, berries, cinnamon and
clove. On the palate, the wine
is deliciously smooth, round
and harmonious with soft
tannins supporting ripe fruit
and berry sensations that
linger on the tongue. If not as
powerful and long-lived as the
traditional style of Barolo, this
Nebbiolo should remain
elegantly drinkable for at least
a decade.

Serving
- 17–18°C, decanting wine
  more than four years old.
- Ample glass (Burgundy
  type).
- Ossobuco (veal shank),
  beef braised in Nebbiolo,
  game birds *in civet*
  (marinated in wine) and
  served with a veil of
  powdered chocolate.

Sorì San Lorenzo
Barbaresco DOCG 🍷

Producer
Gaja
Via Torino 36A
12050 Barbaresco
(Cuneo)
Tel. 0173 635158
Fax 0173 635256
gajad@tin.it

Owner
Gaja family

Founded
1859

Chief winemaker
Guido Rivella

Vineyard managers
Giorgio Culasso and
Mauro Abrigo

Production
About 12,000 bottles
from choice vintages,
including 500 magnums
and 100 double
magnums

Vintages
1999 1998 1997 1996
1995 1990 1989 1988
1985 1982 1979 1978
1971 1970

Price
● ● ● ●

Note
From the 1996 vintage
on, Sorì San Lorenzo
will be classified as
Langhe Nebbiolo DOC
and not Barbaresco
DOCG

Angelo Gaja's boundless energy, charismatic flair and elevated prices have made him Italy's most admired and discussed winemaker. As Piedmont's pre-eminent producer, Gaja would have at least five candidates for top honors among Italian red wines. But his sentimental favorite is Sorì San Lorenzo, the Barbaresco from the 1967 vintage that became his first wine to carry the name of a single vineyard.

"Over time Sorì San Lorenzo has always rewarded us with quality, even from mediocre vintages," says Angelo, who notes that the wine shows unique depth and harmony over time. Some critics may prefer other single-vineyard Barbaresco Sorì Tildin or Costa Russi or the more recently conceived Barolo Sperss or Conteisa Cerequio or the Cabernet Sauvignon called Darmagi. Some even predict that Gaja will surpass his Piedmontese masterpieces with wines from his properties at Bolgheri and Montalcino in Tuscany.

But Angelo and resident winemaker Guido Rivella admit to having a special feeling for Sorì San Lorenzo, a wine from the 1989 vintage that had a book dedicated to it: *The Vines of San Lorenzo* by the American author Edward Steinberg. Gaja built his reputation on Barbaresco in wines that show the basic power and depth of the Nebbiolo grape but with richer color, fuller fruit, better balance and more refined style than before.

In 2000, Angelo announced his stunning decision to declassify single-vineyard Barbaresco and Barolo to the category of Langhe Nebbiolo DOC, keeping only the basic Barbaresco as DOCG to "uphold the family tradition."

Gaja owns 26 properties covering 83 hectares in the Alba area for an annual production of about 300,000 bottles a year. Beyond Barbaresco and the now declassified Barolo, he makes wines that qualify under Langhe DOC: Dolcetto (Sito Cremes), Barbera (Sito Rey), a blend of Nebbiolo, Merlot and Barbera (Sito Moresco), Cabernet Sauvignon (Darmagi), Chardonnay (Gaia & Rey, see page 108, and Rossj-Bass) and Sauvignon Blanc (Alteni di Brassica).

Piedmont

Grapes
Nebbiolo 100%, hand picked in October.

Vineyard
Sorì San Lorenzo, a plot of 3.92 hectares in calcareous clay soils on slopes facing south at 260 meters of altitude at the southeastern edge of the village of Barbaresco on land that once belonged to the parish of San Lorenzo in Alba. The vines, of an average age of 21 years, are planted at a density of 2,600 per hectare and trained in the Guyot cordon method.

Vinification and aging
Grapes are stemmed and soft crushed and the must fermented for 15–20 days in stainless steel vats at just under 30°C. After malolactic fermentation, the wine is aged for 2 years in oak—a part in small new barrels and a part in large traditional casks. The wine, of about 13.5% alcohol, is bottled without filtering and cellared for a year before release.

Style and maturity
Sorì San Lorenzo has fine ruby color showing garnet tones on the rim with age. The bouquet, which heightens over time, recalls violets, vanilla, ripe cherries, cassis and blackberries. Solid structure is marked by uncommon elegance on the palate, with fruit flavors that are rich and vital, yet round, soft and long. From great vintages, the wine begins rounding into form after 5 years and maintains its splendor for a decade or more, reaching peaks of mellow complexity at 12–15 years of age.

Serving
🍷 17–18°C.
🍷 Tall, ample *ballon* (Burgundy type).
🍽 Roast and braised beef, game and poultry, including duck, goose and pigeon. Medium-aged cheeses, such as Bra d'Alpeggio and Castelmagno.

Bruno Giacosa

Santo Stefano di Neive
Barbaresco Riserva DOCG 🍷

Producer
Casa Vinicola
Bruno Giacosa & C.
Via XX Settembre 52
12057 Neive (Cuneo)
Tel. 0173 670 27
Fax 0173 677 477

Owner
Bruno Giacosa

Founded
1900

Winemakers
Bruno Giacosa and
Dante Scaglione

Vineyard manager
Dante Scaglione

Production
An average of 10,000
bottles from select
vintages

Vintages
1999 1998 1997 1996
1995 1990 1989 1985
1982 1978 1971 1967
1964 1961

Price
● ● ●

Bruno Giacosa was perennially portrayed as a staunch traditionalist, whose Barbaresco showed the same sort of power, depth and longevity as the theoretically bigger Barolo. He was known as a *barolista* by admirers of the grand old style of Barolo, though his most distinguished wine has been Barbaresco Riserva Santo Stefano di Neive, exemplified by the 1971, which stood for decades as a monument to Nebbiolo.

Bruno, a pensive, patient man whose reserved manner belies his reputation as one of Piedmont's all-time great winemakers, seems tired of hearing about old styles and new. The fact is that his remodeled family cellars at Neive in the Barbaresco zone are thoroughly up to date. Bruno and resident winemaker Dante Scaglione use stainless steel tanks to ferment wines for a normal 10–15 days on the skins (as opposed to the month or more of the past) and they mature Barbaresco and Barolo in medium-large barrels of French oak from Allier, rather than the ponderous old casks from Slavonia. They do not use the smaller barriques favored by progressives and they continue to age reserve Barbaresco and Barolo (which carry wine-red labels instead of white) for three years in casks, somewhat longer than the norm.

Bruno, who only recently bought some vineyards of his own, is known for his intimate knowledge of *terroirs*. This has enabled him to acquire grapes for a range of some of the most admired wines of Piedmont, produced at the rate of about 450,000 bottles a year. From Barbaresco, he favors the crus of Asili, Gallina di Neive and, of course, Santo Stefano di Neive. For Barolo, he excels with Falletto and Vigna Rionda from Serralunga and Villero from Castiglione Falletto. He also makes fine Barbera d'Alba, Dolcetto d'Alba, Nebbiolo d'Alba and Grignolino d'Asti. The graceful white Roero Arneis and exquisite sparkling Bruno Giacosa Extra Brut show the versatility of a winemaker who might best be described as an enlightened craftsman.

Piedmont

Grapes
Nebbiolo 100%, hand picked in October.

Vineyard
Santo Stefano, a plot of 4.5 hectares in calcareous clay soils on slopes facing southwest at 300 meters of altitude in the commune of Neive in the northern part of the Barbaresco zone. The vines, of an average age of 26 years, are planted at a density of 3,500 per hectare and trained in the Guyot cordon method.

Vinification and aging
Grapes are stemmed and soft crushed and the must fermented for 10–15 days on the skins in stainless steel vats at 25–32°C. After malolactic fermentation in oak casks, the wine is aged for 36 months in casks of French oak from Allier ranging in capacity from 2,700–10,800 liters. The wine, of about 14% alcohol, is bottled and cellared for 6–12 months before release.

BARBARESCO
DENOMINAZIONE DI ORIGINE CONTROLLATA E GARANTITA
SANTO STEFANO DI NEIVE
1996

N° 5294

Casa Vinicola
BRUNO GIACOSA
ITALIA - NEIVE (PIEMONTE) ITALIA

Style and maturity
Santo Stefano di Neive Riserva has deep ruby-garnet color taking on brick red tones with age. The bouquet becomes splendidly complex as the wine hits its stride at 8–10 years, with scents suggesting violets, blackberries, fine leather, spices and sage. The potent structure is underscored by bracing tannins in a wine that needs time to find its equilibrium and reveal uncommon depth in warm, vital flavors that linger on the palate. From great vintages, life expectancy exceeds 2 decades.

Serving
🍷 18°C.
🍷 Tall, ample *ballon* (Burgundy type).
🍽 Piedmontese meat and game dishes, such as spit-roasted kid, hare *in civet* (marinated in red wine), braised veal; medium-aged cheeses, such as Raschera and Castelmagno.

Montruc
Barbera d'Asti Superiore
DOC ❢

Producer
Franco M.
Martinetti & C.
Corso F. Turati 14
10128 Torino
Tel. 011 8395 937
Fax 011 8106 598

Owner
Franco M. Martinetti

Founded
1974

Winemakers
Giuliano and Elena Noè
and Giancarlo Scaglione

Vineyard manager
Piero Roseo

Production
About 18,000 bottles in
choice years

Vintages
1999 1998 1997 1996
1990 1989 1988 1985

Price
● ●

Franco Martinetti followed his sense of taste into the production of wines that have steadily risen toward the summit in Piedmont. A gourmet from Turin with an unerring palate, Martinetti started making wine on a trial basis in the 1970s. But instead of settling in the Langhe hills of Alba to capitalize on the fortunes of the noble Nebbiolo in Barolo and Barbaresco, he headed for the Monferrato hills of Asti to take up the challenge of raising the status of the bourgeois Barbera.

He was encouraged from the start by the late Giacomo Bologna (see page 36), the patron of modern Barbera, who in turn introduced him to Giuliano Noè and Giancarlo Scaglione, the winemaking team that has been with him in his ventures since. Instead of buying properties, Martinetti, who refers to himself as a cultivator of wine (*vinicultore*) rather than a grower of grapes (*viticultore*), leases vineyards at Vinchio for Barbera and Cabernet and at Gavi for the white of that name.

His Gavi DOCG Minaia and Monferrato Rosso DOC Sulbric (from a blend of Barbera and Cabernet Sauvignon) rank near the top of their categories, but Martinetti's tour de force is the Barbera d'Asti Superiore DOC Montruc, whose name in dialect refers to the crest of a hill. That wine, made since 1985 under the expertise of Noè (now aided by his daughter Elena), has become a model of the new eminence of Barbera with a style that makes one wonder how the variety could have remained so long a commoner.

Martinetti, who produces about 70,000 bottles of wine a year in cellars at Vinchio, Rovereto di Gavi and La Morra, also makes a Barbera d'Asti Bric dei Banditi that is less imposing than Montruc but a sheer delight to drink.

Piedmont

Grapes
Barbera 100%, hand picked in early October.

Vineyard
Montruc, a plot of about 4 hectares of sandy calcareous clays on a slope facing south-southwest at 280 meters of altitude in the community of Vinchio in the Monferrato hills 15 kilometers southeast of Asti. The vines, more than 41 years old, are planted at a density of 4,600 per hectare and trained in the Guyot cordon method.

Vinification and aging
Grapes are stemmed and soft crushed and the must fermented for about 10 days in stainless steel vats at 25–31°C. Malolactic fermentation at 20–21°C without use of sulfur dioxide is followed by 12–14 months of maturing in small barrels of French oak. The wine, of about 13.5% alcohol, is cellared for several months before release.

Style and maturity
Montruc on release shows the deep ruby-violet color of young Barbera, gradually taking on garnet hues with age. Its ample bouquet is fresh and clean with scents of berries and ripe fruit underlined by hints of spice and vanilla. A wine of impressive structure, its full fruit flavors are smoothly dry and perfectly balanced against oak tannins that mingle in the soft, long aftertaste. The wine is already attractive 2 years after the harvest, reaching an elegant prime after 5 or 6 years and maintaining class for well over a decade.

Serving
- 18°C, possibly decanting aged wine.
- Ample *ballon* (Burgundy type).
- Piedmontese beef roast or braised; feathered game, such as pheasant and partridge; aged cheeses, such as Taleggio and Castelmagno.

**Giuseppe
Mascarello**

Monprivato
Barolo DOCG ♥

Producer
Azienda Agricola
Mascarello
Giuseppe e Figlio
Strada del Grosso 1
12060 Castiglione
Falletto (Cuneo)
Tel. 0173 792 126
Fax 0173 792 124

Owner
Mauro Mascarello

Founded
1881

Winemakers
Mauro and Giuseppe
Mascarello, with
Donato Lanati

Vineyard manager
Mauro Mascarello

Production
From 8,500–30,000
bottles a year

Vintages
1999 1998 1997 1996
1995 1993 1990 1989
1985 1982 1978 1974
1971 1970

Price
● ● ●

The French term cru sums up the elements of a vineyard: "site, soil, climate, grape varieties, techniques, quality and reputation," as the eminent enologist Emile Peynaud defined it. Since a precise equivalent doesn't exist in other languages, the term has been widely adopted, though perhaps nowhere outside of France is the concept as deeply rooted as in Piedmont.

Mauro Mascarello can show that his prime vineyard of Monprivato was recorded in the archives of Castiglione Falletto in 1666, almost two centuries before Barolo was conceived as a dry red wine by another French enologist, Louis Oudart. Renato Ratti in the 1990 edition of his respected vineyard map of Barolo rated Monprivato as one of ten "first category" sites.

Mascarello, whose family had owned a part of Monprivato since 1904, first used the name on a label of Barolo from 1970, finally bringing his holdings to a major share of 6 hectares with the purchase of a second plot in 1985. He maintains that Barolo's best vineyards produce wines that are intrinsically rich in flavor with softer, sweeter tannins than from lesser sites. But he insists that yields must be limited to extremes to show virtues that are best maintained by traditional methods of minimal intervention in the cellars.

Monprivato, from a privileged position along Barolo's central valley, shows rare splendor from superior vintages, when it seems to strike a median between the potency of wines from the villages of Monforte and Serralunga to the south and east and the gentility of those from the towns of Barolo and La Morra to the west. Yet from minor vintages Monprivato sometimes fails to rise above the level of the ordinary.

Mauro Mascarello, who owns 17 hectares of vines in the Alba area, has his main cellars at Monchiero west of the Barolo zone. Working with his wife Maria Teresa and son Giuseppe, he makes 40,000–50,000 bottles of wine a year, including Barolo Villero and Santo Stefano di Perno, and Barbera and Dolcetto d'Alba DOC.

Grapes
Nebbiolo 100%, hand picked in mid-October.

Vineyard
Monprivato, a plot of 6 hectares in calcareous clays on slopes facing southwest at 280–350 meters of altitude in the Monprivato area at the western edge of the village of Castiglione Falletto along the central valley of the Barolo zone. The vines, between 21 and 26 years old, are planted at a density of 5,000 per hectare and trained in a short Guyot cordon method.

Vinification and aging
Grapes are stemmed and soft crushed and the musts fermented in stainless steel and cement tanks at 28–30°C for 20–25 days on the skins. After malolactic fermentation in stainless steel tanks, the wine is matured for 4 years in casks of Slavonian oak of 5,000–9,000-liter capacity. After bottling, the wine, of about 13.5% alcohol, is cellared for 5–6 months before release.

Style and maturity
Barolo Monprivato on release after about 5 years shows fine ruby-garnet color, tending toward warm brick red over time. The bouquet is complex with ripe fruit scents mingling with hints of licorice and tobacco. A wine of medium–full body, it shows more elegance than power in fruit sensations finely balanced against tannins in warm, round flavors that gain in complexity and length for a decade and from great vintages can hold well for at least a decade beyond.

Serving
🍷 16–18°C.
🍷 Ample *ballon* (Burgundy type).
🍽 Piedmontese beef and game dishes, lamb and kid roasted with herbs, classic Piedmontese cheeses: Raschera, Bra, Murazzano and Castelmagno.

Nino Negri

5 Stelle
Valtellina Sfursat DOC

Producer
Nino Negri
Via Ghibellini 3
23030 Chiuro (Sondrio)
Tel. 0342 482 521
Fax 0342 482 235
negri@giv.it

Owner
Gruppo Italiano Vini

Founded
1897

Winemaker
Casimiro Maule

Vineyard manager
Casimiro Maule

Production
20,000–25,000 bottles
from choice vintages

Vintages
1998 1997 1996 1995
1994 1990 1989 1988
1986 1983

Price
● ● ●

Valtellina, the Alpine valley near the border of Switzerland, is one of Italy's most scenic wine zones. Vines may have been planted there by the ancient Liguri or Etruscans, whose hand-hewn terraces remain as monuments to human fortitude. The principal vine for centuries has been Nebbiolo, known locally as Chiavennasca, though exactly when (or even if) it arrived from Piedmont is a mystery.

The zone has a two-level appellation topped by Valtellina Superiore DOCG for wines made from at least 95 percent Nebbiolo in the subdistricts of Fracia, Grumello, Inferno, and Sassella. The Superiore wines are especially admired by the Swiss, who import a major share of them.

The second level is Valtellina DOC for wines that contain at least 70 percent Nebbiolo with other varieties permitted: a normal red and a rich Sforzato (from "forced," in reference to drying of grapes in a process similar to that of Valpolicella's Amarone). Sforzato, or Sfursat in dialect, has drawn most of the recent attention to the Valtellina, whose wines had long been overlooked by Italians.

The making of wines from semidried grapes seems to have been practiced here as early as the sixteenth century, when Leonardo da Vinci described them as "very potent." Carlo Negri, whose father Nino in 1897 founded what is today Valtellina's major winery, revived the practice in 1956. Casimiro Maule, who directs the cellars now owned by the Gruppo Italiano Vini, points out that Sfursat has improved remarkably due to new techniques and the use of small oak barrels, which enhances the uncommon array of scents and flavors.

Maule began in 1983 to make the select Sfursat 5 Stelle, the "five stars" reflecting its status as the most decorated wine of Valtellina. Sfursat excels not only in fine vintages but also in years when weather conditions remain dry and cold through months of drying. Nino Negri has 16 hectares of vines and another 20 hectares leased to produce about 700,000 bottles a year of the range of Valtellina wines.

Lombardy

Grapes
Nebbiolo (called Chiavennasca locally) 100%, hand picked between late September and mid-October. Bunches are extended on cane mats in houses where east–west air currents favor drying for 100–130 days.

Vineyards
Various plots in loose, shallow, sandy soils sustained by dry walls on terraces facing south and southeast on steep slopes between 350 and 450 meters of altitude in various parts of the Valtellina. The vines, between 11 and 41 years old, are planted at densities of about 3,600 per hectare and trained in a Guyot simple curtain method with ascending vegetation.

Vinification and aging
The semidried grapes are stemmed and soft crushed and the musts fermented at 27–30°C for 10–15 days in stainless steel vats with rotating paddles. Malolactic fermentation occurs naturally in oak barrels before the wine is matured for 16 months in new barriques of French oak. The wine, of 14.5–15% alcohol, is bottled and cellared for 6 months before release.

Style and maturity
5 Stelle has deep ruby-garnet color, taking on tinges of brick red with age. The bouquet is complex with scents reminiscent of prunes, raisins, vanilla, coffee, dried rose petals and toasted hazelnuts. The wine is extremely concentrated and vigorous on the palate, yet harmonious with rich fruit flavors offset by ample acidity and soft wood tannins that add a spicy aspect to the smooth, warm flavors. The wine reaches a prime at 8–12 years, though great vintages such as 1997 and 1989 should retain splendor for two decades.

Serving
🌡 18°C, decanting wines more than 5 years old.
🍷 Ample crystal *ballon* (Burgundy type).
🍽 Roast beef and Alpine game; *sciatt* (buckwheat fritters with cheese and grappa); braised rump steak with polenta; the Valtellina cheese called Bitto.

Prunotto

Pian Romualdo
Barbera d'Alba DOC ❢

Producer
Prunotto
Regione San
Cassiano 4/G
12051 Alba (Cuneo)
Tel. 0173 280 017
Fax 0173 281 167
prunotto@
areacom.it
www.prunotto.it

Owner
Marchesi Antinori

Founded
1904

Winemaker
Gianluca Torrengo

Vineyard manager
Gianluca Torrengo

Production
About 20,000 bottles
annually

Vintages
1999 1998 1997 1996
1990

Price
●

Alfredo Prunotto was one of the most admired vintners who bought grapes from choice vineyards in the Alba area in the early part of the twentieth century. The winery's reputation was enhanced by his successor Beppe Colla, who also led the local producers' consortium and the order of *cavalieri* dedicated to the legendary white truffles and wines of Alba.

Although Prunotto owned no vines, Beppe Colla became an Italian pioneer in citing vineyards on labels. He began with the 1961 vintage from which, along with Barolo from venerated sites, Prunotto released a Barbera Cru Pian Romualdo di Monforte d'Alba. That move marked Beppe as a believer in Barbera decades before the variety became fashionable. Previously, growers had exploited the vine's vigor and adaptability to make red wines for everyday. But recently, Barbera has undergone a revival that threatens the supremacy of Nebbiolo, source of Barolo and Barbaresco. Thanks to Prunotto, the high vineyard of Pian Romualdo, just beyond the southeastern fringe of the Barolo zone, ranks as a premier cru of Barbera d'Alba.

In 1989, Marchesi Antinori of Florence (see page 252) acquired a major share of Prunotto, taking full control in 1994 when Beppe Colla retired. But the Tuscan house, directed by Marchese Piero Antinori's daughter Albiera, has maintained the traditional tone of Prunotto, while gradually acquiring vineyards in the hills of Alba and neighboring Asti.

Today the winery owns 42 hectares of vines, which account for a fair share of total production of about 600,000 bottles a year. These take in a full range of Alba wines, including Barolo from Bussia and Cannubi, Barbaresco from Bric Turot, as well as single-vineyard Barbera, Dolcetto and Nebbiolo DOC. The firm also makes Moscato d'Asti DOCG and two single-vineyard versions of Barbera d'Asti: Costamiole and Fiulot.

Piedmont

Grapes
Barbera 100%, hand picked in mid-October.

Vineyard
An extension of 35 hectares in pale calcareous clay soils on slopes oriented toward the south at about 500 meters of altitude in the Pian Romualdo area at the eastern extreme of the commune of Monforte d'Alba. The vines, of an average age of 31 years, are planted at a density of 4,000 per hectare and trained in the Guyot cordon method.

Vinification and aging
Grapes are stemmed and soft crushed and the must fermented in stainless steel tanks at 29°C for 12 days on the skins. After malolactic fermentation, the wine is matured for 12 months, partly in 5,000-liter casks and partly in 500-liter tonneaux and 225-liter barriques of French oak. The wine, of about 13% alcohol, is bottled and cellared for 4 months before release.

Style and maturity
Barbera Pian Romualdo has a bright ruby-violet color and ample bouquet marked by scents of ripe fruit, berries and spices. The wine is fairly full and firm in body with buoyant fruit sensations nicely balanced by a bracing streak of acidity in warm, smooth flavors that refresh the palate. If most appealing in 4–5 years, the wine will maintain style for at least a decade.

Serving
🌡 17°C.
🍷 Ample tulip-shaped glass.
🍽 Piedmontese dishes: *carne cruda* (marinated raw beef), *agnolotti* pasta envelopes with meat sauce, the rich and exotic stew known as *finanziera*.

Rabajà
Barbaresco DOCG 🍷

Producer
Azienda Agricola Rabajà
di Bruno Rocca
Via Rabajà 29
12050 Barbaresco
(Cuneo)
Tel. 0173 635 112
Fax 0173 635 112

Owner
Bruno Rocca

Founded
1978

**Winemaker and
vineyard manager**
Bruno Rocca

Production
About 18,000 bottles a
year

Vintages
1999 1998 1997 1996
1995 1990 1989 1988
1985 1983 1982

Price
● ● ●

B runo Rocca has asserted his claim to the vineyard of
Rabajà by making it the name of his family estate in the
village of Barbaresco. As he explains: "Rabajà, before being
the name of a famous cru of Barbaresco, was the name of our
house and its pertinent vineyards." The outspoken Bruno
cannot insist on exclusivity, however, since his 4 hectares
don't cover the entire historic expanse of Rabajà. But he has
been vainly campaigning for years to prevent use of the name
on Barbaresco from other plots.

The first bottles to carry the name Rabajà came from the
Produttori del Barbaresco cellars in the early 1970s, when the
Rocca family conferred grapes to that admirable cooperative.
In 1982, Bruno kept enough grapes to make a small amount
of Rabajà of his own. With the 1985 vintage, he left the
Produttori cooperative and used his choice grapes to make
several thousand bottles of Rabajà. But by then the name had
become so prestigious that others took advantage of the lack
of official vineyard limits and specific regulations to label
Barbaresco from other places as Rabajà.

The controversy continues. Recently, Bruno has amplified
and modernized his cellars and revised his techniques to
produce about 18,000 bottles a year of what is not only the
acknowledged best Barbaresco Rabajà but one of the finest
Nebbiolo wines of Piedmont. He has achieved a wine of
contemporary balance and tone, while retaining the
extraordinarily rich bouquet and elegant flavors that
characterized Rabajà in the past. In style, the wine bears a
striking resemblance to Barbaresco from the adjoining
vineyards of Bricco Asili (see page 36) and Camp Gros
Martinenga (see page 44).

From a total of 6.5 hectares of vines, Bruno Rocca
produces about 40,000 bottles of wine a year, including
regular Barbaresco, Barbaresco Coparossa, DOC Barbera
d'Alba and Dolcetto d'Alba Trifolè and Langhe Chardonnay
Cadet.

Piedmont

Grapes
Nebbiolo 100%, hand picked in the first half of October.

Vineyard
Rabajà, a plot of about 4 hectares in calcareous marl mixed with tufa and sand on a slope facing southwest at 300 meters of altitude in the commune of Barbaresco. The vines, of an average age of 26–31 years, are planted at a density of 4,000 per hectare and trained in the Guyot cordon method.

Vinification and aging
Grapes are stemmed and soft crushed and the musts fermented on the skins for 5–9 days in stainless steel vats at 28–32°C. After malolactic fermentation in wooden containers, the wine, of about 13.5% alcohol, is matured for 15–18 months in 225-liter barrels of French oak, then bottled and cellared for 10 months before release.

Style and maturity
Barbaresco Rabajà when released in the 3rd year after the harvest has bright ruby-garnet color that tends toward brick red with age. The bouquet is uncommonly rich and flowery, with scents reminiscent of violets, roses, berries, spices and vanilla. On the palate, the wine shows good weight and harmony with impressive depth of flavors that amplify and lengthen over time. Inherent elegance is well expressed after 5–6 years, though the wine from top vintages tends to reach an aristocratic peak after a decade or more.

Serving
🌡 18°C.
🍷 Ample *ballon* (Burgundy type).
🍽 Piedmontese meat dishes, such as filet of beef braised in Barbaresco, lamb or kid roasted with herbs; local cheeses, such as Bra, Castelmagno and Raschera.

Albino Rocca

Vigneto Brich Ronchi Barbaresco DOCG ❢

Producer
Azienda Agricola
Rocca Albino
Via Rabajà 15
12050 Barbaresco
(Cuneo)
Tel. 0173 635 145
Fax 0173 635 921
www.italywines.com

Owner
Albino Rocca

Founded
1968

Winemakers
Angelo Rocca with
Giuseppe Caviola

Vineyard managers
Albino and Angelo
Rocca

Production
About 18,000 bottles in
choice years

Vintages
1999 1998 1997 1996
1995 1993 1990

Price
● ●

The sudden success of Vigneto Brich Ronchi rewards the efforts of Albino Rocca and, above all, his son Angelo, in raising to prominence the once obscure Ronchi vineyard area of Barbaresco. Vigneto Brich Ronchi first appeared on a label from the 1990 vintage, when the Rocca family decided it was time to declare their crus as neighbors had been doing.

That wine had just been released when, in 1994, wine journalist Alessandro Masnaghetti published his authoritative map rating vineyards of the commune of Barbaresco in three categories: *grande valore, ottimo valore* and *buon valore* (great, very good and good). Masnaghetti rated part of Ronchi (with three sub-zones) as *buon valore* and part as "not particularly suited to Nebbiolo for Barbaresco"—in other words, a third growth at best. Masnaghetti did, however, mention Brich Ronchi as a new estate wine noting that he preferred to evaluate it after further verification.

Since then, Masnaghetti and other critics in Italy and abroad have given high marks to Vigneto Brich Ronchi from the 1993, 1995, 1996 and 1997 vintages, assessments occasionally matched by Albino Rocca's other previously unsung cru, Loreto. Angelo Rocca strives for perfection in vineyards and cellars with a fastidiousness that brings out the best in his terrains. Yet there is no denying that the class shown by Vigneto Brich Ronchi in the 1990s also reflects an intrinsic value of the vineyard that seems certain to be acknowledged in coming years with a move up a notch or two in the rankings. The Rocca family recently acquired a bit more land there, so production should increase from 18,000 bottles to about 23,000 in coming years.

From 10 hectares of vines, Albino Rocca now produces a total of about 60,000 bottles a year, including the excellent DOC Barbera d'Alba Gepin, Dolcetto d'Alba Vignalunga and two versions of white Cortese: Langhe Bianco DOC La Rocca (oak fermented) and Cortese La Rocca, a *vino da tavola.*

Piedmont

BARBARESCO
Denominazione di origine controllata e garantita

1996

VIGNETO BRICH RONCHI

Imbottigliato all'origine dal produttore
Estate bottled by
ROCCA ALBINO
Barbaresco Italia

750 ML e

ITALIA
PRODUCT OF ITALY

Alc 14% BY VOL

Grapes
Nebbiolo 100%, hand
picked in early October.

Vineyard
Brich Ronchi, a plot of
3.8 hectares in calcareous
clay soils on slopes facing
southeast at 270 meters
of altitude at the crest of
the Ronchi vineyard area
in the commune of
Barbaresco. The vines, of
an average age of
21 years, are planted at a
density of 3,500–4,000
per hectare and trained in
the Guyot cordon
method.

Vinification and aging
Grapes are stemmed and
soft crushed and the
musts fermented for
about 15 days at
34–36°C in stainless steel
tanks designed to extract
maximum color and
flavor components in 3
days of contact with the
skins. After malolactic
fermentation, the wine,
of about 14% alcohol, is
matured for 20 months
in 225-liter barrels of
French oak from Alliers,
Tronçais and Nevers (a
third new annually).
After bottling without
cold stabilization,
clarifying or filtering, the
wine is cellared for at
least 2 years before
release.

Style and maturity
Barbaresco Brich Ronchi when
released in the fourth year
after the harvest has fine ruby
color that shows garnet tones
on the rim with time. The
ample bouquet recalls violets,
ripe cherries, cassis and vanilla.
Solid structure is underlined
by rich and vital fruit flavors
balanced by mellow wood

tannins that give the wine
unusual *souplesse* and
impressive length on the
palate. From great vintages, the
wine approaches a prime at
5–6 years, though it should be
expected to maintain its vigor
for at least another decade.

Serving
- 18°C, decanting the wine
  2 hours earlier.
- Ample crystal glass
  (Burgundy type).
- Filet of beef braised in
  Barbaresco, *lepre in salmì*
  (hare marinated in red
  wine and stewed with
  herbs), as well as aged
  cheeses.

Vigna Big
Barolo DOCG ❢

Producer
Podere Rocche dei
Manzoni di Valentino
Località Manzoni
Soprani 3
12065 Monforte d'Alba
(Cuneo)
Tel. 0173 784 21
Fax 0173 787 161

Owners
Iolanda and Valentino
Migliorini

Founded
1974

Winemakers
Valentino Migliorini and
Giuseppe Albertino

Vineyard manager
Giorgio Botto

Production
About 15,000 bottles in
fine years

Vintages
1999 1998 1997 1996
1995 1993 1990 1989
1988 1985 1982

Price
● ● ●

Valentino Migliorini is one of few outsiders to have gained full membership in Barolo's patriarchal wine establishment. When he and his wife Iolanda bought Rocche dei Manzoni in 1972 and started renovating the farm, they were treated with suspicion as free-spending restaurateurs from Emilia who didn't even speak the local dialect. But Valentino, being too bold, too bright and too gregarious to ignore, quickly became a big wheel in Barolo.

He pioneered small barrels of French oak, first used for the trend-setting Nebbiolo-Barbera blend called Bricco Manzoni. He was the first to plant Chardonnay—for the barrel-fermented L'Angelica, as well as for Valentino Brut Zero, Piedmont's best sparkling *blanc de blancs* (see page 118). Yet, as he bought up choice vineyards and built majestic cellars (along with a palatial tower and an Olympic-sized swimming pool), Valentino never lost sight of his first love: Barolo.

He bottled his first single-vineyard Barolo, Vigna d'la Roul, from 1974, following in 1982 with Vigna Big. The Big comes from Bighi, name of a former owner, but it also describes the dimensions of a Barolo that for the time being tops Valentino's list. Probably not for long, however, since vines of Cappella di Santo Stefano at Perno, one of the top historic sites of Barolo, have yet to reach full potential, and the acquisitions of Madonna Assunta-La Villa at Castelletto, Ciabot d'August at Ginestra and Pianpolvere Soprano at Bussia promise even more splendor in years to come.

Iolanda gave up the restaurant in Emilia years ago to work full time with Valentino and sons Alfonso and Rodolfo, who produce more than 200,000 bottles a year from about 50 hectares of vines. The list includes DOC Barbera d'Alba (Sorito Mosconi and Vigna La Cresta), Dolcetto d'Alba (Vigna Matinera) and Langhe Rosso Pinònero (Pinot Nero) and Quatr Nas (a unique blend of Nebbiolo, Barbera, Pinot Nero and Cabernet).

Piedmont

Grapes
Nebbiolo 100%, hand picked in early October.

Vineyard
Vigna Big, a plot of about 2 hectares in sandy calcareous clays on a slope facing south at 350 meters of altitude in the Mosconi area of the commune of Monforte in the southeastern part of the Barolo zone. The vines, of an average age of 31 years, are planted at a density of 4,000 per hectare and trained in the Guyot cordon method.

Vinification and aging
Grapes are stemmed and soft crushed and the musts fermented in stainless steel tanks at 30°C for 2 weeks on the skins. After malolactic fermentation, the wine of about 14% alcohol is matured for 2 years in small barrels of French oak and bottled and cellared for a year before release.

Style and maturity
Barolo Vigna Big has deep ruby color, taking on garnet tones over time. The bouquet is full and vital with scents reminiscent of violets and berries and hints of vanilla and tar. On the palate, it has imposing weight and fine balance, with concentrated fruit sensations set off by sweet tannins in smooth, opulent flavors that linger on the tongue. The wine reaches peaks between 7 and 12 years, but great vintages retain rich complexity for 15 years or more.

Serving
🍴 16–18°C, after decanting.
🍷 Ample glass (Bordeaux type).
🍽 Grilled lamb and kid with Mediterranean herbs; Barbary duck roast with chestnuts; aged cheeses, such as Gorgonzola *naturale* and Castelmagno.

Luciano Sandrone

Cannubi Boschis Barolo DOCG 🍷

Producer
Azienda Agricola
Sandrone Luciano
Via Pugnane 4
12060 Barolo (Cuneo)
Tel. 0173 560 021
Fax 0173 562 39
info@sandroneluciano.
com

Owner
Luciano Sandrone

Founded
1978

Winemaker
Luciano Sandrone

Vineyard manager
Luca Sandrone

Production
About 12,000 bottles in
fine years

Vintages
2000 1999 1998 1997
1996 1995 1990 1989
1987 1986 1985

Price

Luciano Sandrone strives for perfection with an innovative spirit and an air of Old World gentility that make him one of the most admired and amiable producers of Barolo. He was the cellarmaster at the historic house of Marchesi di Barolo in 1977 when he bought his first vineyard, a parcel of the vaunted Cannubi site known as Boschis.

Between 1978 and 1984, Luciano issued the wine as simply Barolo, but with the great 1985 vintage he started to call it Cannubi Boschis. That name has since become a legend in Barolo, as Luciano Sandrone has become one of Italy's most praised winemakers.

In the late 1980s, Luciano left his first job and went independent, working with his brother Luca, a vine specialist, and aided by his daughter Barbara. Gradually they acquired more plots and built spacious modern cellars on the edge of Barolo, enabling them to move from the original cramped quarters near the center of town and expand production to about 80,000 bottles a year.

Luciano, as a leader of the new school of winemaking in Barolo, aims for rapid extraction of components that heighten the color, structure, bouquet and flavor of wines rounded out in small barrels of French oak to give them a decidedly contemporary style. Sandrone's Barolo Le Vigne, from plots at Barolo and Monforte d'Alba, can be just as impressive in some years.

From 8 hectares of vineyards, they also make outstandingly rich and ripe Barbera d'Alba and Dolcetto d'Alba. They acquire grapes from the Roero hills to the north to make the admirable Nebbiolo d'Alba DOC Valmaggiore.

Piedmont

Grapes
Nebbiolo 100%, hand picked in mid-October.

Vineyard
Cannubi Boschis, a plot of 2 hectares in sandy calcareous clay soils on steep slopes facing south and southeast at 250–290 meters of altitude in the Cannubi area of the commune of Barolo at the heart of the Barolo zone. The vines, of 26–31 years of age, are planted at a density of 5,000–5,500 per hectare and trained in the Guyot cordon method.

Vinification and aging
Grapes are stemmed and soft crushed and the musts fermented at no more than 32°C in stainless steel tanks for up to 20 days, including 5–7 days on the skins. After natural malolactic fermentation, the wine, of 13.5–14% alcohol, is matured for 24 months in 600-liter barrels of French oak and bottled and cellared for a year before release.

Style and maturity
Barolo Cannubi Boschis when released in the fourth year after the harvest has deep ruby-violet color, taking on garnet tones over time. The bouquet is vital and complex with scents reminiscent of violets, ripe cherries, blackberries, spices and vanilla. On the palate, it has outstanding weight and balance, with concentrated fruit sensations in smooth, round, opulent flavors that linger on the tongue. The wine approaches a peak in 5–6 years, but retains style for at least a decade beyond.

Serving
🍷 16–18°C.
🍷 Ample glass (Burgundy type).
🍴 Piedmontese meat and game dishes, such as kid roast with herbs, and venison braised in Barolo, as well as aged cheeses, in particular the pungent Castelmagno.

Bric dël Fiasc
Barolo DOCG 🍷

Producer
Azienda Vitivinicola
Paolo Scavino
Via Alba Barolo 59
12060 Castiglione
Falletto (Cuneo)
Tel. 0173 62 850
Fax 0173 62 850
e.scavino@onw.net
www.italywines.com

Owner
Enrico Scavino

Founded
1921

Winemaker
Enrico Scavino

Vineyard manager
Enrico Scavino

Production
About 12,000 bottles in
choice years

Vintages
1999 1998 1997 1996
1995 1993 1990 1989
1988 1985 1982 1978

Price
● ● ●

Fiasco, the Italian term for flask as well as for flop, as in English, is also the name of a slope that descends sharply from the edge of the town of Castiglione Falletto toward the central valley of Barolo. Lorenzo Scavino acquired vineyards there in 1921. After his death, his sons split the property, Alfonso calling his estate Azelia, Paolo calling his simply Paolo Scavino. The latter included 2 hectares of vines at the crest of what is known in the local patois as Bric dël Fiasc.

The wine that has carried that curious name since 1978 has risen to the summit of Barolo, thanks to the awesome drive and self-discipline of Paolo's son Enrico. As a reformist with a prophetic nature, Enrico Scavino sees considerable room for improvement in wines from all the native vines of Piedmont. But most of his endless toil in vineyards and cellars is dedicated to the higher cause of Nebbiolo for Barolo.

Gradually Enrico has acquired more plots to produce Barolo from the famed Cannubi and Rocche dell'Annunziata sites, while creating a blend called Carobric. From 13 hectares of vineyards, he produces about 80,000 bottles a year, including excellent DOC Barbera d'Alba and Dolcetto d'Alba.

None of the others quite equals the splendor of Bric dël Fiasc, which even from lesser vintages shows uncommon concentration, harmony and poise, the results of low yields, studied extraction of coloring, flavoring and structural components and fining in French oak.

Enrico, who greets praise for his wines with the same sort of skeptical expression with which others field criticism, insists that his winemaking leaves plenty of room for improvement. He explains that his is a generation of transition charged with leading Piedmontese wine from an erratic past toward an illustrious future. "Barolo will always be different from the other great wines of the world," he once said. "But when we reach our optimum, it will be second to none."

Piedmont

Grapes
Nebbiolo 100%, hand picked in mid-October.

Vineyard
Bric dël Fiasc, a plot of 2 hectares in calcareous clay soils of a type known as tortoniana on steep slopes facing south and west at 270 meters of altitude in the Fiasco area of the commune of Castiglione Falletto along the central valley of the Barolo zone. The vines, 27 years of age, are planted at a density of 4,500 per hectare and trained in an arched Guyot cordon system.

Vinification and aging
Grapes are stemmed and soft crushed and the musts fermented at 25–30°C in stainless steel tanks for 10–15 days, remaining on the skins long enough for optimum extraction of coloring and structural components. After natural malolactic fermentation, the wine, of about 14% alcohol, is matured for 2 years in 220-liter and 350-liter capacity barrels of French oak (half new, half used once) and bottled and cellared for a year before release.

Style and maturity
Barolo Bric dël Fiasc when released in the fourth year after the harvest has deep ruby-violet color, taking on garnet tones over time. The bouquet is elaborate with scents reminiscent of violets, ripe plums, blackberries and spices. On the palate, it combines rich structure and concentration with round, opulent fruit flavors braced by mellow wood tannins that enhance the long, smooth finish. The wine approaches a prime in 7–10 years, but from great vintages can remain splendid for 20–25 years.

Serving
🌡 19–20°C.
🍷 Ample *ballon* (Burgundy type).
🍽 Roast beef, lamb and kid; game dishes, such as grouse, hare and venison braised or stewed in Barolo; aged cheeses, in particular Parmigiano Reggiano.

Coste & Fossati
Dolcetto d'Alba DOC ❢

Producer
Azienda Agricola
G.D. Vajra
di Vaira Aldo
Via delle Viole 25
12060 Barolo (Cuneo)
Tel. 0173 562 57
Fax 0173 563 45
gdvajra@tin.it

Owners
Aldo and Milena Vaira

Founded
1972

Winemaker
Aldo Vaira

Vineyard manager
Aldo Vaira

Production
About 10,000 bottles
a year

Vintages
2000 1999 1998 1997
1995 1990 1989

Price
● ●

Aldo Vaira likes to do things in his own way, which perhaps explains why he spells his last name with an "i" though his father Giuseppe Domenico Vajra, who founded the estate, used the "j" (the letters are interchangeable in Italian). This free spirit may also explain why he installed stained glass windows in his cellars and why he takes the supposedly lesser wines of Barbera, Dolcetto and Freisa as seriously as Barolo.

After taking a doctorate in agriculture, Aldo Vaira taught at the school of enology in nearby Alba for a time before returning full time to the family cellars at the village of Vergne on the high western edge of the Barolo zone. The vineyard of Bricco delle Viole is the source of Barolo as well as Barbera d'Alba, wines of weight and substance with the added blessing of being appealing when young. That's partly because Aldo has studiedly restrained use of wooden barrels for aging to retain full fruit sensations in his wines.

Dolcetto d'Alba Coste & Fossati from fine vintages tends to be the most impressive wine of the estate and sometimes of the entire appellation. It is named for two vineyards where the Vajra/Vaira family selected and propagated the best old clones of Dolcetto. Unlike the majority of wines from the variety, Coste e Fossati gains depth and complexity with age. Yet, despite its majestic dimensions, this Dolcetto is a sheer pleasure to drink.

The surprises don't stop there. Freisa, a variety normally used for light, bubbly reds, in Aldo's hands becomes a still wine of unprecedented size and style. It's so out of character that he jestingly named it Kyè (for *chi è?*—or who's that?).

He also makes two whites under Langhe DOC, a Chardonnay without oak that combines dynamic power with a supple, fruity style and a Riesling with richness of fruit and aroma rarely sensed outside of Alsace or the Rheingau. Aldo and wife Milena own 20 hectares of vines to make a total of about 90,000 bottles of wine a year.

Piedmont

Grapes
Dolcetto 100%, hand picked in late September.

Vineyards
Two plots of 2 hectares each in calcareous clay soils of a type known as tortoniana: Coste di Vergne on slopes facing south at 440 meters and Fossati on slopes facing southeast at 460 meters, both on the western edge of the commune of Barolo. The vines, of an average age of 21 years, are planted at a density of more than 5,000 per hectare and trained in the Guyot cordon system.

Vinification and aging
Grape bunches are selected in cellars before being stemmed and soft crushed and the musts fermented at 28°C in stainless steel tanks for 2–3 weeks on the skins. After natural malolactic fermentation, the wine, of about 13.5% alcohol, is matured for 8 months, 30% in casks of Slavonian oak, 5% in small barrels of French oak (used once) and the rest in stainless steel, then bottled and cellared for 2 months before release.

Style and maturity
Dolcetto Coste & Fossati on release about a year after the harvest has deep ruby-purple color and fresh, grapy fragrance with hints of black cherries, blackberries and violets. Full and round on the palate, it combines ripe cherry and plum flavors with a chocolate-like bittersweet quality and mellow tannins that give a lift to an unusually long finish for a Dolcetto. The wine reaches a prime in 3–7 years, though it can be impressive for up to a decade.

Serving
🍷 16–18°C.
🍷 Medium-sized glass.
🍽 Piedmontese salami; *agnolotti* pasta envelopes with meat sauce; *coq au vin* (rooster braised in red wine); cheeses such as Tuma and Robiola di Roccaverano.

Rocche
Barolo DOCG 🍷

Producer
Vietti
Piazza Vittorio Veneto 5
12060 Castiglione
Falletto (Cuneo)
Tel. 0173 628 25
Fax 0173 629 41
vietti@il-vino.com

Owners
Vietti-Currado and
Cordero families

Founded
1900

Winemakers
Alfredo and Luca
Currado

Vineyard managers
Mario Cordero and
Luca Currado

Production
About 6,500 bottles and
65 magnums in choice
years

Vintages
2000 1999 1998 1997
1996 1995 1990 1989
1988 1985

Price
● ● ●

Note
Vintages previous to
1995 were labeled as
Barolo Rocche di
Castiglione

Alfredo Currado, who became the winemaker after his graduation from Alba's school of enology in 1951, married Luciana Vietti in 1957 and took command of the small cellars at Castiglione Falletto that had been in her family since 1900. Vietti has since become one of the most admired names in Piedmontese wine, further illuminated by a new generation represented by son-in-law Mario Cordero and son Luca.

Their prime emphasis has always been on single-vineyard Barolo from such prized sites as Brunate at La Morra, Lazzarito at Serralunga d'Alba and Villero on the other side of Castiglione Falletto. The original and still most esteemed Barolo comes from Rocche, a vineyard overlooked from the terrace of the headquarters of the Vietti winery and Currado family home.

Alfredo upholds a traditional style of Barolo in wines of vigorous constitution that acquire regal bearing through aging in large casks of Slavonian oak. But, a few years ago, when the cellars were expanded by excavating steep slopes below Castiglione's 11th-century castle, Luca and Mario made sure that the trappings were strictly state-of-the-art. They installed small barrels of French oak for maturing other wines, notably Barbera that can match Barolo in size and constitution.

Alfredo was long noted for his astute selections of grapes from growers in Barolo and other zones around Alba. But over time the family has acquired vineyards to extend holdings to 22 hectares, which provide more than two-thirds of the total production of about 200,000 bottles a year. Included in the recent purchases were vineyards of Barbera d'Asti for the acclaimed wines called La Crena and Tre Vigne.

Vietti production extends to DOCG Barbaresco Masseria, DOC Barbera d'Alba Scarrone and Dolcetto d'Alba Lazzarito, as well as white Roero Arneis and luscious bubbly Moscato d'Asti. The Vietti labels illustrated by artist Gianni Gallo have won almost as many awards as the wines.

Piedmont

Grapes
Nebbiolo 100%, hand picked in mid-October.

Vineyard
Rocche, a plot of 1.6 hectares in calcareous clay soils on slopes facing southeast at 350 meters of altitude on the southern edge of the village of Castiglione Falletto at the heart of the Barolo zone. The vines, of about 46 years of age, are planted at a density of 4,600 per hectare and trained in the Guyot cordon method.

Vinification and aging
Grapes are stemmed and soft crushed and the musts fermented for about 13 days on the skins at 30–32°C in stainless steel tanks, with frequent pumping over the cap. After malolactic fermentation, the wine, of 13.5–14% alcohol, is matured for 24 months in large casks of Slavonian oak and bottled and cellared for about a year before release.

Style and maturity
Barolo Rocche when released in the 4th year after the harvest has intense ruby color, taking on garnet and orange tones over time. The bouquet is ample and complex with scents reminiscent of violets, dried roses, leather and tar. On the palate, it has impressive weight and rich fruit sensations with a tannic grip that mellows as flavors gain depth and length with time. The wine approaches a prime in 4–8 years, but retains class for a decade or two beyond.

Serving
🌡 20°C, after opening 2 hours earlier or decanting.
🍷 Ample glass (Burgundy type).
🍽 Piedmontese meat and game dishes, such as beef braised in Barolo, hare *in civet* (marinated in red wine), and aged cheeses, such as Castelmagno.

Roberto Voerzio

Vigneto Pozzo dell'Annunziata Barbera d'Alba Riserva DOC

Producer
Azienda Agricola
Roberto Voerzio
Località Cerreto 1
12064 La Morra
(Cuneo)
Tel. 0173 509 196
Fax 0173 509 196

Owner
Roberto Voerzio

Founded
1986

Winemaker and vineyard manager
Roberto Voerzio

Production
About 1,350 magnums
(1.5 liter) from choice
vintages

Vintages
1999 1998 1997 1996

Price
● ● ● ●

Roberto Voerzio makes small quantities of some of the most admired wines of Alba by working his vines with a resolve that might be considered fanatical were it not for his perennially youthful spirit and easygoing manner. His Barolo Brunate and Cerequio come from parcels of those vaunted vineyards of La Morra, wines that have won high marks and widespread attention. From the adjacent site of La Serra, Roberto makes a fine Barolo of the name and the prized Langhe DOC Vigna Serra, a blend of Nebbiolo with Barbera.

Like other Barolo producers of his generation, Roberto grew up with an abiding faith in Nebbiolo as the nonpareil of Piedmontese varieties. But his leanings of late have been toward Barbera, a vine no longer relegated to second-class status. His new devotion has been built on the strength of a Barbera from Vigneto Pozzo dell'Annunziata, where he limits grape yields from the densely planted vines to almost ridiculously low levels. Roberto readily admits that this Barbera from the 1997 vintage overshadowed his Barolos in sheer grandeur—if not necessarily in depth and complexity (though that remains to be seen).

The wine may be assessed as being too big in structure, too concentrated in color and extract and too strong (ranging around 15 percent alcohol). Yet, though it exceeds the conventional quotas of a dry red wine, this jumbo Barbera delivers an initial wallop and lingers on the palate with extraordinary finesse. It seems fitting that Roberto bottles Vigneto Pozzo dell'Annunziata in magnums that carry a whopping price. "I'm in no rush to sell it," he admits. "To tell the truth, I'm hoping that for once I'll have a few bottles left to enjoy in my old age."

Roberto, aided by his wife Pinuccia, cultivates 10 hectares (7 of his own and 3 leased) to produce about 35,000 bottles a year, including the excellent Dolcetto d'Alba DOC Priavino and Barolo of recent vintages from Capalot and Sarmassa, soon to be complemented by a wine from Rocche dell'Annunziata.

Piedmont

Grapes
Barbera 100%, hand picked in mid-October.

Vineyard
A plot covering 7,000 square meters in calcareous clay soils on a slope facing southeast at about 370 meters of altitude in the Pozzo dell'Annunziata area of the commune of La Morra. The vines were planted in 1990 at a density of 8,000 per hectare and trained in a short Guyot cordon method that permits yields of about 600 grams of grapes per vine.

Vinification and aging
Grape bunches are selected in vineyards and cellars before being stemmed and soft crushed and the must fermented in stainless steel tanks at 32–35°C for 10–12 days on the skins. Malolactic fermentation follows immediately in barrels before the wine is matured for 18 months in barriques of French oak (two-thirds renewed annually). The wine, of 14.5–15% alcohol, is bottled and cellared for several months before release.

Style and maturity
Vigneto Pozzo dell'Annunziata on release has deep, dense ruby-violet color and generous bouquet marked by scents of fruit and berries mingling with hints of spices and vanilla. The wine's immense dimensions strike the palate with an impact that is quickly assuaged by lively acidity and a flush of oak tannins that come together in unexpected harmony of smooth flavors that linger on the tongue. The wine should reach a prime in 5–6 years, though it seems to have the attributes to maintain class for well over a decade.

Serving
🍴 16–17°C.
🍷 Ample tulip-shaped glass.
🍽 Piedmontese dishes, such as kid roast with herbs, *gran bollito misto* (simmered beef and veal served with a variety of sauces) and *fonduta* (fondue made with Raschera cheese).

Riserva Vittorio Moretti Franciacorta DOCG Extra Brut ♀

Producer
Bellavista
Via Bellavista 5
25030 Erbusco (Brescia)
Tel. 030/7762000
Fax 030/7760386
bellavista@terramoretti.it
www.terramoretti.it

Owner
Vittorio Moretti

Founded
1977

Chief winemaker
Mattia Vezzola

Vineyard manager
Franco Farimbella

Production
About 7,000 bottles in exceptional years

Vintages
1995 1991 1988 1984

Price
● ● ● ●

Vittorio Moretti personifies the enterprise that made Franciacorta Italy's leading zone for bottle-fermented sparkling wine. A wealthy construction magnate, Moretti bought the vast Bellavista estate in 1977 and began planting vineyards amid fields and woods of Lombardy's Alpine lake country. "I figured that, if nothing else, wine would be an interesting hobby," says Moretti. "But when I realized that we were creating something special, it became a passion."

Bellavista's surge to prominence began with the arrival in 1981 of Mattia Vezzola as winemaker with a no-limits quest for quality that has always focused on the vineyards. Mattia points out that conditions in the rolling glacial moraine of Franciacorta are practically ideal for the Pinots and especially Chardonnay, which prevails in Bellavista's sparkling wines. The range of Franciacorta DOCG takes in the popular Cuvée Brut and the vintage (*millesimato*) Gran Cuvée Brut, Gran Cuvée Pas Opéré, Gran Cuvée Rosé and Gran Cuvée Satèn. The term Satèn, first applied by Bellavista to the gently bubbly wine known as *crémant* in French, is now used generally in Franciacorta.

Grapes for special cuvées are crushed in old-style wooden basket presses for base wines partly matured in oak barrels to make them richer and more complex. The paragon is Riserva Vittorio Moretti, an austerely dry Extra Brut that gains stature from long contact with the yeasts in the bottle.

Bellavista's total production of about 800,000 bottles from 117 hectares of vines includes still wines led by Terre di Franciacorta Bianco DOC Uccellanda and Convento dell'Annunciata (from vineyards around the monastery of that name) and the red Solesine (Cabernet-Merlot) and Casotte (Pinot Nero). The Terra Moretti group also owns the Contadi Castaldi winery that makes fine Franciacorta DOCG of good value. The Moretti family also owns the relais hotel of L'Albereta, which houses the restaurant of renowned chef Gualtiero Marchesi.

Lombardy

Grapes
Chardonnay 61%, Pinot
Nero 39%, hand picked
in September.

Vineyards
Choice plots of the
Bellavista estate in glacial
soils of calcareous clay on
slopes facing south and
southeast at 150–350
meters of altitude at the
villages of Erbusco,
Nigoline, Torbiato and
Colombaro in the
western part of the
Franciacorta zone. Vines,
of an average age of 21
years, are planted at a
density of 5,000 per
hectare and trained in the
Guyot cordon method.

Vinification and aging
Whole grape bunches are
crushed gently in wooden
basket presses and the
free-run musts separated
from the skins are
fermented at 18°C, part
in small oak barrels and
part in stainless steel vats.
Base wines undergo
partial malolactic
fermentation and a
portion is matured for 6
months in barriques. The
cuvée remains on the
yeasts for at least 5 years
in bottle before hand
riddling and disgorging.
The wine, of about
12.5% alcohol, is topped
up with the same wine
before cork sealing. It is
released about 6 years
after the harvest.

Style and maturity
Franciacorta Riserva Vittorio
Moretti on release about 6
years after the vintage has
bright gold color with yellow
highlights and lively, persistent
streams of fine bubbles.
Aromas are vital with yeast,
fruit and vanilla sensations
mingling with scents
reminiscent of rosemary, bay
and citrus. Flavors are
vivacious due to still lively
acidity, yet fruity and elegant
with hints of toasted nuts in a
fine, smooth finish. The wine
reaches a prime between 10
and 15 years.

Serving
🍷 8–9°C.
🥂 Tall, ample flute (vintage
Champagne type).
🍽 Shellfish *antipasto*; risotto
with freshwater prawns or
chanterelle mushrooms; sea
bass or flounder baked in a
crust of sea salt.

Bertelli

Producer
Poderi A. Bertelli
Frazione San Carlo 38
14055 Costigliole
d'Asti (Asti)
Tel. 0141/966137
Fax 02/58316166
ebertelli@tiscalinet.it

Owner
Alberto Bertelli

Founded
1975

Winemaker
Alberto Bertelli

Production
About 3,500 bottles in
favorable years

Vintages
1999 1998 1997 1996
1993 1990

Price
● ● ●

Giarone
Piemonte DOC
Chardonnay ♀

Chardonnay has risen rapidly in Italy since the 1960s, when it was recognized as a variety distinct from the Pinots with which it had previously been identified. The first wave of modern Chardonnay from Friuli-Venezia Giulia and Trentino-Alto Adige was made following new methods of cold fermentation in stainless steel tanks. That may explain the lack of personality that made it barely distinguishable from the rampantly popular Pinot Grigio.

In the 1980s, inspired producers began selecting clones of Chardonnay in Burgundy and limiting grape yields to build character in wines fermented and matured in small barrels of French oak. An early advocate of the style in Piedmont was Alberto Bertelli, who made his Chardonnay from the Giarone vineyard from the 1987 vintage.

Alberto, a physician who took over the estate from his father Aldo in the late 1970s, cites evidence that Chardonnay was grown at Costigliole d'Asti in the late eighteenth century. Curious, since even the French have had trouble tracing its ancestry that far. But there's no question that the variety takes well to the calcareous clay soils and sunny but relatively cool conditions of Piedmont's Langhe hills. For sheer size Giarone can match the blockbuster Chardonnays of California, yet aromas and flavors show a refinement closer in nature to whites of Burgundy's Côte de Beaune.

The range of Bertelli wines reflects the eclectic tastes of a man who has developed his estate into a miniature international research center. From 8 hectares of vines, Alberto makes about 20,000 bottles a year, nearly all exported. DOC wines are Barbera d'Asti Giarone, Montetusa and San Antonio Vieilles Vignes, Monferrato Bianco I Fossaretti (Sauvignon) and Monferrato Rosso I Fossaretti (Cabernet) and Mon Mayor (Cabernet and Nebbiolo). Three others are simply *vini da tavola*: white Saint Marsan (Marsanne and Roussanne), red Saint Marsan (Syrah) and Plissè (a Traminer made in an impressively long-lived late-harvest version).

Piedmont

Grapes
Chardonnay 100%, hand picked in late September.

Vineyard
A plot of 2 hectares in calcareous clay soils on slopes facing west at about 250 meters of altitude at a place called Giarone in the San Carlo area of the commune of Costigliole d'Asti. The vines, of an average age of 13 years, are planted at a density of 4,500 per hectare and trained in a modified Geneva double curtain method with canopies draped downward.

Vinification and aging
Grapes are soft crushed and the musts are clarified cold and fermented for about 2 months at no more than 27°C in small barrels of French oak, where malolactic fermentation occurs during 10 months on the lees. The wine, of about 14% alcohol, is bottled and cellared for 10 months before release.

Style and maturity
Giarone Chardonnay when released about 2 years after the harvest has deep straw yellow color with golden highlights and distinctive aromas with scents reminiscent of acacia blossoms, tropical fruit, honey and toasty oak. Amply structured with plush texture, its mellow fruit flavors combine with hints of vanilla and toasted hazelnuts in a long, smooth finish. The wine usually reaches a prime at 3–4 years, though it can gain depth and complexity for up to a decade.

Serving
- 12–15°C, after decanting.
- Tulip-shaped glass (Chardonnay type).
- Baked yellow peppers with tuna stuffing; *tajarin* noodles with rabbit and mushroom sauce; turbot roasted with red onions.

Bruna

Le Russeghine
Riviera Ligure di Ponente DOC
Pigato ♀

Producer
Azienda Agricola Bruna
Via Umberto I 81
18028 Ranzo (Imperia)
Tel. 0183/318082
Fax 0183/318082

Owner
Maddalena Capello

Founded
1970

Winemakers
Riccardo Bruna and
Valter Bonetti

Vineyard manager
Diego Passaniti

Production
About 22,000 bottles a
year

Vintages
1999 1998 1997 1990
1988

Price
●

The Pigato vine seems to thrive almost exclusively in the peaceful Arroscia valley near the seaside town of Albenga in Liguria's western Riviera. It was once believed that the variety came from Greece or that it was related to the Vermentino that arrived in Liguria from the island of Sardinia. But some seem convinced that Pigato is indigenous to the Arroscia valley, where it is planted on sunny slopes in well-drained clay soils known in dialect as *le russeghine* due to their reddish complexion.

The variety, whose name refers to the *pighe* or dark blotches on the skins of its golden grapes, makes white wine of remarkable character. Yet bottles were rarely found beyond Liguria's capital of Genoa until Bice and Agostino (Pippo) Parodi at their small estate of Cascina Feipù dei Massaretti produced a Pigato that was too fine to escape national attention.

Their success encouraged other growers in the area, chief among them Riccardo Bruna, a man quietly dedicated to proving the nobility of Pigato. Bruna calls his main vineyard Le Russeghine, source of the rich, elegant Pigato that is generally acknowledged to be the current best. A close rival is the Pigato Villa Torrachetta, from the property at the nearby town of Ortovero inherited by his wife Maddalena Capello. Yet Riccardo and Maddalena, who are dedicated to natural farming with minimal intervention, are convinced that they can achieve greater heights with Pigato. To prove it, they designated a selection from the 1999 vintage of 2,500 bottles of a Pigato Riserva known as U Baccan, which won raves in early tastings.

From 4.5 hectares of vines, the Bruna estate produces about 34,000 bottles of wine a year under the Riviera Ligure di Ponente DOC. Besides Pigato, there is also a light, fruity red Rossese, also from the vineyard of Le Russeghine.

Liguria

Grapes
Pigato 100%, hand picked in late September or early October.

Vineyard
Grapes come predominantly from Le Russeghine, a plot of 3 hectares in reddish clay soils on a gravel base on gradual slopes facing south-southwest at about 200 meters of altitude at Borgo di Ranzo in the Arroscia valley of the Ligurian Apennines about 20 kilometers west of Albenga. Vines, of an average age of 31 years, are planted at a density of 5,500 per hectare and trained in an espalier method.

Vinification and aging
Grapes are soft crushed and the musts macerated with the skins at cold temperatures for 24–36 hours followed by fermentation at 20°C for 10 days in stainless steel tanks. The wine, of about 12.5% alcohol, undergoes malolactic fermentation and settling during 7 or 8 months in tanks, after which it is bottled and cellared for at least 3 months before release.

Style and maturity
Pigato Le Russeghine on release in the second year after the harvest has bright straw yellow color and full aromas with scents reminiscent of ripe peaches and apricots mingling with hints of sage, honey and apple blossoms. Fresh fruit sensations prevail on the palate in a wine of rich structure and smooth flavors that linger on the palate. The wine reaches a prime in about 2 years and maintains class for a year or 2 beyond.

Serving
- 12–14°C.
- Tulip-shaped glass (Chardonnay type).
- *Totano* (squid) stuffed with herbs; *burrida di stoccafisso* (spicy stockfish soup); rabbit braised with olives and pine nuts.

Ca' dei Frati

Brolettino
Lugana DOC ♀

Producer
Azienda Agricola Ca' dei
Frati
Via Frati 22
25010 Lugana di
Sirmione (Brescia)
Tel. 030/919468
Fax 030/919468
info@cadeifrati.it
www.cadeifrati.it

Owner
Pietro Dal Cero and
family

Founded
1939

Winemaker
Alberto Musatti

Vineyard manager
Bruno Minotto

Production
60,000 bottles a year

Vintages
1999 1998 1997 1995
1993 1990

Price
●

Lugana is a place on the southern shore of Lake Garda where glaciers scraped out a plateau that ascends into low rolling hills to form a natural amphitheater historically suited to vines. They say that wines from Lugana were appreciated in Roman times and that Andrea Bacci, sixteenth-century scientist and personal physician of Pope Sixtus V, praised the exquisite Trebulani (now Trebbiano) from the area.

Today much Lugana is produced in volume and consumed as a zesty, easy-to-like white in the resorts around Garda. But, when treated with deference, the Trebbiano di Lugana vine, which seems to be related to Verdicchio of the Marches, can make wines of real character in the sunny, calcareous terrains tempered by cooling breezes off the lake. Proof is provided by the Dal Cero family, whose Ca' dei Frati estate extends around an old Carmelite monastery in the heart of Lugana at the base of the Sirmione peninsula.

The winery was founded in 1939 by Domenico Dal Cero, whose grandson Pietro and his children Igino, Gian Franco and Anna Maria have brought new dignity to Lugana DOC. Their basic Lugana I Frati is fragrant, smoothly fruity and, like all Dal Cero wines, fairly priced. Select Trebbiano grapes go into Brolettino, partly fermented and matured in small oak barrels to take on unexpected style. Brolettino from top vintages is called "Grandi Annate" and matured for 15 months in oak and longer in bottle to assume the sort of depth and complexity that rates description as aristocratic.

From 45 hectares of vines, Ca' dei Frati produces about 400,000 bottles a year, including a bottle-fermented sparkling Lugana DOC Brut called Cuvée dei Frati, delicate pink Garda Classico DOC Chiaretto I Frati, IGT Benaco Bresciano white Pratto (from Trebbiano, Chardonnay and Sauvignon) and red Ronchedone (Cabernet and Merlot), and sweet white Tre Filer (from Trebbiano, Chardonnay and Sauvignon).

Lombardy

Grapes
Trebbiano di Lugana 100%, hand picked in October.

Vineyards
Grapes are selected from 2 plots—I Frati of 5.84 hectares and Ronchedone of 9 hectares—in calcareous clay soils at about 60 meters of altitude on the glacial plain at Lugana on the southern edge of Lake Garda. Vines, ranging in age from 5–41 years, are planted at densities of 2,750 and 5,250 per hectare and trained in the Guyot and double Guyot cordon methods.

Vinification and aging
Grapes for Brolettino are soft crushed and the musts separated from the skins begin to ferment in stainless steel vats, completing alcoholic and malolactic fermentation during 10–12 months in small barrels of French oak. The wine, of 12.5–13% alcohol, is bottled and cellared for at least 3 months before release. Brolettino "Grandi Annate," of about 13% alcohol, remains in barriques (half new, half used once) for 15 months followed by 2 years in bottle before release.

Style and maturity
Lugana Brolettino "Grandi Annate" on release in the fourth year after the vintage has bright green-gold color and rich floral aromas with scents reminiscent of peaches, toasted nuts, spices and vanilla. Well structured, full and round on the palate, it combines richness and freshness in a long, smooth finish. The wine reaches a prime between 4 and 5 years.

Serving
🌡 9–10°C.
🍷 Tulip-shaped glass (Chardonnay type).
🍴 Baby octopus in chickpea-rosemary purée; roast lake trout from Garda; chicken salad with rucola and sun-dried tomatoes.

Cuvée Annamaria Clementi Franciacorta DOCG

Producer
Ca' del Bosco
Azienda Agricola
Via Case Sparse 20
25030 Erbusco (Brescia)
Tel. 030/7766111
Fax 030/7268425
cadelbosco@cadelbosco.
com

Owner
Ca' del Bosco
directed by Maurizio
Zanella

Founded
1968

Winemaker
Stefano Capelli

Vineyard manager
Luigi Reghenzi

Production
7,400 bottles in vintage
years, plus a limited issue
of magnums and
jeroboams (4.5 liters)

Vintages
1996 1993 1990

Price
● ● ● ●

Ca' del Bosco burst on the scene in the late 1970s, when Maurizio Zanella, a teenager with a family fortune behind him, hired André Dubois, a cellarmaster from Epernay, to show the world that Italy could make sparkling wine to rival Champagne. Maurizio has led the way in Franciacorta since, though he insists that his wines have distinct personality. "Comparisons with Champagne are inevitable," he admits, "but, rather than a rival, Franciacorta should be considered a valid alternative."

The estate built its early reputation on bubbly wines of unsurpassed style that originate entirely in 125 hectares of vineyards. In the 1970s, Maurizio planted vines at a density of 10,000 per hectare, unprecedented in northern Italy. One result was a Brut di Pinot Nero from 1980 that illustrates how a *blanc de noirs* can maintain depth and elegance over two decades. Still, Maurizio emphasizes Chardonnay in sparkling wines that age in cellars with an underground dome in stone that resembles the cupola of an ancient cathedral.

His Franciacorta DOCG Brut, Extra Brut Dosage Zero and Satèn (entirely Chardonnay) rank with Italy's finest sparklers, though the showpiece is Cuvée Annamaria Clementi (named for Maurizio's mother). Base wines are matured in oak barrels to make them richer and more complex. Normally Cuvée Annamaria Clementi remains 5½ years on the yeasts, but a millennium bottling of the 1990 vintage in jeroboams remained on the yeasts for 8 years.

Ca' del Bosco produces 650,000–850,000 bottles a year of wines about evenly split between sparkling and still. The signature red Maurizio Zanella (see page 38) is a model Cabernet-Merlot blend. Pinèro from some vintages has been Italy's most impressive Pinot Noir. With Terre di Franciacorta DOC Chardonnay, Maurizio achieves a style that falls somewhere between Burgundy and California that could stand with the finest of each.

Grapes
Chardonnay 60%, Pinot Bianco 20%, Pinot Nero 20%, hand picked in early September.

Vineyards
Plots totaling 2.5 hectares in stony glacial moraine on gradual slopes facing south-southeast at 220 meters of altitude on the Ca' del Bosco estate east of the town of Erbusco in the southwestern part of the Franciacorta zone. Vines, of an average age of 11 years, are planted at a density of 10,000 per hectare and trained in the Guyot and spurred cordon methods.

Vinification and aging
Select grape bunches are crushed gently in pneumatic presses and fermentation starts in stainless steel vats. The liquid is transferred to small barrels to complete alcoholic fermentation and natural malolactic fermentation during 6 months in oak. The cuvée is assembled in the spring and the wine bottled for at least 5½ years on the yeasts at 12°C before hand riddling and disgorging. The wine, of about 12.5% alcohol, receives a dose of wine matured in oak barrels with a dash of sugar before cork sealing.

Style and maturity
Franciacorta Cuvée Annamaria Clementi on release more than 6 years after the vintage has luminous straw yellow color with old gold and topaz highlights and remarkably abundant and persistent streams of fine bubbles. Aromas are rich and complex with scents reminiscent of apricot, peach and apple mingling with hints of toasted nuts, honey, vanilla and yeasts. Similar sensations prevail on the palate in a sparkling wine that combines strength of character with extraordinary elegance, reaching a prime between 7 and 12 years from the harvest.

Serving
🍴 9–10°C.
🍷 Tall, ample flute (vintage Champagne type).
🍽 Seafood *antipasti;* risotto with scampi or freshwater prawns; roast sea bass; poultry with creamy sauces; a superb aperitif.

Caudrina

La Galeisa
Moscato d'Asti DOCG ♀

Producer
Azienda Agricola
Caudrina
Strada Brosia 20
12053 Castiglione
Tinella (Cuneo)
Tel. 0141/855126
Fax 0141/855008

Owner
Romano Dogliotti

Founded
1940

Winemakers
Romano and Alessandro
Dogliotti with Giuliano
Noè

Vineyard managers
Romano, Sergio and
Marco Dogliotti

Production
About 24,000 bottles a
year

Vintages
The most recent

Price
●

Production of Asti is dominated by large cellars geared to supply the world with the most popular of sweet sparkling wines. But what really pleases Piedmontese palates is the wine that shares the DOCG: the gentler, more fragrant and more exquisitely fruity Moscato d'Asti made on a relatively small scale by artisans.

By artisans I do not mean simple country folk who labor in dingy cellars the way their grandfathers did, for the art of Moscato d'Asti is as sophisticatedly up to date as are the mass production methods of Asti Spumante. An early master of the art was Romano Dogliotti, a strapping farm boy who got the hang of the new technology in the 1970s to become a leader in the field at his Caudrina estate at Castiglione Tinella.

Romano's father Redento had grown Moscato since the early 1940s, but sold the grapes to Asti houses. When Romano joined him in the 1960s, they made a bit of bottle-fermented Moscato. Big cellars had begun to use pressurized, temperature-controlled stainless steel tanks called *autoclave* to streamline operations for fresher, more stable Asti Spumante.

Romano adjusted the method to Moscato d'Asti, keeping the musts below 0°C to be fermented at intervals to provide wine of exquisitely fresh aroma and flavor. Fermentation is arrested when alcohol reaches 5.5 percent (instead of 7 percent minimum for Asti), leaving the wine sweeter with less carbon dioxide pressure (1.7 atmospheres maximum to Asti's 3 minimum). Romano's success inspired a generation of growers with vineyards in the steep eastern Langhe hills, where the finest Moscato is made. With the 1987 vintage, he created the single-vineyard La Galeisa, an archetype of modern Moscato d'Asti.

Romano works with his wife Bruna and sons Alessandro, Sergio and Marco to produce about 160,000 bottles of wine a year, including another fine Moscato d'Asti called La Caudrina. La Selvatica is a fully sparkling Asti. DOC reds are Barbera d'Asti La Solista and Montevenere and Dolcetto d'Alba Campo Rosso.

Piedmont

Grapes
Moscato Bianco di Canelli 100%, hand picked in mid- to late September.

Vineyards
La Galeisa covers about 4 hectares in sandy calcareous clay soils on steep slopes facing west-southwest at 280–340 meters of altitude at Castiglione Tinella in the Langhe hills of southern Piedmont. Vines, of an average age of 31 years, are planted at a density of 4,500 per hectare and trained in the Guyot cordon method.

Vinification and aging
Whole grape bunches are gently squeezed in pneumatic presses and the free-run must is chilled, filtered and held below freezing in tanks. Fermentation is set off by inoculating the musts with select yeasts and heating them to about 20°C in *autoclave*, pressurized stainless steel tanks. When the alcohol reaches 5.5% (with about the same percentage of residual sugar), the wine is rapidly chilled to below freezing to block the fermentation. Bottling takes place in sterile conditions and the wine is left for about 15 days before release.

Style and maturity
Moscato d'Asti La Galeisa should be consumed within months of bottling (never more than a year from the harvest) when it shows pale straw color with greenish tinges and a joyous flow of fine bubbles. Blossomy Moscato fragrance triumphs in scents reminiscent of sage leaves, rennet apple, raspberry and hints of citrus, honey and musk. Flavors are full and round, as fruity as fresh grapes with a mellow sweetness offset by an apple-like tang and a buoyant but gentle effervescence that exits with a refreshing tingle on the tongue.

Serving
🍸 8–10°C.
🍷 Tulip-shaped, of medium size.
🍽 Zabaglione made with Moscato d'Asti; hazelnut and almond pastries and cakes; *macedonia* (fruit cocktail) of fresh strawberries and peaches.

Brut Collezione
Franciacorta DOCG ♀

Producer
Azienda Agricola
Gian Paolo e
Giovanni Cavalleri
Via Provinciale 96
25030 Erbusco (Brescia)
Tel. 030/7760217
Fax 030/7267350
cavalleri@cavalleri.it
www.cavalleri.it

Owner
Giovanni Cavalleri

Founded
1967

Winemakers
Gianpaolo Turra and
Pierluigi Calabria

Vineyard manager
Gianpaolo Turra

Production
About 13,000 bottles
and 500 magnums in
vintage years

Vintages
1997 1995 1994 1993
1991 1990 1988 1986
1985 1983

Price
● ● ●

Franciacorta was transformed from an unheralded wine zone into "Italy's miniature Champagne" virtually overnight by producers whose progressive vision seems perhaps more Californian than Italian. But that doesn't mean that contemporary wine barons lack a sense of history. Giovanni Cavalleri heads the family winery at the town of Erbusco, where an ancestor, Jacobinus de Cavaleris, settled in the fourteenth century and where another, Giuseppe Paolo Cavalleri, made a neat profit from wine in the late nineteenth century.

Yet when Franciacorta became a DOC zone in 1967, Giovanni Cavalleri admits that he and his father Gian Paolo were still selling wines by the demijohn. "The next year we bottled Franciacorta Rosso and white Pinot, both still wines," he recalls. "The challenge of producing sparkling wines was formidable, so I waited until I was certain that we could make something truly valid."

The cellars shifted from the family *palazzo* (now Erbusco's municipal hall) to a modern mansion on the edge of town that also houses the state-of-the-art winery. Cavalleri works with his daughter Giulia and faithful cellarmaster Pierluigi Calabria in fashioning what is roundly acknowledged to be one of Italy's most impressive ranges of sparkling wines. The exemplar is Brut Collezione, a vintage *blanc de blancs* (pure Chardonnay) of uncommon finesse and character.

From 37 hectares of vines, Cavalleri produces about 280,000 bottles of wine a year, including Franciacorta DOCG Brut, Pas Dosé, Satèn and Rosé Collezione. Still wines take in Terre di Franciacorta DOC Bianco (including Vigna Rampaneto and Vigna Seradina) and Rosso (led by Vigna Tajardino) and Sebino IGT Merlot called Corniole.

Cavalleri, a financier who has also headed the Franciacorta producers' consortium, admits that from a purely economic point of view wine would not be considered a particularly smart investment. But, he adds, "I don't know of any other kind of work that provides greater satisfaction."

Lombardy

Grapes
Chardonnay 100%, hand picked in the first half of September.

Vineyards
Plots totaling 13.93 hectares in stony glacial moraine on slopes facing south and west at 250–287 meters of altitude on the Cavalleri estate at the edge of the town of Erbusco in the southwestern part of the Franciacorta zone. Vines, of an average age of 16 years, are planted at a density of 4,000–5,000 per hectare and trained in a spurred cordon method.

Vinification and aging
Grapes are soft crushed and the free-run musts (50% of the weight) are fermented at no more than 20°C for 10 days in stainless steel vats. Base wines undergo partial malolactic fermentation before being assembled and bottled for 4 years on the yeasts. After hand riddling and disgorging, the wine, of about 12.5% alcohol, receives a dose of wine from the same year matured for 6–7 months in oak barrels. Bottles are cork sealed and cellared for 3–6 months before release.

Style and maturity
Franciacorta Brut Collezione on release about 5 years after the vintage has bright straw color with golden highlights and lively, persistent streams of fine bubbles. Aromas are richly fruity yet refined with hints of yeast and bread crust. Flavors are delicately dry and soft with elegant fruit sensations and velvety texture in a long finish that leaves the palate refreshed. The wine reaches a prime at about 7 years after the harvest and maintains style for another decade.

Serving
🌡 10°C.
🍷 Tall, ample flute (vintage Champagne type).
🍽 *Antipasto* and salads based on shellfish; risotto with shrimp and zucchini; charcoal-grilled scampi.

Bussiador
Langhe Bianco DOC ♀

Producer
Poderi Aldo Conterno
Località Bussia 48
12065 Monforte d'Alba
(Cuneo)
Tel. 0173/78150
Fax 0173/787240
www.il-vino.com

Owner
Aldo Conterno

Founded
1969

Winemakers
Stefano and Franco
Conterno

Vineyard manager
Stefano Conterno

Production
7,800 bottles a year

Vintages
1999 1998 1997 1995
1993

Price
● ● ●

P iedmont's wine establishment has long been known for a staunch sense of tradition. Nowhere in Italy is respect for the past more evident than in the Langhe hills around the town of Alba, where growers maintain a stubborn attachment to their native vines for red wines aged in massive casks of oak from Slavonia. When, a couple of decades ago, progressives (or traitors or heretics as they were sometimes called at the time) planted Chardonnay and Cabernet and began maturing their new-style wines in small barrels of French oak, traditionalists were scandalized. Among the skeptics was Aldo Conterno, a leading producer of Barolo (see page 48).

But, today, Aldo admits that the progressive thinking of his sons Franco and Stefano has influenced his own philosophy of winemaking. Chardonnay has been planted in the family vineyards of Bussia, long a sanctuary of Nebbiolo, Barbera and Dolcetto. And the once dreaded barriques, as they are popularly known in Italy, have gained a place in the Conterno cellars.

"But they are not used for Barolo," vows Aldo, who declares that as long as he's in charge the "king of wines" will be aged in casks of Slavonian oak. As for Chardonnay, Aldo allows that the French vine has filled a gap in a zone that previously didn't have a dry white wine to offer. But it also accentuated a gap between generations of the Conterno family.

"The boys insisted on Chardonnay in barriques and that's fine," says Aldo. "But I like pure fruit sensations in a white wine." The result is two versions, both of which qualify as Langhe Bianco DOC: tank-fermented Printaniè and barrel-fermented Bussiador.

Each type has its advocates and some, like myself, admire both. But if forced to choose, I'd give the nod to Bussiador as a Chardonnay of uncommon depth and opulence enhanced by that gentle kiss of oak that Burgundians call *boisé*.

Piedmont

Grapes
Chardonnay 100%, hand picked in early September.

Vineyards
Plots covering 2.72 hectares in calcareous marl with layers of sand on slopes facing south at about 420 meters of altitude in the Bussia area of the commune of Monforte in the heart of the Barolo zone. The vines, of an average age of 15 years, are planted at a density of 4,200 per hectare and trained in the Guyot cordon method.

Vinification and aging
Grapes are soft crushed and the musts begin fermenting at 16–18°C in stainless steel tanks and continue in new barrels of French oak, where malolactic fermentation occurs during 8–12 months on the lees. The wine, of about 13.5% alcohol, is bottled and cellared for 7 or 8 months before release.

Style and maturity
Bussiador when released about 2 years after the harvest has bright straw yellow color with golden highlights and ample bouquet with scents reminiscent of tropical fruit, butter, honey and vanilla. Flavors are rich, round and finely balanced with a range of fruit flavors (apple, citrus, pineapple) and hints of toasted hazelnut in a long, smooth finish. The wine usually reaches a prime at 3–4 years and retains class for 2–3 years beyond.

Serving
- 12–16°C.
- Tulip-shaped glass (Chardonnay type).
- Baked yellow peppers with a tuna stuffing; *tajarin* (noodles with rabbit and leeks); risotto with porcini mushrooms.

Producer
Giuseppe Contratto
Via G.B. Giuliani 56
14053 Canelli (Asti)
Tel. 0141/823350
Fax 0141/824650
info@contratto.it
www.contratto.it

Owners
Antonella and Carlo
Micca-Bocchino

Founded
1867

Winemaker
Giancarlo Scaglione

Vineyard manager
Gianluca Scaglione

Production
10,000–15,000 bottles a
year

Vintages
1999 1998 1997 1996
1995

Price
● ●

Contratto

De Miranda
Metodo Classico
Asti DOCG ♀

The Moscato vine was recorded in Piedmont in 1203, though only in the nineteenth century did producers around Asti make sparkling wines from its sweetly aromatic grapes. Giuseppe Contratto, who founded a winery at Canelli in 1867, was a pioneer of Asti Spumante. Gran Pin, as he was known, modified the Champagne method of a second fermentation in bottle to suit the peculiarities of Moscato Bianco. The challenge was to retain the fragrant sweetness that characterizes Asti while preventing the yeasts that create bubbles from fermenting the wine out dry (and building enough pressure to break the bottle).

Eventually convenient tank fermentation methods replaced the complicated twists and turns of the Champagne method as Asti grew to become the world's most popular sweet sparkling wine. Only Contratto resisted, making a rare *metodo classico* that was considered the best of Asti in the 1970s. But as the company built its line of dry sparkling wines from Pinot and Chardonnay grapes, the classic Asti vanished.

In 1994, Contratto was acquired by Antonella and Carlo Micca-Bocchino, the sister–brother team that made Bocchino a leading name in grappa. With admirable spirit, they revived bottle-fermented Asti from a vineyard known as De Miranda under direction of the eminent winemaker Giancarlo Scaglione. Techniques differ from those of classic *brut* in that the base wine, matured in oak, goes into bottle before alcoholic fermentation is complete and the *tirage* on the yeasts is shorter to retain natural sweetness. The result is once again the most elegant example of Asti.

Contratto's production of 250,000–300,000 bottles a year is led by a range of *metodo classico* wines based on Pinot Nero or Chardonnay: Brut, Bacco d'Oro, For England, Brut Riserva Giuseppe Contratto and Brut Rosé Riserva Giuseppe Contratto. The firm also makes DOCG Barolo (Tenuta Secolo), Barbaresco (Tenuta Alberta), Moscato d'Asti (Tenuta Gilardino) and DOC Barbera d'Asti (Solus Ad and Panta Rei).

Piedmont

Grapes
Moscato Bianco 100%, hand picked when very ripe in late September.

Vineyards
De Miranda covers 2 hectares in calcareous clay soils on slopes facing south-southwest at about 350 meters of altitude at Cassinasco south of the town of Canelli in the Langhe hills of southern Piedmont. Vines, of an average age of 36–41 years, are planted at a density of 7,000 per hectare and trained in the Guyot cordon method.

Vinification and aging
Grape bunches individually selected in the cellars macerate with the juice briefly before soft crushing. The musts are fermented slowly for 4–6 months in small barrels of French oak (Allier and Tronçais) until alcohol reaches 6%. The base wine is cold stabilized in stainless steel tanks before going into individual bottles with select yeasts for at least 9 months to become sparkling. Bottles are hand riddled and disgorged in small batches and the wine, of about 7.5% alcohol and 8.5% residual sugar, is cork sealed and released soon after.

Style and maturity
Asti De Miranda Metodo Classico on release in the second year after the vintage has bright straw color with golden highlights and a creamy, persistent flow of fine bubbles. The exhilarating fragrance of Moscato prevails in scents reminiscent of fresh sage and apricots with hints of honey, yeast, anise and vanilla. Flavors are sweet and mellow with plush fruit flavors offset by delicate acidity and buoyant effervescence with a hint of toasted hazelnut in a smooth finish. The wine hits its stride at 3–4 years and maintains style for a couple of years beyond.

Serving
🍴 8–10°C.
🍷 Tulip-shaped glass of medium size.
🍽 Zabaglione made with aged Marsala; *panna cotta* (molded cream dessert); *bonèt* (coffee-flavored custard cake).

Frissonière-Les Crêtes Cuvée Bois Vallée d'Aoste DOC Chardonnay ♀

Producer
Azienda Agricola
Les Crêtes
Località Villetos 50
11010 Aymavilles
(Aosta)
Tel. 0165/902274
Fax 0165/902758

Owners
Costantino Charrère and
Jolanda Plat

Founded
1989

Winemakers
Vincent Grosjean and
Massimo Bellocchia

Vineyard manager
Carlo Bataillon

Production
About 5,000 bottles a
year

Vintages
1999 1998 1997 1995

Price
● ● ●

Costantino Charrère had already built a fine reputation with his own estate at Aymavilles when he joined brothers Franco and Paolo Vai, noted restaurateurs, to found the winery of Les Crêtes in 1989. With enologist Vincent Grosjean, they set about perfecting wines from local varieties of Valle d'Aosta, while experimenting with Chardonnay, Pinot Noir and Syrah from neighboring France.

The brothers Vai have departed, but Costantino Charrère has acquired choice new vineyards, including the heights of Les Crêtes, where the cellars of the region's model winery are located. From 13 hectares on steep slopes and terraces, Les Crêtes produces from 110,000–130,000 bottles of wine a year, all named for vineyards and most classified under the comprehensive Valle d'Aosta (Vallée d'Aoste in French) DOC.

More than just local curiosities are the red wines from Fumin (Vigne La Tour), Petit Rouge (as Torrette Vigne Les Toules) and Petite Arvine, a variety shared with Switzerland's Valais (as Vigne Champorette). Charrère's mastery of Syrah is evident in the increasingly acclaimed Côteaux La Tour. Although he admits to being strongly influenced by Burgundy, Costantino so far has posed no threat to the crus of the Côte d'Or with his Pinot Noir from Vigne La Tour. His success with Chardonnay is another matter.

Clones of Chardonnay, selected in Burgundy, are planted in the high vineyards of Frissonière and Les Crêtes above the towns of Saint-Cristophe and Aymavilles. Quantities have been purposely limited as the winemakers experiment with two styles of Chardonnay: one made in stainless steel tanks and the other fermented and matured on the lees in barrels as Cuvée Bois.

To tell the truth, I find it hard to choose between the two. The tank version shows Alpine freshness in its exquisite fruit–acid balance. Cuvée Bois has the depth and complexity of the grand Chardonnays, though to my taste a tad less of toasty oak on the nose and palate would bring it a step closer in style to a top Montrachet or Meursault.

Valle d'Aosta

Grapes
Chardonnay 100%, hand picked in early October.

Vineyards
Two plots in loose sandy glacial moraine at 550–600 meters of altitude: Frissonière of 1.8 hectares facing south and Les Crêtes of 1.2 hectares facing north, the first in the commune of Saint-Cristophe and the second in the commune of Aymavilles in the western sector of Valle d'Aosta. The vines were planted in 1991 at a density of 6,500 per hectare and trained low in the Guyot cordon method.

Vinification and aging
Grapes are soft crushed and the musts fermented in 300-liter barrels of French (Alliers and Tronçais) and American oak, where malolactic fermentation occurs during 10 months with frequent stirring of the lees (*bâtonnage*). The wine, of about 13% alcohol, is bottled and cellared for 6 months before release.

Style and maturity
Chardonnay Frissonière-Les Crêtes Cuvée Bois when released in the second year after the harvest has deep straw yellow color with golden highlights and ample bouquet with scents reminiscent of tropical fruit, butter, honey, toasty oak and vanilla. Flavors are rich, round and finely balanced with a range of fruit flavors (apple, citrus, pineapple) and hints of toasted hazelnuts in a long, smooth finish. The wine reaches peaks in 4–5 years, though it seems to have the elements to improve longer.

Serving
- 12–15°C, opening bottle 2 hours earlier.
- Tulip-shaped glass (Chardonnay type).
- Risotto *alla valdostana* (with Fontina and Parmigiano); brook trout with butter and almonds; poached Maine lobster.

Chambave Moscato Passito Vallée d'Aoste DOC ♀

Producer
La Crotta di
Vegneron
Piazza Roncas 2
11023 Chambave
(Aosta)
Tel. 0166/46670
Fax 0166/46543
LaCrotta@libero.it

Owner
Cooperative winery

Founded
1980

Winemaker
Andrea Costa

Vineyard supervisor
Stefania Dozio

Production
About 6,000 bottles a
year

Vintages
1999 1998 1997 1996
1995

Price
● ●

The vineyards of Valle d'Aosta are still often planted on terraces hewn out of stone on slopes along the Dora Baltea River, flowing down from Mont Blanc. La Crotta di Vegneron is one of the region's six cooperatives formed by growers whose tiny plots don't render enough to justify individual cellars. Its 130 members between them cultivate a mere 33 hectares of vines for a production of a bit over 200,000 bottles a year.

The wines of La Crotta di Vegneron (Cave of the Winegrower) are models of quality and consistency, thanks to persevering work in the vineyards supervised by agronomist Stefania Dozio and enologist Andrea Costa. Nearly all of the wines are covered by the comprehensive DOC known as Valle d'Aosta, or Vallée d'Aoste in the provincial French, taking in 22 categories with names in either language or both.

The range takes in such familiar varieties as Gamay, Pinot Noir and Müller-Thurgau, though the most intriguing wines come from vines that Aostans call their own. These include the *rouges* of the towns of Chambave and Nus, the latter of which is also the home of a Malvoisie that seems to be a local strain of Pinot Gris. The pride of Chambave, where La Crotta is located, is the aromatic Moscato or Muscat that is made in two styles, one an unusual dry type and the other a luscious Passito from grapes partly dried after the harvest.

The local variety of Moscato may have been introduced by the Romans, whose colony of Augusta Prætoria became the city of Aosta. They say that Napoleon enjoyed the wine on his frequent jaunts through the valley.

Chambave's Moscato acquired a measure of renown in recent times thanks to the work of Ezio Voyat, who doubled as a winemaker and croupier at a local casino. La Crotta di Vegneron has become the lone producer of a DOC wine that is so rare and exquisite that the only way to be sure to taste it is to visit its vineyards of Valle d'Aosta amid the splendor of Europe's highest peaks.

Valle d'Aosta

Grapes
Moscato Bianco (or di Chambave) 100%, hand picked in late September and dried on cane mats until they have lost 40% of their weight through evaporation.

Vineyards
Various plots covering about 10 hectares in total in loose sandy soils on slopes oriented toward the south at 400–600 meters of altitude in the communes of Chambave, Chatillon, Saint Vincent, Saint Denis and Verraye in the east-central sector of Valle d'Aosta. The vines, ranging in age from 5–31 years, are planted at densities of 5,000–6,000 per hectare and trained low in the Guyot cordon and *alberello* bush methods.

Vinification and aging
The shriveled grapes are crushed and the musts separated from the skins before fermenting for 21 days at 20°C in stainless steel tanks, where malolactic fermentation occurs during several months of maturation. The wine, of 15–16.5% alcohol (of which 3.5% is in residual sugars), is bottled and cellared until release about a year after the harvest.

Style and maturity
Chambave Moscato Passito on release about a year after the harvest has bright straw yellow color with golden highlights and splendid Muscat aromas with scents reminiscent of roses, dried fruit, peaches and Alpine herbs. On the palate, it is round and fairly rich with a clean sweetness braced by refreshing acidity and smooth fruit flavors that linger on the tongue. At a prime after a year, the wine can retain its vital aromas and flavors for a few years beyond.

Serving
🍷 10–12°C.
🍷 Tall tulip-shaped glass.
🍴 Aostan sweets, such as *martin sec* pears stewed in red wine, almond biscuits called *tegole* and butter crisps known as *torcetti*.

Walter De Battè

Cinque Terre
DOC ♀

Producer
Azienda Vitivinicola
Walter De Battè
Via Trarcantu 25
19017 Riomaggiore (La
Spezia)
Tel. 0187/920127
Fax. 0187/920844

Owner
Walter De Battè

Founded
1991

Winemakers
Walter De Battè with
Giorgio Baccigalupi

Vineyard manager
Walter De Battè

Production
About 3,000 bottles a
year (plus Sciacchetrà)

Vintages
1999 1998 1997 1996

Price
● ●

Cinque Terre refers to the "five lands" or villages of Corniglia, Manarola, Monterosso, Riomaggiore and Vernazza along the rugged Ligurian coast north of the Gulf of La Spezia. The splendor of a landscape of terraced vineyards rising from the sea contributed to the legend of the wines of Cinque Terre, which, though made in precious quantities, were widely admired in the past.

The ancient Liguri people began carving terraces out of rock walls to create vineyards that have been worked over the ages by farmers whose toils have been described as heroic. But, in modern times, ever fewer have been willing to face such hardships, as terraces have become increasingly overgrown with brush and brambles. Still, the days of heroic viticulture aren't quite over, thanks to the persistence of an aging generation of *vignaioli* and, perhaps most admirably, to a determined young man named Walter De Battè.

Walter, who works parcels of land known in dialect as *pàstini* overlooking Riomaggiore, has rapidly emerged as Cinque Terre's most accomplished winemaker. A firm believer in the historic varieties of Bosco, Albarola and Vermentino, Walter limits yields of his old vines to painstakingly low levels and selects grapes to make a mere 3,000 bottles of wine a year.

In his tiny cellars, Walter might be depicted as an enlightened progressive, using small oak barrels to mature his Cinque Terre into a wine of unprecedented polish, depth and aging capacity. He also makes a bit of fine Sciacchetrà, the sweet version of Cinque Terre from the same grapes left to dry after the harvest.

Walter De Battè isn't alone in his dedication to Cinque Terre. Also located at Riogmaggiore are the respected cellars of Forlini e Cappellini and the Cooperativa Agricola, which groups growers from the five villages. In addition, Piero Lugano of the Enoteca Bisson at Chiavari also makes admirable Cinque Terre.

Liguria

Grapes
Bosco 65%, Albarola 25%, Vermentino 10%, hand picked in late September to early October.

Vineyards
Parcels known as Donega, Lirta, Casen and Novale of 6,640 square meters in sandy, stony, acidic soils on steep terraces oriented toward the southeast at 100–250 meters above the Ligurian Sea at the village of Riomaggiore. The vines were planted 60–70 years ago at a density of 4,000–5,000 per hectare and trained in a low-trellised pergola method.

Vinification and aging
Grapes are soft crushed and the juice macerated with the skins for 24 hours in stainless steel tanks cooled from 20–10°C. The clarified must is inoculated with yeast cultures and about 60% ferments in stainless steel at 18–19°C for 12–13 days and the rest in 100–225-liter barrels of oak (Allier, Cher, Tronçais and Slavonia) for 8 or 9 days. The wine, of about 13% alcohol, remains on the lees, stirred periodically in a process known as *bâtonnage*, until April before blending and bottling in July.

Style and maturity
Cinque Terre De Battè on release about a year after the harvest has bright straw-yellow color with golden highlights and decisive aromas with scents reminiscent of yellow plums, spices, wild herbs and vanilla. On the palate, it is round and smooth with flavors that recall ripe plums, honey and toasted nuts in a long finish. The wine reaches a prime about 20 months after the harvest and can gain in style for 3 or 4 years beyond.

Serving
🍷 12–14°C.
♀ Ample glass.
🍽 Oysters and raw or poached shellfish; mussels with a breadcrumb and spice stuffing; rabbit roast with olives and herbs.

Forteto della Luja

Producer
Azienda Agricola
Forteto della Luja
Bricco Casa Rosso 4
14050 Loazzolo (Asti)
Tel. 0141/831596
Fax 0141/831596
fortetodellaluja
@inwind.it

Owner
Giancarlo Scaglione

Founded
1826

Winemaker
Giancarlo Scaglione

Vineyard manager
Gianni Scaglione

Production
About 4,000 half bottles
(0.375-liter) a year

Vintages
1999 1998 1997 1996
1995 1994 1993 1990
1988 1985

Price
● ● ●

Forteto della Luja Vendemmia Tardiva Piasa Rischei Loazzolo DOC

G iancarlo Scaglione may look like a leading man, though he's always had a way of shining behind the scenes. After taking an honors degree in enological science from the University of Turin, Giancarlo headed winemaking operations at the sparkling wine house of Gancia for a time before striking out on his own. As a consultant he stands behind some of the most admired wines of Piedmont, including the Barbera called Bricco dell'Uccellone created with Giacomo Bologna in 1982.

Giancarlo has a little farm at Loazzolo high in the Langhe hills south of Asti, where his wife's family had grown Moscato grapes to sell to the *spumante* houses of nearby Canelli. In 1985, encouraged by Giacomo Bologna, he made a sweet wine from late-harvested Moscato matured in small oak barrels in the grotto of Forteto della Luja, the stone farmhouse that dates to 1600. The wine was as luscious as it was rare and Giancarlo packaged it accordingly in a tall, slim bottle with a black strip label wrapped around it in a spiral.

Being a gregarious type, Giancarlo talked his neighbors into producing similar wines following strict requirements under what was approved as Loazzolo DOC. The crème de la crème is Forteto della Luja's single-vineyard Piasa Rischei, in which half of the Moscato grapes are picked normally and dried on mats and half are harvested late after *Botrytis cinerea* or "noble rot" sets in. During the extended alcoholic-malolactic fermentation, an oxidation process occurs that protects the wine as it concentrates sweet Moscato flavors and develops the beguiling bouquet that noble rot affords.

Giancarlo has once again moved to the background, leaving Forteto della Luja in the skilled hands of son Gianni and daughter Silvia to produce about 40,000 bottles a year from 8 hectares of vines at Loazzolo and Santo Stefano Belbo. The other wines are Moscato d'Asti DOCG Piasa San Maurizio, Piemonte DOC Pian dei Sogni (late-harvested Brachetto) and Monferrato Rosso DOC Le Grive (Barbera and Pinot Nero).

Piedmont

Grapes
Moscato Bianco 100%, hand picked: half in late September–early October and dried on cane mats until December; half left on the vine to develop *Botrytis cinerea* and harvested in early November.

Vineyard
Piasa Rischei, a plot of 9,200 square meters in calcareous marls on slopes facing southwest at 470 meters of altitude at Loazzolo in the Langhe hills south of Asti. The vines, planted 63 years ago at a density of 8,000 per hectare, are trained low in the Guyot cordon method.

Vinification and aging
The late-harvested grapes are crushed in a traditional oak press and remain with the skins for 24 hours before the must is settled for 18 hours and lightly filtered. The dried grapes are crushed in December and the musts blended with those of the late-harvested grapes in the spring. Slow alcoholic and malolactic fermentation occur in small oak barrels over 20 months at temperatures ranging from 10°C in winter to 18°C in summer. The wine, of about 11.5% alcohol with 14% residual sugar, is bottled and cellared for 6–8 months before release.

Style and maturity
Piasa Rischei on release in the third year after the harvest has deep yellow color with golden highlights and bouquet of uncommon richness and complexity with scents reminiscent of ripe fruit, citrus, dried figs, honey, spices and vanilla. On the palate, it is round and concentrated, voluptuously sweet yet clean and fresh with concentrated fruit and hints of honey and toasted nuts in flavors that linger on the palate. Superb at 8–12 years, the wine seems to have the stuff to shine for half a century.

Serving
🍷 10°C with sweets, 16°C with cheese.
♀ Tall tulip-shaped glass.
🍽 *Foie gras*; strong aged cheeses (Gorgonzola, Castelmagno); Piedmontese nougat; after-dinner sipping.

Gaja

Gaia & Rey
Langhe DOC ♀

Producer
Gaja
Via Torino 36A
12050 Barbaresco
(Cuneo)
Tel. 0173/635158
Fax 0173/635256
gajad@tin.it

Owner
Gaja family

Founded
1859

Chief winemaker
Guido Rivella

Vineyard managers
Giorgio Culasso and
Mauro Abrigo

Production
About 18,000 bottles
a year

Vintages
1999 1998 1997 1994
1992 1990 1987 1984

Price
● ● ● ●

One of the secrets behind Angelo Gaja's success is his penchant for surprises. His history of unpredictable behavior can be traced to the 1970s, when he took over the family winery at Barbaresco where father Giovanni had made only red wine in the great Piedmontese tradition.

With Giovanni busy being mayor, Angelo began replanting vineyards, not only in the standard Nebbiolo, Barbera and Dolcetto, but, secretly, in Cabernet Sauvignon, Chardonnay and Sauvignon Blanc. When his father discovered the Cabernet in a plot historically known for Nebbiolo, he muttered *Darmagi* (what a shame). That became the name of the wine.

Although branded as a heretic, Angelo carried his folly a step further, installing small barrels from France beside the ponderous casks of Slavonian oak that had aged Piedmontese wines for ages. His first Chardonnay, from the 1983 vintage, was called Gaia & Rey after his daughter Gaia and the maiden name of his paternal grandmother Clotilde Rey.

Many of the world's great Chardonnays are fermented in oak, but Angelo and resident winemaker Guido Rivella prefer to use stainless steel tanks before maturing the wine in barrels. "Barriques help to give wines clearer fruit definition and a supple complexity that results in more sophisticated flavors," says Angelo. "But I use them with moderation, because I want my wines to have authentic character without appealing to the international taste for oaky Chardonnay." To meet his exacting standards, Angelo buys split oak in northern and eastern Europe, weathers the wood outside the winery and has a cooper make barrels to his specifications. The personalized style is also evident in a Chardonnay called Rossj Bass and a fine Sauvignon Blanc called Alteni di Brassica—all classified under Langhe DOC.

Those are the white wines in the Gaja repertoire, at least for now. His most recent surprises have come in declassifying his top wines as DOCG under Barbaresco and Barolo (see page 54).

Piedmont

Grapes
Chardonnay 100%, hand picked in September.

Vineyard
A plot of 3.6 hectares in marly calcareous clays on slopes facing west at 350 meters of altitude at the village of Treiso in the Barbaresco zone. The vines, planted 23 years ago at a density of 5,600 per hectare, are trained in the Guyot cordon method.

Vinification and aging
Grapes are stemmed and soft crushed and the must fermented without selected yeasts at 18–20°C for about 4 weeks in stainless steel tanks. After spontaneous malolactic fermentation, the wine is matured for 6–8 months in new, small barrels of oak from France, Austria, Poland, Hungary and Russia. The wine, of about 13.5% alcohol, is bottled and cellared for at least 4 months before release

Style and maturity
Gaia & Rey on release in the second year after the harvest has bright straw yellow color with golden highlights and exquisite aroma with scents reminiscent of tropical fruit, ripe apples, butter and vanilla. Well structured and velvety in texture with ripe fruit sensations buttressed by ample acidity, the wine has deep, elaborate flavors that linger through an elegant finish. Prime drinking begins at 3–4 years, though top vintages remain impressive for more than a decade.

Serving
🍷 12°C.
🍷 Ample tulip-shaped glass (Bordeaux type).
🍽 *Vitello tonnato* (veal with tuna sauce); risotto with asparagus tips; *orata in guazzetto* (gilt-head bream in a light tomato sauce).

Ottaviano
Lambruschi

Producer
Azienda Agricola
Ottaviano Lambruschi
& C.
Via Olmarello 28
19030 Castelnuovo
Magra (La Spezia)
Tel. 0187/674261
Fax 0187/674261

Owners
Ottaviano and Fabio
Lambruschi

Founded
1973

Winemaker
Giorgio Baccigalupi

Vineyard managers
Fabio and Ottaviano
Lambruschi

Production
5,000–6,000 bottles
a year

Vintages
1999 1998

Price
●

Vigneto Costa Marina
Colli di Luni
Vermentino DOC ♀

The theory that Vermentino arrived in Italy from Spain via Sardinia is questioned by vine historian Mario Fregoni, who surmises that the variety originated in the Middle East and was brought by Greeks to Liguria around the sixth century BC. As evidence, he cites the *lastra di Luni,* a stone tablet showing a bunch of grapes strikingly similar to modern Vermentino. Luni, a port city founded in 177 BC by the Romans, later disappeared in the flood plain of the Magra river to re-emerge as an archaeological site that gives its name to the area southeast of the port of La Spezia.

The modern wine zone of Colli di Luni has earned a reputation for Vermentino, thanks primarily to the stubborn dedication of Ottaviano Lambruschi at his small estate above Castelnuovo Magra. The zone extends from Liguria into Tuscany around the city of Carrara in whose renowned marble quarries Ottaviano worked for 30 years before saving enough money to buy some land and realize his dream of becoming a winemaker.

He cleared wooded slopes and in 1973 planted 3 hectares of vineyards. Aided by consulting enologist Giorgio Baccigalupi, Ottaviano bottled his first Vermentino in 1982. Two years later it won the prize called Rönseggin d'Öu as the best wine of Liguria and since then there has never been enough to meet demand.

Ottaviano has been joined by his son Fabio, who studied agronomy and brought innovative spirit to the estate. In 1991, they bottled their first Vermentino from a single vineyard called Costa Marina because it has a fine view of the coast and the Ligurian Sea. Costa Marina is generally acknowledged to be the finest Vermentino of Liguria, though their Sarticola, partly matured in oak, can be a close rival from certain vintages.

From 5 hectares of vines (2 hectares rented), they produce 25,000–30,000 bottles a year, including a regular Vermentino and Rosso Il Maniero (from Sangiovese with Cabernet and Merlot) all classified as Colli di Luni DOC.

Liguria

OTTAVIANO LAMBRUSCHI

Colli di Luni
DENOMINAZIONE DI ORIGINE CONTROLLATA

Vermentino

VENDEMMIA 1999
Costa Marina

Prodotto e imbottigliato dall'Azienda Agricola
OTTAVIANO LAMBRUSCHI & C.
Castelnuovo Magra (Italia)

75 cl.   13% vol.

Grapes
Vermentino 100%, hand picked in stages in late September.

Vineyard
Vigneto Costa Marina of 1.7 hectares in clay soils with stony deposits on a steep terraced slope facing southeast at 250 meters of altitude at Marciano in the commune of Castelnuovo Magra in the southeastern corner of the Colli di Luni DOC zone in the foothills of the Lunigiana range of the Apennines overlooking the Ligurian Sea. The vines, of an average age of 26 years, are planted at a density of about 4,000 per hectare and trained in the Guyot cordon method.

Vinification and aging
Grapes are soft crushed and the musts fermented at 18–21°C for 20–25 days in stainless steel tanks. The wine, of about 13% alcohol, undergoes malolactic fermentation in tanks before being bottled and cellared for about a month until release.

Style and maturity
Costa Marina Vermentino on release in the spring after the harvest has bright straw yellow color with green-gold highlights and decisive aromas with scents reminiscent of ripe apples, citron, wild herbs and flowers. On the palate, it is round and smooth with ripe fruit flavors buoyed by refreshing acidity and a hint of toasted nuts in a clean, mellow finish. The wine reaches a prime about a year after the harvest but has the character to show well for a year or 2 beyond.

Serving
🌡 12–14°C.
🍷 Tulip-shaped glass (Sauvignon type).
🍽 *Testaroli* (tiny crepes boiled like pasta and served with pesto); *buridda* (fish soup with tomato and spices); turbot roast with artichokes and potatoes.

Brut Satèn
Franciacorta DOCG ♀

Producer
Azienda Agricola
Monte Rossa
Via Luca Maurenzio 14
25040 Bornato di
Cazzago San Martino
(Brescia)
Tel. 030/725066
Fax 030/7750061
info@monterossa.
com
www.monterossa.
com

Owner
Paola Rovetta

Founded
1972

Winemakers
Cesare Ferrari and
Emanuele Rabotti

Vineyard managers
Paola Rovetta and
Emanuele Rabotti

Production
About 25,000 bottles
a year

Vintages
Non-vintage

Price
● ●

Paolo Rabotti is the man behind the scenes at Monte Rossa, the estate nominally owned by his wife Paola Rovetta and directed by his son Emanuele. Paolo, an agricultural entrepreneur from Emilia, admits that when they bought the historic villa in 1972, he had no intention of making wine and even considered replacing vines with other crops.

But Paola had other ideas for the gentle slopes on a rise overlooking the town of Bornato where the stately villa was built by the Rossa family in the fifteenth century adjacent to the medieval watchtower erected by the Oldofredi dukes. She gradually extended vineyards with choice varieties for sparkling wines while reviving olives in the mild microclimate of Monte Rossa. She also made a wine aficionado of Paolo, who became president of the Franciacorta producers' consortium from 1990–1993.

Yet it must be acknowledged that Monte Rossa's recent surge is due primarily to their son Emanuele, who works with veteran enologist Cesare Ferrari in giving the wines special style and definition. The emphasis is on Franciacorta DOCG as Brut, Brut Satèn, Brut Rosé, Sec and in two vintage (*millesimato*) versions: Extra Brut and Cabochon Brut.

Cabochon, whose base wines of Chardonnay and Pinot Nero are partly matured in oak barrels, remains on the yeasts for at least 4 years to develop the depth, complexity and elegance to rank as Monte Rossa's premier sparkler. But the gently effervescent (*crémant*) type that is called Satèn in Franciacorta is without doubt one of the most seductive bubbly wines I've tasted lately. The blend of Chardonnay with about 40 percent of Pinot Bianco results in a fragrant, fruity wine of uncommon grace and surprising versatility with foods.

From 25 hectares of vines, Monte Rossa produces 150,000–180,000 bottles of wine a year, including Terre di Franciacorta DOC Bianco (Ravellino) and Rosso (Cèp).

Lombardy

Grapes
Chardonnay 60%, Pinot Bianco 40%, hand picked in late August or early September.

Vineyards
Various plots among 25 hectares of vines in stony glacial moraine on slopes at an average of 274 meters of altitude on the Monte Rossa estate at Bornato in the heart of the Franciacorta zone. Vines, of an average age of 13 years, are planted at a density of 6,000 per hectare and trained in a spurred cordon method.

Vinification and aging
Grapes are soft crushed and the free-run musts fermented at 18–20°C for 8–21 days, partly in stainless steel vats and partly in oak barrels. Base wines are assembled and bottled for at least 24 months on the yeasts, which are calibrated to produce a wine of about 4.5 atmospheres of pressure (as opposed to 6 atmospheres for fully sparkling wine). After hand riddling and disgorging, Satèn, of about 12.5% alcohol, is topped up with a *liqueur d'expédition* of 8–9 grams per liter before cork sealing.

Style and maturity
Monte Rossa Franciacorta Brut Satèn on release has bright straw yellow color with greenish highlights and abundant *perlage* in streams of fine bubbles. Aromas are fresh, clean and balanced with vital fruit and floral sensations mingling with hints of herbs and yeast. Satèn caresses the palate with a gentle effervescence that elevates ripe fruit flavors in perfect harmony with acidity in a wine of uncommonly mellow elegance that should maintain style for at least 5 years.

Serving
- 8–10°C.
- Tall, ample flute (Champagne type).
- *Prosciutto* and salame; lasagne with mushrooms and béchamel; risotto with asparagus tips; dishes based on salmon, veal or chicken.

Marco Negri
Moscato d'Asti DOCG ♀

Producer
Azienda Agricola Negri
Strada Piazzo 14
Frazione Boglietto
14055 Costigliole d'Asti
(Asti)
Tel. 0141/968596
Fax 0141/968596
negrimar@tin.it

Owner
Marco Negri

Founded
1991

Winemaker
Donato Lanati

Vineyard managers
Albino Morando and
Sebastiano Massone

Production
About 25,000 half-liter
bottles a year, plus
magnums

Vintages
The most recent

Price
●

Muscat represents one of the most important families of vines, with varieties dispersed since antiquity around the Mediterranean and beyond. The noblest of the breed is considered to be the small-berried type known in Italian as Moscato Bianco or Moscato di Canelli after the town in Piedmont that is the center of the sparkling Asti industry.

The Piedmontese, who export most *spumante*, covet the gentler, more fragrant Moscato d'Asti from vineyards in the steep Langhe hills between the Belbo and Tanaro rivers in the provinces of Asti and Cuneo. What might be described as Moscato's Côte d'Or extends from the villages of Mango and Neviglie north to the town of Costigliole d'Asti, where in 1990 Marco Negri, a psychiatrist from Liguria, bought vineyards.

Marco, whose family has a prominent olive oil business at Imperia, had become a connoisseur and collector of the wines of France and Piedmont. By the late 1980s, tiring of shrinking heads, he made up his mind to become a winemaker. Marco admits that Costigliole wasn't his first choice of sites. But after looking in vain for a special place in Barolo, he decided to try his hand with Moscato. He built cellars in time for the 1993 vintage and within a couple of years his Marco Negri signature wine had risen to the front ranks of Moscato d'Asti.

Considerable credit was due to Donato Lanati, the genial winemaker who deserves the star status accorded him well beyond his native Piedmont. But Marco is convinced that they can do better. The challenge is to express Moscato's richness of aromas and flavors to the hilt without compromising the exquisite freshness that makes it unique among the world's sweet wines.

From 15 hectares of vines, Marco Negri produces about 50,000 bottles a year of Moscato d'Asti DOCG, including a second selection called Marsilio. For the moment, that's the extent of production, though friends hint that Marco is still looking for that special place in Barolo.

Piedmont

Grapes

Moscato Bianco di Canelli 100%, hand picked in September.

Vineyards

Grapes are selected from 2 plots covering about 11 hectares in calcareous clay and tufaceous soils on slopes facing different directions at about 250 meters of altitude in the Boglietto area south of Costigliole d'Asti in the Langhe hills of southern Piedmont. Vines, of an average age of 21 years, are planted at densities of 5,000–5,500 per hectare and trained in the Guyot cordon method.

Vinification

Whole grape bunches are gently squeezed in pneumatic presses and the free-run must is chilled, filtered and held below freezing in tanks. Fermentation is set off by inoculating the musts with select yeasts and heating them to 14–20°C in *autoclave* (pressurized stainless steel tanks) for 10–20 days. When alcohol reaches 4.5–5% (with about 7% of residual sugar), the wine is rapidly chilled to block the fermentation. Sterile filtration eliminates all yeasts before bottling.

Style and maturity

Moscato d'Asti Marco Negri should be drunk within months of bottling (never more than a year from the harvest) when it shows limpid straw-yellow color with greenish tinges and a creamy flow of fine bubbles. Aromas of blossoms and fresh fruit are sensational in scents that also recall sage, honey and primrose. Flavors are full and round with mellifluous sweetness offset by a citrus-like acidic tang and plush effervescence that lends finesse to the wine's grapy freshness.

Serving

🍷 8–10°C.

♀ Bowl-shaped Champagne *coupe*.

🍴 Hazelnut and almond pastries, biscuits and cakes; *panna cotta* (Piedmontese cooked cream with caramel); fresh fruit sorbets.

Orsolani

Sulé
Caluso Passito DOC ☿

Producer
Azienda Agricola
Vitivinicola Orsolani
Via Michele Chiesa 12
10090 San Giorgio
Canavese (Torino)
Tel. 0124/32386
Fax 0124/32386
orsolani@tiscalinet.it

Owner
Gian Francesco Orsolani

Founded
1894

Winemakers
Gian Francesco Orsolani
with Donato Lanati

Vineyard manager
Gian Luigi Orsolani

Production
3,000–6,000 half bottles
(0.375-liter) in favorable
years

Vintages
1997 1996 1995 1994
1993 1990 1988 1985
1982 1979

Price
● ●

Note
The name Sulé has been
used since 1995 for the
Caluso Passito previously
called La Rustìa

After emigrating to America in the late nineteenth century, Giovanni Orsolani and his wife Domenica returned to their hometown of San Giorgio Canavese and opened an inn, Locanda Aurora, where they served wine from the family vineyards. The Orsolani winery has grown over the generations to become the most respected source of the dry white and sparkling Erbaluce di Caluso and the rare and prized sweet Caluso Passito.

The estate is now run by Giovanni's great-grandson Gian Francesco, who works with his son Gian Luigi and enologist Donato Lanati in bringing contemporary style to wines from an antique vine. It isn't known if the Romans grew Erbaluce, which became the prevalent variety in the low-slung hills of the Canavese glacial amphitheater north of Turin. But their methods of cultivation were so practical that they remain largely intact to this day in a low trellised system known as pergola *canavese*.

The Orsolani family put prime emphasis on Erbaluce with the advent of DOC in 1967 for Caluso, the name of the main town in the area. They also produced a sparkling Erbaluce, a revelation in 1968 that led to eventual inclusion in the appellation. In 1985, they introduced the crisply dry Erbaluce called La Rustìa, a name that also came to apply to the Caluso Passito made from grapes dried over the winter.

With the 1995 vintage, the name was changed to Sulé, dialect for *solaio*, the loft where grapes dry. Often during the damp cold of February some of the drying grapes are attacked by *Botrytis cinerea*, the "noble rot" that concentrates aromas and flavors in a wine of exquisite sweetness.

The Orsolani family has 6.5 hectares of vines and harvests grapes from another 8.5 hectares to produce about 100,000 bottles of wine a year. The range includes single-vineyard dry Caluso DOC Vignot Sant'Antonio and San Cristoforo and classic method Cuvée Storica, also in a Gran Riserva version.

Piedmont

Grapes
Erbaluce di Caluso
100%; ripe, healthy
bunches hand picked in
mid-September are
arranged in wooden
boxes placed in an
aerated loft (the *solaio* or
sulé) to dry until mid-
March.

Vineyards
Plots covering 2 hectares
in loose glacial moraine
on slopes facing south
and southeast at about
250 meters of altitude in
the Macellio area of the
commune of Caluso in
the Canavese hills about
35 kilometers north of
Turin. Vines, of an
average age of 31 years,
are planted at densities of
about 2,500 per hectare
and trained in the
traditional trellised
pergola *canavese* method.

Vinification and aging
The dried grapes are
crushed in wooden
basket presses and the
musts separated from the
skins ferment for several
months at 18–20°C in
225-liter barrels of
French oak (Allier). The
wine matures for about 3
years in barrels, which are
topped up regularly
during the gradual
process of evaporation.
The wine, of about 13%
alcohol with 17% of
residual sugar, is bottled
and cellared for a year
until release.

Style and maturity
Caluso Passito Sulé on release
more than 4 years after the
harvest has bright amber color
with copper-bronze highlights.
The bouquet is rich and
complex with scents
reminiscent of dried fruit
(raisins, figs, prunes), honey,
vanilla and a hint of citrus. On
the palate, it is full and
concentrated, opulently sweet
and velvety in texture, yet with
a welcome freshness in
sensations of fruit, nuts and
honey that linger on the
tongue. Each vintage develops
differently; from great ones,
the wine can hold virtues for
30 years or more.

Serving
- 14–15°C, opening the
bottle 15 minutes earlier.
- Small, bulbous glass with
long stem.
- Gorgonzola (*naturale*) or
aged Piedmontese Toma
with acacia honey; hazelnut
and fruit pastries; after-
dinner sipping.

Rocche dei Manzoni

Producer
Podere Rocche dei Manzoni di Valentino
Località Manzoni Soprani 3
12065 Monforte d'Alba (Cuneo)
Tel. 0173/78421
Fax 0173/787161

Owners
Iolanda and Valentino Migliorini

Founded
1974

Winemakers
Valentino Migliorini and Giuseppe Albertino

Vineyard manager
Giorgio Botto

Production
About 20,000 bottles in fine years

Vintages
1999 1998 1997 1996
1995 1993 1992 1990
1989

Price
● ● ●

Valentino Brut Zero Vino Spumante Metodo Classico ♀

Valentino Migliorini is an outsider who has become a major figure in Barolo (see page 70). But he's been noted even longer for the bubbly wines that he began making with his father Adamo in the 1960s, when they had a restaurant called Da Valentino at Caorso, a Po River town in Emilia.

They bought grapes in the hills of nearby Piacenza, long noted for wines that fizz. The local Trebbiano and Malvasia made pleasant enough bubbly, but as the restaurant moved up scale, Valentino and his wife Iolanda decided that they ought to offer something classier to guests, whose tastes ran toward Champagne (or "Zahmpahnya," as the jovial Valentino pronounces it).

They experimented successfully with the classic bottle fermentation method using mainly Pinot Noir from Lombardy's Oltrepò Pavese to create the first Valentino Brut in the 1970s. By then they had acquired the Rocche dei Manzoni estate in Barolo, where conditions also turned out to be favorable for Pinot Noir and especially Chardonnay. Their first estate-bottled sparkling wine was Valentino Brut Riserva Elena (named for Valentino's late sister) of 70 percent Chardonnay with Pinot Noir.

Valentino was the first producer of Barolo to use French oak for maturing wines, including the barrel-fermented Chardonnay called L'Angelica. In 1989, he decided to make Piedmont's first estate-bottled Chardonnay sparkler from grapes grown in his vineyards for a base wine fermented and matured in new barrels. The result was Valentino Brut Zero, in reference to the French term *dosage zéro* to describe wine that receives no *liqueur d'expédition* after disgorging but is topped up with the same wine from an earlier vintage.

Brut Zero is a *blanc de blancs* of uncommon stature, richly fruity and full of flavor, though it does have an evident oaky aspect that takes years to diminish as the wine becomes mellow and complex. Guests at Da Valentino would have loved it, but Iolanda closed the restaurant years ago to join her husband in Barolo.

Piedmont

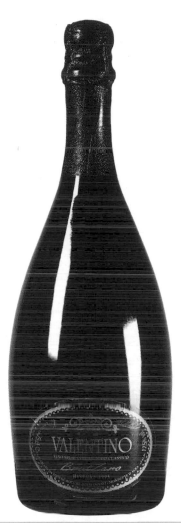

Grapes
Chardonnay 100%, hand picked in late August and early September.

Vineyards
Choice plots covering 3 hectares in sandy calcareous soils on slopes facing north and east at the localities of Manzoni Soprani, Santo Stefano di Perno and Madonna Assunta di Castelletto in the community of Monforte in the Barolo zone. Vines, of an average age of 23 years, are planted at a density of 5,000 per hectare and trained in the Guyot cordon method.

Vinification and aging
Grape bunches selected in the cellars are crushed gently and the free-run musts separated from the skins are fermented at 16–18°C in new small oak barrels where they also undergo malolactic fermentation and mature for about 7 months. The base wine is assembled and bottled with the yeasts for at least 3 years before hand riddling and disgorging. The wine, of about 12.5% alcohol, is topped up with an older version of Brut Zero before cork sealing and further cellaring of about 8 months.

Style and maturity
Valentino Brut Zero on release in the fifth year after the vintage has bright gold color with yellow highlights and lively, persistent streams of fine bubbles. Aromas are vital with ripe fruit and vanilla sensations mingling with scents of yeast, pastry, herbs and oak. Flavors are full and round in a wine of uncommonly rich texture with a long, smooth finish enhanced by vivacious effervescence. The wine reaches a prime between 7 and 8 years but has the stature to last considerably longer.

Serving
🌡 8°C.
🍷 Tall, ample flute (vintage Champagne type).
🍽 Choice cold cuts, such as *prosciutto, culatello, coppa*; liver pâtés; dishes based on seafood, poultry, and veal with sauces.

Saracco

Moscato d'Autunno
Moscato d'Asti DOCG ♀

Producer
Azienda Agricola
Paolo Saracco
Via Circonvallazione 6
12053 Castiglione
Tinella (Cuneo)
Tel. 0141/855113
Fax 0141/855360
info@paolosaracco.com
www.paolosaracco.com

Owner
Paolo Saracco

Founded
1985

Winemaker
Paolo Saracco

Vineyard manager
Paolo Saracco

Production
About 20,000 bottles
a year

Vintages
1999 1998 1997 1996
1995

Price
●

F ranco Colombani, the late lamented apostle of genuine food and wine, introduced me to the Moscato d'Asti of Saracco in the 1980s. At his Albergo del Sole in Lombardy Franco had acquired nearly all of the annual thousand or so bottles of Saracco's traditional type of Moscato. It was made by a method that involved continual filtering of the fermenting musts to remove yeasts and arrest the process with the alcohol level at about 5 percent, leaving the wine fizzy and sweet. It was a bit cloudy and dense and Franco served it from a decanter to leave the dregs in the bottle, but that Moscato with its hues of tarnished gold was an ambrosia never to be forgotten.

Paolo Saracco, who took over the estate at Castiglione Tinella from his father Giovanni in 1985, continued to make the traditional Moscato for a time. But trends favored new methods in pressurized tanks that resulted in the brighter, fresher, more delicate Moscato d'Asti of today. Paolo, a graduate of the enological institute at Alba, went modern for practical reasons. He was expanding vineyards, so production was growing, and the new methods were more efficient and reliable than the old, with its risks of disharmonious scents and flavors and carbon dioxide build-ups that exploded corks.

The estate was founded in the early 1900s by his great-grandfather Luigi, who was known as Lupo (wolf, now the family symbol). Paolo, known as something of a lone wolf himself, has strived to retain some of the old-time character in his Moscato d'Autunno. Almost alone among producers of Moscato, he recommends aging bottles for five or six years, as the color deepens and texture thickens and aromas and flavors become mellow and complex.

From 23 hectares of vines, Paolo produces about 225,000 bottles a year, dominated by a regular Moscato d'Asti and including three admirable whites that qualify under Langhe DOC: Prasuè (Chardonnay), Bianch del Luv (oak-fermented Chardonnay) and Graffagno (Riesling, Sauvignon and Chardonnay).

Piedmont

SARACCO
1999

MOSCATO D'ASTI
DENOMINAZIONE DI ORIGINE CONTROLLATA E GARANTITA
IMBOTTIGLIATO NELLA ZONA DI ORIGINE DALLA
AZIENDA AGRICOLA PAOLO SARACCO - CASTIGLIONE TINELLA (ITALY)

Grapes
Moscato Bianco di
Canelli 100%, hand
picked in mid-September.

Vineyards
Grapes are selected in
various plots covering
about 3 hectares in soils
of marl and chalky tufa
veined with sand on
slopes facing different
directions at about 350
meters of altitude in the
commune of Castiglione
Tinella in the Langhe
hills of southern
Piedmont. Vines, of an
average age of 31 years,
are planted at a density of
6,000 per hectare and
trained in the Guyot
cordon method.

Vinification
Grapes are gently
squeezed in pneumatic
presses and the free-run
must is chilled, filtered
and held below freezing
in tanks. Fermentation is
set off by inoculating the
musts with yeast cultures
and heating them to
about 18°C in *autoclave*,
pressurized stainless steel
tanks. When the alcohol
reaches 5% (with about
7% of residual sugar), the
wine is rapidly chilled to
below freezing to block
the fermentation.
Bottling takes place in
sterile conditions and the
wine is left for 2 months
before release.

Style and maturity
Moscato d'Autunno on release
within months of the harvest
shows pale straw color with
greenish tinges and steady
streams of fine bubbles.
Aromas are full and ripe with
scents reminiscent of green
apple, pears, blossoms, honey,
citrus fruit and sage.
Refreshingly round and
smooth on the palate, the
sweetness characterized by
ripe fruit flavors is offset by
lively acidity and gentle
effervescence. The producer
recommends aging the wine
for 5–6 years to assume the
dense, mellow qualities of old-
time Moscato.

Serving
8–10°C.
Bowl-shaped Champagne
coupe.
Sliced fresh peaches
topped with Moscato;
martin sec pears stewed in
Barolo; fresh fruit sorbets;
meliga (cornmeal) cookies.

La Scolca

Soldati La Scolca Brut Millesimato Vino Spumante di Qualità

Producer
Azienda Agricola
La Scolca
Strada Rovereto 170R
15066 Gavi
(Alessandria)
Tel. 0143/682176
Fax 0143/682197
info@scolca.it
www.scolca.it

Owner
Giorgio Soldati

Founded
1919

Winemaker
Giorgio Soldati

Vineyard manager
Athanase Fakorellis

Production
About 5,000 bottles in
outstanding years

Vintages
1995 1993 1991 1987
1984

Price
● ● ●

Gavi was elevated to DOCG in 1998, thanks in part to the enterprise of producers around the town of that name in southeastern Piedmont. But the appellation owes its lasting fame to Gavi dei Gavi La Scolca.

That legend was created by Vittorio Soldati at Villa La Scolca when he began in the 1960s to make still wine from Cortese grapes that had previously served as a bulk source of *spumante.* The results were so appealing that he issued a top wine with a dignified dark label as "Gavi dei Gavi." The "king of kings" connotation aptly expressed supremacy, since some experts rated it as the finest white of Italy. Its success set off a boom in production. As competition grew, La Scolca was obliged to downgrade Gavi dei Gavi to Gavi di Gavi, like other wines of the town. Yet, despite admirable group efforts behind the rise to DOCG, Gavi as a still white has failed to win expected critical acclaim. Cortese's subtle fruit and pronounced acidity lack the appeal provided by richer, rounder wines from Chardonnay and other noble varieties.

In the 1970s, Vittorio Soldati was joined by his son Giorgio, a passionate winemaker determined to keep production at artisan levels. He resumed making sparkling wines from Cortese, but using the *champenoise* method of long maturation on the yeasts to achieve unprecedented finesse. The version that qualities as Gavi DOCG offers strong evidence that pure Cortese is better suited to sparkling wine than still.

Giorgio's crowning achievement is Soldati La Scolca Brut Millesimato, based on Cortese but with another component that remains secret. Aged on the lees for 7 years (up to 10 in a reserve version), it stands as one of Italy's most elegant sparklers with character that clearly distinguishes it from wines based on Pinots and Chardonnay.

From 35 hectares of vines, La Scolca makes about 375,000 bottles a year. These include still versions of Gavi DOCG, led by La Scolca D'Antan, which shows the opulence of a decade of aging and the freshness of a younger wine.

Piedmont

Grapes

Cortese and other
varieties (secret), hand
picked in mid-September.

Vineyards

Plots covering 3 hectares
in marl and sandy clay
soils on slopes facing
south-southwest at about
350 meters of altitude in
the Rovereto area
northwest of the town of
Gavi. Vines, of an average
age of 31 years, are
planted at a density of
4,200–4,500 per hectare
and trained in the Guyot
cordon method.

Vinification and aging

Grapes are cooled down,
gently crushed and left in
contact with skins and
pulp for about an hour
before being transferred
to tanks to be settled
naturally. The musts are
fermented at 12–14°C
for 3–4 weeks in stainless
steel tanks, followed by
natural malolactic
fermentation. The wine is
bottled with select
indigenous yeasts for at
least 7 years before hand
riddling and disgorging.
Bottles are topped up
with the same wine, of
about 12% alcohol,
before cork sealing.

Style and maturity

Soldati La Scolca Brut
Millesimato on release about
8 years after the vintage has a
brilliant pale gold color and
persistent, vivacious beads of
minuscule bubbles. Aromas are
delightful, suggesting tropical
fruit, butterscotch, spices,
honey and toasted hazelnuts.
Flavors are cleanly dry yet full,
round and velvety with hints
of pineapple and almonds in a
wine of extraordinary finesse
that revitalizes the palate. The
wine reaches a prime soon
after release but style remains
for years.

Serving

🍷 8°C.

🍸 Tall, ample flute (vintage
Champagne type).

🍽 Dishes based on fish,
poultry and veal; *cappon
magro*, an elaborate
seafood specialty of Liguria.

La Spinetta

Bricco Quaglia
Moscato d'Asti DOCG ♀

Producer
Azienda Agricola
La Spinetta
Via Annunziata 17
14054 Castagnole delle
Lanze (Asti)
Tel. 0141/877396
Fax 0141/877566
laspinetta@vinobit.it

Owners
Rivetti brothers

Founded
1981

Winemaker
Giorgio Rivetti

Vineyard managers
Rivetti brothers

Production
About 60,000 bottles a
year

Vintage
The most recent

Price
●

Brothers Bruno, Carlo and Giorgio Rivetti took charge of their small family farm in 1981 and built La Spinetta into a leader of Moscato d'Asti from choice vineyards in the Langhe hills around Castagnole delle Lanze. No one did more to propagate the cult of fine Moscato than Giorgio Rivetti in his tireless travels around Italy selling La Spinetta's single-vineyard wines: Biancospino, Bric Lapasot, Muscatel Vej, San Rümu and, above all, Bricco Quaglia.

But Giorgio soon fell in with a crowd of producers from other parts of the Langhe in whose sanctimonious way of reasoning the only real wine is red. Duly indoctrinated, Giorgio and his brothers began buying up vineyards for Barbera, Nebbiolo and other red varieties, while expanding cellars and installing new French barriques row upon row.

They started with a tasty Barbera d'Asti Ca' di Pian, though the first red to make an impact was Pin, a blend of Nebbiolo with Barbera and Cabernet that carries the nickname of their father Giuseppe and now qualifies as Monferrato Rosso DOC. Then came the acclaimed Barbaresco DOC from the vineyards of Gallina and Starderi with the term Vürsù and a rhinoceros shown on the labels. Gallina is also the source of a jumbo Barbera d'Alba DOC.

At last report La Spinetta had 84 hectares of vines with production programmed to grow beyond the current 320,000 bottles a year. The brothers and their families are all active in the estate, though the energetic Giorgio makes not only the wine but the cardinal decisions. And he sees the future as progressively red.

Critics have been so enthusiastic about La Spinetta's red wines that they seem to have all but forgotten the once pre-eminent bubbly whites. Many critics, that is, not quite all. To me the familiar label of Bricco Quaglia with its portrait of a quail remains the hallmark of Moscato d'Asti.

Piedmont

Grapes
Moscato Bianco di Canelli 100%, hand picked in mid-September.

Vineyard
Bricco Quaglia covers about 10 hectares in medium-textured calcareous clay soils on steep slopes facing south at 300–400 meters of altitude between Castagnole delle Lanze and Coazzolo in the Langhe hills of southern Piedmont. Vines, of an average age of 31 years, are planted at a density of 6,000 per hectare and trained in the Guyot cordon method.

Vinification
Whole grape bunches are gently squeezed in pneumatic presses and the free-run must is chilled, filtered and held below freezing in tanks. Fermentation is set off by inoculating the musts with select yeasts and heating them to about 18°C in *autoclave*, pressurized stainless steel tanks, for about 20 days. When the alcohol reaches 4.5% (with about 7% of residual sugar), the wine is rapidly chilled to below freezing to block the fermentation. Bottling takes place in sterile conditions and the wine is left for 2 months before release.

Style and maturity
Moscato d'Asti Bricco Quaglia on release within months of the harvest shows pale straw color with greenish tinges and an ebullient flow of fine bubbles. Aromas are full and persistent with scents reminiscent of ripe apples and pears, acacia blossoms, honey and sage. Full and round on the palate, the mellow sweetness characterized by ripe fruit flavors gets a tonic lift from vital acidity and gentle effervescence. Aromas and flavors continue to evolve enticingly for about a year in the bottle.

Serving
🌡 8–10°C.
🍷 Bowl-shaped Champagne *coupe*.
🍴 *Bonèt* (coffee-flavored custard cake); hazelnut ice cream with nougat; zabaglione made with Moscato d'Asti.

Uberti

Producer
Azienda Agricola
Uberti G. & G.A.
Via Enrico Fermi 2
25030 Erbusco (Brescia)
Tel. 030/7267476
Fax 030/7760455

Owners
G. Agostino Uberti and
wife Eleonora Pagani

Founded
1793

Winemaker
Cesare Ferrari

Production
About 6,000 bottles in
vintage years

Vintages
1995 1993 1991 1988

Price
● ● ●

Comarí del Salem Franciacorta DOCG Extra Brut ♀

Erbusco has become Franciacorta's premier wine town in terms of quality and quantity, thanks to the dynamic leadership provided by the relatively large estates of Ca' del Bosco and Bellavista. Yet some much smaller estates have moved ahead in a quiet way with wines that have come to rank with the cream of Franciacorta.

A prime example is Uberti, the estate named for a family that has been farming in Erbusco since 1793. Agostino Uberti, current head of the household, learned the winemaking craft from his uncle Giovanni, though the style of his Franciacorta is also due to the master touches of Cesare Ferrari, the dean of local consulting enologists who has been working with him since 1975.

From 18 hectares of vines (some leased), Uberti produces about 110,000 bottles of wine a year processed in deep cellars created especially for the long evolution of classic sparkling wines. These include Franciacorta DOCG Brut and Extra Brut (both with superior versions known as Francesco I), Rosé and a gently bubbly Satèn that lives up to the name Magnificentia. The wine of greatest stature is Comarí del Salem, an Extra Brut from Chardonnay and Pinot Bianco grapes grown in a poetically named vineyard. Comarí refers to the son of a *comare* (godmother), who owned the plot in a place called Salem (which refers to peace). Part of the base wines are matured in oak barrels before the cuvée goes into bottle for at least four years on the yeasts to attain extraordinary depth and finesse.

Uberti also produces fine Terre di Franciacorta DOC—Bianco (Frati Priori and Maria Medici) and Rosso—complemented by an IGT Rosso dei Frati Priori (Cabernet Sauvignon).

Lombardy

Grapes
Chardonnay 75%, Pinot Bianco 25%, hand picked in September.

Vineyards
Comarí del Salem, a plot of 2.1 hectares in gravelly glacial soils on gradual slopes facing south at 220 meters of altitude at the town of Erbusco in the southwestern part of the Franciacorta zone. Vines, of an average age of 19 years, are planted at a density of 2,200 per hectare and trained in a modified version of the high espalier system known as Sylvoz.

Vinification and aging
Grapes are soft crushed and the musts fermented at 18–20°C for 8–10 days, 15% in small oak barrels and the rest in stainless steel vats. The cuvée is assembled and the wine goes into bottle for at least 4 years on the yeasts before hand riddling and disgorging. The wine, of about 12.5% alcohol, is topped up with a light *liqueur d'expédition* before cork sealing. It is released about 5 years after the harvest.

Style and maturity
Franciacorta Brut Comarí del Salem on release about 5 years after the vintage has pale straw yellow color with greenish highlights and lively, persistent streams of fine bubbles. Aromas are ample and round with ripe fruit and floral sensations mingling with hints of yeast, fresh herbs, citrus and vanilla. Flavors are full and vivacious with fine balance between fruit and acids and hints of toasted nuts in a long, smooth finish. The wine reaches a prime between 10 and 15 years.

Serving
- 8–10°C, chilled in an ice bucket.
- Tall, ample glass.
- Pasta and risotto with vegetables and seafood; roast lake tench with polenta; *vitello tonnato* (veal with creamy tuna sauce).

The Northeast

Trentino-Alto Adige, Veneto, Friuli-Venezia Giulia,
Emilia-Romagna

Three regions of northeastern Italy are known collectively as the Tre Venezie or simply Venezie, due to historical links with the Venetian Republic. Veneto, Friuli-Venezia Giulia and Trentino-Alto Adige have vines in common, notably the international elite of Chardonnay, Cabernet, Merlot, Sauvignon and the Pinots. But each also has distinguished native varieties.

The fourth region, Emilia-Romagna, has always stood apart from its neighbors, though in recent times the source of bubbly red Lambrusco has earned a measure of respect for still reds and whites.

Veneto's Verona area is known for white Soave and red Valpolicella and Amarone, all from native varieties. To the east in Venice's region, the international varieties prevail, with the notable exception of Prosecco that makes bubbly wines in the hills near Treviso.

Friuli-Venezia Giulia is esteemed for the whites of Collio, Colli Orientali del Friuli and Isonzo from a range of varieties, notably the native Tocai, though reds are also impressive.

Trentino-Alto Adige, which takes in the formerly Austrian South Tyrol, excels with still whites from a range of varieties, including the native Gewürztraminer, though reds from the local Teroldego and Lagrein can also be outstanding.

PRODUCERS

Trentino ♥ Foradori 140, Pojer & Sandri 150, San Leonardo 156; ♀ Cesconi 180, Ferrari Fratelli Lunelli 194, Metius 214, Pojer & Sandri 222 **Alto Adige** ♥ Hofstätter144, Muri-Gries 148; ♀ Abbazia di Novacella 166, Arunda Vivaldi 170, Produttori Colterenzio 182, Peter Dipoli 188, Hofstätter 200, Alois Lageder 206, Cantina Produttori San Michele Appiano 230, Cantina Produttori di Termeno 234, Tiefenbrunner 236, Elena Walch 244 **Veneto** ♥ Allegrini 130, Bertani 132, Bolla 134, Dal Forno 142, Masi 146, Quintarelli 152, Tedeschi 158; ♀ Anselmi 168, La Cappuccina 176, Col Vetoraz 184, Gini 196, Inama 202, Maculan 212, Pieropan 220, Ruggeri 228 **Friuli-Venezia Giulia** ♥ Walter Filiputti 138, Russiz Superiore 154, Villa Russiz 164; ♀ Bastianich 172, Borgo del Tiglio 174, La Castellada 178, Cantina Produttori Cormons 186, Girolamo Dorigo 190, Livio Felluga 192, Gravner 198, Vinnaioli Jermann 204, Lis Neris 208, Livon 210, Miani 216, Pierpaolo Pecorari 218, Rocca Bernarda 224, Ronco del Gelso 226, Schiopetto 232, Venica 238, Vie di Romans 240, Villa Russiz 242 **Emilia-Romagna** ♥ Castelluccio 136, Vigneto delle Terre Rosse 162, La Tosa 160; ♀ Fattoria Zerbina 246

Talento Trento DOC metodo classico sparkling wine at Ferrari Fratelli Lunelli

Allegrini

La Poja
Monovitigno Corvina
Veronese IGT ♥

Producer
Azienda Agricola
Allegrini
Via Giare 9–11
37022 Fumane di
Valpolicella
(Verona)
Tel. 045 683 2011
Fax 045 770 1774
info@allegrini.it

Owner
Allegrini family

Founded
1854

Winemakers
Franco Allegrin

Vineyard managers
Walter Allegrini and
Stefano Chioccioli

Production
14,000 bottles in choice
years

Vintages
2000 1999 1998 1997
1996 1995 1993 1990
1988 1985 1983

Price
● ● ●

If Allegrini has become the most admired name in Valpolicella, it's because a hard-working farm family went about acquiring choice vineyards, quietly defying the mercenary mentality that compromised Verona's wine industry for decades. The late Giovanni Allegrini began growing grapes after World War I and gradually, with his children Walter, Marilisa and Franco, turned his farm into a full-fledged wine estate.

Today, from about 70 hectares of vines, Allegrini produces the classic wines of Valpolicella with dedication and artistic flair, led by exemplary Amarone (dry) and Recioto (sweet) made from grapes dried after the harvest to concentrate substance and flavors. Wines from the vineyards of La Grola and Palazzo della Torre were once classified as Valpolicella Classico Superiore, but today they qualify under Veronese IGT.

Amarone and Recioto come from a blend of Corvina Veronese with Rondinella and Molinara grapes. But Giovanni Allegrini knew that Corvina on its own would make a noble wine even without drying the grapes, and with his enologist son Franco developed La Poja from the 1983 vintage. La Poja is the name of the summit of the vineyard of La Grola, a crest ideally exposed to sun and breezes from Lake Garda with calcareous soils that include 17 percent active limestone, a factor in the unique personality of the wine.

Franco Allegrini matured La Poja in small barrels of French oak, giving it nuances of bouquet and flavor that brought new dimensions to the red wines of Verona. La Poja, now classified as Veronese IGT, is richer and fuller than Valpolicella. It isn't intended to match the sheer might of Amarone, yet it has similar opulence and complexity with unique elegance in the harmonious fruit sensations that make it eminently appealing with food.

Veneto

Grapes
Corvina Veronese 100%, hand picked in late October when fully mature.

Vineyard
La Poja, a choice parcel of La Grola, covers 2.65 hectares of stony calcareous soils on the southeastern incline of a crest at 327 meters of altitude near Sant'Ambrogio at the western edge of the Valpolicella zone. The vines, of an average age of 18 years, are planted at a density of 4,200 per hectare and trained in a double Guyot cordon method.

Vinification and aging
Grapes are stemmed and soft crushed and the juice fermented for about 10 days in stainless steel tanks at temperatures ranging from 25–30°C. After malolactic fermentation, the wine is matured for 18 months in new 225-liter barrels of oak from Allier in France. The wine, of about 13.5% alcohol, is lightly filtered before bottling and cellared for about 18 months before release.

Style and maturity
La Poja shows a deep mulberry color when young, gradually evolving toward ruby-garnet with age. The bouquet has an intense ripe fruit aspect, enhanced by floral scents and suggestions of vanilla and spices. Even when young (3–5 years), the wine fills the mouth with warm, velvety sensations, richly fruity with hints of plums and cherries offset by a tang reminiscent of bitter chocolate on the finish. With age, as the bouquet heightens, flavors expand and lengthen, achieving maximum harmony between 8 and 15 years.

Serving
🌡 17–18°C.
🍷 Tall, ample glass (Burgundy type).
🍽 Roast and stewed beef, pork and game, such as venison or boar, as well as aged cheeses from the Venetian Alps, notably Asiago and Monte Veronese.

Bertani

Amarone Classico Superiore Recioto della Valpolicella DOC 🍷

Producer
Cav. G.B. Bertani
Località Novare
37020 Arbizzano di
Negrar (Verona)
Tel. 045 601 1211
Fax 045 601 1222
upr@bertani.net
www.bertani.net

Owner
Bertani family

Founded
1857

Winemaker
Paolo Grigolli

Vineyard manager
Giulio Grobberio

Production
About 90,000 bottles a
year

Vintages
1995 1994 1993 1990
1988 1985 1983 1979
1974 1968 1967 1964
1962

Price
● ● ●

Note
Vintages to come will be
labeled as Amarone della
Valpolicella DOC

P atience explains the often splendid Amarone of Bertani, the venerable Veronese winery that boasts the greatest collection of old vintages available to the public. Amarone comes from the same Corvina, Rondinella and Molinara varieties as Valpolicella, but the grapes are concentrated by drying in aerated lofts at the family's Villa Novare in the hills northwest of Verona. During four months of drying on cane mats, the grapes develop traces of *Botrytis cinerea*, the "noble rot" that gives the powerful wine its peculiar grace.

Winemaker Paolo Grigolli explains that Amarone can be made only from choice vintages: success depends not only on fine weather during the season but also on the requisite cold, dry conditions for drying later. The concentrated grapes are fermented into wine that goes into oak casks for at least seven years, from some vintages even longer. (A batch of the original 1959 vintage was in wood for 27 years before bottling in 1987.) Grigolli explains that the wine in cask re-ferments each spring as part of the residual sugar is converted to alcohol and glycerin. This annual revival gives Amarone its opulence of color, bouquet and flavor and the capacity to maintain attributes over time as perhaps no other natural (as distinguished from fortified) red wine. Yet ultimate aging potential isn't known, since early vintages are still vital.

Bertani lists 14 vintages of Amarone dating from 1990 (the latest in commerce) back to 1962.

From 130 hectares of vines and 50 hectares under company direction, Bertani produces about 2 million bottles of wine a year at cellars at Novare, Grezzana and Monteforte d'Alpone (for Soave). These include Valpolicella, Bardolino and Soave (all Classico Superiore) DOC, as well as Valpolicella Valpantena Secco Bertani and sparkling Recioto; IGT white Le Lave (Garganega and Chardonnay) and Catullo Rosso (Cabernet and Corvina). A recent IGT is Villa Novare Albion, a pure Cabernet Sauvignon that from the 1996 vintage triumphed as the top-ranked Italian wine in the 1999 Vinexpo competition in Bordeaux.

Veneto

Grapes
Corvina 70%, Rondinella 25%, Molinara 5%; the ripest, healthiest bunches are hand picked in late September and early October and placed on cane mats for 4 months of *appassimento*.

Vineyards
Various plots totaling about 25 hectares in calcareous marls at 100–250 meters of altitude at Fumane, Marano and Novare in Valpolicella Classico. The vines, ranging in age from 6–31 years, are planted at a density of 2,500–5,000 per hectare and trained in either the trellised pergola or spurred cordon method.

Vinification and aging
Drying grapes lose about a third of their weight as juice and sugars concentrate. They are soft crushed and the musts fermented in cement tanks at 20–25°C for about 6 weeks, including 2 weeks of maceration with the skins. The wine is aged for about 7 years in medium-sized casks of Slavonian oak, during which time the malolactic fermentation takes place naturally. The wine, of about 15% alcohol, is bottled and cellared for a year before release.

Style and maturity
Bertani Amarone is issued no sooner than 9 years after the harvest, when approaching a prime. Its deep ruby-garnet color takes on brick red tones with a further decade or two of age. The bouquet is ornate, with suggestions of ripe cherries and jam, spices, vanilla, balsam and woodsmoke. The wine has an opulence on the palate that has been described as "symphonic," with ripe fruit flavors bolstered by a sweet aspect reminiscent of Port and a hint of walnut and bitter chocolate in its lingering aftertaste.

Serving
🍷 18–20°C, opening the bottle several hours earlier.
🍷 Ample glass (Burgundy type).
🍽 Wines of 10–15 years with roast and stewed beef, pork and game and ripe and sharp cheeses. Old vintages are suited to sipping after meals.

Bolla

Producer
Fratelli Bolla
Piazza Cittadella 3
37122 Verona
Tel. 045 867 0911
Fax 045 867 0912
bolla@bolla.it
www.bolla.it

Owner
Brown-Forman
Beverages Worldwide

Founded
1883

Chief winemaker
Elio Novello

Vineyard coordinator
Giannantonio Marconi

Production
An average of 140,000
bottles a year

Vintages
1996 1995 1993 1990
1989 1988 1985 1983
1979 1974

Price
● ●

Amarone della Valpolicella Classico DOC ❢

The name Bolla is linked worldwide to Soave, the popular white wine from the town near Verona where the family cellars were founded by Abele Bolla in 1883. But it's not widely known that Bolla, which is now American owned, made the first commercial version of Amarone from the 1950 vintage and is still the largest producer of that red wine regarded as the Herculean version of Valpolicella.

Legend has it that Amarone was first made by accident when a batch of what was intended to be sweet Recioto "escaped" and the wine's sugars fermented out so that it became dry—or, if compared to what it was intended to be, *amaro* (bitter), or, in a big way, *amarone*. Bolla gradually built production, soon followed by others as the wine gained international prestige.

Bolla's old vintages prove that Amarone over time maintains its endowments as do few other red wines. The reason seems to be that it derives from dried grapes with an abundance of tannins and polyphenolic substances, notably resveratrol, an antioxidant reputed to help preserve the wine while benefiting the human cardiovascular system. Bolla winemaker Elio Novello notes that Amarone has about double the resveratrol levels of normal red wines, due to the unusually high ratio of grape skins to juice and the extraction that takes place during a long fermentation at low temperature. He points out that the phenomenon occurs only in wines from grapes that are "over-ripened naturally" and not in grapes artificially dehydrated in ovens or drying chambers.

Beyond Amarone and Soave Classico, Bolla is a major producer of Valpolicella Classico, Bardolino, Bianco di Custoza and various IGT wines, including varietal Cabernet Sauvignon (Creso), Merlot (Colforte) and Chardonnay (Lunaie), among a total of about 18 million bottles a year.

In January 2000, Fratelli Bolla came under sole ownership of the American Brown-Forman corporation, ending more than a century of family control.

Veneto

Grapes

Corvina and Corvinone prevail along with Rondinella; the ripest, healthiest bunches are hand picked in early October and dried in airy rooms on cane mats until mid-February.

Vineyards

Grapes come from Negrar, Marano and Fumane in the Valpolicella Classico zone, selected from growers with plots totaling about 150 hectares in marly clay soils at 380–420 meters of altitude. The vines, of an average age of 26 years, are planted at a density of 2,500–3,000 per hectare and trained in the traditional trellised *pergoletta* system.

Vinification and aging

The dried grapes are soft crushed and the musts macerated for 20 days with the skins at 4–5°C before being fermented at 15–17°C for 20–25 days in stainless steel tanks. The wine goes immediately into new oak casks to mature for 24–36 months, during which malolactic fermentation takes place naturally during the summer. The wine, of about 14% alcohol, is bottled and cellared for another year before release.

Style and maturity

Bolla Amarone has deep garnet-red color with scents of bitter cherries, spices and tobacco in its rich bouquet, nuances that carry over into smooth, balanced flavors. A wine of authoritative weight and firm structure, its fruit sensations are attractively expressed at 5–6 years of age, though it gains in depth, complexity and length on the palate if kept in ideal cellar conditions for another decade or more.

Serving

- 17–18°C, decanting three hours ahead of time.
- Tall glass (Syrah type).
- Richly flavored meat and game dishes, such as roast venison or beef braised in Amarone; aged cheeses, such as ripe Taleggio or sharp Gorgonzola naturale.

Castelluccio

Ronco delle Ginestre
Vino da Tavola della provincia
di Forlì 🍷

Producer
Azienda Agricola
Castelluccio
Via Tramonto 15
47015 Modigliana
(Forlì)
Tel. 0546 942486
Fax 0546 942486

Owner
Company headed by
Remigio Bordini

Founded
1975

Winemaker
Vittorio Fiore

Vineyard manager
Remigio Bordini

Production
About 10,000 bottles
from choice vintages

Vintages
1999 1998 1997 1996
1995 1992 1990 1986
1985 1982

Price
● ●

The Sangiovese vine in Romagna was once considered congenitally inferior to its noble cousin across the Apennines in Tuscany—a view long held by more than just Tuscans. The wine referred to affectionately in Romagna's dialect as *sansvez* was described as hearty, zesty, earthy, tangy, with scarcely a nod in the direction of genteel until the early 1980s when the "Ronco" reds emerged from Castelluccio.

Ronco refers to a terraced plot typical of the crest above the town of Modigliana, where in 1975 Gianvittorio Baldi planted clones of Sangiovese selected by vine expert Remigio Bordini. Baldi hired the noted enologist Vittorio Fiore to style the wines in French barriques, an extravagance that shocked other producers and resulted in Sangiovese that was too special to carry the routine Romagna DOC. The trio of Ronco dei Ciliegi (cherry trees), Ronco Casone (big house) and Ronco delle Ginestre (wild broom) drew praise from critics, though some tasters found the wines to be out of line in typology and price for what was, after all, Romagnan Sangiovese.

Baldi and Fiore pushed ahead boldly, creating the oak-fermented Sauvignon Blanc called Ronco del Re (king) that caused a stir with its sovereign style and princely price. But, controversial as they were at the beginning, the wines of Castelluccio sparked a revolution in Romagna's concepts of winemaking that heralded a new day for Sangiovese.

Castelluccio has passed from the Baldi family to a team headed by Bordini and Fiore, who have replaced Ronco Casone with Ronco della Simia (dialect for monkey) from selected clones of Sangiovese that have raised the quality level of the trio to new heights. Top ratings usually go to Ronco delle Ginestre, perhaps the first Sangiovese of Romagna to rate description as super.

Castelluccio's production of about 70,000 bottles annually from 13 hectares of vines includes Sangiovese di Romagna DOC Le More and an IGT white called Lunaria, from Sauvignon Blanc.

Emilia-Romagna

Grapes
Sangiovese, hand picked in late October.

Vineyard
Ronco delle Ginestre of about 2 hectares of terraced calcareous clay soils at 350–410 meters of altitude on slopes above the town of Modigliana. The vines, first planted in 1975 and renewed gradually since 1990, vary in density from 4,500–6,000 per hectare for those trained in the Guyot spurred cordon and up to 7,000 per hectare for recent spur-trained *alberello*.

Vinification and aging
Grapes are stemmed and soft crushed and the must fermented in stainless steel vats at natural temperatures for 15–30 days, the duration depending on the vintage. After malolactic fermentation, the wine is matured for 18–24 months in 350-liter barrels of French oak. The wine, of 13–13.5% alcohol, is bottled and cellared for a time before release.

Style and maturity
Ronco delle Ginestre has dense ruby color when young, retaining dark tones as it evolves toward garnet. The wine is robust and generous in bouquet with clean scents suggesting wild berries, vanilla and toasted almonds. On the palate it has firm structure bolstered by acids and tannins that lend vigor to fresh fruit flavors, which are most intense after about 5 years, though they take on impressive complexity and length with a decade or more of age.

Serving
🍷 16°C.
♀ Medium-sized glass (Chianti type).
🍽 Romagnan pasta dishes, such as *garganelli* envelopes with meat sauce or *gramigna* curls with duck sauce; roast or grilled beef, lamb and kid.

Walter Filiputti

Pignolo
Colli Orientali del Friuli
DOC ❢

Producer
Azienda Agricola
Walter Filiputti
Piazza Abbazia 15
Località Rosazzo
33044 Manzano (Udine)
Tel. 0432 759 429
Fax 0432 759 887
w_filiputti@triangolo.it

Owner
Walter Filiputti

Founded
1995

Winemaker
Walter Filiputti

Vineyard manager
Marco Simonit

Production
About 7,500 bottles
a year

Vintages
2000 1999 1997 1996

Price
● ● ●

Walter Filiputti, beyond his accomplishments as a winemaker, is the author of the most important contemporary books on the wines of Friuli-Venezia Giulia. He combines scholarship with a talent for description and a passion for Friuli's wines that invites readers to share his predilections. His personal pride is Pignolo, an ancient vine that had almost vanished by 1984 when he began diffusing cuttings through the vineyards of Abbazia di Rosazzo, the abbey in whose imposing stone tower he makes his home.

Today, Walter asserts that "Pignolo is the absolute greatest red wine for aging among the autochthonous varieties of Friuli." No argument from me, but the problem is that, after a drawn-out dispute with former partners over use of the name Abbazia di Rosazzo, Walter began making wines under his own label only in 1995. So the Walter Filiputti Pignolo isn't old enough to prove his point, even if early evidence is entirely convincing.

Pignolo was cited as a vine in 1398 by a certain Francesco di Carrara of Padua, who asked permission of the Signoria of Venice to take 20 barrels of the wine home from Friuli for health reasons. In 1823, *Pignul* was described in a Venetian catalog as a black wine made from very juicy grapes of aromatic sweetness. Professor Giovanni Dalmasso in 1931 described Pignolo as a *vino di lusso*.

"Deluxe" is also Walter's term for a wine that stands apart from all others, including the Pignola or Pignol of Lombardy. He has gradually propagated Pignolo around the abbey so that there are now 6,600 vines from which he expects to make 7,000–8,000 bottles a year soon.

Walter's current production of about 150,000 bottles a year includes DOC Colli Orientali del Friuli Sauvignon, Ribolla Gialla, sweet Picolit; two blends of Rosso called Broili di Filip (Merlot, Cabernet, Refosco) and Ronco dei Benedettini (Merlot, Cabernet Franc) and blends of Bianco: Poiesis (Tocai, Chardonnay, Pinot Bianco, Picolit) and Ronco del Monastero (Tocai, Malvasia, Ribolla Gialla).

Friuli-Venezia Giulia

Grapes
Pignolo 100%, hand picked in late October.

Vineyards
Adjacent plots covering 0.96 hectare in Eocene marl on slopes facing south at 180 meters of altitude at Abbazia di Rosazzo in the commune of Manzano in the southern part of the Colli Orientali del Friuli DOC zone. The vines, of an average age of 21 years, are planted at a density of 4,000–8,000 per hectare and trained in the Guyot cordon method.

Vinification and aging
Grapes are stemmed and soft crushed and the musts fermented in stainless steel tanks at 28–30°C for 8–10 days on the skins. After malolactic fermentation, the wine, of about 13% alcohol, matures for 2 years in small barrels of French oak from Allier before being bottled and cellared for another 2 years until release.

Style and maturity
Pignolo has deep ruby color with violet highlights when young (4–5 years), taking on garnet tones over time. A wine of unique personality, it is full and smooth on the palate with elegant balance between fruit and ample tannins, which will sustain vitality of flavors for a decade or more. Most intriguing is the bouquet, which heightens over time to take on scents reminiscent of wild berries and damp earth with hints of morello cherries and wood spice.

Serving
🌡 17–18°C, decanted 30 minutes earlier.
🍷 Medium-sized glass (Chianti type).
🍽 Meat, poultry and game, such as roast woodcock, spit-roasted mallard duck, roast goose with polenta and wild mushrooms, saddle of lamb with basil.

Foradori

Granato
Teroldego Rotaliano DOC

Producer
Azienda Agricola Foradori
Via Damiano Chiesa 1
38017 Mezzolombardo (Trento)
Tel. 0461 601 046
Fax 0461 603 447
foradori@interline.it
www.elisabettaforadori.com

Owners
Gabriella and Elisabetta Foradori

Founded
1935

Winemaker
Elisabetta Foradori

Vineyard manager
Elisabetta Foradori

Production
About 40,000 bottles from choice years

Vintages
1999 1998 1997 1996 1995 1993 1991 1986

Price
●

It's sad to think that the lips of most of the world's wine lovers will never touch Teroldego, because the vine of that name thrives almost exclusively within the limited confines of the gravelly Rotaliano plain in the Alpine province of Trentino. Even there, Teroldego performs in disparate ways, making wine that on the one hand may be youthfully ruby or even prettily pink and on the other hand dark, deep and dense with a capacity to age in a wonderfully unique way.

Among commendable producers of Teroldego, the leader is the family estate of Foradori. Gabriella Foradori ran the winery for years after the death of her husband Roberto. Then daughter Elisabetta took command after graduating from the wine school at nearby San Michele all'Adige.

Elisabetta collaborated for a time with her former husband, a professor of enology who influenced her concepts of winemaking. But she is now busily on her own. When she dresses up, Elisabetta displays the svelte elegance of a fashion model, though she seems more at ease in grape-stained work clothes and boots tramping around vineyards and cellars doing things in her own enlightened way. She has drastically reduced grape yields to far below the maximum levels permitted by law, a policy that has made Granato a Teroldego of uncommon depth and concentration.

Her regular Teroldego Rotaliano DOC is ready in the spring after the harvest as an opulent red of seductive aromas and supple fruit flavors. The protagonist is Granato, named by Elisabetta for the pomegranate, whose rich and concentrated ripe fruit has elements in common with the bouquet and flavors of the wine. Formerly an IGT, Granato became Teroldego Rotaliano DOC with the great 1997 vintage.

From 15 hectares, Foradori makes about 220,000 bottles a year, mainly Teroldego, but also three original wines that qualify under the IGT Vigneti delle Dolomiti: white Myrto (Chardonnay, Pinot Bianco and Sauvignon) and red Ailanpa (based on Syrah) and Karanar (Cabernet with Syrah and others).

Trentino

Grapes
Teroldego 100%, hand picked in early October.

Vineyards
Grapes are selected in 4 plots—Cesura, Morei, Sgarzon and Vignai—of a total of 10 hectares in alluvial gravel and stone soils at 300 meters of altitude on the Rotaliano plain at the confluence of the Adige and Noce rivers 20 kilometers north of the city of Trento. Vines, of an average age of 31 years, are planted in the traditional high pergola at a density of 3,000 per hectare and in Guyot cordon at a density of 6,000.

Vinification and aging
Most grapes are stemmed and soft crushed, though some remain whole at the start of fermentation at 28–30°C for 8–10 days on the skins—partly in stainless steel vats and partly in oak barrels—with frequent pumping over the cap. Malolactic fermentation takes place partly in new oak barrels and partly in tanks. The wine, of about 13% alcohol, is matured for 18 months in new tonneaux of French oak from Allier and Nevers, then bottled and cellared for 6 months until release.

GRANATO
1997
TORADORI

Style and maturity
Granato has a deep violet (almost eggplant purple) color when young, taking on ruby garnet tones with age. The ample bouquet recalls ripe fruit and berries and, as some say, Alpine undergrowth. The exceptional weight and density are rounded out by sweet tannins and voluptuous fruit flavors (pomegranate) that linger on the palate. The wine is appealing after 3–4 years, though great vintages can maintain depth and complexity over 20 years or longer.

Serving
🍴 18°C, after opening at 15–16°C.
🍷 Medium-sized glass (Chianti type).
🍽 Alpine game, such as venison and chamois; braised beef with polenta; Trentino cheeses, such as Nostrano di Malga and Casolet.

Dal Forno

Vigneto di Monte Lodoletta Amarone della Valpolicella DOC ▼

Producer
Azienda Agricola
Dal Forno Romano
Località Lodoletta 4
37030 Cellore d'Illasi
(Verona)
Tel. 045 783 4923
Fax 045 783 4923
az.dalforno@tiscalinet.it

Owner
Romano Dal Forno

Founded
1983

Winemaker
Romano Dal Forno

Production
About 7,000 bottles in
choice years

Vintages
1997 1995 1993 1991
1990 1988

Price

Romano Dal Forno has been depicted as the lone wolf of Valpolicella, an image boosted by the fact that his small estate is located in the Illasi valley far to the east of Verona and the Classico zone, where historically the finest wines of the name originated. But what sets Dal Forno even further apart from the field is the heroic self-discipline that permits no compromises in vineyards and cellars and accounts for wines of singular dimensions.

His Valpolicella, Amarone and Recioto from the vineyards of Monte Lodoletta are monuments to magnitude, matched for sheer size occasionally by Giuseppe Quintarelli (see page 152). But their styles differ markedly, since Quintarelli is a painstaking traditionalist and Dal Forno a painstaking progressive.

Dal Forno's most evident avant-garde technique is his use of entirely new, small barrels to mature Amarone instead of the customary casks of Slavonian oak. He still leaves the wine for more than five years in barriques, though lately he has experimented with limiting wood aging to two years while extending time in bottle to four years to retain greater freshness. If he changes the formula, the evidence will arrive in the coming decade. In the meantime, his admirers (including Italy's most influential critics) continue to be awed by wines that qualify as blockbusters and yet show uncommon finesse.

Dal Forno has increased plantings to 11,000 vines per hectare, a density that surpasses even levels of Burgundy and accounts for the exceptional weight and structure of his wines. For the moment, his 7.5 hectares produce about 22,000 bottles a year of DOC Valpolicella, Amarone and sweet Recioto, all of which carry the name of Vigneto di Monte Lodoletta, along with a luscious white *vino da tavola* called Nettare. But he is also farming a relative's vineyards so production of some of the most sought-after wines of Verona will gradually increase.

Veneto

Grapes
Corvina Veronese 60%, Rondinella 15%, Croatina 15%, Oseleta 10%; the healthiest bunches are hand picked between mid-September and late October and placed on cane mats to dry until early January, when grapes are individually selected.

Vineyards
Various plots of Monte Lodoletta covering 7.5 hectares of stony alluvial soils with 15% lime and 15% clay on slopes at 290 meters of altitude at Cellore in the commune of Illasi in easternmost Valpolicella. The vines, ranging in age from 16–21 years, were first planted at a density of 2,500 per hectare and then at 11,000 per hectare, all trained in a spurred cordon method.

Vinification and aging
The dried grapes are crushed and the musts fermented in stainless steel tanks at 30°C for 8–10 days as the liquid is automatically pumped over the cap. Maturation takes place in small, new oak barrels for 65 months, during which malolactic fermentation occurs naturally. Amarone, of about 15% alcohol, is bottled and cellared for at least a year before release.

Style and maturity
Amarone from Monte Lodoletta is immense in every way, showing deep mulberry color on release (after 7–8 years), evolving toward ruby-garnet with age. The bouquet is rich and ripe with scents of cherries and suggestions of licorice and vanilla. On the palate, the epic dimensions come forth with full fruit sensations and hints of plums and cherries offset by softly sweet tannins that bring warm, velvety sensations to the long finish. The wine reaches peaks of splendor between 10 and 15 years, though it has the stuff to maintain class for decades.

Serving
🍷 16–18°C.
🍷 Ample *ballon* (Burgundy type)
🍽 Cheeses, in particular well-aged grana types: Parmigiano Reggiano, Grana Padano and the Veneto's Vezzana.

144

Hofstätter

Barthenau Vigna Sant'Urbano
Alto Adige Pinot Nero DOC ❢

Producer
Vigneti-Cantina
Vini J. Hofstätter
Piazza Municipio 5
39040 Termeno
(Bolzano)
Tel. 0471 860 161
Fax 0471 860 789
info@
hofstatter.com
www.hofstatter.com

Owner
Foradori Hofstätter
family

Founded
1907

Winemakers
Martin Foradori, Franz
Oberhofer and Martin
Lemayr

Vineyard managers
Martin Foradori and
Hansjörg Weis

Production
About 19,000 bottles
from choice years

Vintages
1998 1997 1995 1993
1990 1989

Price
● ●

Pinot Noir, the heartbreak grape as it's known in California, has created its share of frustration in Italy too. The Burgundy variety is planted fairly widely in the north, where it performs well enough as a base for sparkling wines. As a source of still red wines, however, Pinot Nero (as it's known in Italian) has been generally disheartening. There have been exceptions, though, perhaps most often in a wine called Sant'Urbano after a vineyard at the Hofstätter Barthenau estate in Alto Adige, the Alpine South Tyrol, where the variety is known as Blauburgunder in the local German.

As a devotee of great Burgundy, I can't imagine that in a blind tasting I'd mistake Barthenau Vigna Sant'Urbano for a Clos de Vougeot or Chambertin. Yet this blue-blooded Blauburgunder has style, personality, a decided *gout de terroir* and a by no means negligible history behind it. Pinot Noir was planted 160 years ago at the village of Mazon by Ludwig Ritter Barth von Barthenau, whose villa later came into possession of Hofstätter. That venerable house, founded at the town of Termeno (or Tramin) in 1907 by Josef Hofstätter, was run for years by his nephew Konrad Oberhofer, who in turn passed it on to his son-in-law Paolo Foradori.

A native of Trentino and one of the few South Tyrolean winemakers whose first language is Italian, Paolo has given the winery a progressive image, enhanced by the youthful vigor of his son Martin. Hofstätter produces about 750,000 bottles a year of Alto Adige wines, ranging through varieties as diverse as Lagrein, Chardonnay, Schiava (or Vernatsch), Cabernet, Riesling and Gewürztraminer (outstanding from the vineyards of Kolbenhof – see page 200).

Paolo and Martin devote heartfelt efforts to Blauburgunder from their terraced Sant'Urbano vineyards overlooking the gorgeous valley of the Adige. Their success at Barthenau has inspired neighboring growers, who have made Mazon an Alpine sanctuary of Pinot Noir.

Alto Adige

Grapes
Pinot Nero 100%, hand picked in early October.

Vineyard
Vigna Sant'Urbano, a plot of 3.5 hectares in conglomerate soils (clay, chalk, porphyry, sand, gravel) on terraced slopes at 400 meters of altitude at Barthenau in the village of Mazon at the eastern edge of the Adige valley 25 kilometers south of Bolzano. Vines, of an average age of 60 years, are planted at densities of 4,000–6,500 per hectare, 80% in the traditional high pergola and the rest in the Guyot cordon system.

Vinification and aging
About 80% of the grapes are stemmed and soft crushed and the rest left whole at the start of fermentation of 10–12 days at 28–30°C in stainless steel rotovinification tanks. Malolactic fermentation takes place naturally, followed by maturation for a year in small barrels of French oak and a year in large casks of Slavonian oak. The wine, of about 13% alcohol, is bottled and cellared for another year before release.

Style and maturity
Barthenau Vigna Sant'Urbano has a fine Burgundy garnet color, taking on shadings of mahogany over time. The bouquet is full and round with scents reminiscent of wild berries and herbs, ripe plums, cacao. On the palate it shows medium body and fine balance between acids, wood tannins and fruit flavors that become increasingly warm and seductive while taking on depth and length. Appealing after 5 years, from fine vintages the wine reaches a mellow prime after a decade.

Serving
🍷 15°C.
🍷 Ample *ballon* (Burgundy type).
🍴 Tyrolean dishes, such as *gröstel* (sautéed beef, pork, potatoes and onions) and *gemsenfleisch* (stewed chamois); cheeses, such as Grana Padano and Graukäse.

Brolo di Campofiorin
Rosso del Veronese IGT ▼

Producer
Masi Agricola
Via Monteleone
37020 Gargagnago di
Valpolicella (Verona)
Tel. 045 683 2511
Fax 045 683 2536
masi@masi.it
www.masi.it

Owner
Boscaini family

Founded
1792

Winemakers
Lanfranco Paronetto and
Sergio Boscaini

Vineyard supervisor
Dario Boscaini

Production
About 50,000 bottles in
choice years

Vintages
1997 1996 1995

Price
● ●

Ripasso is a technique used to upgrade Valpolicella by "passing" it over the lees left from newly fermented Amarone (made from partly dried grapes) to create a second fermentation that enriches body and color, while adding dimensions of aroma and flavor. That old custom was revised in 1964 by Nino Franceschetti, then winemaker at Masi, to produce Campofiorin. Since it did not qualify as Valpolicella or Amarone, Campofiorin became a *vino da tavola* of a style that influenced others to make *ripasso* wines of their own.

In 1988, Masi registered "ripasso" for exclusive use on labels worldwide, to the dismay of other producers, who through the Valpolicella consortium have mounted a legal battle to share use of the term. In the meantime, Masi's chief winemaker Lanfranco Paronetto devised a new twist on *ripasso* for a wine from the 1995 vintage called Brolo di Campofiorin. From grapes selected in the vineyards of Campofiorin, 30 percent are dried on mats to develop traces of *Botrytis cinerea,* the "noble rot" that accounts for the lushness of certain wines. The shriveled grapes added whole to the new wine set off a second fermentation that has the same effect as *ripasso* but seems closer to what Tuscans call *governo.* Whatever the technicalities, the wine is a sterling example of ingenuity. Brolo (referring to a walled terrain like a French *clos*) should prove to be more appealing to contemporary palates than the original Campofiorin, which represented "the old Italy of good odors" according to the late literary figure Goffredo Parise.

Masi, owned by Sandro Boscaini and family, controls 160 hectares of vineyards in the Verona area to produce about 2 million bottles of wine a year. These range through Valpolicella, Bardolino and Soave, all Classico Superiore DOC, as well as single-vineyard Amarone and Recioto, including wines from the Serègo Alighieri estate. IGT wines include Toar, an innovative blend of traditional grapes, and Osar, a revival of the Oseleta variety.

Veneto

Grapes
Corvina Veronese
75–80% and Rondinella,
hand picked in late
September–early
October; 30% are left to
dry for 25 days.

Vineyards
Campofiorin and
adjacent plots of 11
hectares in alluvial
calcareous soils with
siliceous rock and gravel
on slopes facing south
and west at 160–175
meters of altitude at
Valgatara in the Marano
valley in the Valpolicella
Classico zone. The vines,
of an average age of
34 years, are planted at a
density of 2,500 per
hectare and trained in
traditional and modified
pergola systems.

Vinification and aging
Grapes are soft crushed
and the yeast-inoculated
musts fermented in
stainless steel vats at
25–28°C for 25 days, 20
on the skins. Partly dried
grapes are added whole
for a second fermentation
at 18–20°C for 15 days
on the skins. After
malolactic fermentation,
the wine, of about 13.5%
alcohol, is matured for
2 years in 600-liter
barrels known as *botti
veronese* (70% French oak
from Allier, 30%
Slavonian oak), and
bottled and cellared for
6 months before release.

Style and maturity
Brolo di Campofiorin has a
deep, bright ruby color and full
bouquet with scents
reminiscent of berries and ripe
cherries, jam and vanilla. The
wine is full, round and velvety
on the palate with rich fruit
sensations and fine balance
and length of flavor. The first
vintage of 1995 was already
impressive after 4 years,
though the wine seems to
have the structure and depth
to maintain class well beyond
a decade.

Serving
🍷 18°C, opening the bottle
an hour earlier.
🍷 Tall, tulip-shaped glass
(Syrah type).
🍽 Pasta, rice and meat dishes:
bigoli noodles with duck
sauce, risotto with porcini
mushrooms, *fegato alla
veneziana* (calf's liver with
onions and polenta).

Abtei Muri
Südtiroler Lagrein Riserva
DOC 🍷

Producer
Klosterkellerei Muri-
Gries di C.
Maffer & C.
Piazza Gries 21
39100 Bolzano
tel. 0471 282 287
fax 0471 273 448

Owner
The Benedictine
Monastery of Muri-Gries

Founded
1845

Winemaker
Christian Werth

Vineyard manager
Walter Bernard

Production
About 30,000 bottles in
choice years

Vintages
1997 1996 1995 1990

Price
●

Note
The DOC may be Alto
Adige or Sudtirolo in
Italian or Südtiroler in
German

As the ancient capital of the South Tyrol, Bolzano (Bozen in the native German) upholds the admirable Austrian tradition of growing vines within the city limits. The wine of renown is Sankt Magdalener (or Santa Maddalena), the zesty red whose terraced vineyards grace the precipitous slopes to the northeast of the urban center. But the wine that lies closest to Bolzano's heart—literally and figuratively—is Lagrein, whose vines are nurtured within the walled "wine gardens" of Gries, the western quarter of the city.

The origins of the vine are not certain, though Lagrein has established its prime habitat at Gries in the sandy clay soils of the alluvial plain formed by the Talvera, Isarco and Adige rivers at a place known in the Middle Ages as Cheller (wine cellar). The Benedictine monks of Muri-Gries have been cultivating Lagrein since 1845 around the monastery, which they took over from the Augustinians, who had converted it from the twelfth-century Castle of Gries.

I first tasted Lagrein in the 1970s with Padre Gregor, the Swiss monk who was then abbot and winemaker. We began with Lagrein Kretzer, a luminous rosé, but the revelation was the dark Lagrein Dunkel, whose deep, opulent bouquet and flavors have lingered in my memory since.

Today the winemaker is Christian Werth, a layman who has given Lagrein unprecedented finesse without sacrificing its time-honored stature in the reserve known as Abtei Muri. Christian prefers Lagrein relatively young, at about five or six years of age, though some admirers attest that it reaches peaks of splendor after a decade.

Klosterkellerei (or Cantina Convento) Muri-Gries owns 32 hectares of vines, including those for Lagrein at Gries and others at Eppan/Appiano west of Bolzano for Alto Adige/Südtiroler DOCs, notably Cabernet and the sweet pink Rosenmuskateller (Moscato Rosa).

Alto Adige

Grapes
Lagrein 100%, hand picked in early October.

Vineyards
Two plots covering 11 hectares in sandy clay soils at 260 meters of altitude in the alluvial plain formed by the Talvera, Isarco and Adige rivers at Gries on the western edge of the city of Bolzano. The vines, of an average age of 29 years, are planted at a density of 4,000–7,000 per hectare and trained in the traditional pergola and Guyot cordon systems.

Vinification and aging
Grapes are soft crushed and the musts fermented in stainless steel vats at 30°C for 10–12 days on the skins. After malolactic fermentation, the wine, of about 12.5% alcohol, is matured for 18–24 months in small barrels of French oak and bottled and cellared for 6 months before release.

Style and maturity
Lagrein Abtei Muri has rich mulberry color that evolves toward ruby-garnet with age. The bouquet is deep and vitally fruity with hints of smoke and leather. Firm and generous in body, it has ample acidity when young with soft tannins behind a full array of fruit flavors (blackberries,

morello cherries) that round out as the wine gains mellow complexity and length, showing a suggestion of tar on the finish. The wine reaches a prime at 5–6 years, though from fine vintages it can maintain virtues for a decade or more.

Serving
🌡 16–17°C.
🍷 Ample glass (Burgundy type).
🍽 Alpine game dishes, such as venison and chamois, served with bread-pork dumplings known as *Knödel* or *canederli*; braised, stewed and roast beef with polenta.

Pojer & Sandri

Rosso Faye
Vigneti delle Dolomiti IGT ♟

Producer
Azienda Agricola
Pojer & Sandri
Località Molini 6
38010 Faedo (Trento)
Tel. 0461 650 342
Fax 0461 65 1100
pojeresandri@
interline.it
www.pojeresandri.it

Owners
Mario Pojer and
Fiorentino Sandri

Founded
1975

Winemaker
Mario Pojer

Vineyard manager
Fiorentino Sandri

Production
8,000–9,000 bottles in
choice years

Vintages
1997 1993 1990

Price
● ●

Pojer & Sandri as a company dates back to 1975, when young Fiorentino Sandri inherited a parcel of vineyards at the Alpine village of Faedo and with his enologist friend Mario Pojer formed a partnership that has proved to be one of the most fruitful in Italian wine. Their first release was an exquisitely scented Müller-Thurgau from 1975, followed by acclaimed whites from Chardonnay and the native Nosiola.

Mario and Fiorentino traveled widely to study winemaking, while acquiring vineyards and building new cellars and a distillery at Faedo. Early success with whites inspired interest in reds, initiated with a Pinot Nero in 1980 that proved to be Burgundian in a refined style. The partners, envisioning a majestic red to head their list, planted Cabernets, Merlot and Lagrein down the hill at San Michele all'Adige, adjacent to the wine school of which they are both alumni.

Rosso Faye emerged with superlatives from the 1990 vintage, following with an even greater fanfare for the 1993, though even in lesser years it shows enviable style. The addition of Lagrein seems to give Rosso Faye an extra dimension that distinguishes it from other Italian reds based on Bordeaux blends. The label, with a painting by the German master Albrecht Dürer from 1502, depicts a plump hare, which Mario and Fiorentino consider a perfect culinary match for their wine.

Faye (the ancient name of Faedo) is also applied to a Chardonnay among the classiest of Italy's oak-fermented whites. From 23 hectares, Pojer & Sandri produce about 240,000 bottles annually, ranging through Trentino DOC varietals (see page 222) to fine bottle-fermented sparkling wine to Essenzia, a sumptuous blend of late-harvested grapes. The distillery is noted for fruit liqueurs and an oak-aged grappa called, appropriately, Divino.

Never content with their achievements, Mario and Fiorentino have acquired an old farm in the high Cembra valley where they are reviving long-neglected vines for a new series of wines.

Trentino

Grapes
Cabernet Sauvignon 50%; Cabernet Franc, Merlot and Lagrein at 15–20% each, hand picked in early October.

Vineyard
Paradisot, 1.3 hectares in shallow soils of calcareous lime mixed with silt, marl and dolomite on a marlstone base on slopes facing south-southwest at 250 meters of altitude in the commune of San Michele all'Adige in northern Trentino. Vines, of an average age of 13 years, are planted at a density of 8,300 per hectare and trained in a trellised spurred cordon and a traditional pergola for Lagrein.

Vinification and aging
Cabernet and Merlot grapes are stemmed and soft crushed though Lagrein remains whole at the start of fermentation in open stainless steel vats at 28–30°C for 8–10 days on the skins with the cap submerged twice daily. Malolactic fermentation takes place in new barrels of French oak, subsequently used for maturation of about a year. The wine, of 12.5–13% alcohol, is stored at 0°C to precipitate tartrates and bottled a year before release.

Style and maturity
Rosso Faye has a deep garnet red color with tinges of dark violet when young. The bouquet is clean and complex with scents recalling wild berries, blackcurrants, cherries, plums and hints of vanilla, roasted coffee beans, pepper and cinnamon. On the palate, the wine shows full body and rich extract, with fruit flavors balanced elegantly by tannins in a long finish that reveals a sweetness reminiscent of licorice. Though seductive from the start, the wine will gain in depth and complexity for a decade or more.

Serving
🌡 18–20°C, decanting only if bottle has sediment.
🍷 Ample glass (Bordeaux type).
🍽 Alpine game, such as hare and venison; roast veal shank with polenta; Trentino cheeses, such as Trentingrana and aged Vezzena.

Valpolicella
Classico Superiore DOC ❢

Producer
Azienda Agricola
Quintarelli Giuseppe
Via Cerè 1
37024 Negrar (Verona)
Tel. 045 750 0016
Fax 045 750 0016

Owner
Giuseppe Quintarelli

Founded
Early 1900s

Winemakers
Giuseppe Quintarelli
and Roberto Ferrarini

Vineyard manager
Giuseppe Quintarelli

Production
About 30,000 bottles
a year

Vintages
1997 1995 1993 1990
1988 1985 1983

Price
● ●

The author and film-maker Mario Soldati, in his entertaining book *Vino al Vino* (1969), tasted a dozen wines before deciding that the Valpolicella of Quintarelli came closest in character to that described by Ernest Hemingway in *Across the River and Into the Trees*. Giuseppe Quintarelli, now in his seventies, continues to make Valpolicella as he did then, with the perseverance in vineyards and cellars that sets his wines apart from all others.

A quiet man with the gentle manner of a country friar, Bepi Quintarelli is looked upon as a sort of folk hero in Valpolicella, though as his friends can attest he is by no means living in the past. It's simply that the philosophical Bepi, after traveling and observing the progressive techniques of others, decided that there was nothing to be gained from changing the methods learned from his father and grandfather.

His Valpolicella—like his even more prized Amarone and IGT red Alzero—has always been noted as bigger and bolder than the rest, with a mouth-filling, rustic goodness that more than makes up for any lack of modern polish. The Valpolicella is bolstered by the *ripasso* method of a second fermentation on the lees of Amarone to give it greater color, structure and aroma. Quintarelli admirers are willing to pay the extra price justified by the long cask aging and sacrosanct devotion to detail that permit such outmoded practices as bottling and labeling wines by hand.

From his 12 hectares of vineyards at Monte Ca' Paletta, Giuseppe Quintarelli makes 50,000–60,000 bottles a year, all with handwritten details printed on plain paper labels. These include DOC Amarone della Valpolicella Classico and Riserva, sweet Recioto della Valpolicella and IGT Alzero (from semidried Cabernet grapes) and amber Amabile del Cerè (from semidried white varieties).

Veneto

Grapes
Corvina 50%, Rondinella 25%, Molinara 5% with Cabernet, Nebbiolo, Croatina, Sangiovese, hand picked in late September and early October.

Vineyards
Plots covering 12 hectares in volcanic soils of calcareous marls and basalt on slopes facing west at 240 meters of altitude at Monte Ca' Paletta in the commune of Negrar in Valpolicella Classico. The vines, of an average age of 31 years, are planted at a density of 2,000–3,000 per hectare and trained in a traditional pergola or Guyot cordon for a plot planted in 1992.

Vinification and aging
Grapes are crushed and the musts fermented with indigenous yeasts in stainless steel and wooden vats at natural temperatures for 7–8 days on the skins. In April, the wine is mixed with the lees of Amarone, which set off a second alcoholic fermentation. Natural malolactic fermentation is followed by about 6 years of aging in casks of Slavonian oak. The wine, of about 13% alcohol, is bottled without filtering and cellared for 6 months before release.

Style and maturity
Quintarelli Valpolicella Classico Superiore when issued 6–7 years after the harvest shows deep, dense ruby color with a trace of garnet on the rim. The bouquet is rich and ripe with scents reminiscent of wild berries, cherry liqueur, pepper and cacao. The wine is unusually full in body for a Valpolicella with opulent flavors of ripe fruit and jam and a hint of bitter chocolate on the finish. At a prime after 8–10 years; some vintages remain vital for 15 years or more.

Serving
- 16–18°C.
- Medium-sized *ballon* (Burgundy type).
- *Pasta e fasioi* (thick pasta and bean soup); *pastissada de caval* (horsemeat stew); *bollito misto* (boiled meats) with *pearà*, Verona's peppery sauce based on marrow and breadcrumbs.

Russiz Superiore

Rosso Riserva degli Orzoni Collio DOC ♉

Producer
Azienda Agricola
Russiz Superiore
Via Russiz 7
34070 Capriva del Friuli
(Gorizia)
Tel. 0481 991 64
Fax 0481 960 270
info@marcofelluga.it
www.marcofelluga.it

Owner
Marco Felluga and
family

Founded
The ancient estate was
acquired in 1967

Winemakers
Giovanni Di Mastro
with Donato Lanati

Vineyard manager
Bolis Princic

Production
About 15,000 bottles in
choice years

Vintages
1999 1997 1996 1995
1994 1993 1990 1988

Price
● ●

Marco Felluga was a pioneer of the reformation of the 1960s and 1970s that uplifted Friuli-Venezia Giulia from an isolated vineyard region into the promised land of Italian white wine. Since then Marco, like many of his fellow Friulians, has realized that the gentle hills of Collio along the border of Slovenia have a similar aptitude for reds.

Marco, from a family of vintners from Isola d'Istria (now in Slovenia), founded a winery of his own at Gradisca d'Isonzo in 1956. Business grew as the whites of Friuli acquired a reputation, enabling Marco to buy Russiz Superiore, an ancient estate with a vast spread of land. Instead of simply replanting the *ronchi* (terraces), he reshaped the contours to provide ideal exposure and drainage for vines. Eventually he planted 64 hectares in select varieties with a sense of innovation that gave Collio a telling boost toward supremacy.

The first wines to emerge from the 1975 vintage were white, but Marco knew that Cabernet and Merlot had eminent potential. In those days, Friuli's reds were for the most part youthfully fruity and round, wonderfully drinkable but rather simplistic in comparison with heavier, more complex wines from other places. Marco, soon joined by son Roberto and daughter Patrizia in running the estate, continued to strive for greater things.

In 1988, they blended Cabernets Sauvignon and Franc with Merlot in the first wine to qualify as Collio Rosso Riserva DOC. They called it Rosso Riserva degli Orzoni after the former owners, the Counts Orzoni, who had singled out vineyards for red wines on the estate in the eighteenth century. Matured in small oak barrels to achieve greater color, structure and style, the wine has become the hallmark of Russiz Superiore.

The estate produces about 200,000 bottles a year of Collio DOC, including white Pinot Bianco, Pinot Grigio, Sauvignon, Tocai Friulano, Verduzzo and Bianco Russiz Disôre (a blend based on Pinot Bianco), as well as red Cabernet Franc and Merlot.

Friuli-Venezia Giulia

Grapes
Cabernet Sauvignon 80% with Cabernet Franc and Merlot, hand picked in October.

Vineyards
Grapes are selected in various plots in soils of marl and sandstone on terraced slopes at about 150 meters of altitude at Russiz Superiore in the commune of Capriva del Friuli at the heart of the Collio DOC zone. The vines, of an average age of 16 years, are planted at a density of 7,000 per hectare and trained in the Guyot cordon method.

Vinification and aging
Grapes are stemmed and soft crushed and the musts fermented in stainless steel tanks at 30°C for 2 weeks on the skins. After malolactic fermentation, the wine, of about 13% alcohol, matures for 18 months in small oak barrels before being bottled and cellared for a year until release

Style and maturity
Riserva degli Orzoni when released about 5 years after the harvest has dark ruby color with a hint of mulberry and garnet highlights on the rim. The bouquet is deep, round and full with clean fruit and floral scents and well-integrated notes of wood spice and vanilla. On the palate it has good structure with a tannic underpinning that goes nicely with long, smooth flavors of fruit, berries and chocolate. Attractive on release, the wine should retain class for well over a decade.

Serving
🌡 18°C.
🍷 Ample glass (Bordeaux type).
🍽 Friulian meat and game dishes, such as filet of venison with myrtle berries, stuffed veal shank braised in red wine, rack of lamb with thyme.

San Leonardo
Vallagarina IGT ♗

Producer
Marchese Carlo
Guerrieri Gonzaga –
Tenuta San Leonardo
38060 Borghetto
all'Adige (Trento)
Tel. 0464 689 004
Fax 0464 682 200
info@sanleonardo.it
www.sanleonardo.it

Owner
Marchese Carlo
Guerrieri Gonzaga

Founded
1724

Winemaker
Giacomo Tachis

Vineyard manager
Luigino Tinelli

Production
About 85,000 bottles a
year

Vintages
1998 1997 1996 1995
1993 1991 1990 1988

Price
● ●

My early encounters with Cabernets and Merlots of Trentino provided scents of bell peppers and cut grass along with tangs of under-ripe fruit accented by the likes of choke cherries and bitter almonds. I naively attributed those traits to a peculiar *goût de terroir* of the terraced vineyards of that Alpine region. But it has since been pointed out that the Bordeaux varieties introduced early in the twentieth century had not been well selected (Cabernet Franc and the lesser Carmenet prevailed) and that overcropped vines trained over high pergolas were so lush that leaf canopies inhibited ripening of grapes.

The wines of Tenuta San Leonardo had won moderate praise by the 1970s when Carlo Guerrieri Gonzaga inherited the estate that had come into his family in the nineteenth century. Carlo, who traces his lineage to the Gonzaga dynasty that ruled Mantua from the fourteenth to the seventeenth centuries, took a degree in enology and worked at estates in France before joining his father Anselmo in running the winery. He knew that the wines could be better, but he wasn't aware of how dramatically they could improve until, after observing production of Sassicaia (see page 326), he began working with enologist Giacomo Tachis.

Carlo produced a blend of Cabernet Sauvignon and Cabernet Franc with Merlot from the 1983 vintage, calling it San Leonardo after the chapel in the walled hamlet of the estate that surrounds the site of a tenth-century monastery. Since then, he has introduced select clones of those varieties, training vines in a spurred cordon for lower yields of riper, healthier grapes. Tachis provided the cellar mastery, including maturation in small barrels of French oak.

San Leonardo has grown steadily in stature to rank among the finest Bordeaux blends of Italy, while dispelling my suspicions that tastes of the earth in Trentino could be somehow less than noble. From 18 hectares of vines, Tenuta San Leonardo produces about 120,000 bottles of wine a year, including Trentino DOC Merlot.

Trentino

Grapes
Cabernet Sauvignon 60%, Cabernet Franc 30%, Merlot 10%, hand picked in October.

Vineyards
Grapes are selected from the estate's 18 hectares of vines in loose, sandy alluvial soils on slopes facing southwest at 160 meters of altitude along the Adige River at Borghetto in the commune of Avio in the Vallagarina at the southernmost point of Trentino. The vines, ranging in age from 11–26 years, are planted at a density of 5,500 per hectare and trained in a double spurred cordon method.

Vinification and aging
Grapes are stemmed and soft crushed and the musts fermented in concrete tanks at no more than 30°C for 13–15 days, followed by prolonged maceration on the skins. After malolactic fermentation, the wine, of about 13% alcohol, is matured for 6 months in casks of Slavonian oak and then for 20 months in small barrels of French oak, part new and part used, then bottled and cellared for at least 8 months before release.

Style and maturity
San Leonardo when young has ruby-mulberry color of excellent tone and intense bouquet with enticing fruity ripeness and peppery notes that become composed with time. On the palate, it is nicely balanced between dry and mellow, with full body and bracing firmness on the tongue and acids and tannins in line for steady development. Attractive after 4–5 years, with age it takes on a smooth, long finish with hints of chocolate and tobacco similar to fine Bordeaux.

Serving
🍷 18°C.
🍸 Tall, ample glass (Bordeaux type).
🍽 Roast venison with bilberries, *carne salà* (salt-cured beef) and white beans, goose stewed with shallots and potatoes.

Fratelli Tedeschi

Producer
Agricola Fratelli
Tedeschi
Via Giuseppe
Verdi 4
37020 Pedemonte di San
Pietro in Cariano
(Verona)
Tel. 045 770 1487
Fax 045 770 4239
tedeschi@
tedeschiwines.com
www.tedeschiwines.com

Owner
Renzo Tedeschi and
family

Founded
1824

Winemakers
Renzo and Riccardo
Tedeschi

Vineyard managers
Renzo and Riccardo
Tedeschi

Production
About 3,000 half-liter
bottles in choice years

Vintages
1997 1996 1995 1990
1989 1988 1985 1981
1980 1978 1976 1974
1970 1969 1964

Price
● ●

Capitel Monte Fontana
Recioto della Valpolicella Class
DOC ❢

The appellation Recioto della Valpolicella applies only to the original sweet version of a wine made from grapes dried after the harvest, though it once included an appendix for Amarone, the dry counterpart of more recent conception. Mounting prestige and popularity have earned Amarone della Valpolicella a distinct designation to avoid confusion with Recioto, which now stands alone and too often neglected.

Both types derive from the basic Valpolicella blend of grapes, dried for months on cane mats to concentrate sugars and flavoring elements. Production of Recioto involves painstaking practices, including a slow, cool fermentation arrested naturally by filtering out active yeasts when the alcohol reaches about 15% so that residual sugars remain to make the wine sweet. There is also a bubbly version, popular around Verona, though the most convincing Recioto della Valpolicella is still and opulently sweet yet buoyantly vigorous on the palate, as exemplified by the Capitel Monte Fontana of Fratelli Tedeschi.

Renzo Tedeschi, who heads the family winery now in its sixth generation, works with son Riccardo and daughters Antonietta and Sabrina to produce a range of Valpolicella Classico wines. The estate makes considerably more Amarone, but Recioto is a labor of love that results in a mere 3,000 half-liter bottles a year. Despite the shortage, Capitel Monte Fontana has won a wealth of honors, including a place among the six best entrants in the International Wine Challenge of London in 1987.

Tedeschi has 7 hectares of vines, acquiring grapes from trusted growers to produce about 300,000 bottles a year. These include DOC Valpolicella Classico Superiore Capitel dei Nicalò, Amarone Capitel Monte Olmi and La Fabriseria. *Vini da tavola* include Capitel San Rocco Rosso and the excellent new Rosso la Fabriseria. "Capitel" refers to the tiny chapel or shrine that marks choice vineyards in the hills of Verona.

Veneto

Grapes

Corvina 30%, Corvinone 30%, Rondinella 30%, Molinara, Dindarella, Negrara, Rossignola together 10%; bunches hand picked in early October are dried in airy rooms on cane mats for about 4 months.

Vineyard

Monte Fontana, a plot of 1 hectare in glacial moraine with calcareous clay and stony red soils on steep terraced slopes facing southeast at 150 meters of altitude. The vines, of an average age of 31 years, are planted at a density of 2,000 per hectare on the terraces and trained in the traditional trellised pergola *trentina* system.

Vinification and aging

The dried grapes with their stems are crushed and the musts macerated with the skins at 5°C as temperatures rise naturally to 10–11°C, setting off fermentation that continues at 15–18°C in tall, narrow stainless steel tanks, the process covering about 40 days. The wine, of about 15% alcohol with 5–6% residual sugars, doesn't undergo malolactic fermentation before maturing for 18 months in 500-liter capacity oak barrels. It is bottled and cellared for at least 6 months before release.

Style and maturity

Capitel Monte Fontana has bright ruby-red color with scents reminiscent of raspberries, currants, blackberries and vanilla in a rich bouquet. Those nuances carry over into smooth, balanced flavors in a wine of weight and structure whose sweetness is braced by ample tannins and acids leaving the finish long and clean. The wine maintains fresh fruit sensations up to a decade, after which more complex, spicy flavors prevail.

Serving

- 13–15°C, decanting old vintages.
- Medium–small tulip-shaped glass (Port type).
- Meat dishes with sweet-sour sauces; fruit tarts; strawberries with balsamic vinegar; blue cheeses, such as Gorgonzola, Stilton and Roquefort.

La Tosa

Vignamorello
Colli Piacentini Gutturnio
DOC ❢

Producer
Azienda Agricola La Tosa
Località La Tosa
29020 Vigolzone
(Piacenza)
Tel. 0523 870 727
Fax 0523 870 358
latosa@libero.it

Owners
Stefano and Ferruccio
Pizzamiglio

Founded
1980

Winemakers
Stefano Pizzamiglio with
Piero Ballario

Vineyard manager
Stefano Pizzamiglio

Production
3,500–8,000 bottles
from choice vintages

Vintages
1999 1998 1997 1995
1991 1988

Price
●

The ancient Romans, who founded the city of Piacenza on the Po, appreciated the wine from the hills that taper from the Apennines south of the city. Among remnants, the Romans left behind a silver wine pitcher known as a *gutturnium*. That name was adopted as Gutturnio by modern producers in the Colli Piacentini to identify a unique blend of Barbera and the locally prized Bonarda.

At first Gutturnio, like most wines of Piacenza, was bubbly and softly sweet, combining the zesty acidity of Barbera with the plush fruit of Bonarda. The blend also turned out to be amply suited to a still, dry wine of impressive breadth and depth and, from some estates, even a touch of elegance. The serious type of Gutturnio is typified by the Vignamorello of La Tosa, the small estate of brothers Stefano and Ferruccio Pizzamiglio.

Stefano is a man of strong convictions, one of which is that wines are made in the vineyard and merely guided to completion in the cellar. He holds yields of Vignamorello to drastically low levels, discarding about 40 percent of the grape bunches in August.

DOC rules for Gutturnio favor Barbera in a blend that permits no more than 45 percent of Bonarda. Stefano would prefer to emphasize the latter because of the natural softness of its wines and the richness of components that account for flavor and color. The 1998 Vignamorello had such ripe, concentrated qualities that he decided not to mature it in wood, as he had previous vintages. But Stefano knows that his vineyards can do better.

From 10 hectares, La Tosa makes about 80,000 bottles a year, including Colli Piacentini DOC Sauvignon, fizzy white Valnure and mellow Malvasia Sorriso di Cielo. Recently the other wines have been overshadowed by a Cabernet Sauvignon called Luna Selvatica that has won raves from the critics. But in the long run La Tosa stands a better chance of distinguishing itself in the world of wine with Gutturnio Vignamorello.

Emilia-Romagna

Grapes
Barbera 55%, Bonarda
45%, hand picked in late
September to early
October.

Vineyard
Vignamorello of 1.5
hectares in soils of clay
and silt on terrain sloping
from north to south at
210 meters of altitude at
La Tosa in the commune
of Vigolzone in the Nure
valley at the heart of the
Colli Piacentini zone.
The vines, of an average
age of 21 years, are
planted at a density of
2,500 per hectare and
trained in a Guyot
cordon method.

Vinification and aging
Grapes are stemmed and
soft crushed and the
must fermented in
stainless steel vats at
28–30°C for about 10
days. After induced
malolactic fermentation,
the wine, of 13–14.5%
alcohol, used to be
matured for a few
months in part in a
2,500-liter capacity cask
of French oak and part in
stainless steel vats, then
bottled and cellared for
4–6 months before
release. From the 1998
vintage the wine was not
aged in wood.

Style and maturity
Gutturnio Vignamorello at its
prime from 3–5 years has a
deep purple color with ruby
highlights on the rim. The
bouquet is full and ripe with
scents reminiscent of berries
and violets. On the palate, it is
unusually opulent with ripe
fruit sensations supported by a
firm base of acids and soft
tannins that lend a certain
depth and length to flavors.
The wine can retain mellow
elegance for about 8 years.

Serving
🍾 18–20°C.
🍷 Medium glass (Chianti
type).
🍽 *Pisarei e faseu* (tiny gnocchi
with beans and tomato);
Barbary duck stuffed with
chestnuts; filet of beef
braised in Gutturnio.

Vigneto delle Terre Rosse

Il Rosso di Enrico Vallania Colli Bolognesi Cabernet Sauvignon DOC

Producer
Vigneto delle Terre Rosse
di Enrico Vallania
Via Predosa 83
40069 Zola Predosa
(Bologna)
Tel. 051 755 845
Fax 051 618 7210
gival@iol.it
www.simnet.italia.com

Owners
Vallania family

Founded
1961

Winemakers
Luigino Casagrande with
Giovanni and Elisabetta
Vallania

Production
6,000–8,000 bottles
from choice vintages

Vintages
1999 1998 1997 1996
1995 1993 1992 1990
1988 1987 1985 1983
1979

Price
● ●

Enrico Vallania was an exceptional man, a physician who taught himself to make wines that brought new dignity to the hills of Bologna. When he inherited the Terre Rosse farm in 1961, the Colli Bolognesi provided light, zesty wines for quaffing to the city that was long considered the gastronomic capital of Italy. Even red wines from the hills were known to be fizzy and often a shade sweet, considered the ideal foil to the pasta, pork, butter and cheese dishes that glorified the local diet.

Doctor Vallania had other ideas about wine, formulated by his experiences with the elite of Bordeaux and Burgundy. On his property was a huge vine, dating back a century or so, that turned out to be a particular clone of Cabernet Sauvignon. He patiently propagated cuttings through the vineyards and began to make the wine that came to symbolize the estate named for its ferrous red soils.

Enrico Vallania knew he couldn't imitate Margaux or Lafite, so instead he fashioned a wine of substance and style that he could drink every day. His Cabernet was vigorous and refreshing, full of fruit and flavor but without the elaborate nuances of the classics of that variety because he refused to age it in wood.

The same principles applied to his supple, zesty Merlot and Pinot Nero, as well as to white wines from Chardonnay, Pinot Bianco and Grigio, Malvasia, Riesling, Sauvignon Blanc and Viognier.

On Enrico's death in 1985, son Giovanni and daughter Elisabetta took over Terre Rosse, aided by their mother Adriana. From 20 hectares of vines they produce about 100,000 bottles a year of Colli Bolognesi DOC wines, led by the Cabernet Sauvignon that has come to be known as Il Rosso di Enrico Vallania Cuvée. Lately Luigino Casagrande has become consulting winemaker and Giovanni's son Enrico has begun to follow the footsteps of his grandfather through the vineyards and cellars of Terre Rosse.

Emilia-Romagna

Grapes
Cabernet Sauvignon, hand picked in late October to early November.

Vineyard
A plot of 3 hectares in calcareous clay soils rich in ferrous mineral salts at 150–250 meters of altitude on slopes facing south at Terre Rosse near the town of Zola Predosa at the northern edge of the Colli Bolognesi zone. The vines, part planted 22 years ago at a density of 5,000–6,000 per hectare and part planted 14 years ago at 7,000 per hectare, are trained in an espalier method.

Vinification and aging
Grapes are stemmed and soft crushed and the must fermented in stainless steel vats at 25–27°C for 20 days. After natural malolactic fermentation, the wine, of 13–13.5% alcohol, is stored for years in stainless steel vats and bottled and cellared for 6 months before release.

Style and maturity
Il Rosso di Enrico Vallania Cuvée has bright ruby color when released about 4 years after the harvest, taking on garnet tones with age. The bouquet is clean and generous with scents suggesting ripe plums and berries and hints of bell pepper. On the palate it is full and round with smooth texture underpinned by tannins that lend vigor to warm fruit flavors with a hint of bitter chocolate in the long finish. The wine retains its mellow, velvety qualities for 10–15 years.

Serving
🌡 14–16°C, opening the bottle 30 minutes earlier.
🍷 Ample glass (Bordeaux type).
🍽 Tagliatelle noodles with Bolognese meat sauce; *bollito misto* (boiled meats with green sauce); roast saddle of lamb.

164

Villa Russiz

Graf de La Tour
Collio Merlot
DOC 🍷

Producer
Azienda Agricola
Villa Russiz
Via Russiz 6
34070 Capriva del Friuli
(Gorizia)
Tel. 0481 800 47
Fax 0481 809 657
villarussiz@
villarussiz.it
www.villarussiz.it

Owner
Istituto A. Cerruti-Villa
Russiz

Founded
1869

Winemaker
Gianni Menotti

Vineyard manager
Gianni Menotti

Production
About 3,500 bottles in
outstanding years

Vintages
1998 1997 1995 1994
1993

Price
● ● ●

Villa Russiz was founded by the French Count Théodore de La Tour and his Austrian wife Elvine Ritter in 1869, when the northeastern corner of Italy was under rule of the Hapsburgs of Vienna. Graf de La Tour, as he was known by the Austrians, planted vineyards with Merlot, the Pinots and Sauvignon Blanc from his homeland and built the vaulted cellars still used by the winery. After World War I, the countess left the property to the Italian state to become an orphanage that carries the name of its founder Adele Cerutti.

The wine tradition continued and in recent decades Villa Russiz has re-emerged as one of Friuli's premier estates. Credit for that goes to Edino Menotti, who ran the winery for years, and his son Gianni, the current director, winemaker and vineyard specialist.

The wines of Villa Russiz, which all qualify under the DOC of Collio Goriziano (or simply Collio), are predominantly white, in keeping with Friuli's modern reputation. The standout is Sauvignon, which Gianni Menotti selects in top years as Sauvignon de La Tour (see page 242).

The reds are Cabernet and Merlot. When I first visited Villa Russiz in the late 1970s, Edino Menotti let me taste those wines, which I recalled as being deliciously soft and fruity in the flush of youth—in keeping with what was then the style in Collio. But recently Gianni Menotti has selected Merlot from outstanding vintages to be aged to aristocratic splendor as Graf de La Tour. The wine is excruciatingly rare and precious, but it's so plush and elegant that it seems to be inspiring a new breed of Merlot in Friuli.

Villa Russiz has 30 hectares of vines to produce about 180,000 bottles a year of Collio DOC, including Pinot Bianco, Pinot Grigio, Ribolla Gialla, Riesling, Sauvignon, Tocai Friulano and sweet Verduzzo.

Friuli-Venezia Giulia

Grapes
Merlot 100%, hand picked in early October.

Vineyards
Grapes are selected in plots of 1.5 hectares in marl-rich soils on slopes facing south at about 100 meters of altitude at Russiz in the commune of Capriva del Friuli at the heart of the Collio DOC zone. The vines, of an average age of 31 years, are planted at a density of 4,500 per hectare and trained in the Guyot cordon method.

Vinification and aging
Grapes are stemmed and soft crushed and the musts fermented in stainless steel tanks at 30°C for 15 days on the skins. After natural malolactic fermentation in barriques, the wine, of about 13% alcohol, matures for 2 years in new 225-liter barrels of French oak and is bottled and cellared for at least 6 months before release.

Style and maturity
Merlot Graf de La Tour on release about 3 years after the harvest has deep ruby-mulberry color and immense bouquet with scents reminiscent of ripe plums and blackcurrants, winter violets and hints of wood spice and vanilla. A wine of ample structure, it fills the mouth with concentrated fruit and berry sensations, mellow wood tannins and a hint of bitter chocolate in a long, velvety finish. The first vintage of 1993 is approaching a prime, but it could age as gracefully as a grand Pomerol.

Serving
- 20°C, after decanting an hour earlier.
- Ample glass (Bordeaux type).
- Friulian meat and game dishes, such as roast veal shank with polenta and filet of venison with Savoy cabbage; Montasio cheese from Carnia.

Abbazia di
Novacella

Sylvaner
Sudtirolo Valle d'Isarco
Bressanone DOC ♀

Producer
Abbazia di Novacella
Via Abbazia 1
39040 Varna (Bolzano)
Tel. 0472/836189
Fax 0472/837305
weine@kloster-neustift.it
www.kloster-neustift.it

Owners
Canonici Regolari
Agostiniani

Founded
1142

Winemaker
Celestino Lucin

Vineyard manager
Urban von Klebelsberg

Production
About 100,000 bottles a
year

Vintages
1999 1997 1995 1992
1990 1989

Price
●

Note
The DOC may be Alto
Adige or Sudtirolo in
Italian or Südtiroler in
German

A bbazia di Novacella, the splendid Augustinian
monastery known as Chorherrenstift Neustift in the
native German of the South Tyrol, was founded in 1142 as a
hospice for pilgrims crossing the nearby Brenner Pass on the
way to Rome. The abbey complex houses chapels, cloisters,
libraries, galleries, gardens and orchards. But the main
attraction seems to be the *cantina*, where tourists arrive by
the busload to sip the rarefied whites of the high Isarco or
Eisack valley, further identified under the Sudtirolo DOC by
the name of the town of Brixen or Bressanone.

The adjacent vineyards, among the most northerly of Italy,
are planted in Riesling, Gewürztraminer and Pinot Grigio, as
well as varieties that excel at these heights: Müller-Thurgau
and the Veltliner and Sylvaner which are extremely rare in
Italy. Once popular in Germany, Sylvaner, spelled with an "i"
there, is still the base of the Franken wines of Franconia. It is
esteemed in Alsace as Sylvaner, where it grows mainly in
flatlands along the Rhine. In Italy, it is planted almost
exclusively in the Isarco valley, where the Alpine climate seems
to account for its steely dry, gracefully aromatic qualities.

Sylvaner is the prime wine of Abbazia di Novacella, whose
cellars are believed to be the oldest of the South Tyrol. Urban
von Klebelsberg, the abbey's amiably urbane administrator,
explains the philosophy as "keeping things as natural and
traditional as possible." Winemaker Celestino Lucin has
access to modern equipment, but he rounds out the Sylvaner
in massive oak casks following an old custom here. Von
Klebelsberg once described the wine's style as "a modern
interpretation of baroque."

Abbazia di Novacella has 17 hectares of vines, including
those at the Marklhof estate near Bolzano, source of
respected red Lagrein and a rare sweet Rosenmuskateller.
With acquisitions from growers, the cellars produce about
450,000 bottles a year, much of it sold on the premises to
wine-bibbing pilgrims who venture across the Brenner Pass
to the sunny side of the Alps.

Alto Adige

Grapes
Sylvaner 100%, hand picked when very ripe in late October.

Vineyards
Grapes are selected from plots totaling 17 hectares in stony glacial moraine mixed with sand and silt on slopes facing south-southeast at 600–720 meters of altitude in the communes of Varna-Novacella, Rasa and Bressanone in the northern part of the Valle d'Isarco subdistrict of the Alto Adige DOC zone. Vines, of an average age of 16 years, are planted at densities of 6,000–7,000 per hectare and trained in the Guyot cordon method.

Vinification and aging
Grapes are crushed gently and the musts macerate briefly with the skins before fermenting in stainless steel vats at 20°C for about 10 days. Malolactic fermentation is avoided during a period on the lees— partially in 3,000-liter oak casks—for 6 months. The wine, of about 12.5% alcohol, is bottled and cellared for a month before release.

Style and maturity
Abbazia di Novacella Sylvaner on release has pale straw yellow color with greenish highlights and graceful aromas with scents reminiscent of apples, peaches, lemons and Alpine herbs. Crisp and clean in flavor, its lively acidity buoys aromatic fruit sensations that are amplified as they linger on the tongue. Though often preferred in its youth, certain vintages with time acquire elegantly mellow fragrance and flavor.

Serving
🌡 12–14°C.
🍷 Tulip-shaped glass (Riesling type).
🍽 Tyrolean salami and *Speck* (smoked pork flank); gnocchi with goat's cheese and mountain herbs; Alpine brook trout.

Anselmi

I Capitelli
Passito Bianco
Veneto IGT ♀

Producer
Roberto Anselmi
Azienda Agricola
Via San Carlo 46
37032 Monteforte
d'Alpone (Verona)
Tel. 045/7611488
Fax 045/7611490

Owner
Roberto Anselmi

Founded
1948

Winemaker
Roberto Anselmi

Vineyard manager
Roberto Anselmi

Production
11,000–11,500 bottles
and 10,000 half bottles
annually

Vintages
1999 1998 1997 1996
1993 1992 1991 1990
1988 1986

Price
● ● ●

Note
The wine through the
1997 vintage was labeled
I Capitelli Recioto di
Soave

Roberto Anselmi's role in elevating the class and style of Soave had made his name a symbol of an appellation that had finally begun to acquire prestige after decades of exploitation. His single-vineyard Soave Classico Superiore Capitel Croce, Capitel Foscarino and San Vicenzo inspired a new breed of winemakers in the zone east of Verona. Anselmi's Recioto di Soave I Capitelli, conceived in 1986, ranked with the most admired of sweet wines. But Roberto's leadership was more of an exemplary than an active nature. He, like the other middle-aged lion of Soave, Leonildo Pieropan (see page 220), had refused to join the producers' consortium, pointing out that there was far too great a gap in scope and motives between small estates and cellars turning out awesome quantities of what has been known around the world for decades as "the most Italian of white wines."

The consortium, after a successful bid to raise Recioto di Soave to DOCG in 1998, launched a similar campaign for Soave—all Soave, including both the growing portion of dignified Classico from the hills and the bulk of often wishy-washy plonk from the plains. Roberto, insisting that Soave from the vast majority of producers doesn't merit a guarantee, announced in 2000 that his wines would no longer carry the appellation, adding that he had ceased to issue I Capitelli as Recioto di Soave DOCG.

The decision shocked Verona's wine establishment but left Roberto feeling liberated: "Now I'm free to make wine the way I like and call it what I please without facing the contradictions of a denomination."

Roberto has planted most of his 70 hectares in Soave Classico at high density to make wines of greater depth of character. I Capitelli, from Garganega grapes dried after the harvest, combines concentration with a smooth, fresh style that makes it among the most delightful of sweet wines to drink. Production of about 350,000 bottles a year, now entirely IGT, includes a fine Cabernet Sauvignon called Realda.

Veneto

Grapes
Garganega 100%, hand picked when very ripe in October. Bunches are individually selected and separated in the cellars before drying on cane mats in well-ventilated drying rooms for 3–4 months.

Vineyards
Grapes are selected from plots totaling 70 hectares in volcanic tufa and calcareous soils on slopes oriented to the south at 200–350 meters of altitude in the communes of Monteforte d'Alpone and Soave east of Verona. Vines, of an average age of 16 years, are planted at a density of 6,000 per hectare and trained in a spurred cordon method.

Vinification and aging
Dried grapes are crushed and the dense, murky musts are settled before fermenting for 15 days at 20°C in small oak barrels or stainless steel tanks, depending on the vintage. The wine, of about 12.5% alcohol with 10.2% of residual sugar, is matured in small barrels of French oak for 12 months, then bottled and cellared for 1–3 years before release.

Style and maturity
I Capitelli Passito on release about 3 years after the harvest has bright straw-gold color with amber-copper highlights. The bouquet is rich and composed with scents reminiscent of elderberries, cherries, apricots, vanilla, cinnamon and blossoms. On the palate, it is cleanly sweet with round, mellow qualities braced by refreshing acidity in flavors of great complexity and a long, smooth finish. Persuasive from the start, the wine reaches a prime after a decade and promises to maintain style for at least another.

Serving
- 12–14°C.
- Medium-sized glass with narrow top.
- Foie gras; lobster Americaine; ripe cheeses such as Gorgonzola or Taleggio; torta sbrisulona (cornmeal-almond crumb cake).

Cuvée Marianna Extra Brut Sudtirolo DOC Talento Metodo Classico ♀

Producer
Arunda Vivaldi
Via Centro 53
39010 Mölten/Meltina
(Bolzano)
Tel. 0471/668033
Fax 0471/668229
arunda@dnet.it

Owners
Josef and Marianne
Reiterer

Founded
1979

Winemaker
Josef Reiterer

Production
About 4,500 bottles
annually

Vintages
Non-vintage sparkling
wine

Price
● ●

Note
The DOC may be Alto
Adige or Sudtirolo in
Italian or Südtiroler in
German

After studying at the wine institute at Geisenheim in Germany's Rheingau, Josef Reiterer worked for years as a technical adviser for a noted manufacturer of enological equipment. In 1976, he decided to put his experience into practice as a *négoçiant-manipulant* of sparkling wines by the Champagne method, buying Chardonnay and Pinot Noir grapes in the Adige valley and processing them in a cellar at his home village of Mölten (Meltina) at 1,200 meters of altitude in the South Tyrolean Alps.

Josef, who called his winery Arunda, released his first 10,000 bottles in 1979. I met him soon after that at a wine fair in Bolzano, where he wore a Tyrolean loden jacket and bibbed leather knee britches while merrily serving flutes of his Alpine bubbly. Hearing my praise, the bespectacled Josef grinned like a schoolboy and invited me to visit the cellars.

Mölten can be reached by road via a series of hairpin curves, but the express route is by cable car. After a visit to what Josef believes to be the highest sparkling wine cellar in Europe (but I wonder if there is another winery that lofty anywhere), we settled into the cozy *stube* of his home, where his wife Marianne served Arunda Brut and Extra Brut with slices of the smoked pork flank called *speck* and crisp rye flatbread.

Since then, Josef has created a blend of barrel-aged Chardonnay with Pinot Noir called appropriately Cuvée Marianna. Long aging on the yeasts accounts for the depth and complexity of a wine that also shows the buoyancy and finesse that Josef credits to the Alpine atmosphere.

Production of about 70,000 bottles a year is entirely *metodo classico* under the Alto Adige/Südtiroler DOC and further identified as Talento, a trademark used by an association of producers in northern Italy. In 1982, Josef made an arrangement with Ignazio Miceli of Sicily to sell his wines in Italy under the trade name Vivaldi, a north–south union that has proved to be propitious.

Alto Adige

Grapes
Chardonnay 80%, Pinot Nero 20%, hand picked in September (the Pinot Nero a year after the Chardonnay).

Vineyards
Grapes are acquired from growers with hillside plots along the Adige valley, the Pinot and most Chardonnay from calcareous clay soils around Buchholz (Pochi) and Salorno south of Bolzano, and some Chardonnay from plots in medium-textured porphyritic soils in the Terlano area northwest of Bolzano. Vines are trained in the traditional trellised pergola and the Guyot method.

Vinification and aging
Grapes are stemmed, soft crushed, separated from the skins then fermented in stainless steel tanks at 18°C for 2 weeks. The Chardonnay is matured in small barrels of French oak for a year then assembled with Pinot Nero from the latest vintage in a cuvée that remains in bottle on the yeasts for 50 months before riddling, disgorging and topping up with wine from the same batch. After cork sealing, the wine, of about 12% alcohol, is cellared for a few months before release.

Style and maturity
Vivaldi Cuvée Marianna on release about 5 years after the cuvée is assembled shows luminous straw yellow color with golden highlights and abundant, steady streams of fine bubbles. Aromas are ample and complex with scents reminiscent of baked apple, acacia honey, toasted nuts, vanilla and yeasts. Rich and vital on the palate, its smooth, round fruit flavors are buoyed by lively acidity in a sparkling wine that reaches a peak about a year after release and retains finesse well beyond.

Serving
- 6–8°C.
- Tall, ample flute (vintage Champagne type).
- Speck (smoked pork flank); Alpine brook trout braised with white wine and butter; mazzancolle (jumbo shrimp) with leek and cream sauce.

Bastianich

Tocai Friulano Plus
Colli Orientali del Friuli
DOC ♀

Producer
Azienda Agricola
Bastianich
Frazione Casali Ottelio
33040 Premarriacco
(Udine)
Tel. 0432/675612
Fax 0432/675612

Owner
Joseph V. Bastianich

Founded
1998

Winemakers
Emilio Del Medico with
Maurizio Castelli

Vineyard manager
Maurizio Castelli

Production
About 2,000 bottles
from 1998, 6,000 bottles
from 1999

Vintages
1999 1998

Price
● ●

In terms of status, experience and scope of production, Bastianich and Tocai Friulano Plus would not merit mention here. But the outstanding potential of this new estate gives me the opportunity to review a star of the future.

Joseph Bastianich, the owner, is a young American, son of Felice and Lidia, who went to the United States from Friuli-Venezia Giulia after leaving their native Istria (now in Slovenia). They opened the Felidia restaurant in New York and Lidia Bastianich, as an author and lecturer, became a recognized authority on Italian food and wine in America. Joseph followed the lead, opening the highly successful Becco, Babbo, Lupa and Esca restaurants in New York.

The family retained ties to Friuli and, in 1998, Joseph bought the farm at Buttrio in the Colli Orientali zone with 6 hectares of old vines planted in native and international varieties. His first production of about 15,000 bottles emphasized the natives, including Colli Orientali DOC red Pignolo and Refosco Plus (neither yet released) and the white Tocai Friulano Plus, which made such a splash in New York that the waves rippled back to Italy.

Consultant Maurizio Castelli, working with winemaker Emilio Del Medico and manager Wayne Young, devised a new twist on the Tocai routine, leaving 15 percent of the grapes on the vine to be harvested late. The musts are saturated with oxygen before being fermented and added to the original wine as what Joseph calls the *piccolo bambino* (little baby). The "Plus" boosts the aromas, flavors and body of Tocai to new levels of opulence.

They also made DOC Pinot Grigio and *vino da tavola* Vespa Bianco (oak-fermented Chardonnay with Picolit and Sauvignon) and Vespa Rosso (Merlot with Refosco). Joseph's original aim was to supply the family restaurants, but he became so enthusiastic about winemaking that he quickly expanded, leasing another 9 hectares of vineyards that will soon provide enough wine to open up a market in Italy.

Friuli-Venezia Giulia

Grapes
Tocai Friulano 100%, hand picked in mid- to late September; 15% left on the vine is harvested later in October.

Vineyard
Grapes are selected from 1 hectare of vines in marl and sandstone soils known as *ponca* on a crest facing south at 180 meters of altitude at Premariacco in the southern part of the Colli Orientali del Friuli zone. The vines, about 40 years old, are planted at a density of 3,000 per hectare and trained in an arched double cordon.

Vinification and aging
Grapes are soft crushed and the musts macerated with the skins before fermenting at natural temperatures (around 25°C) for about 20 days in stainless steel vats. Musts from the late harvested grapes are saturated with oxygen (hyperoxygenation) and fermented in tanks, then blended with the previous batch and left on the lees until March without undergoing malolactic fermentation. The wine, of about 13.5% alcohol, is bottled with the waning moon in July and cellared for 6 months until release.

Style and maturity
Bastianich Tocai Friulano Plus on release in the 2nd year after the harvest has bright straw yellow color with pale green highlights and exuberant aromas that recall ripe apricot and peach, mandarin orange and spices. Well structured and round on the palate, it has impressive depth of flavors of ripe fruit and nuts and a fresh, smooth finish. Prime drinking is normally from 2–3 years for Tocai, though the producers predict a life span as long as for whites of Burgundy and Alsace.

Serving
- 10°C, chilled briefly in an ice bucket.
- Ample tulip-shaped glass.
- Pasta with shrimp and zucchini; roast chicken, rabbit and veal dishes; cheeses such as Taleggio, Asiago or Friuli's Montasio.

Ronco della Chiesa
Collio DOC ♀

Producer
Azienda Agricola Borgo
del Tiglio
Via San Giorgio 71
34070 Brazzano di
Cormons (Gorizia)
Tel. 0481/62166
Fax 0481/630845

Owner
Nicola Manferrari

Founded
1981

Winemaker
Nicola Manferrari

Vineyard manager
Nicola Manferrari

Production
About 4,000 bottles in
choice years

Vintages
1999 1998 1994 1993
1990

Price
● ● ●

Tocai, the beloved white variety of Friuli-Venezia Giulia, has been ordered to change its name by a European Union ruling that gave precedence to Hungarian Tokaji (or Tokay), which, curiously, is a wine but not a vine. Almost as deflating to local egos was the confirmation that Tocai Friulano is not a native, as was long believed, but is actually Sauvignon Vert or Sauvignonasse, a common cousin of France's Sauvignon Blanc.

Nicola Manferrari, whose Ronco della Chiesa has stood as a model Tocai for years, is deeply upset by these "misfortunes." Nicola, who left his job as a pharmacist to take over the family farm in Collio on the death of his father in 1981, recalls that Tocai was practically all that Borgo del Tiglio grew then. As a child, he loved its sweet yellow grapes, but comparative tastings of local wines were largely negative.

Farmers, who appreciated Tocai's productivity and abundance of sugar, picked grapes early to maintain acidity. Thus wines lacked personality but made a refreshing *tajut,* as the glassful served in local inns is known. Nicola decided to try treating Tocai like its "aristocratic cousins" Chardonnay and Sauvignon Blanc. He succeeded with greater plant density and lower yields while respecting the vine's biological equilibrium in the precipitous plot of Ronco della Chiesa, named for the little church beside the property.

Ronco della Chiesa has an elegance that reveals Tocai's hidden nobility. "I will never abandon this grape without a name, because it is the grape of my childhood," vows Nicola. "Humble, generous and unfortunate as it is, I still love it more than its aristocratic and, perhaps, overbearing cousins."

From 8.5 hectares of vines at Brazzano, Ruttars and Ca' delle Vallade, Borgo del Tiglio makes about 40,000 bottles a year, including Collio DOC Chardonnay and Malvasia and the IGT Rosso della Centa, an outstanding Merlot. Studio di Bianco, a meditated blend of Tocai, Riesling and Sauvignon, shows remarkable depth of flavor over time.

Friuli-Venezia Giulia

Grapes
Tocai Friulano 100%, hand picked in late September or early October.

Vineyard
Ronco della Chiesa, a plot of 1.2 hectares in alternating strata of marl and sandstone known as *flysch di Cormons* on a steep slope facing southwest at about 120 meters of altitude at the base of Monte Quarin at Brazzano di Cormons on the western edge of the Collio zone. The vines, of an average age of 41 years, are planted at a density of 4,000 per hectare and trained in the arched double cordon known as *doppio capovolto*.

Vinification and aging
Grapes are soft crushed and the musts separated from the skins to ferment in part in stainless steel vats and in part in small barrels of French oak (most used once before), though length and temperatures vary according to vintage, as does the limited degree of malolactic fermentation. The wine, of about 13.5% alcohol, remains on the lees for 6–9 months of maturation in small barrels before being bottled and cellared for 6 months until release.

Style and maturity
Ronco della Chiesa on release in the 2nd year after the harvest has straw yellow color with pale green highlights and delicate, blossomy aromas that recall apricots and pears with hints of citrus and toasted almonds. Well structured and round in texture, flavors of ripe fruit and nuts show impressive depth with a trace of bitter almond in a long, smooth finish. Prime drinking is normally from 2–3 years, though top vintages can be splendid beyond.

Serving
🌡 8–10°C.
🍷 Tulip-shaped glass (Chardonnay type).
🍽 *Frico* (fried crisps of Montasio cheese); barley and bean soup; green asparagus with eggs and grated Parmigiano.

La Cappuccina

Fontégo
Soave Superiore DOC ♀

Producer
Azienda Agricola La
Cappuccina
Via San Brizio 125
37030 Costalunga di
Monteforte d'Alpone
(Verona)
Tel. 045/6175840
Fax 045/6175755
lacappuccina@la
cappuccina.it
www.lacappuccina.it

Owners
Pietro and Sisto Tessari

Founded
1988, though the estate
has been in the family
since 1890

Winemaker
Pietro Tessari

Vineyard manager
Sisto Tessari

Production
About 20,000 bottles
annually

Vintages
1999 1997 1994 1990

Price
● ●

Amid the talk of a renaissance of Soave, it's worth remembering that only a fraction of the wine produced could actually be considered of premium class. Italy's most popular white wine fills some 75 million bottles a year, but only about a fifth of the volume comes from the hills of Soave Classico. The rest—usually clean and fresh but too often innocuous—comes from low inclines and plains that surround the historic zone.

Wine snobs may insist that if it isn't Soave Classico, it isn't worth drinking, but a conspicuous exception must be made for La Cappuccina. That estate, named for a fifteenth-century Capuchin chapel on the property, is owned by the Tessari family, whose vineyards along the lower slopes of the Alpone valley lie just outside the Classico zone. Brothers Sisto and Pietro Tessari, who divide vineyard and cellar duties, are as dedicated to the greater glory of Soave as are their neighbors up the hill. But low altitude precludes the higher designation.

La Cappuccina's 28 hectares of vineyards, farmed following biological standards that exclude chemical pesticides, herbicides and fertilizers, produce about 150,000 bottles of wine a year. The emphasis is on Soave DOC, produced in a regular type and in the Superiore versions of Fontégo (a single-vineyard wine) and San Brizio (a selection fermented and matured in barriques). Although both could stand proudly with the cream of Soave Classico Superiore, from recent vintages I've developed a fondness for Fontégo, for its full fruit sensations balanced by lively acidity and a purity of line that doesn't need oak to show depth and finesse.

I've also been impressed by the sumptuous Recioto di Soave DOCG Arzimo, as well as the IGT Verona Sauvignon and red Campo Buri (Cabernet Franc with Cabernet Sauvignon) and Madégo (Cabernet Sauvignon with Cabernet Franc and Merlot).

Grapes
Garganega 90% and
Chardonnay, hand picked
in mid-September
(Chardonnay) and early
October (Garganega).

Vineyard
Fontégo, a plot of 3
hectares in medium-
textured volcanic soils
with calcareous clays at
the base of a slope facing
southeast at 80 meters of
altitude in the commune
of Montecchia di Crosara
in the northeastern part
of the Soave zone. Vines,
of an average age of 16
years, are planted at a
density of 4,000 per
hectare and trained in a
spurred cordon method.

Vinification and aging
Whole bunches of grapes
are soft crushed and the
musts separated from the
skins and chilled to
precipitate solid matter
before fermenting at
18°C for about a week in
stainless steel tanks. The
Garganega and
Chardonnay, vinified
separately, are blended
and matured for about 7
months in tanks,
undergoing malolactic
fermentation if it occurs
naturally. The wine, of
about 12% alcohol, is
bottled and cellared for at
least 2 months before
release.

Style and maturity
Soave Superiore Fontégo on
release about a year after the
harvest has bright straw
yellow color with greenish
highlights and full aroma with
floral notes and scents
reminiscent of apples, citrus
and hazelnuts. On the palate it
is fresh and round with
mellow fruit qualities balanced
by lively acidity in a long,
smooth finish. The wine
approaches a prime soon after
release, but can show style for
5 or 6 years.

Serving
🌡 12°C.
🍷 Medium tulip-shaped glass
(Chardonnay type).
🍽 *Bigoli* noodles with salted
sardines; risotto creamed
with Monte Veronese
cheese and nettles; rolled
filets of Val d'Alpone guinea
fowl with chard sauce.

178

La Castellada

Bianco della Castellada Collio DOC

Producer
Azienda Agricola La
Castellada
Località Oslavia 1
34070 Gorizia
Tel. 0481/33670
Fax 0481/33670

Owners
Giorgio and Nicolò
Bensa

Founded
1985

Winemakers
Giorgio and Nicolò
Bensa

Vineyard managers
Giorgio and Nicolò
Bensa

Production
11,000–12,000 bottles
in favorable years

Vintages
1999 1998 1997 1996
1995 1994 1992

Price
● ● ●

White wines from elaborate blends of varieties have become a specialty of Friuli-Venezia Giulia, inspired by the archetypal Vintage Tunina of Silvio Jermann (see page 204). Bianco della Castellada is the brainchild of Giorgio and Nicolò Bensa, who blend Pinot Grigio, Chardonnay and Sauvignon Blanc with a trace of Tocai Friulano in one of the most admired wines of the genre.

The Bensa brothers founded La Castellada in 1985, after inheriting vineyards at Oslavia from their father, who had a trattoria there. They had built a reputation for their single varietal wines by 1992, when they composed the blend that propelled them to stardom. Bianco della Castellada debuted as a *vino da tavola* and went on to become Venezia Giulia IGT. With the 1997 vintage, it qualified as Collio DOC when the rules were modified to include wines from blends of any of the varieties approved under the appellation.

Giorgio and Nicolò are neighbors and, as some might say, soul brothers of Josko Gravner (see page 198). Like Josko, they ferment and mature all of their wines in oak barrels, selling the whites two years after the harvest and the reds after four or five years. They continue to make excellent Chardonnay and Sauvignon from certain vintages, but, like Josko, their ideal is to produce only Ribolla Gialla as an indigenous varietal and use the others in blends.

Since current production from 8 hectares of vines is only about 24,000 bottles a year, the idea of concentrating on estate wines seems to make sense. Also, as they point out, achieving a successful blend requires a greater measure of creativity than interpreting the character of a single variety. Bianco della Castellada is one of the few composites based on Pinot Grigio, which with the Chardonnay seems to account for the mellow ripeness of flavor, though the brothers credit Sauvignon Blanc as the key to aroma. Its twin is Rosso della Castellada, from Cabernet Sauvignon and Merlot matured for three years in barrels.

Friuli-Venezia Giulia

Grapes

Pinot Grigio 40–45%, Chardonnay 30%, Sauvignon 20–25%, Tocai Friulano (when included) 5%, all hand picked, the Pinot Grigio in early September, the others later in the month.

Vineyards

Grapes are selected from the oldest vines in 4 hectares of crumbly marl and sandstone soils on slopes facing various directions at 145–175 meters of altitude at Oslavia in the commune of Gorizia in the eastern part of the Collio zone. The vines, 26–31 years old, are planted at densities of 4,000–6,000 per hectare and trained in the Guyot and double Guyot cordon methods.

Vinification and aging

Grapes are stemmed and soft crushed and part of the must is macerated with the skins before fermentation in 225-liter oak barrels (a third new and the rest used once or more) at natural temperatures for 20–25 days. The wine, of about 14% alcohol, remains on the lees in barriques for a year, followed by 6–7 months in stainless steel tanks before being bottled and cellared for 6 months until release.

Style and maturity

Bianco della Castellada on release about 2 years after the harvest has deep straw yellow color with golden highlights and rich aromas with scents reminiscent of ripe fruit and berries, herbs and caramel. The initial impact on the palate is forceful, due to solid structure and ample alcohol, though flavors emerge as full and round with sensations of ripe fruit combined with notes of butter and vanilla in a long, smooth finish. The wine reaches a prime of mellow complexity in about 4–5 years, though top vintages show style well beyond.

Serving

- 12–16°C.
- Tulip-shaped glass (Chardonnay type).
- Risotto with shellfish; filet of John Dory with green asparagus; roast guinea fowl with a chestnut stuffing.

Pinot Grigio
Trentino DOC ♀

Producer
Cesconi
Via Marcon 39
38015 Pressano (Trento)
Tel. 0461/240355
Fax 0461/240355
cesconi@cr-surfing.net

Owners
Paolo Cesconi and sons

Founded
1995

Winemakers
Roberto and Lorenzo
Cesconi

Vineyard managers
Alessandro and Franco
Cesconi

Production
About 5,000 bottles
a year

Vintages
1999 1998 1997 1996

Price
● ●

The family winery of Cesconi has rapidly emerged with some of the most acclaimed varietal whites of Italy. Paolo Cesconi and sons Alessandro, Franco, Roberto and Lorenzo run the estate that on paper was founded in 1995, when they started bottling wines. Before that grapes from the Cesconi vineyards went to the admirable cooperative of LaVis. But the family archives reveal that ancestors began planting vines in 1751 on the same hillsides above the village of Pressano, north of Trento.

Independence was inspired by Roberto, after experiments with small batches of grapes grown on the property: Chardonnay, Pinot Bianco, Pinot Grigio, Traminer Aromatico (Gewürztraminer), Sauvignon Blanc and the local Nosiola. Production from 1995 was 8,000 bottles, greeted with such enthusiasm that the next year's output soared to 20,000. The sudden success prompted the family to replant part of their 6 hectares of vines at Pressano and lease another 6 hectares near Lake Garda in the western part of Trentino, where they planted Cabernet, Merlot and Syrah. By 1999, they had reached 65,000 bottles, though in their newly expanded cellars they expect to produce about 90,000 bottles in the future.

Little about the Cesconi operation would seem to distinguish it from others, yet their wines have an intensity and depth of aromas and flavors that project them above the field. The entire range is admirable, though I've been especially impressed by the Pinot Grigio made following elemental methods of modern winemaking without the use of oak.

Cesconi has given new dignity to an overworked variety of French origin that has enjoyed overwhelming popularity in northeastern Italy for more than two decades. Their Pinot Grigio has a richness of tone and a purity of line that are worthy of the superlatives it has been winning. The secret seems to lie in the vineyards, where the four brothers work with a dedication that has been described as fanatical.

Trentino

Grapes
Pinot Grigio 100%, hand picked in late September.

Vineyard
A plot of 8,000 square meters in potassium-rich sedimentary soils on a sandstone base on slopes facing west at 300 meters of altitude at Costa di Pressano in the commune of LaVis about 10 kilometers north of Trento. Vines, of an average age of 14 years, are planted at a density of 3,600 per hectare and trained in the trellised pergola *trentina* system. New plantings at greater density are in the Guyot cordon method.

Vinification and aging
Grapes are soft crushed and the musts fermented at 18–22°C in stainless steel vats. Malolactic fermentation is avoided and the wine, of about 13.5% alcohol, is settled for a few months before bottling.

Style and maturity
Cesconi Trentino Pinot Grigio on release has straw yellow color with glints of old gold and copper. Aromas are full and enticing with scents reminiscent of ripe pears and Alpine herbs and flowers. On the palate it is uncommonly full and round with rich fruit flavors (apples and pears) underlined by bracing citrus-like acidity in a clean, mellow, long finish. Seductive from the start, the wine should retain style for 3–5 years.

Serving
- 10°C.
- Tulip-shaped glass (Chardonnay type).
- Potato gnocchi with chanterelle mushrooms; lake trout *in carpione* (fried and marinated with herbs); stewed snails with polenta.

Produttori
Colterenzio

Cornell Chardonnay
Alto Adige DOC ♀

Producer
Produttori
Colterenzio
Strada del Vino 8
39050 Cornaiano
(Bolzano)
Tel. 0471/664246
Fax 0471/660633
info@colterenzio.com
www.colterenzio.com

Owners
Cooperative directed by
Luis Raifer

Founded
1960

Winemakers
Wolfgang Raifer with
Donato Lanati

Vineyard supervisor
Luis Raifer

Production
About 20,000 bottles a
year

Vintages
1999 1998 1997 1995
1990

Price
● ●

Note
The DOC may be Alto
Adige or Sudtirolo in
Italian or Südtiroler in
German

Colterenzio is the Italian name of the South Tyrolean village of Schreckbichl, where, in 1960, 28 vineyard owners founded what today ranks as one of Italy's most admired cooperative cellars. Director Luis Raifer backs an uncompromising quest for quality with Teutonic drive and discipline in a winery that represents 310 growers with 320 hectares of vines in choice Alto Adige sites.

In a bilingual Alpine province where cooperatives dominate production, Luis Raifer, in the 1980s, was among the first to see the potential of the long neglected market represented by the rest of Italy. Kellereigenossenschaft Schreckbichl, as it was known, was selling most wines labeled in German as Südtiroler DOC. The change of direction paid off handsomely for Produttori Colterenzio, whose wines labeled as Alto Adige DOC have won admirers from the Alps to Sicily.

Production of about 1.2 million bottles a year is sold in three distinct lines. Linea Classico is a range of varietal wines at moderate prices. Linea Praedium takes in vineyard and estate selections, notably Chardonnay Conte Coreth, Merlot Siebeneich and Pinot Bianco Weisshaus. Special bottlings of Cabernet Sauvignon and Sauvignon are called Lafoa.

Linea Cornell represents an elite of wines that reflect the Raifer policy of limiting grape yields to absolute minimums. The range includes Chardonnay, Gewürztraminer, Moscato Rosa, Lagrein Schwarzhaus, Pinot Nero Schwarzhaus, Cornelius Bianco (from Pinots and Chardonnay) and Cornelius Rosso (from Cabernet Sauvignon and Merlot).

Success in Italy has inspired Colterenzio to set its sights on North American and British markets. "We've been too provincial up to now," admits Luis. "It's time for Alto Adige to take a global approach to wine." Colterenzio's strategy seems to be summed up in Cornell Chardonnay, which combines concentration and complexity of aromas and flavors with a deft kiss of oak certain to lend it international appeal.

Alto Adige

Grapes
Chardonnay 100%, hand picked in early to mid-September.

Vineyards
3 plots of about 4 hectares in total in gravelly soils with a high content of chalky clay on slopes at 400–450 meters of altitude in the commune of Cornaiano in the Überetsch area of the Adige valley southwest of Bolzano. Vines, of an average age of 13–16 years, are planted at a density of 6,000 per hectare and trained in the Guyot cordon system.

Vinification and aging
Grapes are soft crushed and the musts macerated with the skins at cold temperatures for 24 hours followed by fermentation at 22–24°C for about 3 weeks in new 225-liter barrels of French oak (Allier, Nevers and Tronçais). The wine, of about 13% alcohol, remains on the lees where it undergoes malolactic fermentation during 10 months in barrels, followed by bottling and cellaring for a further 10 months before release.

Style and maturity
Cornell Chardonnay on release nearly 2 years after the harvest has bright moon yellow color with golden highlights and fine, complex bouquet with scents reminiscent of tropical fruit and vanilla. Flavors are dry, round and neatly balanced with hints of ripe apple and toasted almond in a long, smooth finish. The wine usually reaches a prime at 4–5 years, though it will retain mellow complexity for several years beyond.

Serving
🍷 12°C.
🍷 Tulip-shaped glass (Chardonnay type).
🍴 *Knödel* (bread dumplings) in broth with melted cheese; brook trout braised with almonds; roast sea bass with porcini mushrooms.

184

Prosecco di Valdobbiadene Superiore di Cartizze DOC ♀

Col Vetoraz

Producer
Col Vetoraz Spumanti
Via Tresiese 1
31040 Santo Stefano di
Valdobbiadene (Treviso)
Tel. 0423/975291
Fax 0423/975571
colvetoraz@libero.it

Owner
Francesco Miotto

Founded
1992

Winemaker
Loris Dall'Acqua

Vineyard manager
Loris Pasetto

Production
20,000 bottles a year

Vintages
Non-vintage sparkling
wine

Price
● ●

The Prosecco vine seems to have originated near the Adriatic port of Trieste as the source of the ancient Roman wine called Pulcinum. It was planted long ago in the lovely hills north of Venice between the towns of Valdobbiadene and Conegliano, where in 1868 Antonio Carpenè introduced the Champagne method to Italy.

Prosecco took well to bubbles. But, having a delicate constitution, it turned out to be better suited to a rustic type of bottle fermentation briefer than the classic method. It gained popularity as a softly sweet to off-dry fizz of sunny golden hue sold in bottles with corks fastened by strings. In modern times, the Charmat method of fermentation in sealed tanks has transformed Prosecco into a crystal-clear wine that is usually dry and fully sparkling. It is often served locally from a pitcher or decanter, though Venetians normally sip it from a small glass as what they call affectionately an *ombra* or *ombretta*.

Wine from an area known as Cartizze, noted for a graceful sweetness, was historically considered the finest of Prosecco. The DOC for Prosecco di Conegliano/Valdobbiadene granted in 1971 included the category of Superiore di Cartizze for wine from the localities of San Pietro in Barbozza, Santo Stefano and Saccol in the commune of Valdobbiadene.

The steep hillsides of Cartizze cover 106 hectares, enough to produce an absolute maximum of just over a million bottles. But not long ago production of "Cartizze" was estimated at several times that volume in wines that were often steely dry and devoid of personality. Controls have stiffened, but the recent improvement in Cartizze, and Prosecco in general, is due to the integrity of a growing number of producers.

Among them, Col Vetoraz makes Prosecco di Valdobbiadene of admirably consistent class with a Cartizze of contemporary balance and tone but with the elegant sweetness and depth of aromas and flavors that recall the best of the good old days.

Veneto

Grapes
Prosecco 100%, hand picked in early October.

Vineyards
Plots totaling 1 hectare in carbonic clay soils derived from limestone on steep slopes of varying exposures at about 330 meters of altitude in the delimited Cartizze vineyard area east of the town of Valdobbiadene. Vines, of 16–21 years of age, are planted at a density of 2,000–2,200 per hectare and trained in the *doppio capovolto* (double arched) cordon system.

Vinification and aging
Grapes are soft crushed and the musts clarified cold before fermenting at 18–20°C for 10 days in stainless steel vats. The base wine is inoculated with select yeasts and sugar that set off a second fermentation that lasts for 30–45 days at low temperature in sealed tanks. The sparkling wine, of about 11.5% alcohol, is filtered and cold stabilized before bottling, then cellared for at least 30 days until release.

Style and maturity
Col Vetoraz Superiore di Cartizze on release about a year after the harvest has pale straw green color and lively streams of fine bubbles. Aromas are blossomy fresh and fruity with scents reminiscent of ripe apples, apricots and peaches. The wine is softly sweet and fresh with exhilarating effervescence to enhance graceful fruit flavors that linger on the palate through a smooth, mellow finish. It reaches a prime at a year from the vintage and maintains style for at least 2 years beyond.

Serving
🍶 8°C.
🍷 Medium-sized flute (Champagne type).
🍽 Ideal as an aperitif, it also goes well with desserts, such as *crema fritta* (fried cream custard) and the crunchy butter cake called *torta sabbiosa*.

**Cantina
Produttori
Cormons**

Vino della Pace
Vino da Tavola di Cormons ♀

Producer
Cantina Produttori
Cormons
Via Vino della Pace 31
34071 Cormons
(Gorizia)
Tel. 0481/62471
Fax 0481/630031
info@cormons.com
www.cormons.com

Owners
Cooperative directed by
Luigi Soini

Founded
1968

Winemakers
Luigi Soini and Rodolfo
Rizzi

Vineyard managers
Luigi Soini and
Gianni Rover

Production
9,000–12,000 bottles a
year

Vintages
1999 back to 1985

Price
● ●

Note
Older vintages are prized
by collectors for their
unique labels

In a nation known for idiosyncratic wines, Vino della Pace stands as the most exotic. The "Wine of Peace" was conceived in honor of international brotherhood by Luigi Soini, cellarmaster of the Cantina Produttori Cormons cooperative winery in Friuli-Venezia Giulia. In 1983, Soini talked his associates into planting the first vines in the 2-hectare Vigna del Mondo beside the winery, and in September 1985 they harvested the first grapes in a festive atmosphere. The next spring, the original Vino della Pace was bottled with labels designed by Italian artists Enrico Baj, Zoran Music and Arnaldo Pomodoro and sent to heads of state and religious leaders with messages of peace.

Letters of appreciation have arrived from such figures as Mikhail Gorbachev, Pope John Paul II, Queen Elizabeth, Bill Clinton and the Russian cosmonaut Valery Polyakov, who drank a toast of Vino del Pace in space that made the *Guinness Book of Records*. Producers from many nations contributed vines to the "World Vineyard," which has more than 550 varieties to rank as one of the most important viticultural collections on earth.

Since the wine comes from grapes of all species and colors, it was most practical to make a white wine by separating the juice from the skins, explains Soini. "Of course, it's a curiosity and each vintage is a little different, but we make it with serious dedication."

Each year three artists do a label for Vino della Pace, which is made in quantities ranging between 9,000 and 12,000 bottles. Contributors have included Robert Rauschenberg, Yoko Ono, Joe Tilson, Aligi Sassu, Miguel Berrocal, Philippe Garel and Matias Quetglas.

Cantina Produttori Cormons has 198 members with 382 hectares of vines for a total production of about 3.2 million bottles a year. These include a range of Collio and Friuli Isonzo DOC, though Vino della Pace remains the showpiece. "Sure, it's attracted attention to our cellars," says Soini. "But above all it represents a noble cause that we feel deeply about."

Friuli-Venezia Giulia

Grapes
More than 550 varieties, hand picked in late September.

Vineyard
La Vigna del Mondo covers 2 hectares in alluvial and glacial soils of sand and gravel on a stone base rich in potassium and phosphorous on a plain at 45 meters of altitude in the commune of Cormons at the northern edge of the Isonzo valley. The vines, planted at intervals starting in 1983 at a density of about 3,000 per hectare, are trained in the cordon sytems known as Guyot and Cappuccina and in part in the high espalier system known as Sylvoz.

Vinification and aging
Grapes are stemmed and soft crushed and left at room temperature for 3 or 4 hours to be oxygenated and enriched with enzymes before the must is separated, cooled and inoculated with yeasts for fermentation lasting about a month at 18°C in stainless steel tanks. The wine, of about 12% alcohol, is racked, clarified and stabilized and left in tanks until the following September, when it is bottled during a ceremony.

Style and maturity
Vino della Pace on release in September of the year after the harvest has bright lemon yellow color with golden highlights and delicate floral and fruit scents. On the palate, it is round and smooth with flavors of ripe fruit and toasted almond nicely balanced by bracing acidity. Prime drinking is normally from 1–2 years after the harvest.

Serving
🌡 12–14°C.
🍷 Tulip-shaped glass (Chardonnay type).
🍴 *Antipasti*, pasta and rice dishes based on seafood, vegetables and mushrooms. Especially recommended for toasts to peace.

Peter Dipoli

Voglar
Alto Adige DOC Sauvignon ♀

Producer
Peter Dipoli
Via Vadena 12
39055 Laives/Leifers
(Bolzano)
Tel. 0471/954227
Fax 0471/954227

Owner
Peter Dipoli

Founded
1987

Winemaker
Peter Dipoli

Vineyard manager
Peter Dipoli

Production
About 13,000 bottles
annually

Vintages
1999 1998 1997 1996

Price
● ●

Note
The DOC may be Alto
Adige or Sudtirolo in
Italian or Südtiroler in
German

Peter Dipoli was already a noted figure in wine before he became a producer. After graduating from the regional agricultural institute at San Michele all'Adige, Peter worked for years as a wine dealer and got to know the vineyards of France as well as those of Italy. He opened a wine bar, Johnson & Dipoli, at the town of Egna, consulted with restaurateurs on their cellars and fed writers inside information that made them seem like experts. Blessed with an unerring palate and a searching mind, he might have qualified as the South Tyrol's resident wine guru—except that he was rarely at home.

Then, in 1987, Peter, who came from a family of grape and apple growers, decided to return to his roots. He acquired land on steep slopes above the village of Cortaccia, where the popular red wine variety known as Vernatsch or Schiava had prevailed for ages, and promptly removed the vines trained onto picturesque pergolas. In their place, he planted Sauvignon Blanc to be trained in a low cordon method in the chalky soils that he'd noted as being similar to those found in vineyards along France's Loire Valley, where the variety reaches heights of quality.

Before planting, Peter had carefully analyzed conditions and concluded that the cool mountain terrains favored slow ripening of grapes to retain full varietal aromas and lively acidity. "My aim was to make a Sauvignon with complex tropical fruit aromas and not the vegetal traits that too often characterize the variety in Italy." The result is Voglar, an Alpine Sauvignon Blanc that could be taken for a fine Sancerre or Pouilly-Fumé.

In lower, warmer vineyards near the town of Magrè, Peter planted Merlot and Cabernet Sauvignon for a fine Bordeaux-style red called Iugum. At his new cellars at Egna, he produces just over 20,000 bottles a year of wines designed to reflect his ideals. But being his own greatest critic, the skeptical Peter knows that the best is yet to come.

Alto Adige

Grapes
Sauvignon Blanc 100%,
hand picked in late
September or early
October.

Vineyards
Plots of 0.8 hectare
owned and 1.6 hectares
leased in chalky soils of
sandy lime with a heavy
concentration of
dolomite on slopes facing
east, northeast and south
at 550–600 meters of
altitude at Penon in the
commune of
Cortaccia/Kurtatsch in
the southwestern part of
the South Tyrolean
Unterland. The vines
were planted between
1988 and 1991 at
densities of 5,000–7,000
per hectare depending on
the slope grade and
trained in the Guyot
cordon method.

Vinification and aging
Grapes are soft crushed
and the musts are
separated from the skins
and fermented at 22°C
for about 10 days,
partially in stainless steel
tanks and partially in
large acacia wood casks.
The wine, of about
12.5% alcohol, matures
on the lees in the same
containers until May,
when it is bottled and
cellared until release in
September.

Style and maturity
Voglar Sauvignon on release
about a year after the harvest
shows pale yellow color with
greenish highlights and ample
aroma marked by scents
reminiscent of tropical fruits,
spices and acacia blossoms
with a hint of smoky gunflint.
Flavors are fresh and
harmonious in a wine of
smooth texture with ripe fruit
sensations offset by vital
acidity that provides a palate-
cleansing finish. At a prime in
2–3 years, the wine has the
structure to hold style for a
few years beyond.

Serving
🌡 12°C.
🍷 Tulip-shaped glass
(Sauvignon type).
🍽 Asparagus with butter and
grated Parmigiano;
spaghetti *con le vongole*
(small clams); turbot with
tomato, eggplant and basil
sauce.

Girolamo Dorigo

Vigneto Ronc di Juri
Colli Orientali del Friuli DOC
Chardonnay ♀

Producer
Azienda Agricola
Girolamo Dorigo
Via del Pozzo 5
33042 Buttrio (Udine)
Tel. 0432/674268
Fax 0432/673373
girdorig@tin.it

Owner
Girolamo Dorigo

Founded
1966

Winemaker
Roberto Cipresso

Vineyard manager
Marco Simonit

Production
About 10,000 bottles
a year

Vintages
1999 1998 1997 1996
1990

Price
● ●

Girolamo Dorigo left his insurance business in 1966 to devote himself full time to wine with the purchase of two vineyards: Ronc di Juri at Buttrio and Montsclapade at Premariacco in the Colli Orientali del Friuli zone.

His aim was to elevate wines from Friuli's native vines to new levels of class, which he has succeeded in doing. But a fascination with the wines of France prompted frequent trips to Bordeaux, Burgundy and beyond. He planted Cabernet, Chardonnay, Merlot, the Pinots and Sauvignon at greater density than was usual for Friuli, while continuing to cultivate a full array of native vines with such meticulous care that his vineyards resemble manicured gardens.

Girolamo's son Alessio has joined the quest for perfection. Their practices of severe pruning, heavy thinning of grape bunches and rigid harvest selection result in extremely low yields and wines of remarkable concentration. They are just as diligent in the cellars, where the arrival of Roberto Cipresso as consulting enologist has hailed a contemplated return to traditional practices, such as fermenting red wines in open wooden casks instead of stainless steel vats. As they explain: "Modern methods can make a wine that is technically perfect but lacking soul."

From 30 hectares of vines, they produce 120,000–150,000 bottles a year of wines about equally divided between Friulian and French varieties. Worthy natives are red Pignolo, Refosco, Schioppettino and Tazzelenghe and white Ribolla Gialla, Tocai Friulano, Verduzzo and Picolit from grapes dried after the harvest. But their most admired wines have a French connection: the red Montsclapade, from Cabernets Sauvignon and Franc with Merlot, and Chardonnay Ronc di Juri.

The rise of Ronc di Juri to rank among Italy's top Chardonnays illustrates the Dorigo spirit. From the difficult 1998 vintage, the wine was fermented and aged for months in new barrels of French oak, but only half was deemed worthy of the final blend. Needless to say, that half had soul.

Grapes
Chardonnay 100%, hand picked when very ripe at intervals in mid- to late September.

Vineyard
A plot of 2.8 hectares in marly soils known as *flysch di Cormons* on low slopes at 124 meters of altitude in the Ronc di Juri vineyard in the commune of Buttrio at the southeastern edge of the Colli Orientali del Friuli zone. The vines, of an average age of 16 years, are planted at a density of 8,600 per hectare and trained in the Guyot cordon system.

Vinification and aging
Grapes are soft crushed and the musts decanted spontaneously over 12 hours and pumped to new barrels of French oak to ferment at 18–22°C for about 10 days. Malolactic fermentation follows in the same barriques, where the wine on the lees for 10–11 months is stirred periodically in what is known as *bâtonnage*. Each barrel must be judged worthy of the final blend of a wine of about 14% alcohol that is bottled and cellared for 10–12 months before release.

Style and maturity
Ronc di Juri Chardonnay on release in the second year after the harvest has bright straw yellow color with golden highlights and rich aromas reminiscent of ripe peaches with hints of spice and vanilla. Amply structured and round in texture, flavors of ripe fruit linger on the palate in a long, smooth finish that brings out the mellow, warm qualities of the wine. Prime drinking is normally from 3–5 years, though top vintages can remain splendid beyond.

Serving
🍷 12–15°C.
🍷 Ample glass (Burgundy type).
🍽 *Foie gras; zotui* (baby cuttlefish) with white polenta; filet of sea bass with wild mushrooms.

Livio Felluga

Terre Alte
Colli Orientali del Friuli DOC
Rosazzo Bianco

Producer
Livio Felluga
Via Risorgimento 1
34070 Brazzano di
Cormons (Gorizia)
Tel. 0481/60203
Fax 0481/630126
info@liviofelluga.it
www.liviofelluga.it

Owner
Livio Felluga and family

Founded
1956

Winemakers
Stefano Chioccioli and
Lorenzo Regoli

Vineyard managers
Daniele Cocetta with
Stefano Chioccioli

Production
About 60,000 bottles in
favorable years

Vintages
1999 1998 1997 1996
1995 1993 1992 1990
1989

Price
● ● ●

Livio Felluga in his late eighties might be considered the grand old man of Friulian winemakers, except that in spirit he seems to be among the youngest. The secret to his perennial youth may lie in his inquisitive mind and lively sense of humor and the fact that he works with his children Maurizio, Elda and Andrea in the winery that he founded in 1956 at Brazzano on the edge of the town of Cormons.

Livio grew up in a family of vintners from Isola d'Istria (now in Slovenia) and, like his younger brother Marco (owner of Russiz Superiore – see page 154), acquired vineyards in the hills of Friuli in the 1950s and 1960s. In those days wines weren't identified as DOC, so Livio, to express his love of the land, put an antique map on his labels to indicate the place of origin. The map remains the symbol of one of Italy's most admired estates with a production of about 700,000 bottles a year exclusively from 135 hectares of vineyards in the Collio and Colli Orientali del Friuli zones.

Livio's early favorites were Pinot Grigio, which he made in the mellow old style called *ramato* in reference to its coppery color, and Picolit, Friuli's legendary sweet wine. But, as he acquired choice vineyards in such places as Ruttars, Oleis and Rosazzo, the range expanded to cover white and red wines from native and foreign vines. The prime wine is Terre Alte, a blend of Tocai, Pinot Bianco and Sauvignon inspired by Livio's son Maurizio in 1982, when he was starting out as sales manager. The name refers to the high terrains of Rosazzo, a special subdistrict in the Colli Orientali del Friuli DOC zone.

Terre Alte seems to have risen another step in stature after the arrival of Stefano Chioccioli as winemaker, though the entire range of Livio Felluga wines are noted for style and personality. Varietals under Colli Orientali del Friuli DOC are Tocai Friulano, Pinot Grigio, Sauvignon, Pinot Bianco (Illivio), Refosco del Peduncolo Rosso and an outstanding Picolit Riserva, as well as Rosazzo Rosso (Sossò).

Friuli-Venezia Giulia

Grapes
Tocai Friulano, Pinot Bianco, Sauvignon Blanc in about equal parts, hand picked in late September.

Vineyards
Various plots of about 8 hectares in crumbly marl and sandstone soils (known locally as *ponca*) on slopes oriented toward the west at 60–80 meters of altitude at Rosazzo in the commune of Manzano in the southern part of the Colli Orientali del Friuli zone. The vines, of an average age of 21 years, are planted at a density of 5,000 per hectare and trained in the Guyot cordon method.

Vinification and aging
Grapes are stemmed and soft crushed and the musts are macerated briefly with the skins before fermenting in stainless steel tanks at 19°C for 15 days. The wine, of about 13.5% alcohol, remains on the lees in tanks for a time without undergoing malolactic fermentation before being bottled and cellared for at least a year until release. Starting in 1999, part of the Tocai was matured for 8 months in barrels undergoing malolactic fermentation.

Style and maturity
Terre Alte on release in the second year after the harvest has bright straw yellow color and ample aroma in which scents reminiscent of ripe peaches, honey, blossoms and sage can be detected. Flavors are soft and round in a wine of fine balance with a bracing vein of acidity to heighten sensations of fruit and nuts evident in a long, smooth finish. At a prime after 2–3 years, the wine can remain elegant for a decade.

Serving
🍷 12–15°C.
🍷 Tulip-shaped glass (Chardonnay type).
🍽 *Boreto alla graisana* (Grado fish soup), risotto with wild hops and an herb called *sclopit;* sea bass baked in a crust.

Ferrari
Fratelli Lunelli

Giulio Ferrari
Riserva del Fondatore
Talento Trento DOC

Producer
Ferrari Fratelli Lunelli
Via del Ponte di Ravina
15
38040 Trento
Tel. 0461/972311
Fax 0461/913008
info@cantineferrari.it
www.cantineferrari.it

Owner
Lunelli family

Founded
1902

Chief winemaker
Mauro Lunelli

Vineyard manager
Marcello Lunelli

Production
About 35,000 bottles in
vintage years

Vintages
1992 1991 1990 1989
1988 1986 1985 1983
1982 1980 1979

Price
● ● ● ●

Giulio Ferrari, born in 1879 when Trento was part of the Austro-Hungarian Empire, studied viticulture in France, where he learned the secrets of Champagne. He knew that Trento's sunny Alpine climate could favor sparkling wine production and on his return home in 1902 planted vines from Champagne on his family's terraced slopes.

The first release of Ferrari "Champagne" (as it could be called then) amounted to about a thousand bottles, though a similar quantity was discarded as he adapted the *méthode champenoise*. Ferrari was a perfectionist who considered winemaking an art, evident in his high prices and the prizes won in competitions around the world. By 1952, production had reached 8,800 bottles, but supply was running so far behind demand that Ferrari decided to sell to Bruno Lunelli, who had a wine bar in Trento.

Lunelli borrowed money to build the business, offering top prices to growers to supply him with Chardonnay. Giulio Ferrari continued for a time as the maestro behind Italy's most prestigious sparkling wines. Production had reached 100,000 bottles by 1969, when Bruno Lunelli turned over the business to his five children, including Franco and Gino, the managers, and Mauro, winemaker. Ferrari Fratelli Lunelli has since built modern cellars on the edge of Trento while building the output to 4.3 million bottles a year, all qualified as Talento Trento DOC for *metodo classico* sparkling wines.

The range takes in Brut, Maximum Brut, Rosé, Demi-Sec, Perlè Brut and Perlè Rosé. The prestigious cuvée is Giulio Ferrari Riserva del Fondatore, a *blanc de blancs* (pure Chardonnay) conceived in 1972 in homage to the founder. The wine remains on the yeasts in bottle for at least 8 years, a practice generally reserved for top Champagnes that explains its extraordinary finesse and longevity.

Lunelli also makes still wines from estates under Trentino DOC: Chardonnay (Villa Margon and Villa Gentilotti), Sauvignon (Villa San Nicolò), Pinot Nero (Maso Montalto) and Rosso (Maso Le Viane).

Trentino

Grapes
Chardonnay 100%, hand picked in late September.

Vineyard
Maso Pianizza covering about 10 hectares in soils of sand, gravel and calcareous clays on slopes facing south-southwest at 500–550 meters of altitude near the city of Trento. Vines, of an average age of 16 years, are planted at a density of 4,500 per hectare and trained in the trellised pergola *trentina* system.

Vinification and aging
Grapes are soft crushed and the free-run musts fermented with selected yeasts at about 19°C for 12 days in stainless steel vats. A partial malolactic fermentation is induced with select bacteria. The cuvée is assembled and the *tirage* of cane sugar and select yeasts is added to the wine that remains in bottle for at least 8 years before hand riddling and disgorging. The wine, of about 12% alcohol, receives a *liqueur d'expédition* before being cork sealed and cellared until release.

Style and maturity
Giulio Ferrari Riserva del Fondatore on release about 9 years after the vintage has bright straw color with golden highlights and vivacious *perlage* in steady streams of fine bubbles. The bouquet is deep with the elegant Chardonnay fruit mingling with hints of honey, vanilla, yeasts and spices. On the palate it is round and harmonious with ripe fruit flavors underlined by sensations reminiscent of honey, flowers and spices as the finish becomes increasingly long and velvety over 10–15 years or more.

Serving
🌡 9–10°C, after 20 minutes in an ice bucket.
🍷 Tall, ample flute (vintage Champagne type).
🍽 *Antipasti* based on shellfish, eggs and vegetables; charcoal-grilled scampi; it makes a fine aperitif.

Gini

Contrada Salvarenza Vecchie Vigne Soave Classico Superiore DOC ♀

Producer
Azienda Agricola Gini
Via G. Matteotti 42
37032 Monteforte
d'Alpone (Verona)
Tel. 045/7611908
Fax 045/6101610

Owners
Sandro and Claudio
Gini

Founded
1980

Winemaker
Sandro Gini

Vineyard manager
Sandro Gini

Production
About 15,000 bottles
annually

Vintages
1999 1998 1997 1995
1993 1990

Price
● ●

The familiarity of Soave as a contemporary white tends to obscure the fact that it has a rather dignified history that dates back to the ancient Romans, who supposedly traded its wines around the Mediterranean. The town of Soave got its name from the Swabians, a Germanic people who settled there in the sixth century and probably started building the landmark castle that was completed by the Della Scala lords in the Middle Ages.

In modern times, Soave earned a reputation as *the* fish wine of Venice, though that, in turn, led to rampant popularity and the mass production that tarnished the image.

The new generation of Soave producers might prefer to forget the legends and get on with meeting the considerable challenge of making world-class white wine from the native Garganega variety, sometimes blended with a bit of Chardonnay. Brothers Sandro and Claudio Gini are in the vanguard of the Soave revolution, yet they look back with pride to 1852 when their ancestor Giuseppe Gini bought a vineyard at a place called Salvarenza, where the family apparently had land as early as the 1700s.

The advantage of having some of the oldest vineyards of Soave Classico is evident in the depth of aromas and flavors of their Contrada Salvarenza Vecchie Vigne, made from very ripe grapes from vines planted on the slopes of Monte Froscà 60 years ago. Yet Sandro, the winemaker, uses thoroughly progressive techniques, fermenting the wine in barrels of French oak and leaving it on the lees for months to attain dimensions and aging capacity that are extraordinary for Soave. A close rival is their Soave Classico Superiore La Froscà, from slightly younger vines.

From 25 hectares of vineyards, the Gini brothers make about 150,000 bottles a year, including a regular DOC Soave Classico Superiore, fine DOC Recioto di Soave (Col Foscarin and Renobilis) and Veneto IGT Chardonnay (Sorai), Sauvignon (Maciete Fumé) and Pinot Nero (Campo alle More).

Veneto

Grapes
Garganega 90% and Chardonnay, hand picked in late October.

Vineyard
Salvarenza, a plot of 4 hectares in volcanic tufaceous soils on a base of white calcareous stone on slopes of Monte Froscà facing southeast at 150 meters of altitude in the commune of Monteforte d'Alpone in the southeastern part of the Soave Classico zone. Vines, of an average age of 60 years, are planted at a density of 4,000 per hectare and trained in the traditional pergola *veronese* method.

Vinification and aging
Grapes are soft crushed and the musts macerated briefly with the skins before being chilled to precipitate solid matter and fermented at 16–18°C for about 20 days in 228-liter capacity barrels of French oak from Allier, Tronçais and Vosges. Malolactic fermentation is induced if deemed beneficial during 9 months of maturing on the lees in barrels (half new, half used once). The wine, of about 13.5% alcohol, is bottled without filtering and cellared for 6 months before release.

Style and maturity
Soave Classico Superiore Contrada Salvarenza Vecchie Vigne on release in the second year after the harvest has deep straw yellow color with green-gold highlights and richly complex aromas reminiscent of ripe peaches and pineapple with hints of cinnamon, almonds and vanilla. On the palate, it is ripe and round with mellow fruit qualities supported by a vein of acidity that adds vivacity to the long, smooth finish. The wine approaches a prime at 3–5 years, but retains class for a decade or more.

Serving
🌡 12–14°C.
🍷 Medium tulip-shaped glass (Chardonnay type).
🍽 *Bigoli* noodles with *granseola* (spider crab); risotto with scampi and zucchini flowers; pheasant braised with raisins and spices.

Ribolla Gialla
Collio DOC ♀

Producer
Azienda Agricola Josko
Gravner
Via Lenzuolo Bianco 9
34070 Oslavia (Gorizia)
Tel. 0481/30882
Fax 0481/30882

Owner
Josko Gravner

Founded
1901

Winemakers
Josko Gravner with
Marco Simonit

Vineyard managers
Josko Gravner with
Marco Simonit

Production
Not disclosed

Vintages
1998 1997 1995 1994
1993

Price
● ● ●

Francesco (Josko) Gravner recently wrote a book recounting his life in wine. The album, in Italian and Slovenian, which Josko or Joško uses with equal fluency, is a heartfelt account by a winemaker of profound conviction.

It opens with an anecdote that says more about the man than anything I could compose. He writes of a rainy summer day, years ago, when the grapes were turning color. Suddenly a hailstorm struck, a "wall of ice", as he puts it. As he cursed the heavens and the toils of a farmer, his old uncle Franc told him calmly: "Joško, nature gives us all that we have. At times it has the right to take something away." "That day I understood," he recalls, "and that's where my story began."

The Gravner family has been farming for three centuries at Oslavia, a village in the hills above Gorizia on the border of Slovenia, though the estate's first bottled wines date to 1973. After 1977, when Josko took charge, his Chardonnay and Sauvignon showed splendid fruit sensations in vital aromas and flavors to rank with Italy's finest.

In the 1990s, as he planted vines at higher densities and lower yields, Josko began using open oak vats exclusively for fermentation at natural temperatures and extended aging of wines in large barrels to three years. His whites assumed uncommon stature and, like Josko, uncompromising character. They are sometimes criticized as laden with oak and lacking fruit and acidity, but they endure as monuments to the integrity of a man who has strongly influenced others.

Josko, who is experimenting with fermentation and aging in terracotta *amphorae*, now limits his wines to four: Rosso Gravner and Rujno (both based on Cabernets and Merlot), Breg (a blend of Sauvignon, Chardonnay, Pinot Grigio and Riesling Italico) and Ribolla Gialla. He admits that it took him 20 years to understand an antique vine so stubborn that it needs to be tamed little by little. As others make their marks with varieties of familiar names and flavors, Josko with stubborn courage advocates the uniqueness of Ribolla.

Friuli-Venezia Giulia

Grapes
Ribolla Gialla 100%,
hand picked in October.

Vineyards
Grapes are selected in
various plots in crumbly
marl and sandstone soils
(known as *ponca*) on
slopes oriented toward
the south at about 150
meters of altitude at
Oslavia in the commune
of Gorizia in the eastern
part of the Collio zone.
The vines, some between
30 and 60 years old, are
planted at densities of
4,000–10,000 or more
per hectare and trained in
the arched Cappuccina
and Guyot cordon
methods and recently in
the head-trained *alberello*.

Vinification and aging
Grapes are crushed and
the musts ferment on the
skins for 5–12 days in
open-topped oak vats at
natural temperatures and
without the use of
selected yeast cultures,
followed by 3 years of
aging in large oak casks,
during which time
malolactic fermentation
occurs. The wine, of
about 12% alcohol, is
bottled without
clarification or filtering.

Style and maturity
Gravner Ribolla Gialla on
release about 3 years after the
harvest has deep straw yellow
color with golden highlights
and subdued aromas with
scents reminiscent of ripe
peaches, dried apricots and
hints of vanilla and caramel
from the oak. The initial
impact on the palate is rather
stark and dry, though when
held on the tongue, warm, soft
flavors emerge with a certain
sweetness that remains
through the finish. The wine
seems to need years more to
round into form, though the
producer vows that it will
improve with time.

Serving
🌡 14–16°C.
🍷 Medium-sized glass
(Sauvignon type).
🍽 *Jota* (rich bean, potato and
sauerkraut soup); *cjalçons*
(pasta envelopes with a
sweet-sour squash filling);
spicy fish soups.

Kolbenhof
Alto Adige DOC
Gewürztraminer ♀

Producer
Vigneti-Cantina
Vini J. Hofstätter
Piazza Municipio 5
39041 Termeno
(Bolzano)
Tel. 0471/860161
Fax 0471/860789
hofstätter@
hofstätter.com
www.hofstätter.com

Owner
Foradori Hofstätter
family

Founded
1907

Winemakers
Martin Foradori, Franz
Oberhofer and Martin
Lemayr

Vineyard managers
Martin Foradori and
Hansjörg Weis

Production
About 40,000 bottles
from choice years

Vintages
1999 1998 1997 1995
1993 1990 1989 1987

Price
● ●

Note
The DOC may be Alto
Adige or Sudtirolo in
Italian or Südtiroler in
German

Winemakers of Alto Adige (the South Tyrol or Südtirol in the native German) will tell you that Gewürztraminer takes its name from the village of Tramin (Termeno in Italian). But that is only half of the story, according to the English author Jancis Robinson. She explains that Traminer was the original vine that produced grapes with pale green skins at Tramin around AD 1000, but that the variety found its way to the Rhine valley where it mutated into a version with dark pink berries that made wine of greater color, body and aroma. *Gewürz*, which means spiced or perfumed in German, was prefixed, and Gewürztraminer became the official name in Alsace, where its wines reach heights of opulence.

The superior mutation eventually returned to Italy, where it is called Traminer Aromatico and is often confused with its common cousin Traminer. Even at Tramin, where true Gewürztraminer gained the upper hand, the wine tended to be freshly fruity and fragrant but decidedly dainty. A turning point came in the mid-1980s, when comparative tastings with Alsatian Gewürz blew the local lightweights away, as witnesses recall.

From the 1987 vintage, Paolo Foradori, head of the Josef Hofstätter winery, began selecting grapes from the venerable Kolbenhof vineyard at the village of Söll (Sella) overlooking Tramin to make a wine of greater substance. Through the 1990s, as his son Martin joined the effort, Kolbenhof has gained not only weight but depth and affluence of aromas and flavors to stand with the most stylish of Gewürztraminers. Still, as Paolo points out with a trace of hometown pride, the Gewürz of Tramin has character traits that differentiate it from Alsatians.

Hofstätter produces about 650,000 bottles a year of Alto Adige DOC wines, ranging through varieties as diverse as Lagrein, Chardonnay, Schiava (or Vernatsch), Cabernet, Riesling, Pinot Grigio and Pinot Nero (for Barthenau Vigna Sant'Urbano, described on page 144).

Alto Adige

Grapes
Gewürztraminer 100%, hand picked in the 2nd week of October.

Vineyard
Kolbenhof, a plot of about 6 hectares in gravelly calcareous clay soils on terraced slopes at 390 meters of altitude at the locality of Söll (Sella) in the commune of Tramin (Termeno) on the western side of the Adige valley 23 kilometers southwest of Bolzano. Vines, of an average age of 46 years, are planted at densities of 4,000–6,500 per hectare and trained in the traditional pergola (70%) and Guyot cordon system.

Vinification and aging
Grapes are soft crushed and separated from the skins and the musts ferment at about 20°C for 8–10 days in stainless steel tanks. Malolactic fermentation takes place naturally, followed by maturation for about 6 months in part in tanks and part in large casks of Slavonian oak. The wine, of about 13.5% alcohol, is bottled and cellared for a time before release.

Style and maturity
Kolbenhof Gewürztraminer on release in the year after the harvest has deep straw yellow color with old gold highlights and opulent aroma with scents reminiscent of mountain roses and tropical fruit accented by spicy, vaguely smoky notes. Full and round on the palate, its rich fruit sensations (lychee, pineapple) are buoyed by a vein of acidity in a long, smooth finish with a hint of almond at the end. Impressive after a year or 2, the wine gains mellow elegance for a decade or more.

Serving
- 12–13°C.
- Tulip-shaped glass (Alsatian type)
- Wild salmon, braised or grilled; turbot in cream sauce; liver pâté; raw oysters; Thai cuisine.

Inama

Vulcaia Après
Vino da Tavola Dolce ♀

Producer
Azienda Agricola Inama
Via IV Novembre 1
37047 San Bonifacio
(Verona)
Tel. 045/6104343
Fax 045/6131979
inama@inama
aziendaagricola.it
www.inamaazienda
agricola.it

Owner
Giuseppe Inama

Founded
1991

Winemakers
Giuseppe and Stefano
Inama

Vineyard manager
Stefano Inama

Production
About 1,200 bottles and
6,000 half bottles (0.375
liter) in favorable years

Vintages
1998 1997 1995 1992

Price
● ● ●

I nama emerged in the 1990s as a new phenomenon of Soave, though, as it turns out, the reputation had been decades in the making. Giuseppe Inama, who had a farm at San Bonifacio in the plains, bought vineyards in the hills of Soave Classico in the 1960s, long before prices became prohibitive. His main acquisition was 25 hectares at Monte Foscarino, now recognized as one of Soave's leading sites.

It wasn't until 1991, when his son Stefano took charge, that the wines of Inama were sold in bottles. From 30 hectares of vines, the estate now produces some 250,000 bottles a year of wines that range beyond Soave. Stefano, known for his bold ambitions and passion for experiments, has shown enviable skill with the native Garganega in Soave Classico Vigneti di Foscarino and Vigneto du Lot, both oak fermented. He has also succeeded admirably with Chardonnay, in Campo dei Tovi, and Cabernet Sauvignon, in Bradisismo.

But his first love seems to be Sauvignon Blanc, which he produces in two versions: the dry Vulcaia Fumé and the sweet Vulcaia Après. When he planted the vines on Monte Foscarino, he tried different clones and training methods before deciding on the Geneva double curtain devised in America. Stefano depends on low yields and late harvesting of concentrated grapes for wines whose personalities express the nature of their terroirs. He credits the distinct floral and mineral notes of his Sauvignons to the volcanic soils that explain the Vulcaia in both names.

Although Vulcaia Fumé recalls the smoky aspects attributed to Pouilly-Fumé, the overall style seems closer to that of an oak-matured white Bordeaux. Vulcaia Après (French for "after" in reference to late harvesting or after-dinner sipping) may have points in common with Sauternes in aroma and flavor, though its graceful sweetness makes it much more refreshing to drink.

Veneto

Grapes

Sauvignon Blanc 100%, hand picked when very ripe in mid-October.

Vineyards

Grapes are selected from plots of about 3.5 hectares in basalt soils of volcanic origin on slopes oriented south-southwest at 150 meters of altitude at Monte Foscarino in the Soave Classico zone in the commune of Monteforte d'Alpone. Vines, of an average age of 11 years, are planted at a density of 4,500 per hectare and trained in the Geneva double curtain system in which two parallel cordons are trained downward in twin canopies.

Vinification and aging

The late-harvested grapes are crushed and the musts macerate with the skins for about 3 hours before being cold stabilized for 24–36 hours and fermented for about a week at 15°C, in part in small barrels of French oak (part new and part used once). After racking and filtration, the wine, of 12.5% alcohol with about 12% of residual sugar, matures in barriques for 9 months before being bottled and cellared for about 6 months until release.

Style and maturity

Vulcaia Après on release in the second year after the harvest has bright straw yellow color with golden highlights and intense aromas with scents reminiscent of citrus blossoms, tropical fruit and spices with an underlying smoky gunflint aspect. On the palate, it is cleanly sweet with round, mellow qualities and rich fruit sensations braced by refreshing acidity in flavors of impressive depth and length. Though attractive from the start, the wine promises to retain class for a decade or more.

Serving

🌡 10–12°C.

🍷 Medium-sized glass with narrow top.

🍽 Aged cheeses, such as Monte Veronese d'Allevo or Asiago with honey; Venetian sweets, such as *fregolotta*, *crema fritta* and *zaleti*.

204

Vinnaioli Jermann

Vintage Tunina
Venezia Giulia IGT ♀

Producer
Vinnaioli Jermann
Via Monte Fortino 21
34070 Villanova di Farra
(Gorizia)
Tel. 0481/888080
Fax 0481/888512

Owner
Silvio Jermann

Founded
In 1881, when the
Jermann family arrived
from Austria

Winemaker
Silvio Jermann

Vineyard manager
Silvio Jermann

Production
50,000–60,000 bottles a
year

Vintages
1999 1998 1997 1996
1995 1990 1989

Price

When, in 1975, Silvio Jermann concocted a curious blend of grapes from a vineyard in the Collio zone of Friuli-Venezia Giulia, he had no idea that Vintage Tunina was to become Italy's most acclaimed white wine of the twentieth century. Silvio had begun to make the single-varietal whites that were building Collio's reputation, but the creative young man aspired to something unique. The memory of his grandfather making wines from field blends of various grapes inspired Vintage Tunina.

The components seemed oddly incongruous: Sauvignon Blanc and Chardonnay with the native Ribolla Gialla, Malvasia Istriana and Picolit. Still, even though they mature at different times with varying degrees of sugar and acidity and make wines of diverse personalities, Silvio found that when picked very ripe they complemented each other in the blend.

The nickname Tunina (for Antonia) belonged to the previous owner of the vineyard, as well as to the housekeeper who became Casanova's lover. Silvio, who likes romantic names, prefixed Vintage for a ring of authority in English.

Vintage Tunina was conceived as a creature of cold steel and remains so. Yet it has weight, depth, complexity, a rare capacity to age, and, like all Vinnaioli Jermann wines, is deliciously easy to drink. No other Italian white wine has accumulated the critical praise and decorations that have been lavished on Vintage Tunina. Yet Silvio takes honors in his stride as he strives in his quietly intense way to bring all of his wines closer to perfection.

From 67 hectares of vines, the Jermann *vinnaioli* (grape growers) produce about 400,000 bottles a year, taking in a full array of varietals and blends, mostly white, but also reds, some finished in oak. Most would qualify as Collio DOC, but Silvio avoids the appellation. Highlights are Dreams (oak-fermented Chardonnay once known as "Where the Dreams Have no End..."), the intricate white blends of Capo Martino and Vinnae and the red Pignacolusse (Pignolo) and Red Angel (Pinot Nero).

Friuli-Venezia Giulia

Grapes
Sauvignon Blanc and Chardonnay with Ribolla Gialla, Malvasia Istriana and Picolit (percentages vary from year to year), hand picked in late September.

Vineyards
Grapes are selected from 2 plots covering 12 hectares in crumbly marl and sandstone soils on slopes tapering from southwest to northeast at 100–120 meters of altitude on Monte Fortino, the isolated rise in the Isonzo valley that is the southernmost sector of the Collio DOC zone. The vines, of an average age of 16 years, are planted at densities of 5,000–6,000 per hectare and trained in the *cappuccina* arched double cordon system.

Vinification and aging
Grapes are soft crushed and separated from skins and stalks and the musts fermented with indigenous yeasts for 40–50 days at 14–16°C in stainless steel tanks. Malolactic fermentation occurs naturally as the wine, of about 13% alcohol, remains on the lees in tanks for 8–10 months before being bottled and cellared for 3 months until release.

Style and maturity
Vintage Tunina on release in the second year after the harvest has brilliant straw yellow color with golden glints and elaborate aromas with scents reminiscent of acacia blossoms, ripe peaches, tropical fruit, herbs and spices. On the palate, it is full and round with fresh fruit sensations heightened by an acidic vein that mellows through a long finish as elements come together in perfect harmony. Time brings out the depth and complexity of a wine that reaches a vital prime in 6–8 years but continues to reveal its majesty well beyond a decade.

Serving
- 12–14°C.
- Tulip-shaped glass (Chardonnay type).
- *Antipasti* and pasta dishes with crustaceans and mollusks; freshwater crayfish with aromatic herbs; rabbit braised with white wine and tarragon.

Lehenhof
Alto Adige DOC
Terlaner Sauvignon ♀

Producer
Alois Lageder Tenuta
Löwengang
39040 Magrè/Margreid
(Bolzano)
Tel. 0471/809500
Fax 0471/809550
info@lageder.com
www.lageder.com

Owner
Alois Lageder

Founded
1855

Chief winemaker
Luis von Dellemann

Vineyard supervisor
Alois Lageder

Production
7,000–10,000 bottles
annually

Vintages
1999 1997 1995 1991

Price
● ●

Alois Lageder, whose great-grandfather of the same name founded the cellars at Bolzano in 1855, personifies the new vibrancy in Alto Adige's once staid wine community. The cheery red wines that represent the bulk of the South Tyrol's production are still shipped to nearby Austria, Switzerland and Germany. But in the 1980s, Alois fashioned a formidable range of modern wines led by single-vineyard and estate selections and pioneered premium markets in the rest of Italy and abroad.

Alois, who works with his sister Wendelgard and her husband Luis von Dellemann, the chief enologist, has renovated the Löwengang estate at Magrè as an ecological winery. Systems rely on solar energy and natural gravity flow. The philosophical Alois explains that they don't think so much in terms of producing wines as educating them in the cellars after helping nature to provide the healthiest of grapes.

The winery owns 17 hectares of choice vineyards and has contracts with growers with another 130 hectares to produce about a million bottles a year. These cover a complete range of Alto Adige DOCs, divided into classics, single-vineyard and estate wines. Space doesn't permit a complete review of the 28 wines, so I'll single out some favorites.

The stylish Löwengang Chardonnay was the first white of Alto Adige to be fermented and matured in barrels of French oak—a practice criticized by competitors who later followed suit. The Römigberg estate produces a zesty red Caldaro and a splendid Cabernet Sauvignon called Cor Römigberg. Exemplary varietals are the single-vineyard Pinot Grigio Benefizium Porer, Pinot Bianco Haberlehof and Sauvignon Lehenhof. The Lehenhof vineyard above the town of Terlano has produced Sauvignon of marked character since 1974, though recently it seems to have taken on a new touch of elegance due to a final rounding out in massive oak casks.

Alois Lageder also own Casòn Hirschprunn, an estate in Magrè with 32 hectares of vineyards for blends of premium reds and whites.

Alto Adige

Grapes
Sauvignon Blanc 100%,
hand picked in the
second half of September.

Vineyard
Lehenhof, a plot of 2
hectares in medium-
textured volcanic
porphyritic soils on a
slope facing south at
400–500 meters of
altitude at Montigl in the
commune of Terlano
along the Adige valley
between Bolzano and
Merano. The vines,
ranging in age from
11–44 years, are planted
at a density of 2,700 per
hectare and trained in the
trellised pergola system.

Vinification and aging
Grapes are soft crushed
and the musts are
separated from the skins
and fermented at 18°C
for about 3 weeks in
stainless steel tanks.
Malolactic fermentation
occurs during 5 months
on the lees in stainless
steel tanks, followed by 4
months of rounding out
in large casks of
Slavonian oak. The wine,
of about 12.5% alcohol,
is bottled and cellared for
a year before release.

Style and maturity
Lehenhof Terlaner Sauvignon
on release in the second year
after the harvest shows pale
yellow color with greenish
highlights and ample aroma
marked by scents reminiscent
of tropical fruit, spices and
sage. Flavors are clean and
harmonious with fresh fruit
sensations offset by vital
acidity in a wine of full
structure with a long, smooth
finish. After reaching an
aromatic peak in about 3
years, the wine retains mellow
complexity for at least 3 years
beyond.

Serving
🍷 12–14°C.
🍸 Tulip-shaped glass
(Sauvignon type).
🍽 *Antipasti* based on seafood
and vegetables; asparagus
with butter and grated
Parmigiano; grilled prawns;
dishes based on poultry or
rabbit.

Lis Neris

Producer
Azienda Agricola
Lis Neris
Via Gavinana 5
34070 San Lorenzo
Isontino (Gorizia)
Tel. 0481/80105
Fax 0481/809592
lisneris@lisneris.it
www.lisneris.it

Owner
Alvaro Pecorari

Founded
1879

Winemaker
Alvaro Pecorari

Vineyard manager
Alvaro Pecorari

Production
About 10,000 bottles a
year

Vintages
1999 1998 1996

Price
● ●

Dom Picol
Friuli Isonzo DOC
Sauvignon ♀

When, not long ago, the hills of Collio Goriziano and Colli Orientali del Friuli emanated as Italy's new sanctuary of white wine, the plain to the south formed by the Isonzo river was still considered red wine territory. But, as demand for whites grew, producers in the gravelly flatlands planted Chardonnay, Sauvignon Blanc and other chic varieties that launched Friuli Isonzo as a full-fledged rival of the hill zones.

A prime mover of the reformation was Alvaro Pecorari, who in the 1980s took over the farm that had been in his family since 1879. Although trained as an architect, Alvaro quickly mastered the vintner's craft, buying vineyards and renovating cellars as part of his grand design. He changed the estate name to Lis Neris, after the first vineyard planted by his ancestors, now the source of a red wine from Merlot and Cabernet that seems to be his personal favorite.

To my taste, the white wines of Lis Neris are every bit as impressive. At the top is the Friuli Isonzo DOC triumvirate of Gris (Pinot Grigio), St. Jurosa (Chardonnay) and Dom Picol (Sauvignon), selections fermented in oak. They are all round and mellow with uncommon depth of aromas and flavors, though the ultimate class of each depends on the fortunes of the vintage. If forced to pick one, it would have to be Dom Picol, a wine that over the years has proved the merits of Sauvignon Blanc on what have come to be regarded as the privileged plains of Isonzo.

From 34 hectares of vines, Alvaro produces about 200,000 bottles a year, including a second-tier range of Friuli Isonzo varietal whites that do not go into wood but can be as satisfying to drink as the big three. He also makes two sweet wines: Confini (from late-harvested Pinot Grigio) and Tal Lûc (from Verduzzo Friulano and Riesling grapes dried after the harvest).

Friuli-Venezia Giulia

Grapes
Sauvignon Blanc 100%, hand picked in mid- to late September.

Vineyards
Grapes are selected in 3 plots—Picol, Jurosa and Gris—totaling 8.5 hectares in gravelly calcareous soils on plains at about 60 meters of altitude in the commune of San Lorenzo Isontino in the northern sector of the Friuli Isonzo zone. The vines, of an average age of 10 years, are planted at a density of 5,200 per hectare and trained in the Guyot cordon system.

Vinification and aging
Grapes are soft crushed and the musts fermented at 20–22°C for about 15 days in 500-liter barrels of French oak, where the wine remains for 9 months with occasional stirring of the lees (*bâtonnage*). The wine, of about 13% alcohol, is bottled and cellared for about 6 months until release. In certain vintages, the musts are macerated with the skins briefly before fermentation.

Style and maturity
Dom Picol Sauvignon on release in the second year after the harvest has bright straw yellow color with golden highlights and rich aromas reminiscent of ripe pears with hints of sage, honey and vanilla. Full in structure and round in texture, mellow flavors of ripe fruit are underpinned by a vein of acidity in a wine of depth and complexity with a velvety finish. At a prime at about 2 years, the wine can retain class for some time beyond.

Serving
🍷 12°C.
🍷 Tulip-shaped glass (Sauvignon type).
🍴 Risotto di Marano (with shrimp, squid and mussels); *astice* (rock lobster) in a spicy tomato sauce; roast turbot.

Livon

Braide Alte
Vino da Tavola ♀

Producer
Azienda Agricola
Livon
Via Montarezza 33
Frazione Dolegnano
33048 San Giovanni al
Natisone (Udine)
Tel. 0432/757173
Fax 0432/757690
livon@livon.it
www.livon.it

Owners
Antonino and Valneo
Livon

Founded
1964

Winemaker
Rinaldo Stocco

Vineyard manager
Elvio Zorzini

Production
About 11,000 bottles a
year

Vintages
1999 1998 1997 1996

Price
● ●

Dorino Livon used profits from his lumber business to buy vineyards in Collio and Colli Orientali del Friuli in the 1960s before those zones attained DOC status. In the 1980s, he was joined by sons Valneo and Tonino, whose acquisitions have arrived at 150 hectares, including prime sites in the hills and an extension in the plains.

Valneo and Tonino brought a change of philosophy to a house previously known more for quantity than quality, introducing wines from single vineyards managed with devotion and meticulous attention to detail. With winemaker Rinaldo Stocco, they have fashioned a series of crus that have made Livon one of the most admired names in Friuli.

The single-vineyard wines include Collio DOC Pinot Grigio Braide Grande, Chardonnay Braide Mate, Tocai Friulano Ronc di Zorz, Sauvignon Valbuins, Merlot Tiare Mate, Refosco Riûl, Cabernet Franc Arborizza and Colli Orientali DOC Verduzzo Friulano Casali Godia and Schioppettino Picotis. Two blends qualify as *vino da tavola*: Tiareblù (from Merlot and Cabernet) and Braide Alte (Chardonnay and Sauvignon Blanc with Moscato Giallo and Picolit). The Livon brothers' lofty aspirations seem best expressed in Braide Alte, a unique blend of splendidly harmonious aromas and flavors heightened by deft use of oak.

Consistent class carries over to the Livon classic line, a series of Collio and Colli Orientali DOC and Friuli Grave DOC Chardonnay, Pinot Grigio and Sauvignon from Villa Chiopris. Total production in Friuli from family vineyards is about a million bottles a year. Valneo and Tonino also own the Borgo Salcetino estate in Tuscany where they make fine Chianti Classico and a Super-Tuscan called Rossole (Sangiovese with Merlot).

Labels of the cru wines carry a design by the nineteenth-century Russian artist Erté of a mermaid whose tail forms a "C" (for Collio), though her bare breasts once brought censorship from the Bureau of Alcohol, Tobacco and Firearms, which controls U.S. wine imports.

Friuli-Venezia Giulia

Grapes
Chardonnay and Sauvignon Blanc with small and variable percentages of Moscato Giallo and Picolit, hand picked in mid-October.

Vineyards
Plots totaling 3.73 hectares in marl and clay soils on slopes at 150–200 meters of altitude in the commune of Dolegna del Collio in the northwestern part of the Collio DOC zone. The vines, of an average age of 21 years, are planted at a density of about 5,000 per hectare and trained in the double arched *cappuccina* and spurred cordon systems.

Vinification and aging
Grapes are soft crushed and macerated with the skins for 8 hours at cold temperatures before being clarified by decantation and fermented in new barrels of French oak (Allier) at 15°C. The wine, of about 13.5% alcohol, remains in the same barriques on the lees for about 8 months at constant low temperature before being assembled and bottled and then cellared for 12–15 months until release.

Style and maturity
Braide Alte on release about 2 years after the harvest has bright straw yellow color with golden highlights and full aromas reminiscent of apples and blossom with hints of nutmeg, honey and vanilla. Amply structured and richly textured, its ripe fruit flavors take on a buttery quality with suggestions of toasted nuts and bitter almond in a smooth, lingering finish. Prime drinking is normally from 3–4 years, though top vintages can remain splendid well beyond.

Serving
🍷 13–15°C.
♀ Ample glass (Burgundy type).
🍽 Pasta *alla marinara* (with shellfish and tomato sauce); eel stewed with leeks; swordfish or grouper with a tomato-herb sauce.

Maculan

Acininobili
Breganze Torcolato Riserva
DOC ♀

Producer
Azienda Agricola
Maculan
Via Castelletto 3
36042 Breganze
(Vicenza)
Tel. 0445/873733
Fax 0445/300149
maculan@netics.net
www.netics.net/maculan

Owners
Fausto and Franca
Maculan

Founded
1937

Winemakers
Fausto Maculan and
Massimo Dal Lago

Production
About 3,800 half bottles
(0.375-liter) and 200
bottles in outstanding
years

Vintages
1998 1997 1995 1991
1990 1989 1985 1983

Price
● ● ● ●

Note
Acininobili, previously
qualified as Vino Dolce
Naturale, was classified
as Breganze Torcolato
Riserva DOC starting
with the 1995 vintage

Fausto Maculan has transformed his family cellars in the town of Breganze at the foot of the Venetian Alps into a hi-tech workshop where he creates one of Italy's most brilliant arrays of contemporary wines. From 30 hectares of vines and acquisitions from growers with another 40 hectares, Maculan makes about 400,000 bottles of wine a year in 12 types, with the emphasis on varieties covered by Breganze DOC.

Over the years, the Cabernet-Merlot blend of Fratta and the Cabernet Sauvignon and Chardonnay from the Ferrata vineyards have stood out. But quality is unerring through a range that includes dry white Breganze di Breganze from Tocai and Pinots, Riale Chardonnay, Marchesante Merlot and Palazzotto Cabernet Sauvignon.

Fausto, who runs the estate with his sister Franca, is also a specialist in sweet wines, beginning with Dindarello from the Venetian variety of Moscato Fior d'Arancio. In the 1980s, he revived the local tradition of Torcolato, made from Vespaiola, Garganega and Tocai grapes dried after the harvest and aged for 18 months in small oak barrels.

Fausto's passion for sweet wines dates to his boyhood when he used to steal and eat grapes drying in the family loft. Years later, on a visit to Château d'Yquem in Sauternes, he noted that Sémillon and Sauvignon Blanc grapes infected on the vine by *Botrytis cinerea* developed larva-like veils just like some of those drying for Torcolato. In 1983, he began to select grapes shriveled by noble rot one by one from others in the bunches hanging in drying rooms. "It required the patience of a Carthusian monk," he recalls, "but the result was Acininobili."

Fausto explains that *Botrytis cinerea* penetrates the skins and evaporates liquid, lending an exquisite mellifluous quality to wines. He once described Acininobili as a phenomenal wine whose sweetness seduces without overwhelming. Among connoisseurs who agree is the French critic who called it *"L'Yquem d'Italie."*

Grapes

Vespaiola with Garganega and Tocai, hand picked in late September. Choice bunches are attached to cords draped from the ceilings of air-conditioned, ventilated drying rooms until January when grapes infected with *Botrytis cinerea* are individually selected for the wine.

Vineyards

Grapes come from plots totaling 5 hectares in volcanic tufaceous soils on slopes facing south and southwest at 100–200 meters of altitude in the communes of Breganze and Fara about 20 kilometers north of Vicenza. Vines, of 11–26 years of age, are planted at densities of 2,000–5,000 per hectare and trained in the double arched *capovolto* and spurred cordon methods.

Vinification and aging

Dried grapes are crushed and the dense musts are fermented for 3–4 weeks at 20–22°C in stainless steel tanks before maturing for 24 months in new barrels of French oak (Allier). The wine, of about 13% developed alcohol with about 15% of residual sugar, is bottled and cellared for 6 months before release.

Style and maturity

Acininobili on release in the third year after the harvest has bright golden color and elaborate bouquet with scents reminiscent of honey, raisins, figs, apricots, vanilla and spices. On the palate, it is sumptuously rich and mellifluous, yet clean and refreshing due to a vein of acidity that braces flavors of dried fruit and sweet spices through a luxuriously long finish. Seductive from the start, the wine reaches peaks after a decade and maintains style well beyond.

Serving

- 🌡 8–10°C.
- 🍷 Small tulip-shaped glass with long stem.
- 🍽 *Foie gras*; aged cheeses such as Asiago Stravecchio or ripe Gorgonzola; pastries and fruit tarts; after-dinner sipping.

Methius Brut Riserva Talento Trento DOC ♀

Producer
Azienda Vinicola
Metius
Via Romana 8
38016 Mezzocorona
(Trento)
Tel. 0461/605313
Fax 0461/605830
vini@dorigati.it
www.dorigati.it

Owners
Dorigati family and
Enrico Paternoster

Founded
1986

Winemakers
Carlo Dorigati and
Enrico Paternoster

Vineyard manager
Carlo Dorigati

Production
About 10,000 bottles in
vintage years

Vintages
1995 1994 1993 1992
1991 1990

Price
● ● ●

Carlo Dorigati, whose family owns the Fratelli Dorigati estate at the town of Mezzocorona in Trentino, teamed up with his friend and fellow winemaker Enrico Paternoster in 1986 to form a small company specializing in sparkling wine. They decided to call the wine and the winery Methius in reference to Methius Coronae, as Mezzocorona was called in the twelfth century when Trentino was part of the Austrian state of Tyrol. But after a notary had drawn up the documents, they noticed that the company name had been written Metius, without the 'h'.

Fourteen years later, Carlo and Enrico were still patiently going through the legal maneuvers to correct the spelling, a telling comment on the efficiency of the Italian bureaucratic system. "One of these days the winery will also be Methius," Carlo promises. But in the meantime Methius Brut Riserva has risen in status to rank among the most dignified of Italy's classic sparklers.

It is made from Chardonnay and Pinot Nero grapes grown on hillsides at Faedo and Pressano overlooking the Rotaliano plain where the Metius/Methius winery was established in the Dorigati family's vaulted cellars. Barrel aging of part of the base wine and long contact with the yeasts account for uncommon finesse, though Methius Brut Riserva retains fresh fruit qualities that make it a delight to drink for a decade or more.

The wine qualifies under Trento DOC, an appellation that applies only to sparkling wines made by the classic method of a second fermentation in bottle. That DOC also includes the term Talento, a collective trademark used by producers in several regions of northern Italy who belong to the Istituto Talento Metodo Classico.

The Fratelli Dorigati estate, founded in 1858, produces a full range of Trentino DOC wines, including fine Teroldego Rotaliano Riserva Diedri and the refreshing red Rebo, from a cross of Merlot and the local Marzemino.

Trentino

Grapes
Chardonnay 60%, Pinot Nero 40%, hand picked in September.

Vineyards
Plots covering about 2 hectares in calcareous clay soils on slopes facing south-southwest at 350–500 meters of altitude at the villages of Faedo and Pressano in the northern part of the province of Trento. Vines, of an average age of 19 years, are planted at a density of 3,800 per hectare and trained in a short-pruned version of the traditional pergola *trentina*.

Vinification and aging
Grapes are soft crushed and the musts fermented at 15–18°C for 10 days, the Pinot Nero in stainless steel vats and part of the Chardonnay in small oak barrels. Base wines do not undergo malolactic fermentation before the cuvée is assembled in the spring. The wine goes into bottle for 6 years on the yeasts before hand riddling and disgorging. The wine, of about 12.5% alcohol, receives a *liqueur d'expédition* before being cork sealed and cellared for 6–8 months until release.

Style and maturity
Methius Brut Riserva on release about 7 years after the vintage has straw yellow color with golden highlights and ample *perlage* in steady streams of fine bubbles. Aromas are rich and round with ripe fruit and floral sensations mingling with hints of yeast and spices. Flavors are full and mellow with fine balance between fruit and acidity in a long, smooth finish. The wine reaches a prime between 10 and 15 years.

Serving
- 10°C.
- Tall, ample flute (vintage Champagne type).
- Alpine mushrooms with polenta; *strangolapreti* (green gnocchi) with sage and grated Grana cheese; brook trout poached in white wine.

Miani

Producer
Azienda Agricola Miani
Via Peruzzi 10
33042 Buttrio (Udine)
Tel. 0432/674327
Fax 0432/674327

Owner
Enzo Pontoni

Founded
1985

Winemakers
Enzo Pontoni with
Roberto Cipresso

Vineyard manager
Enzo Pontoni

Production
About 2,500 bottles a
year

Vintages
1999 1998 1997 1996
1995 1994

Price
● ● ●

Bianco Miani
Colli Orientali del Friuli DOC
Bianco ♀

Enzo Pontoni of Miani had been described as aloof, defiant, the lone wolf of Friuli, a region renowned for self-styled winemakers. He seemed to fit the image when I met him, a ruggedly built type in faded denims with creases in his tanned face enclosing piercing blue eyes in a gaze worthy of the vintage Clint Eastwood.

The occasion was a blind tasting at Montalcino, a showdown of red wines ranging from Brunello and Super-Tuscans to the cream of Bordeaux, California and Australia, plus oddballs. The oddest, Miani's Vigna Calvari 1996 from the unsung variety of Refosco, won by a notable margin.

Enzo seemed almost embarrassed, attributing success to the good earth, which, as I learned on further digging, he is attached to with a fervor that surpasses reason. He took over his mother Edda Miani's farm in the 1980s and became Friuli's leading apostle of the creed of low yields.

He prunes and thins mercilessly, leaving just two grape bunches per vine, to produce about 9,000 bottles a year from 14 hectares—less than a tenth of the yields permitted under Colli Orientali del Friuli DOC. That explains why Miani wines are uncommonly rich and concentrated, uncompromisingly honest and virtually impossible to obtain.

The first wine I had tasted was Bianco Miani, an exotic blend of Chardonnay, Pinot Grigio, Malvasia and Riesling. That was at Blasut, a trattoria in Friuli, where host Dante Bernardis served one of two remaining bottles from 1994, promising that it would be *fenomenale*. Phenomenal it was, but, as Dante pointed out, the only way to even hope to get a few bottles is to go to Miani and beg.

Enzo makes wine stimulated by confrontations with Roberto Cipresso, a consulting enologist who is no conformist either. The entire range is coveted, from Rosso Miani (Refosco and Tazzelenghe with Cabernet) to the varietals of Tocai Friulano, Sauvignon, Ribolla Gialla and Merlot. The triumphant Vigna Calvari Refosco is so rare that even begging for it won't work.

Friuli-Venezia Giulia

Grapes

Chardonnay 40%, Pinot Grigio 25%, Malvasia Istriana 18%, Riesling Renano 17% (slightly varied from year to year), hand picked in mid-September (Chardonnay, Pinot Grigio) and late September (Malvasia, Riesling).

Vineyards

Plots totaling 2.5 hectares in marl on slopes facing various directions at 100–150 meters of altitude on the rises of Buttrio in Monte in the southern part of Colli Orientali del Friuli. The vines, ranging in age from 10–80 years, are planted at densities of 2,500–4,000 per hectare and trained in the Guyot cordon method.

Vinification and aging

Grapes are soft crushed, and the musts inoculated with yeast cultures are fermented for about 15 days, part at natural temperatures in 500-liter barrels of French oak and part in glass-lined cement vats at about 20°C. Malolactic fermentation may occur spontaneously during 8–9 months of maturing in barrels (half new, half used once). The wine, of about 13.5% alcohol, is bottled and cellared for 3–4 months before release.

Style and maturity

Bianco Miani on release in the second year after the harvest has bright straw yellow color tinged with gold and a spectrum of aromas that recall ripe apricots and apples, honey, vanilla and spices. Potently structured yet round and creamy smooth in texture, flavors are full and mellow with rich fruit sensations underlined by hints of coffee and vanilla. A white of uncommon depth and complexity, it has the substance to shine for well over a decade.

Serving

🌡 14°C.

🍷 Ample tulip-shaped glass with long stem.

🍽 *Prosciutto* from San Daniele with red-fleshed verdello figs; Friulian rice and bean soup; turbot braised in white wine with mussels and clams.

Pierpaolo Pecorari

Soris
Venezia Giulia IGT
Chardonnay ♀

Producer
Azienda Agricola
Pierpaolo Pecorari
Via Tommaseo 36/C
34070 San Lorenzo
Isontino (Gorizia)
Tel. 0481/808775
Fax 0481/808775
a.pecorari@go.nettuno.it

Owner
Pierpaolo Pecorari

Founded
1974

Winemaker
Pierpaolo Pecorari

Vineyard manager
Pierpaolo Pecorari

Production
6,000–8,000 bottles in
favorable years

Vintages
1999 1998 1997 1996
1992

Price
● ●

Pierpaolo Pecorari grew up on a farm in Friuli's Isonzo plains where his family cultivated mainly grains but also fruit trees and vines for a bit of wine. When Pierpaolo took charge in 1974, the wines of Isonzo were not considered special—certainly not the whites, anyway. But being young and something of a dreamer, he decided to plant new vineyards in the trendy varieties that were starting to make an impact in the nearby hills of Collio: Chardonnay, Sauvignon Blanc and Pinot Grigio, along with the Merlot and Refosco that were already at home on the plains.

Today, Pierpaolo Pecorari is one of the acknowledged protagonists of Isonzo, whose white wines are considered to be worthy rivals to those of Collio by a growing number of connoisseurs. Evidently not enough for Pierpaolo, however, who, after complaining about the continuing second-class status of Friuli Isonzo DOC, recently classified his esteemed single-vineyard wines as Venezia Giulia IGT.

Pierpaolo, who cultivates 17 hectares of vines following strict organic standards, produces 80,000–100,000 bottles of wine a year based on a range of varietals under Friuli Isonzo DOC. His single-vineyard whites—Chardonnay Soris, Sauvignon Kolaus and Pinot Grigio Olivers—are matured in 500-liter barrels of French oak, which contribute to their depth and complexity. He also makes a blend of late-harvested Müller-Thurgau and Riesling called Pratoscuro, a Merlot Baolar and a Refosco with a bizarre name, Oh Sweet Were the Hours…, inspired by Beethoven. A new white, issued in late 2000, is Pinot Grigio Altis.

Among this commendable array, I've developed a fondness for the Chardonnay Soris, whose name, aptly enough, comes from *sorriso* (smile). Soris reminds me of a classic white Burgundy, perhaps because it comes from old vines planted in the gravelly soils of Isonzo that seem to account for the elegantly subdued fruit flavors that Pierpaolo has integrated deftly with the oak.

Friuli-Venezia Giulia

Grapes
Chardonnay 100%, hand picked in late September.

Vineyard
Soris, a plot of 1 hectare in gravelly calcareous soils on plains with a gradual taper toward the southeast at about 40 meters of altitude in the commune of San Lorenzo Isontino in the northern sector of the Friuli Isonzo zone. The vines, of an average age of 26 years, are planted at a density of 5,500 per hectare and trained in the Guyot cordon system.

Vinification and aging
Grapes are soft crushed and the musts macerated with the skins briefly before fermenting at 20°C for about 15 days in 500-liter capacity barrels of French oak, where the wine undergoes malolactic fermentation during 10 months on the lees, which are stirred frequently in a process known as *bâtonnage*. The wine, of about 13.5% alcohol, is bottled and cellared for about 6 months until release.

Style and maturity
Soris Chardonnay on release in the second year after the harvest has deep straw yellow color with golden highlights and refined aromas reminiscent of ripe pears and apples with hints of honey, herbs and vanilla. Well structured with round, smooth texture, it has mellow flavors of ripe fruit buoyed by a vein of acidity and a salient mineral-like aspect in a long finish. At a prime at about 3 years, the wine can retain style for another 3 years or more.

Serving
- 13–17°C, preferably decanted.
- Ample glass (Montrachet type).
- Risotto with scampi; octopus stewed with tomato, garlic and herbs; grilled veal sweetbreads.

Pieropan

Producer
Azienda Agricola
Pieropan
Via Camuzzoni 3
37038 Soave (Verona)
Tel. 045/6190171
Fax 045/6190040
pieropan@netbusiness.it
www.pieropan.it

Owner
Leonildo Pieropan

Founded
1890

Winemaker
Leonildo Pieropan

Vineyard manager
Leonildo Pieropan

Production
About 40,000 bottles in
favorable years

Vintages
1999 1998 1997 1995
1993 1990 1988 1985

Price
● ●

Vigneto La Rocca
Soave Classico Superiore
DOC ♀

A search for the words to describe one of my favorite wines resulted in the prosaic summary below (under "Style and maturity"). More apropos would have been the accolade of Englishman Charles G. Bode in *The Wines of Italy* (1956): "It tastes as a very clear sky might taste if one could drink it." Bode referred to Soave in general, but I can't help thinking that he had just sipped a glass of Pieropan.

Yet Leonildo Pieropan, named after his grandfather who founded the estate in 1890, might deny that. Not just because he's admirably modest, but because Nino, as he's known, admits that he began making Soave in a serious way only in the 1970s. He acquired plots in the hills of Soave Classico and introduced the concept of single-vineyard wines, first with Calvarino, then with La Rocca (as the adjacent town castle is known).

Their class was not due simply to superior terrains, but to a combination of factors that set Nino's Soave apart from the rest. He selected clones of the local Garganega and Trebbiano and planted them at high density, reducing yields by sharp pruning and cluster thinning and, not least of all, the use of natural fertilizers in place of the chemicals that had boosted Soave production for decades.

Vigneto La Rocca, fermented and aged with gentle discretion in barrels and casks, is the ultimate expression of pure Garganega, proof that Soave can mature as splendidly as wines from supposedly nobler varieties. Vigneto Calvarino, which includes some Trebbiano, is nearly its match and stands with La Rocca as the best value in Italy's premium whites today.

Nino and his wife Teresita have renovated and expanded cellars at the fifteenth-century Palazzo Pullici in the center of Soave to produce about 300,000 bottles a year from 30 hectares of vines. These include the elegant Recioto di Soave DOCG Le Colombare and the luscious Passito della Rocca (from Sauvignon, Riesling, Trebbiano and Garganega) that some critics consider Pieropan's finest.

Veneto

vigneto
la Rocca 1997

LEONILDO
PIEROPAN
VITICULTORE

SOAVE CLASSICO SUPERIORE

ITALIA

Grapes
Garganega 100%, hand picked when very ripe in late October or early November.

Vineyard
La Rocca, a plot of 5.5 hectares in volcanic soils of alkaline calcareous clays on a slope facing southwest at 220 meters of altitude adjacent to the town castle of Soave. Vines, of an average age of 30 years, are planted at a density of 5,200 per hectare and trained in the traditional pergola *veronese* and spurred cordon systems.

Vinification and aging
Grapes are soft crushed and the musts macerated briefly with the skins before fermenting in 500-liter oak barrels at 20–22°C for 15–20 days, during which time malolactic fermentation takes place. The wine, of about 12.5% alcohol, is matured for 10 months in casks of 2,000-liter capacity and barrels of 500-liter capacity before being bottled and cellared for at least 4 months until release.

Style and maturity
Soave Classico Vigneto La Rocca on release in the second year after the harvest has sunny yellow color with polished brass highlights and rich yet refined floral and fruit aromas with scents reminiscent of melon, peach, mango and hints of primrose and vanilla. On the palate, it is full, round and velvety with perfect balance between fruit sensations and acidity in mellow, complex flavors that linger on the palate. The wine reaches a prime at about 2 years and maintains elegance for another 6 years—or, from great vintages, well beyond that.

Serving
🍷 12–14°C, giving old vintages 15 minutes to breathe in the glass.
♀ Tulip-shaped glass (Chardonnay type).
🍽 *Bigoli in cassopipa* (noodles in shellfish soup); *risi e bisato* (rice with eel); *sepe a' la venessiana* (cuttlefish stewed with tomatoes).

Pojer & Sandri

Producer
Azienda Agricola
Pojer & Sandri
Località Molini 6
38010 Faedo (Trento)
Tel. 0461/650342
Fax 0461/651100
info@pojeresandri.it
www.pojeresandri.it

Owners
Mario Pojer and
Fiorentino Sandri

Founded
1975

Winemaker
Mario Pojer

Vineyard manager
Fiorentino Sandri

Production
60,000–70,000 bottles a
year

Vintages
1999 1998 1997 1996
1995

Price
●

Müller-Thurgau
Trentino DOC ♀

Müller-Thurgau was once believed to be a cross of Riesling and Sylvaner realized by Professor Hermann Müller from the Swiss canton of Thurgau at the German wine institute of Geisenheim in 1882. His aim was to duplicate the nobility of Riesling in a vine with the precocity of Sylvaner. In terms of productivity, he succeeded with flying colors, but Riesling character was largely lost in the Müller-Thurgau wines of the Rheingau.

Eventually, though, the cross found its way to the Alps, where the rarefied atmosphere seemed to revive its spirits. It was planted at the end of World War II in vineyards now owned by Mario Pojer and Fiorentino Sandri at the village of Faedo in Trentino. The first wine released by the now famous partners was the buoyantly crisp and fragrant Müller-Thurgau from 1975, a revelation in an era when Italy's new wave whites tended to be bland, if not downright insipid.

Pojer & Sandri have since become known for bigger wines, such as the oak-fermented Chardonnay Faye and Rosso Faye (see page 150). But Mario and Fiorentino retain a soft spot for Müller, as they affectionately call their firstborn. They have planted vines at heights of up to 750 meters at a place called Palai, while increasing production of one of the most refreshingly zesty of Alpine whites. The cool mountain environment naturally retards ripening and accounts for the wealth of aromas that can rival those of Riesling.

In the meantime, DNA studies have revealed that Müller-Thurgau is a cross of Riesling and Chasselas and has nothing to do with Sylvaner. The partners, though unperturbed by the find, admit that it might make one wonder about proverbial Swiss precision.

From 23 hectares, Pojer & Sandri produce about 240,000 bottles annually, ranging through Trentino DOC varietals to fine bottle-fermented sparkling wine to Essenzia, a sumptuous blend of late-harvested grapes. The distillery is noted for fruit liqueurs and an oak-aged grappa called, appropriately, Divino.

Trentino

Grapes
Müller-Thurgau 100%, hand picked in mid-September.

Vineyards
Plots totaling 7 hectares in soils of calcareous lime mixed with sandstone, silt and dolomite on a marlstone base on slopes facing south-southwest and southeast all above 550 meters, including 80% at Palai at 600–750 meters of altitude in the commune of Faedo in northern Trentino. Vines, from 5–56 years of age, are planted at densities of 4,000–6,000 per hectare, the older trained in the trellised *pergoletta trentina* and the younger in the Guyot or spurred cordon methods.

Vinification and aging
Grapes are stemmed and crushed gently for about 3 hours and decanted statically for 12 hours before the musts, inoculated with yeasts, ferment in stainless steel vats at 18–20°C for 7–17 days. The wine, of about 12.5% alcohol, remains on the lees until December and is held near freezing until April, when it is bottled after bentonite stabilization and filtering. Partial malolactic fermentation is induced in vintages with high acidity.

Style and maturity
Pojer & Sandri Müller-Thurgau on release has a brilliant straw yellow color with greenish highlights and ample aroma with scents reminiscent of apricots, peaches, lemons and mountain herbs. Bright and clean in flavor, the aromatic fruit and mineral sensations are buoyed by lively acidity that leaves the palate thoroughly refreshed. Though normally at its zesty best in a year or 2, certain vintages (notably 1983) acquire the elegance of a fine Riesling or Chablis with time.

Serving
🍶 10–12°C.
🍷 Tulip-shaped glass (Riesling type)
🍽 *Antipasti* based on shellfish, vegetables and herbs; *strangolapreti* (bread and spinach gnocchi) with butter and sage.

Rocca Bernarda

Producer
Azienda Agricola
Rocca Bernarda
Via Rocca Bernarda 27
33040 Ipplis di
Premariacco (Udine)
Tel. 0432/716914
Fax 0432/716273
roccabernarda@tin.it

Owner
Sovrano Militare Ordine
di Malta

Founded
1559

Winemaker
Marco Monchiero

Vineyard manager
Mario Zuliani

Production
About 3,000 half-liter
bottles in favorable years

Vintages
1998 1997 1996 1994
1993

Price
● ● ●

Picolit
Colli Orientali del Friuli
DOC ♀

Picolit was esteemed as one of Europe's great sweet wines in the mid-eighteenth century, when Count Fabio Asquini sold it in hand-made flacons of Murano glass at the rate of 100,000 bottles a year. The pride of Friuli was regarded by some as a rival to Hungary's Tokaji until the late nineteenth century when phylloxera destroyed its vineyards.

At the beginning of the twentieth century, Giacomo Perusini selected surviving vines to replant around his splendid hilltop manor of Rocca Bernarda in the Colli Orientali del Friuli. His son Gaetano increased plantings to the point that modest amounts of wine could be sold. In 1959, the author Luigi Veronelli wrote that the Rocca Bernarda Picolit was to Italy as Château d'Yquem to France. Giacomo's widow Giuseppina, who lived to 103, was admired as the first lady of Italian wine.

Rocca Bernarda Picolit, made in the traditional way from semidried grapes, was coveted and increasingly imitated. But the vine, whose name refers to its small (*piccole*) grapes and scarce yields, suffered from a debilitating pollination malady. Production burgeoned nonetheless, raising doubts about authenticity and causing a fall from favor.

On Gaetano Perusini's death in 1977, Rocca Bernarda was bequeathed to the Sovereign Military Order of Malta. Quality had already lapsed and although other producers fashioned late-harvested Picolit matured in small oak barrels, veterans complained that it was nothing like it used to be.

In the 1990s, the Order hired Piedmontese enologist Marco Monchiero and estate manager Mario Zuliani to return Picolit to its former glory. They are well on the way with a style inspired by both old and new: drying the grapes for a month and maturing the wine in barriques. The 1997 Picolit was named Italy's best sweet wine of 2000 by the *Gambero Rosso* guide.

From 40 hectares of vines, Rocca Bernarda produces about 170,000 bottles a year of Colli Orientali DOC varietals, including a Merlot of notable class called Centis.

Friuli-Venezia Giulia

Grapes
Picolit 100%, hand picked in late October and dried on mats for more than a month.

Vineyards
Grapes are selected from 2 hectares of vines in crumbly marl and sandstone soils on slopes facing south-southwest at 160 meters of altitude at Rocca Bernarda in the Ipplis area of the commune of Premariacco in the south-central part of the Colli Orientali del Friuli zone. The vines, of an average age of 31 years, are planted at a density of 4,000–6,000 per hectare and trained in the Guyot and double-arched *doppio capovolto* cordon methods.

Vinification and aging
The shriveled grapes are soft crushed and the musts decanted at cold temperatures before fermenting at about 20°C for several months in 225 liter oak barrels, in which the wine is then matured for 18 months undergoing malolactic fermentation if it occurs naturally. The wine, of about 13% alcohol with 8–10% of residual sugar, is bottled and cellared for at least 6 months before release.

Style and maturity
Rocca Bernarda Picolit has bright straw yellow color with golden highlights and elegant bouquet with scents reminiscent of apricots, ripe figs, candied citrus and hints of walnuts, acacia honey and vanilla. On the palate, the wine has rich, round, clean sweetness with impressive depth of flavors of ripe fruit and honey in a long, velvety finish. Prime drinking is normally between 5 and 10 years, though the wine should hold its class considerably longer.

Serving
🌡 11°C.

🍷 Long-stemmed, tulip-shaped glass.

🍽 Goose liver; scallops with glazed apples; Gorgonzola, Roquefort or Stilton with honey; green apple tart with Picolit ice cream; meditative sipping.

Ronco del Gelso

Tocai Friulano
Friuli Isonzo DOC ♀

Producer
Azienda Agricola Ronco
del Gelso
Via Isonzo 117
34071 Cormons
(Gorizia)
Tel. 0481/61310
Fax 0481/61310

Owner
Giorgio Badin

Founded
1972

Winemaker
Giorgio Badin

Vineyard manager
Giorgio Badin

Production
About 21,000 bottles a
year

Vintages
1999 1998 1997 1995

Price
● ●

Giorgio Badin owns and runs with youthful energy and devotion the farm that has been in his family for generations. Tocai Friulano has always been the principal variety grown in the vineyards of Ronco del Gelso in the upper plains of the Isonzo river valley, where the play of breezes between the nearby Adriatic Sea and the foothills of the Alps has created an idyllic atmosphere for viticulture.

Giorgio, after taking a diploma in enology and agronomy, bottled his first Tocai in 1988, breaking the family tradition of selling wine in bulk. He also planted other varieties and introduced modern methods of winemaking to build Ronco del Gelso into one of the most admired small estates of Friuli-Venezia Giulia.

His wines, both red and white, are noted for great concentration of aroma, flavor and color and the capacity to maintain their qualities over time. Although Giorgio seems reluctant to describe his practices in detail, it is known that he severely limits yields per vine and harvests grapes when very ripe. His cellar techniques include a process called hyperoxygenation in which the musts are saturated with oxygen and remain free of sulfites during the fermentation. For Tocai, he avoids maturation in barrels, as well as malolactic fermentation to maintain acidity at levels that give the wine its enduring verve.

From 15 hectares of vines, Ronco del Gelso produces about 100,000 bottles a year of wines of admirably consistent class. The Tocai Friulano is exemplary, though unlike many wines from the variety, it needs two or three years of age and a little breathing to show its best. Of similar stature are the Riesling, Sauvignon, Chardonnay, Pinot Grigio Sotto Lis Rivis and the blend called Làtimis (late-harvested Tocai, Pinot Bianco and Riesling). Giorgio Badin shows equal competence with red wines, as evident in fine, rich Merlot and Cabernet Franc.

Friuli-Venezia Giulia

Grapes
Tocai Friulano 100%, hand picked in late September or early October.

Vineyards
Grapes are selected from 3.8 hectares of vines in rich but arid alluvial soils on a gravelly base in rolling plains at about 50 meters of altitude in the commune of Cormons in the northern sector of the Friuli Isonzo zone. Old vines were planted using different methods, but recent plantings of densities up to 7,000 per hectare are prevalently in the Guyot cordon system.

Vinification and aging
Grapes are soft crushed and the musts are saturated with oxygen (hyperoxygenation) but left free of sulfites during fermentation with select yeasts at 18–19°C for 4 or 5 days in stainless steel vats. Malolactic fermentation is avoided during 4 months of maturing in tanks on the lees. The wine, of about 13% alcohol, is bottled and cellared for 2–3 months until release.

Style and maturity
Ronco del Gelso Tocai Friulano on release about a year after the harvest has bright straw yellow color with green highlights and aromas that recall ripe apples, dried figs and citrus with hints of walnuts and toasted almonds. On the palate, the wine has rich, round texture and impressive depth of flavors of ripe fruit and nuts with a bitter trace on the finish that actually enhances the complexity. Prime drinking is normally in 2–3 years, though this Tocai has the stuff to shine longer.

Serving
- 12–14°C, possibly decanting 15 minutes earlier.
- Tulip-shaped glass (Chardonnay type).
- *Prosciutto di San Daniele*; risotto with asparagus tips; brook trout braised with Tocai and almonds.

Ruggeri

Producer
Ruggeri & C.
Via Pra' Fontana
31049 Valdobbiadene
(Treviso)
Tel. 0423/975716
Fax 0423/973304
ruggeri@ruggeri.it
www.ruggeri.it

Owner
Giustino Bisol

Founded
1950

Winemaker
Fabio Roversi

Vineyard manager
Fabio Roversi

Production
About 8,000 bottles a
year

Vintages
1999 1998 1997 1995

Price
●

Giustino B.
Prosecco di Valdobbiadene DO
Extra Dry ♀

The Bisol family has been involved with wine at
Valdobbiadene since 1542, when a map of the area now
known as Cartizze indicated a place called Bisoi. The prime
wine of those enchanting hills is Prosecco, the bubbly aperitif
whose popularity in nearby Venice and Treviso has led to
growing recognition abroad.

In 1989, Giustino Bisol bought out his partner Luciano
Ruggeri and turned over direction of the Ruggeri winery to
his son Paolo, who has accomplished remarkable growth in
terms of both quality and quantity (elements that don't
always go together hereabouts). Paolo Bisol has established a
network of 80 growers who work under the direction of
winemaker Fabio Roversi to supply choice grapes to the firm
for Prosecco di Valdobbiadene, including a Superiore di
Cartizze that stands with the best of the breed (see page 184).
But to my taste the most persuasive wine of the house is the
Prosecco called Giustino B., which Paolo dedicated to his
father in 1995 to celebrate his 50 years of winemaking.

It qualifies as Extra Dry, which under the confusing
nomenclature of sparkling wines means that it is actually a
tad sweet. Or, better, that it has a mellow quality known as
abboccato, meaning more or less mouth filling. That was the
prevalent style of Prosecco in the days when wines were made
by rustic bottle-fermentation methods instead of in the
convenient stainless steel tanks of today. Giustino B. has
impeccably modern fruit-acid balance yet it retains enough
of that traditional mouth-filling goodness to make it a treat
as an *ombra* or *ombretta,* as Venetians call the little glasses of
wine sipped at intervals through the day.

The Ruggeri range of about 1,300,000 bottles a year is
focused on Prosecco di Valdobbiadene DOC in types known
as Gentile and Santo Stefano, Giall'Oro (Extra Dry) and a
still version called La Bastia. The winery also produces
sparkling wines by the classic method from Chardonnay and
Pinot grapes called Ruggeri Brut and Ruggeri Chardonnay.

Veneto

Grapes
Prosecco 100%, hand picked in early October.

Vineyards
Plots totaling about 1 hectare in calcareous clay and sandstone soils on steep slopes facing south at about 350 meters of altitude in the commune of Valdobbiadene. Vines, of various age, are planted at a density of 3,000 per hectare and trained in the espalier and Guyot cordon systems.

Vinification and aging
Grapes are soft crushed and the musts clarified cold before fermenting at 20°C for 8 days in stainless steel vats. The base wine is settled at cold temperature for about 5 months, carefully avoiding malolactic fermentation, before being inoculated with select yeasts that set off a second fermentation lasting about 3 months at 12–14°C. The wine, of about 11% alcohol, is bottled and cellared for 4 months before release.

Style and maturity
Giustino B. Prosecco Extra Dry on release about a year after the harvest has pale straw color with hints of green and lively streams of fine bubbles. Aromas are fresh and fruity with scents reminiscent of ripe apples and acacia blossoms. Flavors are delicately mellow (*abboccato*) and fresh with pleasant fruit sensations that linger on the palate through a soft, smooth finish. The wine reaches a prime at a year from the vintage and maintains style for at least 2 years beyond.

Serving
- 6–7°C.
- Medium-sized flute (Champagne type).
- As an aperitif with *antipasti* based on fish, vegetables and mushrooms; *baccalà mantecato* (creamed salt cod); risotto with red radicchio.

Cantina
Produttori San
Michele Appiano

Sanct Valentin
Alto Adige DOC Sauvignon ♀

Producer
Cantina Produttori San
Michele Appiano
Via Circonvallazione
17–19
39057 Appiano/Eppan
(Bolzano)
Tel. 0471/664466
Fax 0471/660764
kellerei@stmichael.it
www.stmichael.it

Owner
Cooperative headed by
Anton Zublasing

Founded
1907

Chief winemaker
Hans Terzer

Vineyard supervisors
Hans Terzer and Richard
Meraner

Production
About 35,000 bottles in
favorable years

Vintages
1999 1998 1997 1995
1992 1989

Price
● ●

Note
The DOC may be Alto
Adige or Sudtirolo in
Italian or Südtiroler in
German

H ans Terzer took a while to gain his reputation as Alto
Adige's wizard of white wine after he arrived at the
Cantina Produttori San Michele Appiano in 1977. The
venerable Kellereigenossenchaft St. Michael-Eppan, as it is
known to its more than 300 German-speaking members, has
been elevated by Hans into a shining example of why the
cooperatives of the South Tyrol boast the highest quality
standards of Italy.

The young *Kellermeister* imposed strict production
standards for wines in select categories. But it wasn't easy to
coax lower yields out of farmers who grew grapes with the
same lust for quantity that they cultivated apples, the other
cash crop of the Alpine province. Then, as now, the bulk of
South Tyrolean wines were light and breezy reds, notably the
Kalterersee and St Magdalener that have quenched thirsts in
central Europe for decades.

But demand was mounting in Italy for fragrant whites
from mountain vineyards, following the surge to popularity
of Pinot Grigio. In the late 1980s, the San Michele cellars
created the top category of Sanct Valentin, named for a local
castle. The trademark came to apply to barrel-fermented
Chardonnay and Pinot Grigio and richly aromatic
Gewürztraminer and Sauvignon. If compelled to name a
favorite from that elect group, I would probably choose the
Sauvignon, a wine that brings together that variety's
sometimes disparate character traits in splendid harmony.

A second category called Selezioni takes in wines from
specific vineyards and estates, including the Pinot Bianco
Schulthauser that further confirms Hans's mastery with
whites. He's equally inspired by reds, as Sanct Valentin
Cabernet and Pinot Nero attest.

The cellars, housed in an imposing structure of imperial
Austrian factory architecture, produce about 1,500,000
bottles a year from more than 300 hectares of vineyards. The
range covers a category called Classica that takes in a bit of
everything the South Tyrol has to offer at moderate prices.

Alto Adige

Grapes
Sauvignon Blanc 100%, hand picked in late September (10% harvested in October).

Vineyards
Various plots covering 8 hectares in calcareous soils on slopes facing south and southeast at 480–600 meters of altitude in the commune of Appiano in the Überetsch area of the Adige valley southwest of Bolzano. The vines, of an average age of 10 years, are planted at densities of 3,500–5,000 per hectare, about half trained in the Guyot cordon method and half in the trellised pergola system.

Vinification and aging
Grapes are soft crushed and the musts are cold macerated with the skins before being clarified and fermented at 18°C for 7–12 days in stainless steel tanks. Late-harvested grapes (10%) are fermented separately and blended into the wine, which remains 7–8 months on the lees in tanks without undergoing malolactic fermentation. The wine, of about 14% alcohol, is bottled in May and cellared for 8–10 months until release.

Style and maturity
Sanct Valentin Sauvignon on release in the second year after the harvest shows pale straw yellow color with greenish highlights and decisive varietal aroma marked by scents reminiscent of wild elderberries, ripe figs and spices. Flavors are decisively dry and harmonious with vital acidity buoying fresh fruit sensations that linger through a long, smooth finish. The wine reaches a prime in 3 or 4 years but can retain fresh, refined qualities for a decade or more.

Serving
🍴 12°C.
🍷 Tulip-shaped glass (Sauvignon type).
🍽 *Antipasti* based on shellfish; risotto with green asparagus tips and grated Parmigiano; Cantonese seafood and vegetable dishes.

Schiopetto

Producer
Azienda Agricola Mario
Schiopetto
Via Palazzo
Arcivescovile 1
34070 Capriva del Friuli
(Gorizia)
Tel. 0481/80332
Fax 0481/808073
azienda@schiopetto.it
www.schiopetto.it

Owner
Mario Schiopetto

Founded
1965

Winemakers
Giorgio Schiopetto and
Stefano Menotti

Vineyard managers
Giorgio and Carlo
Schiopetto

Production
About 3,300 bottles in
favorable years

Vintages
1999 1998 1997 1996

Price
● ●

Amrità
Collio DOC Pinot Bianco ♀

Mario Schiopetto worked in his father's inn as a youth, serving wines that didn't always satisfy his palate. So, after a period of travel and work, he decided to become a vintner himself. In 1965, he leased the vineyards of the Archbishopric of Gorizia at Spessa di Capriva in a privileged part of Collio and adjusted the new techniques of temperature-controlled fermentation to his own meditated style to produce whites of crystalline purity and polish.

Within a decade Mario Schiopetto had become Italy's most admired producer of white wine. When I met him in 1977, I was struck by the philosophy of a master of technology who upheld the patience and intuition of man as the fundamentals of making fine wine.

Mario continued to set the pace in the 1980s, developing the process of hyperoxygenation of musts to minimize the use of sulfites. But he refused to be caught up by the Italian mania for new barrels of French oak, a reluctance that earned him a label as an enemy of wood and even a conservative. "That wasn't accurate," Mario explained later. "I simply have a distaste for wines dominated by new oak."

By the mid-1990s, with daughter Maria Angela and twin sons Carlo and Giorgio working with him in new cellars, Mario was ready for more revisions. He selected Pinot Bianco, Tocai Friulano and Sauvignon Blanc, varieties that excel at Spessa, for wines fermented and matured at natural temperatures in large casks of Slavonian oak. They were baptized Amrità (Pinot Bianco), Pardes (Tocai) and Tarsia (Sauvignon).

The toast of the trio is Amrità, named for an elixir of immortality in ancient religious rites, an exemplar of the elegance of Pinot Blanc and proof that Mario is still in the forefront of Friulian winemaking. From 22.3 hectares of vines, Schiopetto produces about 220,000 bottles of wine a year, including the blend called Blanc des Rosis (Pinot Bianco, Tocai, Sauvignon and Malvasia) and Collio and Colli Orientali del Friuli varietals.

Friuli-Venezia Giulia

Grapes
Pinot Bianco 100%, hand picked in mid-September.

Vineyard
A plot of 0.8 hectare in clay soils with marl and sand on a slope facing south at about 50 meters of altitude at Sant'Antonio in the Spessa area of the commune of Capriva del Friuli in the southern part of the Collio zone. Vines, of an average age of 21 years, are planted at a density of about 3,500 per hectare and trained in a bilateral Guyot cordon system.

Vinification and aging
Grapes are soft crushed and the musts decanted for about 12 hours before fermenting without the addition of sulfites in 2,500-liter capacity casks of Slavonian oak at natural temperatures for 7 or 8 days. Malolactic fermentation is not induced during 15 months of maturing in the same casks. The wine, of about 13% alcohol, is bottled in December of the year after the harvest and cellared until release in May of the following year.

Style and maturity
Pinot Bianco Amrità on release in the spring of the second year after the harvest has bright straw yellow color with golden highlights and refined aromas that recall ripe apples and pears with hints of herbs and vanilla. Full and round on the palate, it has smooth texture and exquisite balance between elements of fruit, acid and wood that come together in an elegantly complex finish. Prime drinking is normally in 2–5 years, though the wine should retain its style for a decade.

Serving
🌡 12°C, possibly decanting 15 minutes earlier.
🍷 Tulip-shaped glass (Chardonnay type).
🍴 Mixed fry of squid, shrimp and zucchini; Friulian rice and Savoy cabbage soup; breast of guinea fowl with raspberries.

**Cantina
Produttori di
Termeno**

Producer
Cantina Produttori
di Termeno
Strada del Vino 122
39040 Termeno
(Bolzano)
Tel. 0471/860126
Fax 0471/860828
info@tramin-wine.it

Owner
Cooperative headed by
Reinhold Andergassen

Founded
1898

Chief winemaker
Willi Stürz

Vineyard supervisor
Stephan Dezini

Production
About 23,000 bottles
from choice years

Vintages
1999 1998 1997 1996
1995 1993 1990

Price
● ●

Note
The DOC may be Alto
Adige or Sudtirolo in
Italian or Südtiroler in
German

Nussbaumerhof
Südtiroler DOC
Gewürztraminer ♀

The changing attitudes that have revolutionized styles in the wines of Alto Adige are evinced by the recent history of the Cantina Produttori di Termeno. From its founding as Kellerei Tramin in 1898, when the South Tyrol was Austrian, the specialty had been the light red wine from the Vernatsch or Schiava vine that flowed north over the Alps as Kalterersee. That wine, Caldaro in Italian, is named for the pretty lake surrounded by a veritable sea of vines extending through the broad valley of the South Tyrolean Unterland and beyond.

In the 1980s, as the fortunes of Kalterersee declined in the face of mounting demand in Italy for the flowery whites of Alto Adige, growers reluctantly began to replace prolific Schiava vines with Chardonnay, the Pinots, Sauvignon and the Gewürztraminer that is named in part for the town of Tramin (see Hofstätter, page 200). A turning point for the town cooperative came in 1986, when floods mired the cellars in mud and reconstruction resulted in a bigger and better equipped winemaking plant.

Quality has risen steadily through the 1990s, stimulated by young cellarmaster Willi Stürz, whose skills applied to a broad range of wines seem most brilliant with Gewürztraminer. Maso Nussbaumerhof, a 700-year-old farm at Söll (Sella), is the source of a Gewürztraminer that combines the decisively full aromas typical of Alsace with the delightfully fresh fruit flavors of the South Tyrolean tradition.

Nussbaumerhof heads the Cantina's Terminum line, which includes a fine sweet Gewürztraminer from partly dried grapes and exemplary estate selections of Pinot Grigio (Unterebnerhof) and red Lagrein (Urbanhof). The Cantina groups 277 members with 220 hectares of vines, three-quarters of which are still planted in red wine varieties. Production of about 500,000 bottles annually includes a share of Kalterersee Auslese, though most Schiava is sold in bulk. An exception is the single-vineyard wine called Hexenbichler that shows Schiava at its best.

Alto Adige

Grapes
Gewürztraminer 100%, hand picked in late September–early October.

Vineyard
Maso Nussbaumerhof, a plot of 4.2 hectares in calcareous clay and gravelly soils on steep slopes at 400 meters of altitude at the locality of Söll (Sella) in the commune of Tramin (Termeno) on the western side of the Adige valley southwest of Bolzano. Vines, from 10–37 years of age, are planted at densities of 5,000–7,000 per hectare and trained in the Guyot cordon (70%) and traditional pergola systems.

Vinification and aging
Grapes are soft crushed and 10–20% of the musts are macerated cold with the skins before fermenting at 18–21°C for 7–10 days in stainless steel tanks. Malolactic fermentation is avoided during 6 months of maturation on the lees in tanks. The wine, of about 13.5% alcohol, is bottled and cellared for a month before release.

Style and maturity
Gewürztraminer Nussbaumerhof on release in the spring after the harvest has deep straw yellow color with golden highlights and ample aromas with scents reminiscent of roses, ripe peaches and tropical fruit accented by spices. Rich and round on the palate, its ripe fruit sensations are balanced by vital acidity with a hint of almond in a long, smooth finish. The wine reaches a prime between 2 and 4 years, though some vintages hold style longer.

Serving
🍷 10–12°C.
♀ Tulip-shaped glass (Alsatian type).
🍴 *Türteln* (fried rye ravioli with spinach-cumin stuffing); polenta with wild mushrooms; cheese soufflés; goat cheese with herbs.

Feldmarschall von Fenner zu Fennberg Vino da Tavola ♀

Producer
Tiefenbrunner –
Schlosskellerei Turmhof
Via Castello 4
Niclara/Entiklar
39040
Cortaccia/Kurtatsch
(Bolzano)
Tel. 0471/880122
Fax 0471/880433
t@tiefenbrunner.com
www.tiefenbrunner.com

Owner
Herbert Tiefenbrunner

Founded
1848

Winemakers
Herbert and Cristof
Tiefenbrunner

Vineyard manager
Cristof Tiefenbrunner

Production
About 12,000 bottles a
year

Vintages
1999 1998 1990 1989
1988 1985 1983 1979

Price
● ●

Schloss Turmhof, an enchantingly bizarre castle, has served as the Tiefenbrunner family home and cellars since 1848. It is also a mecca for tourists, who sip house wines and munch on sausages and *Speck* in shaded gardens where ponds and ornate statuary lend the surroundings a fairytale air. Owner Herbert Tiefenbrunner goes about his *Kellermeister* duties as he has for nearly 60 years, wearing lederhosen and loden jackets with buckhorn buttons. Son Cristof prefers sweaters and jeans, though the tandem strikes a propitious balance between tradition and progress in wines that rank consistently with the region's finest.

Their emphasis is on whites of enticingly fruity, fragrant qualities, led by Chardonnay, Pinot Grigio and Pinot Bianco. Herbert takes special pride in his aromatic varietals of Gewürztraminer, Riesling, Moscato Giallo and above all the Müller-Thurgau called Feldmarschall. That name honors Franz Philipp Freiherr von Fenner zu Fennberg, founder of the Tyrolean *Kaiserjäger* (Royal Huntsman). The Field Marshal, a native of the village of Fennberg or Favogna, had a summer residence there called Hofstatt, a stone manor in a clearing at a thousand meters in the Alps that is now the site of the South Tyrol's highest vineyard, planted by Herbert in 1972.

The microclimate accounts for Feldmarschall's sublime aromas, but problems such as frost and deer dining on young vines make cultivation a challenge. The wine reached peaks of splendor in the 1980s, but Herbert replanted the vineyard in the early 1990s, so Feldmarschall only returned to its former glory with the 1998 and 1999 vintages.

Cristof, an early advocate of French barrels in Alto Adige, uses them deftly for the Chardonnay called Linticlarus. That name also applies to fine Cabernet Sauvignon, exquisitely sweet Moscato Rosa and a blend of Lagrein, Cabernet and Pinot Noir called Linticlarus Cuvée. From 20 hectares of vines and grapes from trusted growers, Tiefenbrunner produces about 600,000 bottles a year.

Alto Adige

TIEFENBRUNNER

Feldmarschall
von Fenner zu Fennberg

Grapes
Müller-Thurgau 100%,
hand picked in mid-
October.

Vineyard
Hofstatt, a plot of 2
hectares in sandy
calcareous clay soils in an
Alpine meadow at 1,000
meters of altitude at
Favogna in the commune
of Magrè (Margreid) on
the western edge of the
Adige valley 25
kilometers southwest of
Bolzano. Vines, of an
average age of 10 years,
are planted at a density of
7,500 per hectare and
trained in the Guyot
cordon method.

Vinification and aging
Grapes are soft crushed
and the musts separated
from the skins ferment at
18–20°C for about 2
weeks in stainless steel
tanks. The wine, of about
12% alcohol, matures for
8 months on the lees in
tanks before being
bottled and cellared until
release.

Style and maturity
Feldmarschall on release has a
brilliant straw yellow color
with greenish highlights and
intense aroma with scents
reminiscent of apricots,
pomegranates, sage, jasmine
and Alpine flowers. Bright and
steely dry in flavor, the
aromatic fruit and herb
sensations are buoyed by zesty
acidity that refreshes the
palate through a smooth finish.
The wine needs 2 years to
express full aromas and
flavors, though certain vintages
show extraordinary finesse for
well over a decade.

Serving
🍷 10–12°C.
🍷 Tulip-shaped glass (Alsatian
type).
🍽 Spinach gnocchi with
melted Alpine cheese; raw
oysters; *blau forelle* (brook
trout) poached in white
wine with butter and
herbs.

Ronco delle Mele
Collio DOC Sauvignon ♀

Producer
Azienda Agricola
Venica & Venica
Via Mernico 42
34070 Dolegna del
Collio (Gorizia)
Tel. 0481/61264
Fax 0481/639906
venica@venica.it
www.venica.it

Owners
Gianni and Giorgio
Venica

Founded
1930

Winemakers
Giorgio and Giampaolo
Venica

Vineyard managers
Gianni Venica and
Marco Simonit

Production
About 13,000 bottles in
favorable years

Vintages
1999 1998 1997 1996

Price
● ●

Venica & Venica is not a law firm, as the title might suggest, but a wine estate owned by brothers Gianni and Giorgio Venica. The farm is located near Dolegna in the valley formed by the Judrio stream along the border of Slovenia at the northern extreme of the Collio DOC zone. The relatively cool microclimate there is noted as being ideal for apples and white wine varieties, above all Sauvignon Blanc.

Gianni and Giorgio, whose grandfather began farming the property in 1930, have gradually expanded vineyards to 28 hectares, while refurbishing cellars to produce 180,000–200,000 bottles of wine a year. So fine is their Sauvignon—in both a regular version and the single-vineyard Ronco delle Mele—that one might wonder why they bother with other varieties. But the brothers make 16 types of wine, covering most of the gamut of Collio DOC varieties and a couple of IGT blends.

Critics have given top marks to the Sauvignon Ronco delle Mele, named for the apple orchard at the foot of the terraced incline (*ronco* in dialect), which explains the tree depicted on the label. The wine has a green apple crispness when young, though as it matures it takes on the exquisite flavors and fragrance associated with the Sauvignon R3 clone developed at the Rauscedo vine nurseries in Friuli.

Giorgio, the winemaker, keeps things simple in the cellars, fermenting and maturing the Sauvignon in stainless steel and avoiding malolactic fermentation to retain bright acidity and fresh fruit sensations. He made an oak-fermented Sauvignon called Cerò in the past, but prefers the current purity of line.

Among the Venica whites, the Pinot Bianco can rival Sauvignon from some vintages, though the Tocai Friulano, Pinot Grigio and the blend called Vignis (Tocai with Chardonnay and Sauvignon) also show admirable style. Gianni and Giorgio are determined to bring their reds up to the level of the whites, producing Merlot Perilla, Refosco Bottaz and Rosso delle Cime (a blend of Cabernet, Merlot and Refosco).

Friuli-Venezia Giulia

Grapes
Sauvignon Blanc 100%, hand picked in mid-September.

Vineyard
Ronco delle Mele, a plot of 1.9 hectares in crumbly marl and sandstone soils (known locally as *ponca*) on slopes oriented toward the northwest at 100–150 meters of altitude at Cerò in the commune of Dolegna in the northwestern part of the Collio zone. The vines, of an average age of 17 years, are planted at a density of 4,445 per hectare and trained in the double arched *doppio capovolto* cordon method.

Vinification and aging
Grapes are stemmed and soft crushed and the musts are macerated with the skins for 18 hours at 6–8°C before fermenting in stainless steel tanks at 19°C for 10–15 days. The wine, of about 12.5% alcohol, remains on the lees in tanks at least 6 months without undergoing malolactic fermentation before being bottled and cellared for at least 3 months until release.

Style and maturity
Sauvignon Ronco delle Mele on release in the year after the harvest has pale straw yellow color with glints of gold and clean, fresh aromas with scents reminiscent of elderberries, peaches, green peppers and thyme. Flavors are decisively round and harmonious with crisp acidity buoying fresh fruit sensations and a nut-like tang through a long, smooth finish. The wine reaches a prime in about 3 years but retains mellow style for 2–5 years beyond.

Serving
🍶 12°C.
🍷 Tulip-shaped glass (Sauvignon type).
🍴 *Prosciutto di San Daniele*; *datteri* (date shell mussels) with puréed chickpeas; *scampi alla busara* (cooked with white wine, olive oil, garlic and breadcrumbs).

Piere Sauvignon
Friuli Isonzo DOC
Sauvignon ♀

Producer
Azienda Agricola
Vie di Romans
Località
Vie di Romans 1
34070 Mariano del
Friuli (Gorizia)
Tel. 0481/69600
Fax 0481/69600

Owner
Gianfranco Gallo

Founded
1978

Winemakers
Gianfranco Gallo and
Alessandro Sandrin

Vineyard manager
Gianfranco Gallo

Production
About 28,000 bottles in
favorable years

Vintages
1999 1998 1997 1993
1990 1986 1985

Price
● ●

Behind the name Vie di Romans lies an intriguing tale. In 1986, Gianfranco Gallo shipped about 400 cases of wine to the United States with his family and estate name in small letters on the labels. Some bottles reached California, where they were noticed by attorneys for E. & J. Gallo, the world's largest winery, who threatened a suit for unfair competition if they were not withdrawn from the market immediately.

Needless to say, they were. Gianfranco used the trademark Masut (a family nickname) until 1989, when he renamed the estate Vie di Romans for the ancient road linking the Roman towns of Aquileia and Cividale that passed through the property in the Isonzo plains. "It isn't exactly the Appian Way," says Gianfranco, "but it's the name of a place with a certain history."

Gianfranco, whose family had farmed there for nearly a century, transformed Vie di Romans into an oasis of world-class white wine in the gravelly flats previously noted for robust reds. If the white wines of Isonzo are considered worthy rivals of the elite of the adjacent hills of Collio, the credit goes first to Gianfranco Gallo.

From 28 hectares of vines, Vie di Romans produces about 150,000 bottles a year of Friuli Isonzo DOC wines. These range from the Chardonnays called Ciampagnis Vieris and Vie di Romans (which is oak-fermented) to Pinot Grigio Dessimis to Tocai and the blend called Flors di Uis (Malvasia Istriana, Riesling and Chardonnay) to the lone red Voos dai Ciamps (Merlot and Cabernet). To devotees of Vie di Romans, the top choice often narrows down to a showdown of Sauvignons: the pristine Piere or the oak-matured Vieris. The mineral-rich soils of the plot called Piere, dialect for *pietre* (stones), seem to uplift the spirits of a Sauvignon of singular personality and poise, though the fleshier flavors of Vieris may appeal more to international tastes.

Gianfranco still exports wines to the U.S. with the estate name and his own on labels and has had no further complaints from the California clan whose surname he shares.

Friuli-Venezia Giulia

Grapes
Sauvignon Blanc 100%, hand picked in mid-September.

Vineyards
Grapes are selected in plots of 5.5 hectares in gravelly ferruginous soils rich in magnesium and potassium on plains at 33 meters above sea level at Piere in the commune of Mariano del Friuli in the western part of the Friuli Isonzo zone. The vines, of an average age of 17 years, are planted at a density of 6,000 per hectare and trained in the Guyot cordon method.

Vinification and aging
Grapes are soft crushed and the musts are chilled and decanted statically before fermenting at 15–16°C for 20–30 days in stainless steel tanks. Partial malolactic fermentation occurs during 8–9 months of maturing on the lees in tanks. The wine, of about 14% alcohol, is bottled and cellared for at least 8 months before release.

Style and maturity
Piere Sauvignon on release in the second year after the harvest has pale straw yellow color with glints of green and bright, fresh aromas with scents reminiscent of elderberries, tropical fruit, tomato leaves, sage and hints of gunflint. Flavors are mellow and harmonious with vital acidity buoying fresh fruit sensations that expand on the palate through a long, elegant finish. The wine reaches a prime in about 3 years, but top vintages remain stylish for a decade or more.

Serving
🌡 12–15°C, opening bottle 20 minutes earlier.
🍷 Tulip-shaped glass (white Burgundy type).
🍽 *Antipasti* of Adriatic mollusks and crustaceans; risotto with asparagus tips and grated Parmigiano; poached sea bass.

Villa Russiz

Sauvignon de La Tour
Collio DOC Sauvignon ♀

Producer
Azienda Agricola
Villa Russiz
Via Russiz 6
34070 Capriva del Friuli
(Gorizia)
Tel. 0481/80047
Fax 0481/809657
villarussiz@villarussiz.it
www.villarussiz.it

Owner
Istituto A. Cerruti-Villa
Russiz

Founded
1869

Winemaker
Gianni Menotti

Vineyard manager
Gianni Menotti

Production
8,500 to 12,000 bottles
in favorable years

Vintages
1999 1998 1997 1994
1991 1990 1989 1988

Price

Sauvignon Blanc, the Bordeaux variety that apparently arrived in Italy via Piedmont in the early nineteenth century, found its spiritual home in the northeast, notably in Friuli-Venezia Giulia. The vine seemed to have been introduced there by the French Count Théodore de La Tour, who founded Villa Russiz in 1869, when Friuli was under Austrian rule. Graf de La Tour, as he was known, planted Merlot, the Pinots and Sauvignon on the domain, which his widow later left to the Italian state to become an orphanage named for its founder Adele Cerutti.

The tradition was revived in the 1950s by Edino Menotti, who ran the estate for decades, followed by his son Gianni, the current director, winemaker and vineyard specialist. Gianni, who has been carrying out an ambitious program to restore cellars while gradually renewing 30 hectares of vineyards, produces some of the most consistently fine wines of Friuli. Proceeds from sales support the orphanage.

Production of about 180,000 bottles is dominated by whites that qualify as Collio DOC: Pinot Bianco, Pinot Grigio, Ribolla Gialla, Riesling Renano, Sauvignon and Tocai Friulano. From top vintages, Gianni makes a selection called Sauvignon de La Tour, following cellar methods that are enviably simple—no oak and no malolactic fermentation— for a wine that ranks among the maximum expressions of the variety. The pungently herbaceous traits that often characterize Sauvignon are deftly subdued in an elegantly opulent style that is distinctly Friulian.

Just as impressive in some years is the Pinot Bianco, a vine that seems to have found an ideal habitat on the gentle slopes of Russiz and Spessa in the commune of Capriva del Friuli.

Gianni also excels with reds in a fine Collio Cabernet and a Merlot from top vintages aged to aristocratic splendor as Graf de La Tour (see page 164).

Friuli-Venezia Giulia

Grapes
Sauvignon Blanc 100%, hand picked in late September.

Vineyards
Grapes are selected from 2 plots of about 3 hectares in crumbly marl and sandstone soils on slopes oriented toward the south at 40–80 meters of altitude at Russiz in the commune of Capriva del Friuli at the heart of the Collio DOC zone. The vines, of 16–21 years of age, are planted at densities of 4,000–5,000 per hectare and trained in the Guyot cordon method.

Vinification and aging
Whole grape bunches are gently crushed in pneumatic presses and the free-run must is chilled and decanted statically before fermenting at 18–20°C for 10–15 days in stainless steel tanks. Malolactic fermentation is avoided during 5–6 months of maturing on the lees in tanks. The wine, of about 14.5–15% alcohol, is bottled and cellared for 2–3 months before release.

Style and maturity
Sauvignon de La Tour on release in the year after the harvest has pale straw yellow color with greenish highlights and ample yet refined aromas with scents reminiscent of yellow peppers, cantaloupe, citrus and sage. On the palate, it is full and round with rich fruit sensations balanced by bracing acidity and considerable depth of flavors in a long, smooth finish. The wine reaches a prime in about 2 years, but top vintages may retain style up to a decade.

Serving
🌡 13–14°C.
🍷 Tulip-shaped glass (white Burgundy type).
🍽 Prosciutto di San Daniele with figs; frittata with chard, potatoes and onions; turbot braised in white wine with mussels and clams.

Kastelaz
Alto Adige DOC
Gewürztraminer ♀

Producer
Elena Walch
Castel Ringberg &
Kastelaz
39040 Termeno/Tramin
(Bolzano)
Tel. 0471/860172
Fax 0471/860781
walch@cenida.it
www.elenawalch.com

Owner
Elena Walch

Founded
1986 as Elena Walch

Winemaker
Gianfranco Faustin

Vineyard manager
Gianfranco Faustin

Production
About 10,000 bottles
from choice years

Vintages
1999 1997 1995

Price
● ●

Note
The DOC may be Alto
Adige or Sudtirolo in
Italian or Südtiroler in
German

E lena Walch left a career as an architect in 1988 to join her husband Werner at the venerable Wilhelm Walch cellars, founded at Tramin (or Termeno) in 1896. But Elena had no intention of merely helping Werner to maintain the Walch reputation as a respectable producer of the multitude of wines of Alto Adige. The family properties included the estates of Castel Ringberg and Kastelaz, which she has transformed into increasingly admired sources of the premium wines that carry her name.

Leni, as she's known to her friends, began with unexpected grit in the vineyards. Ringberg, overlooking the lovely lake known as Kalterersee, had been planted in the Vernatsch or Schiava used for the cheerful red wine of that name. She extended the range to include Chardonnay, Pinot Grigio, Riesling, Sauvignon, Cabernet Sauvignon and Merlot. But it wasn't just a routine matter of replanting. She removed wooden pergolas with pole arms that had decorated South Tyrolean terraces for centuries and gradually replaced them with rows of vines planted in greater density and trained in the Guyot cordon method.

At Kastelaz, overlooking Tramin, Elena planted the precipitous south-facing slopes with the Gewürztraminer that takes its name (at least in part) from the town. Although vines are still young, Gewürztraminer from Kastelaz has quickly established itself as a contemporary classic of the South Tyrol, with the soaring aromas and opulent fruit flavors that distinguish the variety. Other vineyards at Kastelaz produce first-rate Pinot Bianco, a reserve Merlot and the exquisitely sweet Moscato Rosa.

Elena Walch has 25 hectares of vineyards to produce about 120,000 bottles of wine a year in collaboration with enologist/agronomist Gianfranco Faustin. So successful have been her signature wines that the line has been extended to cover selections from other vineyards, among them the Alto Adige DOC Cabernet called Istrice and the Chardonnay called Cardellino.

Alto Adige

Grapes
Gewürztraminer 100%, hand picked in late September–early October.

Vineyard
Kastelaz, a plot of 5 hectares in calcareous soils, partly clay, on steeply terraced slopes facing south at 400 meters of altitude at the locality of Kastelaz in the commune of Tramin (Termeno) on the western side of the Adige valley southwest of Bolzano. Vines planted in 1994 at a density of 7,000 per hectare are trained in the Guyot cordon method.

Vinification and aging
Grapes are macerated cold with the skins for about 6 hours before being soft crushed and the musts decanted statically and inoculated with yeast cultures to ferment at 20°C for 8 days in stainless steel tanks. Malolactic fermentation is avoided during 5 months of maturation on the lees in tanks. The wine, of about 13.5% alcohol, is bottled and cellared for 2 months before release.

Style and maturity
Gewürztraminer Kastelaz on release in the spring after the harvest has bright yellow color with golden highlights and intense aromas with scents reminiscent of roses, acacia honey, tropical fruit and lychee accented by spices. Full and round on the palate, its concentrated fruit flavors are buffered by vital acidity with a hint of toasted almond in a long, smooth finish. Impressive after a year or 2, the wine gains mellow elegance for a few years longer.

Serving
🍷 10–12°C.
♀ Tulip-shaped glass (Alsatian type).
🍽 Liver pâtés, short pastry flan with leeks and porcini mushrooms; boiled lobster; goat cheeses.

Scaccomatto
Albana di Romagna Passito
DOCG

Fattoria Zerbina

Producer
Fattoria Zerbina di
Maria Cristina
Geminiani
Via Vicchio 11
48010 Marzeno Faenza
(Ravenna)
Tel. 0546/40022
Fax 0546/40275
zerbina@zerbina.com
www.zerbina.com

Owners
Francesco, Cristina and
Vincenzo Geminiani

Founded
1966

Winemaker
Cristina Geminiani

Vineyard managers
Cristina Geminiani and
Franco Calini

Production
About 600 bottles, 3,000
half bottles (0.375-liter)
and 100 magnums in
choice years

Vintages
2000 1998 1997 1996
1994 1992 1987

Price
● ● ●

When Albana di Romagna became Italy's first DOCG white wine in 1987, critics scoffed or cried scandal over a promotion that was viewed elsewhere as richly undeserved. Most Albana then was dry and bland with a languid finish that smacked of marzipan. Regulations also permitted sweet versions that seemed more in keeping with the legends of a wine that was supposedly revered by nobles 15 centuries ago.

The sweetest is Passito, derived from dried or shriveled grapes. That style intrigued Maria Cristina Geminiani, a young lady with a degree in agronomy who had taken charge of her family's Fattoria Zerbina in the hills of Romagna after studying enology at the University of Bordeaux. Experience in Sauternes led to a fascination with *Botrytis cinerea*, the noble rot that accounts for the exquisite sweetness of certain wines. Cristina managed to create conditions for its development on her farm, planting select clones of Albana in places affected by autumn damp and reducing yields to a fraction of permitted levels to concentrate sugars and aromatic and flavoring components in the grapes.

Working then with consulting enologist Vittorio Fiore, Cristina fermented and matured the wine in new barriques of French oak and named it Scaccomatto (Checkmate) for the bold move that, as it turned out, won the first raves for Albana di Romagna DOCG from connoisseurs. Scaccomatto heralded the fortune of Albana Passito as a wine that is now also made admirably by others.

Fattoria Zerbina has 32 hectares of vineyards to produce about 200,000 bottles a year of Romagna's most impressive range of wines. Cristina makes another Albana Passito called Arrocco, along with selections of DOC Sangiovese di Romagna Superiore (Torre di Ceparano, Ceregio, Ceregio Vigna Querce and Riserva Pietramora) and Colli di Faenza DOC white Tergeno (Chardonnay and Sauvignon Blanc). The IGT Ravenna Rosso called Marzieno, a blend of Sangiovese and Cabernet, now wins as much acclaim as Scaccomatto.

Emilia-Romagna

Grapes
Albana di Romagna 100%, hand picked in phases as *Botrytis cinerea* develops between early October and early November.

Vineyards
Grapes are selected from 3 plots (Laghetto, Spagnera and Ginestre) of 4 hectares in total in calcareous clays over a gravelly stratum on slopes facing southwest at about 150 meters of altitude at Marzeno in the commune of Faenza in the heart of the Albana di Romagna DOCG zone. Vines, of 17–22 years of age, are planted at densities of 2,500 per hectare in trellised *pergoletta*, 4,500 in Guyot cordon and 9,500 in more recent spur-trained *alberello*.

Vinification and aging
Grapes with the stems are crushed gently and the musts are clarified at 12–13°C before fermenting at 20°C for 15–21 days in new 225-liter barrels of French oak, in which maturation follows for 16–18 months. The wine, of about 13.5% alcohol with 12% residual sugar, is bottled and cellared for 12 months before release.

Style and maturity
Scaccomatto on release in the third year after the harvest has deep golden color with faint brassy highlights and intense bouquet with scents reminiscent of apricots, peaches, orange marmalade and an enticing bitter hint from the noble rot. Full bodied and concentrated on the palate, its rich fruit flavors and pronounced sweetness are offset by a refreshing vein of acidity that accounts for seductive balance and complexity in the lingering finish. Though impressive after 3–4 years, great vintages should remain vital for at least 2 decades.

Serving
- 13–14°C.
- Tulip-shaped glass (Chardonnay type).
- Foie gras of goose or duck; blue cheeses, such as Gorgonzola or Roquefort; as aperitif or after-dinner sipping.

Central Italy

Tuscany, Marche, Umbria, Lazio, Abruzzo

The regions of central Italy are divided by the Apennine mountains that loom between the Adriatic and Mediterranean seas. To the west, on the Mediterranean side, lie Tuscany, Lazio and landlocked Umbria; to the east, facing the Adriatic, lie Marche and Abruzzo.

Italy's most diffused vine, Sangiovese, is planted in all regions, though that variety reaches aristocratic heights in Tuscany as the source of Chianti, Brunello di Montalcino and Vino Nobile di Montepulciano. Sangiovese is also employed in many of the so-called Super-Tuscans, which may also derive from Cabernet, Merlot and Syrah, whether alone or in blends.

Other noble native red varieties of central Italy are Montepulciano, which excels in Abruzzi and in Rosso Conero in Marche, and Umbria's mighty Sagrantino.

The ancient white varieties of Malvasia and Trebbiano dominate the white wines of the Mediterranean side, notably in Lazio's Frascati and Est! Est!! Est!!! di Montefiascone, Umbria's Orvieto and Tuscany's rich Vin Santo from dried grapes. Trebbiano can also do well on occasion in Abruzzo, though the rising star among Italian white varieties is Verdicchio, grown almost exclusively in Marche.

PRODUCERS

Tuscany ♥ Antinori 252, Argiano 254, Avignonesi 256, Banfi 258, Biondi Santi 260, Boscarelli 262, Capezzana 264, Castell'in Villa 268, Castello dei Rampolla 270, Castello di Ama 272, Castello di Fonterutoli 274, Castello di Monsanto 276, Castello di Volpaia 278, Col d'Orcia 280, Coltibuono 282, Felsina 284, Fontodi 286, Frescobaldi 288, Isole e Olena 290, Manzano 294, La Massa 296, Montevertine 298, Giovanna Morganti 300, Ornellaia 304, Il Poggione 306, Poliziano 308, Le Pupille 310, Querciabella 312, Ricasoli 314, Riecine 316, Ruffino 318, Salvioni 320, San Felice 322, San Giusto a Rentennano 324, Tenuta San Guido 326, Selvapiana 328, Soldera 330, Villa Cafaggio 336; ♀ Falchini 346, Querciabella 362, San Giusto a Rentennano 366, Teruzzi & Puthod 372 **Marche** ♥ Moroder 302, Umani Ronchi 332; ♀ Bucci 338, Coroncino 344, Fazi Battaglia 350, Garofoli 354, Fattoria la Monacesca 358, Santa Barbara 368, Sartarelli 370, Umani Ronchi 374 **Umbria** ♥ Adanti 250, Caprai 266, Lungarotti 292; ♀ Castello della Sala 342, Palazzone 360 **Lazio** ♀ Castel de Paolis 340, Falesco 348, Fontana Candida 352, Tenuta Le Quinte 364 **Abruzzo** ♥ Valentini 334; ♀ Masciarelli 356, Valentini 376

Trebbiano and Malvasia grapes for Vin Santo drying at Selvapiana

Arquata
Sagrantino di Montefalco
DOCG ?

Producer
Azienda Agricola Adanti
Località Arquata
06031 Bevagna (Perugia)
Tel. 0742 360 295
Fax 0742 361 270
cantineadanti@
cantineadanti.com

Owner
Adanti family

Founded
1975

Winemaker
Mauro Monicchi

Vineyard manager
Mauro Monicchi

Production
About 25,000 bottles
from top vintages

Vintages
1999 1997 1994 1993
1990 1988 1985

Price
● ●

Even if wine lovers had heard of Sagrantino di Montefalco when it emerged in 1992 as Italy's twelfth guaranteed appellation, few beyond its home in Umbria have had the chance to taste it. The Sagrantino vine seems to be planted only around the aloof medieval fortress town of Montefalco, though it's uncertain whether it was indigenous or was brought to Umbria by Saracen invaders or by monks following the paths of St Francis of Assisi.

The name comes from *sagra* (Italian for festival or feast), since Sagrantino was by tradition sweet and reserved for celebrations. The practice of *appassimento* (drying grapes before pressing to concentrate sugars and extract) had prevailed in Umbria for ages. But the so-called Sagrantino *passito*, dark purple with explosively sweet fruit and berry flavors, was frustratingly capricious and needed to be consumed quickly.

Sagrantino entered the modern era in the late 1970s, when the late Domenico Adanti hired Alvaro Palini as cellarmaster of his family's Arquata estate. The astute Alvaro brought out the majesty in this mysterious grape by reducing grape yields and modifying techniques to achieve better balance between fruit, tannins and acids in wines which, after maturing slowly in oak casks, continued to age gracefully in bottle.

Adanti's mighty but mellow Sagrantino *secco* became the prototype, exemplified by the 1985 vintage that was still magnificently rich and smooth in 1999. The equally grand 1990 was a winner among DOCG red wines at the Banco d'Assaggio national competition in 1996. The Adanti Sagrantino *passito* is also impressive.

The Arquata estate has 24 hectares of vines for a total production of about 130,000 bottles a year, including the DOC Montefalco Rosso and Bianco and white Grechetto dei Colli Martani. The estate name applies to the IGT Rosso d'Arquata, a blend of Cabernet Sauvignon, Barbera and Merlot that rates as one of central Italy's best values in red wines.

Umbria

Grapes
Sagrantino 100%, hand picked in late October.

Vineyards
Two plots in the community of Bevagna: 2.8 hectares at Arquata on slopes of calcareous clays facing northwest at 230–280 meters of altitude and 2 hectares at Colcimino in sandy calcareous clay soils facing southeast at 360 meters of altitude. The vines, of an average age of 16 years, are planted at a density of about 2,000 per hectare and trained in a spurred cordon method.

Vinification and aging
Grapes are stemmed and soft crushed and the must fermented in stainless steel tanks at just under 30°C, remaining in contact with the skins for 12–14 days as the liquid is pumped over the cap twice daily at first and once daily later. Malolactic fermentation takes place naturally in tanks before aging for 2 years in medium sized casks of Slavonian and French oak. The wine, of 13.5–14% alcohol, is bottled and cellared for about 10 months before release.

Style and maturity
Sagrantino has a dark ruby color when young, taking on garnet hues with age. When fully mature, it has a lavish bouquet of spices and berries and sumptuous flavors that suggest ripe plums and blackberries with a bracing lift of tannins and a long finish that leaves a hint of licorice on the tongue. From top vintages, the wine is approachable after 5 years, reaching a prime between 6 and 15.

Serving
🍶 18–20°C.

🍷 Tall, ample glass (Burgundy type)

🍽 Umbrian meat dishes, such as veal shank roast in a wood-burning oven and spit-roasted pigeon *alla ghiotta* (basted with red wine and herbs), as well as aged Pecorino cheese.

Tignanello
Toscana IGT ♀

Producer
Marchesi Antinori
Palazzo Antinori
Piazza Antinori 3
50123 Firenze
Tel. 055 235 95
Fax 055 235 9884
antinori@antinori.it
www.antinori.it

Owner
Piero Antinori

Founded
1385

Director
Renzo Cotarella

Chief winemaker
Maurizio Angeletti

Vineyard manager
Claudio Pontremolesi

Production
About 300,000 bottles
a year

Vintages
1999 1998 1997 1996
1995 1993 1990 1988
1986 1985 1983 1975
1971

Price
● ● ●

Piero Antinori, whose family traces its winemaking history to 1385, is the dynamic head of the Florentine house of Marchesi Antinori, leader of the modern renaissance in Tuscan wine. His first innovation, Tignanello, is regarded as the most influential wine of Italy's modern era, though its production was clearly inspired by Sassicaia (see page 326), the Tuscan Cabernet which Antinori also launched on the market in the 1970s.

Tignanello's first vintage was 1971, when Sangiovese was blended with Canaiolo and white Trebbiano and Malvasia in a wine that then adhered to the standards of Chianti Classico (where it is produced) but was pointedly kept outside of the appellation. Working with enologist Giacomo Tachis, Antinori upgraded the Tignanello formula in 1975 by blending Sangiovese with about 20% Cabernet Sauvignon, a revelation in style that fostered a generation of red wines known as Super-Tuscans. Cabernet gave a welcome boost to a wine matured in small barrels of French oak, the barriques that were then curiosities in Tuscany but have since become fixtures in cellars up and down Italy. Tignanello takes the name of a large vineyard on the Antinori Santa Cristina estate. Within it lies the plot called Solaia, whose name applies to a blend of Cabernet Sauvignon with Sangiovese at 20%. Solaia was ranked first by the American journal *The Wine Spectator* in its list of top 100 wines of the world in 2000. But Tignanello remains the house's premier wine because of its pivotal role in modern enology and its continuing class as a red whose character is quintessentially Tuscan. Antinori's wine interests extend to Umbria (Castello della Sala—see page 342), Piedmont (Prunotto—see page 64) and Puglia (Vigneti del Sud), as well as California (Atlas Peak) and Hungary (Bátaapáti). But the prime focus remains on Tuscan wines, produced at the rate of 14.5 million bottles a year, recently augmented by the estates of La Braccesca for Vino Nobile di Montepulciano and Pian delle Vigne for Brunello di Montalcino.

Tuscany

Grapes
Sangiovese 80%,
Cabernet Sauvignon
15%, Cabernet Franc
5%, hand picked in late
September early October
(Cabernets usually ripen
a week before
Sangiovese).

Vineyard
Tignanello of 47 hectares
in calcareous marl with
tufaceous deposits on
slopes facing southwest at
350–400 meters of
altitude at the Santa
Cristina estate near
Montefiridolfi in the
northwestern part of the
Chianti Classico zone.
The vines, of an average
age of 21 years, are
planted at a density of
3,500 per hectare and
trained in the Guyot
cordon method.

Vinification and aging
Grapes are stemmed and
crushed and the varieties
are fermented separately
in open oak vats at less
than 30°C—Sangiovese
for 15 days, Cabernets
for 20 days—with
frequent cap submersion.
After malolactic
fermentation in small
barrels of French oak
(part new, part used
once), the batches are
blended and the wine, of
about 13% alcohol, is
returned to barrels for
about 14 months before
being bottled and cellared
for a year until release.

Style and maturity
Tignanello at its prime
(starting at 5–6 years) has
deep ruby color with scents
that recall plums, cassis, vanilla
and, vaguely, tobacco. Structure
is robust yet accessible with
smooth texture and rich fruit
flavors braced by tannins that
give the wine gentle
complexity. With age,

Tignanello takes on a garnet
cast as flavors lengthen and
dimensions broaden, showing
class that holds for at least 20
years from top vintages.

Serving
🌡 17–18°C.
🍷 Ample crystal glass
(Bordeaux type).
🍴 The ideal match for a rare
Florentine beefsteak,
Tignanello also goes nicely
with roast meats, poultry,
game birds and aged Tuscan
Pecorino cheese.

Argiano

Brunello di Montalcino
DOCG ▎

Producer
Argiano
Sant'Angelo
in Colle
53020 Montalcino
(Siena)
Tel. 0577 844 037
Fax 0577 844 210
argiano@ftbcc.it

Owner
Noemi Marone Cinzano

Founded
1980

Winemaker
Giacomo Tachis

Vineyard manager
Giampiero Pazzaglia

Production
About 130,000 bottles
annually

Vintages
1999 1998 1997 1995
1993 1990 1988 1985
1979

Price
● ●

E states that produce both officially classified wines and Super-Tuscans are, in a sense, seeking to balance the best of both worlds. But the practice, routine among progressive producers, can create confusion and conflicts. Consider the case of Argiano, an estate at Montalcino, where the DOCG rules for Brunello permit release of the wine only in the fifth year after the harvest. Argiano's Brunello from the fine 1995 vintage was issued early in the year 2000, months after Solengo, a Toscana IGT from the great 1997 vintage, had been launched to resounding acclaim.

Thus Solengo, a blend of Sangiovese with Cabernet Sauvignon, Merlot and Syrah, eclipsed the debut of a Brunello that might rate as the estate's finest to date. In 1995, Argiano's estate manager Sebastiano Rosa and winemaker Giacomo Tachis selected their best Sangiovese to produce a single Brunello (excluding *riserva*, which had been made in top years previously). The result was a beautifully concentrated wine of great style that might well be considered a prototype for the new era of Brunello di Montalcino. Not only was 1995 the best vintage in Montalcino since 1990, but with that harvest new rules for Brunello reduced required barrel aging from 3.5 years to 2 years, giving winemakers greater leeway in determining the ideal length of maturation.

Brunello and Solengo have restored glory to an estate that has been a landmark since the twelfth century, when its castle dominated the Orcia valley south of Montalcino. All that remains of the castle is a lonely tower known as Argianaccio. Today the estate is centered in a grandiose *palazzo* built in the fifteenth century by the Gaetani Lovatelli family, which, after relinquishing vast tracts of vineyards to neighboring Banfi (see page 258), sold the property in 1980 to Noemi Marone Cinzano (of the Cinzano wine and vermouth family of Turin). Argiano has 50 hectares of vines to produce about 230,000 bottles a year, including Rosso di Montalcino DOC.

Tuscany

Grapes
Sangiovese 100%, hand picked between late September and late October.

Vineyards
Various plots totaling about 22 hectares in stony calcareous marls on slopes facing generally south at an average of 250 meters of altitude in the Argiano area near Sant'Angelo in Colle in the southern part of the commune of Montalcino. The vines, from 11–13 years of age, are planted at a density of 6,900 per hectare and trained in a spurred cordon method.

Vinification and aging
Grapes are stemmed and soft crushed and the musts fermented in stainless steel tanks at 30–32°C for 14–16 days on the skins with frequent pumping over the cap. After malolactic fermentation, the wine is matured for 2 years, half in small barrels of French oak (part new, part used once) and half in casks of Slavonian oak. The wine, of about 13.5% alcohol, is fined with egg whites, bottled without filtering and cellared until release in the fifth year after the harvest.

Style and maturity
Argiano Brunello when released in the fifth year after the harvest has rich ruby-garnet color with scents that recall ripe fruits and berries, flowers, spices and, vaguely, cedar. The structure is ample in a concentrated and compact wine of impeccable balance and style with tannins that are assuaged with time as flavors become deeper and longer. Although impressive on release, the wine should reach an elaborate prime about a decade after the harvest and retain finesse for a decade or more beyond.

Serving
🌡 18–20°C, opening bottle several hours earlier.
🍷 Ample crystal glass (Bordeaux type).
🍽 Beef, lamb, pork or free-range chicken roast in a wood-burning oven; wood pigeon turned on the spit; aged Pecorino cheese.

Vin Santo Occhio di Pernice
Vino da Tavola di Toscana 🍷

Producer
Avignonesi
via di Gracciano
nel Corso 91
53045 Montepulciano
(Siena)
Tel. 0578 757 872
Fax 0578 757 847
avignonesi@avignonesi.it
www.avignonesi.it.

Owner
Company run by Falvo
brothers

Founded
1974

Winemakers
Ettore Falvo and Paolo
Trappolini

Vineyard manager
Ettore Falvo

Production
About 900 half bottles
(0.375-liter) a year

Vintages
The wine is made every
year, though variables
during drying and aging
account for fascinating
differences from vintage
to vintage

Price
●●●●

Brothers Ettore, Alberto and Leonardo Falvo of Avignonesi led the revival of Vino Nobile di Montepulciano in the 1980s with vanguard techniques extended to an array of premium wines that is formidable even by the eclectic standards of Tuscany.

Ettore Falvo directs production of more than 600,000 bottles a year from 110 hectares of vineyards in the communities of Montepulciano and Cortona. The main focus is on Vino Nobile, including Grandi Annate made only in top years, but the prestigious line takes in Super-Tuscan reds called Grifi (Sangiovese-Cabernet Sauvignon), Il Toro Desiderio (Merlot) and Valcapraia (Pinot Nero), as well as opulent whites called Marzocco (Chardonnay) and Il Vignola (Sauvignon Blanc).

Despite its dynamic modern image, Avignonesi has won greatest acclaim for Vin Santo, Tuscany's age-old "holy wine" made in token quantities by methods that Ettore Falvo insists are devoutly traditional. Avignonesi makes two types of Vin Santo, one from white varieties of Malvasia and Trebbiano, the other from red Prugnolo Gentile, the clone of Sangiovese that is also the base of Vino Nobile. The latter, called Occhio di Pernice (Eye of the Partridge, in reference to its ruddy color), may be Italy's most cherished sweet wine, though production rarely surpasses a thousand half bottles a year.

Grapes are methodically dried for six months before crushing instead of the standard three. Bunches are arrayed on *graticci*, cane mats, in the *appassitoio*, a large room whose windows are open when it's cool and dry and closed when it's mild and damp. Moldy grapes are carefully discarded as they shrivel, losing about 70 percent of their original liquid. Ettore Falvo has prolonged barrel aging to ten years instead of the normal two to five to make Vin Santo that is more concentrated in texture and richer and more luscious in flavor, with depth and polish that others only aspire to.

The Vin Santo from white grapes is aged in barrels for eight years. More is produced: about 2,500 half bottles a year.

Tuscany

Grapes
Prugnolo Gentile 100%; only the ripest, healthiest bunches suited to drying are selected in mid-October and transported in crates in refrigerated vans to drying rooms.

Vineyards
I Poggetti, 18 hectares on slopes of medium packed, slightly alkaline soils at about 350 meters of altitude in the community of Montepulciano. The vines, of an average age of 21 years, are planted at a density of 3,500 per hectare and trained in a high spurred cordon.

Vinification and aging
Dried grapes are crushed whole with their stems, and thick, murky musts are put in small oak barrels called *caratelli* on racks in the *vinsantaia*. Bungholes are sealed with wax for 10 years on each 50-liter capacity barrel, which contains about 45 liters of must and 2 liters of *madre*, residue from earlier vintages that guides the transformation into wine. Evaporation during intermittent fermentations results in some 19 liters a barrel of wine of about 15% alcohol with 15 grams per liter of residual sugars.

Style and maturity
Occhio di Pernice has deep ruddy color with glints of amber on the edges. Bouquet is elaborate with suggestions of raisins, dried fruit, spices, herbs and aged Cognac. Flavors are dense and deep with sumptuous sweetness offset by bracing tannins and extraordinary length on the palate. Ultimate aging potential isn't known; all vintages to date are splendid and improving.

Serving
- 18°C.
- Glass with ample bowl and narrow top.
- Occhio di Pernice should be drunk without food, in small sips, as a wine of meditation.

Banfi

Poggio all'Oro
Brunello di Montalcino Riserv
DOCG ❡

Producer
Banfi
Castello di Poggio
alle Mura
53024 Montalcino
(Siena)
Tel. 0577 840 111
Fax 0577 840 444
banfi@banfi.it
www.castellobanfi.com

Owner
Mariani family

Founded
1978

Chief winemaker
Rudi Buratti

Vineyard manager
Maurizio Marmugi

Production
60,000 bottles from
choice vintages

Vintages
1999 1997 1995 1993
1990 1988
1985

Price
● ● ●

B anfi, the largest producer of Brunello di Montalcino with nearly 350,000 bottles a year, is owned by the Mariani family, which built the firm into the prime importer of Italian wines in the United States. The estate, developed by the eminent enologist Ezio Rivella, who recently retired, takes in vast spreads of vines in the southwestern corner of Montalcino around the imposing castle of Poggio alle Mura (now called Castello Banfi).

Banfi specializes in Brunello, in both a regular vintage bottling and a single-vineyard reserve known as Poggio all'Oro (Golden Hill), which was first produced in 1985. That wine, which has won numerous awards in Italy, is especially prized in America, where, at a recent Sotheby's auction in New York, a six-bottle case of the great 1990 vintage sold at $1,380. Equally impressive is the 1993 Poggio all'Oro, which stood out in a vintage that was by no means outstanding over all in Montalcino. Admirers anticipate even greater things when the 1995 and 1997 vintages are issued in 2001 and 2003.

Brothers John and Harry Mariani bought the property at Montalcino in 1978 and commissioned Ezio Rivella to develop what ranks as Italy's most colossal wine estate, a project that hastened the confirmation of the once rare and coveted Brunello as a red wine of international stature.

From the 800 hectares of vines at Montalcino, Banfi produces about 8 million bottles of estate wines a year. These range beyond Brunello and Rosso di Montalcino through reds and whites from varieties that include Cabernet, Merlot, Pinot Noir, Syrah, Chardonnay and Sauvignon Blanc. Some of these qualify under the recent Sant'Antimo DOC for alternative wines of Montalcino. Banfi, which offers impeccable value at all price levels, also produces white Gavi and sparkling wines from vineyards and cellars in Piedmont.

Tuscany

Grapes
Sangiovese 100% (select Brunello clones), hand picked in 2 phases in early October.

Vineyard
Poggio all'Oro covers 24.4 hectares in medium-packed stony soils rich in marine fossils on slopes facing southwest at about 250 meters of altitude at a place called La Pieve in the southwest corner of the commune of Montalcino. The vines, of an average age of 16 years, are planted at a density of 3,600 per hectare and trained in a spurred cordon method.

Vinification and aging
Grape bunches are individually selected before being stemmed and soft crushed and the must fermented for 9 days in stainless steel vats at 27–31°C, followed by another 15 days of maceration with the skins. Malolactic fermentation takes place in stainless steel tanks before aging for 4 years in wood, half in 12,000-liter capacity casks of Slavonian oak and half in new barrels of French oak from Allier. The wine, of about 13.5% alcohol, is bottled and cellared for a year before release.

Style and maturity
Poggio all'Oro when released in the sixth year after the harvest has deep ruby-garnet color and intense bouquet that recalls ripe berries and spices with a hint of violets typical of Brunello. Its decisive impact on the palate is marked by nobly austere tannins that gradually soften as the wine becomes velvety and complex over time with notes of tar and cedar in its lingering aftertaste. The wine reaches peaks at 10–12 years and promises to maintain them for at least another decade.

Serving
🍷 18–20°C.
🍷 Tall, ample glass (Bordeaux type).
🍽 Tuscan beef, lamb and game dishes, such as wild boar stewed in red wine or roast duck, as well as aged Pecorino cheeses from around nearby Siena.

Biondi Santi

Brunello di Montalcino Riserva DOCG ▽

Producer
Tenuta Greppo di
Franco Biondi Santi
Tenuta Greppo
53024 Montalcino
(Siena)
Tel. 0577 848 087
Fax 0577 849 396
biondisanti@
biondisanti.it
www.biondisanti.it

Owner
Franco Biondi Santi

Founded
Mid-19th century

Winemaker
Franco Biondi Santi

Vineyard manager
Franco Biondi Santi

Production
8,000–10,000 bottles in
choice years

Vintages
1999 1997 1995 1993
1990 1988 1985 1983
1982 1981 1975 1971
1970 1969 1968 1964
1955 1945 1925 1891
1888

Price
● ● ● ●

Note
Biondi Santi has
Brunello Riserva for sale
ranging back through
the 1975, 1964, 1955
and 1945 vintages

Brunello di Montalcino in its formative years was synonymous with the name Biondi Santi. The first wine of the name was produced by Ferruccio Biondi Santi in 1888 at the family's Greppo estate, where in the 1860s his maternal grandfather Clemente Santi made an award-winning "Vino scelto (Brunello)." Ferruccio's son Tancredi made the name Brunello famous through his own skills and his astute habit of stashing away bottles of top vintages, including the 1888 and 1891, whose vitality astounded experts more than a century later.

Tancredi's son Franco continues to make Brunello in the grand tradition, selecting only grapes from very old vines for his vaunted Riserva and following vinification and aging techniques that give it an aristocratic aura of earlier times. Competition has increased in a field that now includes about 130 producers of Brunello di Montalcino DOCG, but Biondi Santi stands apart from the crowd for its history and self-imposed standards of winemaking that refuse compromise.

The Brunello Riserva tends to be severe and unyielding in its youth, which is why Franco Biondi Santi insists that great vintages need 20 years or more to begin showing class and why he recommends opening bottles to "breathe" hours before serving. Aeration does help to bring out the uncommon depth and complexity of reserve wines that remain among the most prized and expensive of Italy, in particular those dating back 30 years or more (which the producer will top up with the same vintage and recork at his expense). The cellars of Il Greppo still contain bottles of the Biondi Santi Brunello Riserva from 1925, 1891 and the original 1888, which, though no longer for sale, is valued at 100 million lire (about $50,000/£30,000).

Biondi Santi also produces a regular Brunello di Montalcino 'Annata' and Rosso di Montalcino from younger vines. Average production of the three types is 70,000 bottles a year.

Tuscany

Grapes
Sangiovese Grosso 100%, hand picked in late September.

Vineyards
Grapes for Brunello Riserva come from the Greppo, Pievecchia, Pieri, Buonconsiglio and Greppino plots totaling 20 hectares in stony galestro (schistous) soils with tufaceous clay on slopes oriented toward the northeast, east and south at 400–500 meters of altitude in an area lying about a kilometer southeast of the town of Montalcino. The vines, between 25–80 years of age, are planted at a density of 2,500 per hectare and trained in a spurred cordon method.

Vinification and aging
Grapes for Riserva, selected from older vines, are soft crushed and the musts fermented for 15–18 days in vats of Slavonian oak at 26–33°C, as liquid is pumped over the cap twice daily. The wine is aged in Slavonian oak casks of 800–7,000-liter capacity for 2–3 years, as malolactic fermentation occurs naturally. The wine, of 12.5–13% alcohol, is bottled after light filtering and released starting in the sixth year after the harvest.

Style and maturity
Biondi Santi Brunello Riserva has, on release, a brilliant ruby-garnet color and refined bouquet with subtle scents suggesting iris, vines in bloom and vanilla. The structure is robust with ample tannins that yield ever so gradually as the wine achieves a warm harmony of flavors that seem to become more aristocratically austere with age. The producer has evidence that great vintages maintain integrity for a century, though bouquet and flavor reach optimum levels at between 2 and 3 decades.

Serving
- 18°C, after removing the cork 8 hours ahead of time.
- Ample crystal glass (Bordeaux type).
- Roast and grilled meats and game birds, such as guinea fowl, pigeon or duck.

Boscarelli
Vino da Tavola di Toscana ❦

Producer
Boscarelli
Via di Montenero 28
53040 Montepulciano
(Siena)
Tel. 0578 767 277
Fax 0578 767 277

Owner
Paola De Ferrari Corradi

Founded
1964

Winemaker
Maurizio Castelli

Vineyard manager
Maurizio Castelli

Production
About 6,500 bottles
from choice vintages

Vintages
1999 1997 1995 1993
1990 1988 1985 1983

Price
● ●

My early tastings of Vino Nobile di Montepulciano in the 1960s left me wondering how in the world the "noble" got into the name. For it seemed to me that all the decadence of Tuscan tradition had been trapped in the then available bottles of what had been lauded in the seventeenth century by the poet Francesco Redi as "of all wines king."

Then, in the mid-1970s, Ippolito and Paola De Ferrari Corradi, a young couple from Genoa, quietly introduced new concepts of winemaking at their small Poderi Boscarelli and emerged with perhaps the first modern wines that lived up to the name. Ippolito died all too soon after, but Paola and sons Luca and Niccolò carried on, hiring Maurizio Castelli to make wines that inspired the revival of Vino Nobile.

In 1983, caught up in the wave of innovation that was sweeping Tuscany, they produced a wine called simply Boscarelli of pure Sangiovese matured in barrels of French oak. Though not officially a Nobile, Boscarelli from fine vintages has been the wine that best expresses how Sangiovese (known locally as Prugnolo Gentile) prospers in the privileged terrains of Montepulciano.

Boscarelli from 1985 was the most appealing wine among 27 old vintages presented in the "Taste of Tuscan History" event in Florence in 1996.

From 14 hectares of vines, Poderi Boscarelli produces from 60,000–70,000 bottles of estate wines annually, including Vino Nobile di Montepulciano DOCG and the prized Riserva Vigna del Nocio.

Tuscany

Grapes
Prugnolo Gentile
(Sangiovese) 100%, hand
picked in late
September–early
October.

Vineyards
Two choice plots covering
2 hectares in sandy
alluvial soil with traces of
lime and clay on slopes
facing south-southwest at
320 meters of altitude at
Cervognano on the edge
of the Chiana valley 6
kilometers east of the
town of Montepulciano.
The estate's vines, planted
in 1963 and 1995, range
in density from
2,800–6,000 per hectare
and are trained in a
Guyot cordon method.

Vinification and aging
Grapes are stemmed and
soft crushed and the
musts fermented for
15–25 days in small oak
vats and stainless steel
tanks at 32°C, as the cap
is periodically punched
down with poles by
hand. Malolactic
fermentation takes place
in barrels of French oak
from Allier, Nevers and
Vosges (30–50% new
annually) in which, after
racking, the wine matures
for 18–20 months.
Boscarelli, of about
13.5% alcohol, is bottled
and cellared for at least 6
months before release.

Style and maturity
Boscarelli is rich, round and
concentrated with deep ruby-
garnet color and scents of ripe
fruit, berries and spices
enhanced by a whiff of violets
in its full bouquet. Irresistible
after 7 years, when flavors
show uncommon depth and
scarcely a hint of the austere
tannins that characterized old
wines from Sangiovese, it
develops mellow complexity
while maintaining elegance for
well over a decade beyond.

Serving
🌡 18°C, opening the bottle
2–3 hours ahead of time.
🍷 Tall, ample glass (Bordeaux
type).
🍽 Risotto with porcini
mushrooms; roast, grilled
or braised game; aged
Pecorino cheese from
nearby Pienza.

Villa di Capezzana Carmignan Riserva DOCG ❢

Producer
Tenuta di Capezzana
Via Capezzana 100
59015 Carmignano
(Prato)
Tel. 055 870 6005
Fax 055 870 6673
capezzana@dada.it
www.capezzana.it

Owner
Conte Contini Bonacossi

Founded
Ancient Roman times

Winemaker
Stefano Chioccioli

Vineyard manager
Stefano Chioccioli

Production
10,000–11,000 bottles
in choice years

Vintages
1999 1998 1997 1996
1995 1993 1990 1989

Price
● ●

Note
Beginning in 1998, the
estate will produce only
a single Villa di
Capezzana Carmignano
DOCG from choice
vintages, no longer a
Riserva

It's hard to imagine a wine domain anywhere with the historical credentials of Capezzana, the property developed by the Contini Bonacossi family into the premier estate of Carmignano. The name Capezzana derived from *Capitus,* as it was called by Roman army veterans in the first century BC, when they were assigned land around Carmignano on a hill overlooking Florence from the west. The estate was cited as Capetiana in AD 804 in a document that also referred to its wine and olive oil.

In the fourteenth century, the red Vermiglio of Carmignano was valued above other wines of Tuscany by Francesco Datini, the merchant of Prato, and his friend Lapo Mazzei, who had an estate of his own near Capezzana. In 1716, a decree of Cosimo III de Medici designated Carmignano as one of four wines of controlled name and origin in the Grand Duchy of Tuscany—perhaps the first document in history recognizing official denominations. Records showed that a variety called Uva Francesca, or Cabernet, was planted there in the eighteenth century. That gave historical precedence to the current formula for Carmignano, whose revival as a DOCG in 1991 was a tribute to the prodigious efforts of Ugo Contini Bonacossi.

His family had acquired Capezzana early in the twentieth century and developed lands that today include 100 hectares of vineyards extending around the the historic Medici villa and the other Contini Bonacossi estate of Villa di Trefiano. The Carmignano of Villa di Capezzana blends the native Sangiovese and Canaiolo with Cabernet in a Riserva that stands as a testimonial to an illustrious past.

The estate's total production of about 500,000 bottles a year includes Carmignano DOC red Barco Reale, Rosato (called Vin Ruspo) and Vin Santo, as well as Chianti Montalbano DOCG and an IGT called Ghiaie della Furba, from Cabernet with Merlot.

Tuscany

Grapes
Sangiovese 60%, Cabernet Sauvignon 20%, Canaiolo Nero 10%, other varieties 10%, hand picked in late October and early November.

Vineyards
Plots known as Trote, Sant'Isabella and Cevoli totaling 47 hectares in alberese limestone and schistous galestro soils on slopes oriented toward the southeast, north and southwest at about 200 meters of altitude in the communes of Carmignano and Poggio a Caiano. The vines, from 23–32 years of age, are planted at a density of 4,000–6,500 per hectare and trained in Guyot and spurred cordon methods.

Vinification and aging
Grapes are stemmed and soft crushed and the musts fermented at 28–30°C for 7–9 days, as the liquid is pumped over the cap 5 or 6 times. Malolactic fermentation, started in the same tanks, is completed before the wine is matured in barrels of relatively new oak for the required 2 years. The wine, of 13–13.5% alcohol, is bottled and stored in controlled conditions until release starting 3 years after the harvest.

Style and maturity
Carmignano Riserva on release has ruby-red color with garnet tones and refined bouquet that brings together scents of Sangiovese and Cabernet with hints of berries, resin and spices. Even from great vintages, structure tends more toward elegant than robust, as the wine gradually takes on a warm harmony of flavors. The wine reaches a prime in 6–7 years, though great vintages last for decades, assuming an aristocratic austerity reminiscent of classic clarets.

Serving
🌡 18–20°C.
🍷 Ample tulip-shaped glass (Bordeaux type)
🍽 Roast and grilled beef, lamb, pork and game birds; rabbit stewed with olives; aged Pecorino cheese.

25 Anni
Sagrantino di Montefalco
DOCG ▉

Producer
Val di Maggio
Arnaldo Caprai
Località Torre
06036 Montefalco
(Perugia)
Tel. 0742 378 802
Tel. 0742 378 523
Fax 0742 378 422
info@
arnaldocaprai.it
www.arnaldocaprai.it

Owners
Arnaldo and Marco
Caprai

Founded
1971

Winemaker
Attilio Pagli

Vineyard manager
Francesco Cisani

Production
About 25,000 bottles
from choice vintages

Vintages
2000 1999 1998 1997
1996 1995 1994 1993

Price
● ● ●

Marco Caprai's aim of fashioning Sagrantino di Montefalco for twenty-first century tastes seems to be pretty well on target. His special selection called 25 Anni, created in 1993 to celebrate the Val di Maggio estate's first quarter century in 1996, has won growing acclaim in Italy with sometimes lavish ratings from critics. But Sagrantino as a category is still too rare and exotic to have made an impact abroad.

Caprai, backed by a fortune compiled by his father Arnaldo in the textile industry, works with Attilio Pagli, a Tuscan consulting enologist who has access to the ultimate in equipment, including mounting rows of French barriques, which are gradually replacing the casks of Slavonian oak that long prevailed in Umbria's cellars. Pagli's techniques have somewhat tempered Sagrantino's noted tannic grip on the tongue, while maturing in barriques has lent the wine those touches that are sometimes described as international style.

In other words, 25 Anni combines opulence of bouquet and flavor with the requisite doses of new oak to ensure Umbria's entry to the company of blockbuster reds that seem to have gained the upper hand among the world's wine critics. Yet some tasters find the wine to be too self-consciously modern, as extravagant as the price, which skyrocketed with the early success.

Caprai's dynamic approach contrasts with the calmer progress of other top producers of Sagrantino, Adanti (see page 250) and Antonelli, whose wines have been gaining stature in a less conspicuous manner. Sagrantino may be challenging winemakers' skills and imaginations for years to come, though few experts seem to doubt that the variety has the stuff of greatness.

From 80 hectares of vines, Val di Maggio produces about 750,000 bottles of wine a year, including the sweet Sagrantino Passito (from semidried grapes), Montefalco Bianco and Rosso DOC and a white called Grecante that qualifies as Grechetto dei Colli Martani DOC.

Umbria

Grapes
Sagrantino 100%, hand picked in late September.

Vineyards
Two plots of about 4 hectares in total planted in calcareous clay soils—one facing southeast at 250 meters of altitude at Torre in the commune of Montefalco and one facing southwest at 400 meters at La Valle in the commune of Gualdo Cattaneo. The vines, from 8–21 years of age, are planted at densities of 5,500 and 6,600 per hectare and trained in a spurred cordon method.

Vinification and aging
Grapes are stemmed and soft crushed and the must fermented in part in stainless steel tanks and part in wooden vats at 28–33°C for 15–18 days, remaining in contact with the skins for 12–15 days as the liquid is pumped over the cap twice daily. Malolactic fermentation takes place in new French barrels of oak from Allier, where maturation continues for 29–30 months. The wine, of about 13.5% alcohol, is bottled and cellared for a year before release.

Style and maturity
Sagrantino 25 Anni on release after 4 years has deep ruby color, taking on garnet tones with time. The bouquet is rich and full with sensations of ripe fruit (plums and wild blackberries), spices and vanilla that carry over into powerful yet mellow and velvety flavors with a long finish that leaves a pleasantly bitter tang on the tongue. Ultimate aging potential isn't known for a wine first made in 1993, but signs point to a long and distinguished life.

Serving
🍷 18°C.
♀ Large glass (Bordeaux type).
🍽 Richly flavored meat and game dishes, such as pork roast with rosemary and garlic and hare braised in red wine, as well as aged Pecorino cheese.

Castell'in Villa

Producer
Castell'in Villa
Località
Castell'in Villa
53019 Castelnuovo
Berardenga (Siena)
Tel. 0577 359 074
Fax 0577 359 222
castellinvilla@interfree.it
www.castellinvilla.com

Owner
Coralia Pignatelli

Founded
1968

Winemaker
Coralia Pignatelli

Vineyard manager
Coralia Pignatelli

Production
About 9,000 bottles
from choice vintages

Vintages
1999 1997 1996 1994

Price
● ● ●

Poggio delle Rose
Chianti Classico Riserva
DOCG 🍷

When Greek-born Coralia Ghertsos married Italian Prince Riccardo Pignatelli della Leonessa, she spent most of her time abroad with her ambassador husband. But in 1968 they bought a rundown estate called Castell'in Villa in Chianti as a country retreat and Coralia decided to settle in and try her hand at making wine. Relying on textbooks and help from technicians of the Chianti Classico producers' consortium, she succeeded with more than just amateurish good luck.

"In diplomatic circles, I was able to drink the finest of French wines," recalls Coralia. "But, you know, I quickly fell in love with Sangiovese." Her Chianti soon became so stylish that it drew the attention of Giacomo Tachis, then enologist at Antinori, who has provided friendly advice since. But Coralia, whose husband died in 1985, has always insisted on doing things in her own way, and her wines reflect her feminine intuition and forceful personality.

She ventured beyond Chianti Classico in 1983 with a Super-Tuscan called Santacroce that blends Sangiovese with a touch of Cabernet Sauvignon. But in the early 1990s, she prepared a special plot among her 54 hectares of vines, planted it in pure Sangiovese and called it Poggio delle Rose.

Her first vintage of Chianti Classico Riserva Poggio delle Rose was 1994, a middling year in much of Chianti but an outstanding one for Castell'in Villa. That wine, recently released, had rich, velvety flavors and magnificent bouquet to easily outclass most reserve Chianti from the highly rated 1995 vintage. In fact, *la Principessa*, as she is known around Chianti, skipped 1995 to return with 1996, offering further proof that Castell'in Villa excels in medium years.

Her wines, which include a regular Chianti Classico and Riserva, as well as a delicately sweet Vin Santo, are served at a restaurant on the premises.

Tuscany

Grapes
Sangiovese 100%, hand
picked in late September.

Vineyard
Poggio delle Rose covers
2.7 hectares in soils of
stratified sands mixed
with alluvial stones and
marine deposits at
330–350 meters of
altitude in the commune
of Castelnuovo
Berardenga in the
southeastern part of
Chianti Classico. The
vines, of an average age of
10 years, are planted at a
density of 4,460 per
hectare and trained in a
double Guyot spurred
cordon method.

Vinification and aging
Grapes are stemmed and
soft crushed and the
must fermented in
stainless steel vats at
28–30°C for 10–12 days
on the skins. After
malolactic fermentation,
the wine is matured for
18 months in small
barrels of French oak
from Allier. The wine, of
13–13.5% alcohol, is
bottled and cellared for a
year before release.

Style and maturity
Chianti Classico Poggio delle
Rose has deep ruby-red color
with hints of garnet on the
rim. The bouquet is full and
harmonious with scents
reminiscent of ripe cherries,
blackberries, spices, violets and
roses. On the palate it shows
ample structure with rich fruit
sensations underlined by well-
rounded wood tannins in
flavors that are supple, smooth
and warm after 5 years,
though the wine seems to
have the stature to remain
splendid for 10 or 15 years.

Serving
🌡 18°C.
🍷 Ample glass (Bordeaux
type).
🍴 *Pappardelle alla lepre*
(noodles with hare sauce);
rack of spring lamb roasted
with wild herbs; charcoal-
grilled slabs of Chianina
beef served rare in slices as
tagliata.

Castello dei Rampolla

Vigna d'Alceo
Toscana IGT ♟

Producer
Azienda Agricola Santa
Lucia in Faulle
Via Case Sparse 32
50020 Panzano in
Chianti (Firenze)
Tel. 055 852 001
Fax 055 852 533
castellodeirampolla.cast
@tin.it

Owner
Di Napoli Rampolla
family

Founded
1965

Winemaker
Giacomo Tachis

Vineyard managers
Luca and Maurizia Di
Napoli

Production
13,000–15,000 bottles a
year

Vintages
1998 1997 1996

Price
● ● ● ●

One might imagine that a prince with a splendid castle in Chianti would have ruled his estate with a patrician air, but Alceo Di Napoli Rampolla is remembered fondly as the *principe contadino* who toiled in his vineyards like a hired hand. Castello dei Rampolla is located in the Conca d'Oro, a declivity formed by the Pesa stream beneath the town of Panzano, where some of the finest Chianti Classico originates. But the farmer prince had a fondness for Bordeaux and with his enological mentor Giacomo Tachis chose Cabernet Sauvignon as the base of a wine called Sammarco, after his son Marco, a helicopter pilot killed in a crash.

Sammarco, blended with about 20% of Sangiovese, was one of the noblest Super-Tuscans created in the 1980s. But Alceo wanted to make a wine even closer in character to his models in the Médoc, so in 1990 he began planting Cabernet Sauvignon and Petit Verdot, a minor Bordeaux variety reputed to lend color, fragrance and a vigorous spicy quality to the blend. To give the wine power and concentration, he planted vines at high density to be pruned low in the spur-training method rarely used in Tuscany.

Alceo passed away after the first part of the vineyard was planted, but son Luca and daughter Maurizia have brought it to fruition with a wine that would certainly have made the farmer prince proud. The first vintage of La Vigna d'Alceo, 1996, was greeted with critical raves, inspiring Italy's influential *Gambero Rosso* guide to name it wine of the year in 1999. Long-time admirers of Sammarco concede that La Vigna d'Alceo has somewhat richer, rounder flavors with that mellow quality that the French call *souplesse*.

Castello dei Rampolla has 42 hectares of vines for an annual production of about 140,000 bottles of wine, including DOCG Chianti Classico and a Chianti Classico Riserva that ranks as the estate's third label but wins high praise nonetheless.

Tuscany

Grapes
Cabernet Sauvignon 85%, Petit Verdot 15%, hand picked in late September–early October.

Vineyard
La Vigna d'Alceo of 7 hectares in stony, schistous galestro soils on slopes oriented toward the south at 360 meters of altitude at Santa Lucia in Faulle near the town of Panzano in the heart of Chianti Classico. The vines, planted in 1990 at a density of 8,000–10,000 per hectare, are trained in the low, spur-trained *alberello* method.

Vinification and aging
Grapes are stemmed and soft crushed and the musts fermented for 6 days at 30°C in enameled steel tanks, followed by malolactic fermentation in small barrels of French oak. After racking, the wine, of about 13.5% alcohol, is matured for a year in 225-liter barriques, then bottled and cellared for at least 6 months before release.

Style and maturity
Vigna d'Alceo from the first vintage of 1996 has solid structure, smooth texture and deep ruby color of excellent tone. The bouquet is intense, clean and rich with scents of ripe fruit and spices that already show signs of elegance. Agreeably balanced between dry and sweet, it has a bracingly firm feel on the tongue and a long, smooth finish, with lingering hints of chocolate and tobacco. The wine seems to have exceptional potential to gain in depth and complexity with age.

Serving
🌡 18°C.

🍷 Ample crystal glass (Bordeaux type).

🍽 With noble country fare, such as *pappardelle alla lepre* (noodles with hare sauce), duck braised with olives, goose roast in a wood-burning oven.

Castello di Ama
Chianti Classico DOCG ♟

Producer
Castello di Ama
53010 Lecchi di Gaiole
in Chianti (Siena)
Tel. 0577 746 031
Fax 0577 746 117
amawine@tin.it

Owners
Sebasti, Cavanna,
Tradico and Carini
families

Founded
1972

Winemaker
Marco Pallanti

Vineyard manager
Marco Pallanti

Production
150,000–160,000
bottles a year, including
magnums and double
magnums

Vintages
1999 1998 1997

Price
● ●

Ama, a medieval hamlet in Chianti long noted for its wines and olive oil, was in a state of disrepair in the 1970s when it was acquired by four Roman families with the aim of converting it into a modern estate. They succeeded rapidly, thanks to the wisdom and drive of manager Silvano Formigli and winemaker Marco Pallanti, who put prime emphasis on Castello di Ama's single-vineyard Chianti Classico. That policy went against trends in the 1980s, when the rise of the unclassified Super-Tuscans was in full swing. But they persisted with Chianti Classico from the vineyards of Bellavista, San Lorenzo and eventually La Casuccia and Bertinga, as wines whose distinct personalities respected the nature of their terrains. Those wines headed Castello di Ama's list, even when Vigna L'Apparita, one of Tuscany's first and finest Merlots, began winning critical raves.

Silvano Formigli has moved on, but Marco Pallanti stayed and married estate director Lorenza Sebasti, forming a team that has brought even more luster to Castello di Ama. For years they have been acquiring new plots and redoing old ones, selecting superior clones of Sangiovese and adapting a system known as *lira aperta* (vines trained in the shape of a lyre) to improve the quality of grapes.

From the great 1997 vintage, they consolidated production from four vineyards in a new banner Chianti Classico called, appropriately, Castello di Ama. They have maintained Chianti Classico Bellavista and La Casuccia from top vintages at the rate of about 5,000 bottles each, symbolic quantities compared with the 150,000 bottles of the wine that now represents their domain.

From 90 hectares of vines, Castello di Ama produces a total of about 300,000 bottles of wine a year, including the prized Merlot Vigna L'Apparita, Pinot Nero Il Chiuso and Chardonnay Vigna al Poggio.

Tuscany

CHIANTI CLASSICO

1997

CASTELLO DI AMA

Grapes
Sangiovese 80%, Canaiolo 8%, Malvasia Nera and Merlot 12%, hand picked in late September–early October.

Vineyards
Grapes are selected from 55 hectares of vines in 4 plots—Bellavista, La Casuccia, San Lorenzo, Bertinga—on slopes of stony calcareous clays ranging from 390–530 meters of altitude with varied sun exposure around Ama in the commune of Gaiole in south-central Chianti Classico. The vines, planted between 1964 and 1978 at a density of 3,000 per hectare, are trained in Guyot cordon and the system known as *lira aperta* (in the form of a lyre).

Vinification and aging
Grapes are stemmed and soft crushed and the must fermented in stainless steel vats at no more than 33°C for 23–24 days on the skins. After malolactic fermentation, mainly in small oak barrels, the wine is matured for just over a year in barriques of French oak (40% new and the rest used from 1–3 years). The wine, of about 13% alcohol, is bottled and cellared for a year before release

Style and maturity
Chianti Classico Castello di Ama from the initial 1997 vintage has intense ruby-red color with bouquet that recalls ripe fruit and berries, morello cherries and vanilla. On the palate it shows firm structure with full fruit nicely set off by tannins that will soften as flavors become broader and longer. From the outstanding 1997 vintage, the wine should approach a prime at 5–6 years and retain virtues for at least 15 years.

Serving
🌡 16–18°C.
🍷 Tall, ample glass (Bordeaux type)
🍽 Classic Tuscan meat and poultry dishes, such as charcoal-grilled Chianina beefsteak, skewers of spit-roasted pork and chicken, as well as aged Pecorino cheeses.

Castello di Fonterutoli
Chianti Classico DOCG ❢

Producer
Castello di Fonterutoli
Via Rossini 5
Località Fonterutoli
53011 Castellina in
Chianti (Siena)
Tel. 0577 735 71
Fax 0577 735 757
fonterutoli@fonterutoli.it
www.fonterutoli.it

Owners
Marchesi Mazzei

Founded
1435

Winemaker
Carlo Ferrini

Vineyard manager
Carlo Ferrini

Production
About 100,000 bottles a
year

Vintages
1998 1997 1996 1995

Price
● ●

Among numerous Tuscan families that have made wine for centuries, perhaps the two most intimately linked to Chianti have been the Ricasoli of Brolio (see page 314) and the Mazzei of Fonterutoli. In 1398, Ser Lapo Mazzei, a Florentine notary and jurist, recorded the first sale of a wine called Chianti. Curiously, that wine was white and probably sweet, while today Chianti by law must be red and dry. Ser Lapo's heirs founded Fonterutoli in 1435 and today the estate owned by his namesake ranks among the most illustrious of Chianti Classico.

The modern Lapo Mazzei, who headed the Classico producers' consortium for years, runs Fonterutoli with sons Francesco and Filippo. Like other enlightened producers of post-flask Chianti, they created alternative reds, first a Sangiovese-Cabernet blend called Concerto in 1981 and then a Merlot-Sangiovese blend called Siepi in 1993. In between, they dedicated a reserve to Ser Lapo, a fine Chianti Classico that was unjustly overshadowed by the Super-Tuscans.

Chianti's second-class status troubled the modern Lapo and his sons who wanted to restore luster to the most widely recognized name in Italian wine. They decided to create a Chianti Classico of traditional stature and contemporary style to carry the name Castello di Fonterutoli.

To do so, they sacrificed Concerto, using the Cabernet at 10% to complement Sangiovese selected from their top vineyards: Fonterutoli and Siepi. Winemaker Carlo Ferrini took up the challenge with aplomb, using small oak barrels to fashion 100,000 bottles from the outstanding 1995 vintage and following up from the reputedly weaker 1996 with a wine of equal dignity. Castello di Fonterutoli has become the model for the new millennium for what may come to be known as Super Chianti Classico.

From 62 hectares of vines, the estate produces about 400,000 bottles of wine a year, including regular Chianti and Classico called Fonterutoli and the IGT Siepi and Poggio alla Badiola.

Tuscany

Grapes
Sangiovese 90%,
Cabernet Sauvignon
10%, hand picked in late
September–mid-October.

Vineyards
Grapes are selected from
2 plots: Fonterutoli of
15 hectares on slopes
facing south at 150
meters of altitude and
Siepi of 17 hectares on
slopes facing southwest at
260 meters, both in
rocky soils of limestone
and sandstone in the
commune of Castellina
in the southwestern part
of Chianti Classico. The
vines, between 16 and
26 years old, are planted
at densities of
4,500–6,000 per hectare
and trained in spurred
cordon or the arched
cordon system called
archetto toscano.

Vinification and aging
Grapes are stemmed and
soft crushed and the
must fermented in
stainless steel vats at 33°C
for 18 days on the skins.
After natural malolactic
fermentation, the wine,
of about 13% alcohol, is
matured in small oak
barrels for 16–18
months, then bottled and
cellared for at least 6
months before release.

Style and maturity
Chianti Classico Castello di
Fonterutoli from the 1995 and
1996 vintages shows intense
ruby-red color with bouquet
that recalls ripe fruit and
berries, morello cherries,
spices and vanilla. On the
palate it has rich structure
with well-rounded wood
tannins underpinning fruit
flavors that will continue to
expand, though they are
already nicely balanced and
long on the tongue. The wine
should approach a prime at
5–6 years and maintain its
elegance for at least a decade
beyond.

Serving
🌡 18°C.
🍷 Tall, ample glass (Bordeaux
type).
🍽 Classic Tuscan meat and
poultry dishes, such as
arista (pork loin roasted
with rosemary and wild
fennel) and spit-roasted
game birds, as well as aged
Pecorino cheeses.

Castello di Monsanto

Il Poggio
Chianti Classico Riserva
DOCG ▮

Producer
Castello di Monsanto
Via Monsanto 8
50021 Barberino Val
d'Elsa (Firenze)
Tel. 055 805 9000
Fax 055 805 9049
monsanto@castello
dimonsanto.it
www.castellodimonsanto.it

Owner
Fabrizio Bianchi

Founded
1961

Winemaker
Fabrizio Bianchi

Vineyard manager
Andrea Dal Cin

Production
38,000–40,000 bottles
from choice years

Vintages
1999 1998 1997 1995
1990 1988 1985 1983
1982 1981 1979 1978
1977 1975 1974 1971
1970 1969 1968 1964
1962

Price
● ●

Note
The estate has
an archive of top vintage
bottles dating back to
1962

Monsanto stands today as one of the most admirable estates of Chianti Classico, known above all for Riserva Il Poggio, though also respected for a range of alternative wines that reveal the creative skills of Fabrizio Bianchi. Still, it must be admitted that recognition of Monsanto in Italy came mainly after Il Poggio was discovered in America.

Bianchi, a textile manufacturer from Lombardy who bought the estate with its medieval castle in 1961, arrived with serious ideas about wine and little respect for the status quo of Chianti, which was then amusing the world in straw-based flasks. His ambitions became clear with the first vintage of 1962, when he decided to bottle a Chianti Classico Riserva from his best vineyard, Il Poggio, a pioneering example of a Tuscan cru.

Bianchi admits that he learned by doing, while following French texts on enology, yet that wine made a lasting impression. In 1968, he excluded the white grapes then required in the blend, defying DOC rules to "make a Chianti Classico to compete with the most important red wines of the world."

His accomplishments were publicized by the late Sheldon Wasserman, the American author who in 1985 declared in his unequivocal manner that Monsanto's Riserva Il Poggio was the single finest Chianti Classico. That view was echoed by the influential critic Robert M. Parker, Jr., and upheld by a tasting panel of *The Wine Spectator*. Curiously, recognition has come slowly in Italy from writers who still seem reluctant to give Fabrizio Bianchi his due as a winemaker of foresight and courage who played a key role in uplifting the image of Chianti.

From 70 hectares of vineyards, Bianchi and daughter Laura produce about 400,000 bottles of wine a year, including Chianti Classico and Riserva, IGT Fabrizio Bianchi Sangiovese, Fabrizio Bianchi Chardonnay, Nemo (Cabernet Sauvignon), Tinscvil (Sangiovese-Cabernet) and Vin Santo.

Tuscany

Grapes
Sangiovese 90%, Canaiolo 7%, Colorino 3%, hand picked in mid-October.

Vineyard
Il Poggio, a plot of 5.5 hectares in schistous galestro soils on slopes facing south-southwest at 310 meters of altitude at Monsanto in the commune of Barberino Val d'Elsa on the western edge of Chianti Classico. The vines, of an average age of 31 years, are planted at a density of 4,000 per hectare and trained in the *archetto toscano* arched cordon method.

Vinification and aging
Grape bunches are stemmed and soft crushed and the must fermented in stainless steel vats at 22–27°C for about 18 days on the skins. After malolactic fermentation, the wine is matured for about 18 months in wood (60% in 5,000-liter casks of Slavonian oak and 40% in barriques of French oak used once previously). The wine, of 13.5% alcohol, is bottled and cellared for a year before release.

Style and maturity
Chianti Classico Riserva Il Poggio has bright ruby color tending toward garnet over time with rich scents of ripe fruit, spices and vanilla. On the palate it shows robust structure and expansive flavors bolstered by tannins that soften as the wine gains depth and length and the uncommon grace that characterizes vintages over nearly 4 decades.

Serving
🍴 18°C.

🍷 Tall, ample glass (Burgundy type).

🍽 Red meats and poultry, such as roast beef, rack of lamb, guinea fowl, duck and pigeon.

Castello di Volpaia

Coltassala
Vino da Tavola di Toscana ♟

Producer
Fattoria Castello di
Volpaia di Giovanna
Stianti
Piazza delle Cisterne 1
Località Volpaia
53017 Radda in Chianti
(Siena)
Tel. 0577 738 066
Fax 0577 738 619
info@volpaia.com
www.chianticlassico.com

Owner
Giovannella Stianti

Founded
1967

Winemakers
Maurizio Castelli and
Giovanna Morganti

Vineyard manager
Stefano Borsa

Production
About 25,000 bottles
from choice vintages

Vintages
1999 1998 1997 1995
1990 1988 1985 1982

Price
● ●

Coltassala was an early Super-Tuscan dominated by Sangioveto, a wine noted since its inception for a refinement that sets it apart from bolder reds of Chianti. Elegance is attributed to the lofty vineyards around the splendid hamlet of Volpaia, where sharp day–night temperature variations during ripening account for rarefied qualities in a wine that includes a bit of Mammolo, a variety reputed to lend a scent of violets.

Volpaia, with remnants of a tenth-century castle dominating the upper Pesa valley, was known for Chianti in earlier eras, though it was in 1967 that Raffaello Stianti, a Florentine, bought the main *palazzo* to use as a weekend retreat and hunting lodge. His daughter Giovannella and her husband Carlo Mascheroni soon decided that Volpaia ought to be revived as a wine estate and with the guidance of Maurizio Castelli began renewing vineyards and making wine.

The operation grew, but space was limited in historic stone buildings whose façades and arched doorways couldn't be altered. Undaunted, they removed roofs piece by piece, using cranes to lower vats, casks and presses into position before replacing wooden beams and roof tiles exactly as they were. Today, Volpaia looks much the way it would have in the Middle Ages, though open doors reveal a state-of-the-art winery and olive mill dispersed through ancient rooms.

Castello di Volpaia is owned and run by Giovannella Stianti, though husband Carlo, a Milanese tax lawyer who once sailed across the Atlantic alone, is the dynamo behind one of Chianti's most admired estates. He served as president of the producers' consortium of Chianti Classico in 1998, a role that influenced the decision to bring Coltassala under DOCG with the 1998 vintage.

From 45 hectares of vines, Castello di Volpaia produces about 250,000 bottles of wine a year, including regular Chianti Classico and Riserva, DOC Bianco Val d'Arbia and Vin Santo, and the prestigious IGT called Balifico (Sangioveto with Cabernet).

Grapes
Sangioveto and Mammolo (2–5%), hand picked in early October.

Vineyard
Coltassala is a sector of the estate with 3 hectares of vines in sandy limestone soils at 450 meters of altitude in the Volpaia area of the commune of Radda in the central part of Chianti Classico. The vines, of an average age of 16 years, are planted at a density of 5,800 per hectare and trained in the Guyot spurred cordon method.

Vinification and aging
Grape bunches are individually selected before being stemmed and soft crushed and the must fermented with indigenous yeasts for 14 days in stainless steel vats at 27–30°C, remaining on the skins for another 6 days. After malolactic fermentation, the wine is matured for about 18 months in small barrels of French oak from Allier. The wine, of 13–13.5% alcohol, is bottled and cellared for a year before release.

Style and maturity
Coltassala has deep ruby-red color that takes on garnet tones with age. The refined bouquet recalls ripe blackberries, violets, bay and vanilla. On the palate it has graceful structure and concentrated flavors with vital fruit sensations balanced by adequate acids and tannins. Texture is already smooth and supple after 5 years, though depth and inherent breed come to the fore after a decade.

Serving
- 18°C.
- Ample glass (Bordeaux type).
- Charcoal-grilled beef and free-range chicken; spit-roasted pigeon; aged Pecorino cheeses.

Poggio al Vento
Brunello di Montalcino Riserva
DOCG 🍷

Producer
Tenuta Col d'Orcia
Sant'Angelo in Colle
53024 Montalcino
(Siena)
Tel. 0577 808 001
Fax 0577 808 063
coldorciadirezione@
tin.it

Owner
Francesco Marone
Cinzano

Founded
1973

Winemakers
Pablo Härri with
Maurizio Castelli

Vineyard manager
Giuliano Dragoni

Production
30,000 bottles from
outstanding vintages

Vintages
1997 1995 1993 1990
1988 1985 1983 1982

Price
● ● ●

Count Alberto Marone Cinzano, of Piedmont's Cinzano vermouth and sparkling wine dynasty, acquired Col d'Orcia in 1973 when the Franceschi family began ceding its vast lands around the village of Sant'Angelo in Colle. That was at the beginning of the Brunello boom that witnessed dramatic expansion of vineyards and volumes of wine produced in the once tranquil commune of Montalcino. Col d'Orcia rode the crest of the wave to become one of the largest and most respected producers of Brunello, with a special reputation for the reserve of Poggio al Vento.

Alberto Marone Cinzano's son Francesco now owns the estate directed with aplomb by Edoardo Virano, whose program of development has been coordinated by technical consultant Maurizio Castelli and vineyard manager Giuliano Dragoni. The recent arrival of Swiss-born Pablo Härri as chief enologist after years of directing operations at neighboring Banfi completes a winemaking team with few rivals in Tuscany.

Poggio al Vento, on a gentle rise wafted by breezes that flow between the Orcia valley and the massif of Monte Amiata, was planted in 1974 with clones of Sangiovese selected locally and trained to produce minimum yields. From the fine vintage of 1982, Poggio al Vento was designated as one of the first single-vineyard bottlings of Brunello and has stood since as a model reserve that combines traditional character traits with contemporary appeal.

Col d'Orcia has steadily increased vineyards to cover about 130 hectares, providing grapes for about a million bottles of wine a year. Along with DOCG Brunello, the estate produces DOC Rosso di Montalcino and the sumptuous late-harvest Moscadello di Montalcino DOC called Pascena, along with an outstanding pure Cabernet Sauvignon IGT called Olmaia.

Tuscany

Grapes
Sangiovese 100% (select Brunello clones), hand picked in mid-September.

Vineyard
Poggio al Vento covers 5 hectares in stony calcareous marls with tufaceous deposits on slopes facing south at about 350 meters of altitude near Sant'Angelo in Colle in the southern part of the commune of Montalcino. The vines, planted in 1974 at a density of 2,700 per hectare, are trained in a spurred cordon method.

Vinification and aging
Grape bunches are individually selected in vineyards and cellars before being stemmed and soft crushed and the must fermented on the skins at under 30°C for 20 days in large stainless steel vats with daily breaking of the cap. After malolactic fermentation, the wine, of about 14% alcohol, is matured for 4 years in casks of oak from Allier (France) and Slavonia, then bottled and cellared for at least 15 months before release.

Style and maturity
Poggio al Vento when released in the sixth year after the harvest has deep ruby-garnet color and rich bouquet that recalls blackberries, morello cherries and spices. The wine is full bodied with ripe fruit sensations braced by tannins that gradually soften as flavors gain depth and complexity and extraordinary length on the palate. From great vintages, such as 1988 and 1990, this stately Riserva needs nearly a decade to round into form, though it will maintain vitality for at least another.

Serving
🌡 18°C, decanting.
🍷 Ample crystal glass (Bordeaux type).
🍽 Roast and grilled beef and lamb; wood pigeon braised with Vin Santo; mature Pecorino cheese from nearby Pienza.

Coltibuono

Sangioveto di Toscana
IGT 🍷

Producer
Tenuta di Coltibuono
Località Badia a
Coltibuono
53013 Gaiole in Chianti
(Siena)
Tel. 0577 74 481
Fax 0577 749 235
marketing@
coltibuono.com
www.chianticlassico.com
/coltibuono

Owner
Stucchi-Prinetti family

Founded
1846

Winemakers
Roberto Stucchi-Prinetti
and Luca D'Attoma

Vineyard manager
Roberto Stucchi-Prinetti

Production
20,000–30,000 bottles
from top vintages

Vintages
1999 1997 1995 1994
1990 1989 1988 1985

Price
●●

The tenth-century abbey of Coltibuono is headquarters of an estate where monks made some of the earliest wines of medieval Chianti. Badia a Coltibuono, restored to antique splendor by Piero Stucchi-Prinetti and his wife Lorenza de' Medici, renowned author of books on Italian cooking, was long noted for reserve Chianti of austere virtue. Today their son and daughter, Roberto and Emanuela, make wines of contemporary style at ultramodern vinification and aging cellars adjacent to the main vineyards at Monti, 12 kilometers from the abbey in the southern part of the commune of Gaiole.

The estate's finest wine, Sangioveto, takes the historical local name of Sangiovese. First produced in 1980, it comes from very old vines with scarce yields, accounting for its extraordinary power and durability. It's an IGT, though it could qualify fully as Chianti Classico, for which Badia a Coltibuono is also known, especially for its singular collection of old vintages.

The estate has 50 hectares of vines, notably around the village of Monti, where cellars work on a system of gravity flow instead of pumping, assuring minimal exposure to air during the processes of vinification and aging.

Roberto Stucchi-Prinetti works with consulting enologist Luca D'Attoma in fashioning Sangioveto and other wines of class: Chianti Classico (including a type called RS—Roberto Stucchi) and Chianti Classico Riserva, Val d'Arbia DOC Vin Santo, as well as Sella del Boscone, an oak-fermented Chardonnay. Coltibuono is also renowned for its extra virgin olive oil.

These and other products from the estate are served at the family restaurant adjacent to the abbey, where terraces offer views over olive groves and woods of oak and ilex across the broad Arno Valley to the Apennines.

Tuscany

Grapes
Sangiovese 100%, hand picked in early October.

Vineyards
Various plots covering 5 hectares on slopes of medium-packed *alberese* limestone soils at 230–280 meters of altitude at Monti in the commune of Gaiole in southern Chianti Classico. The vines, of an average age of 50 years, are planted at a density of 5,500–6,000 per hectare and trained in the Guyot spurred cordon method.

Vinification and aging
Grape bunches are individually selected before being stemmed and soft crushed and the must fermented in stainless steel vats at just under 28°C, remaining in contact with the skins for 4–5 weeks. Malolactic fermentation takes place naturally in tanks before aging for a year in small barrels of French oak. The wine, of about 14% alcohol, is bottled and cellared for a year before release.

Style and maturity
Sangioveto has intense ruby-red color with bouquet that recalls raspberries, black currants, tobacco and spices. Its powerful initial impact on the palate is gradually tamed by moderate acidity and tannins that soften over time as rich, fruity flavors become broader and longer. From great vintages, the wines are approachable after 5 years, reaching primes between 10 and 15, though Sangioveto has the stuff to shine for 2 or 3 decades.

Serving
🍷 19–20°C.
🍷 Tall, ample glass (Bordeaux type).
🍽 Classic Tuscan meat dishes: roast and grilled beef, lamb, pork, pigeon, duck; medium to well-aged Pecorino cheeses.

Rancia
Chianti Classico Riserva
DOCG ❢

Producer
Fattoria di Felsina
Strada Chiantigiana 484
53019 Castelnuovo
Berardenga (Siena)
Tel. 0577 355 117
Fax 0577 355 651
felsina@dada.it

Owner
Giuseppe Poggiali

Founded
1966

Winemaker
Franco Bernabei

Vineyard manager
Giovanni Poggiali

Production
30,000–35,000 bottles
from choice years

Vintages
1999 1997 1995 1994
1993 1990 1988 1986
1985

Price
● ●

Felsina, an estate centered in a hamlet founded by the Etruscans on the edge of what became the town of Castelnuovo Berardenga, was acquired in 1966 by Domenico Poggiali as a place in the country that supplied quantities of tasty, if rustic, Chianti.

Poggiali, from Romagna, wasn't aware of Felsina's potential grandeur until 1982, when his son-in-law Giuseppe Mazzocolin, a professor of Greek and Latin from Treviso in the Veneto, decided to leave academia and try to improve the wines. Giuseppe hired Franco Bernabei, a young enologist also from the Veneto beginning to make his mark in Tuscany. Their first feat was Fontalloro, a pure Sangiovese matured in barriques, a wine of might and bearing that quickly rose to star status among the so-called Super-Tuscans.

Giuseppe, intrigued by local traditions, decided that Felsina must also have a special reserve Chianti and in 1983 selected grapes from a farm on the property called Podere di Rancia. That, too, was a pure Sangiovese (despite rules requiring other grapes in the blend), though for the sake of authenticity the Venetian team employed a quaint local practice called *governo all'uso toscano*. That consisted of gathering very ripe grapes after the normal harvest and drying them to add to the fermented wine to make it richer and rounder.

Rancia combines the integrity of a classic reserve Chianti with contemporary weight and style in a way that few other wines of Tuscany do. Felsina also produces Maestro Raro, a pure Cabernet Sauvignon that rivals Fontalloro among Super-Tuscans, as well as an oak-fermented Chardonnay called I Sistri. With the acquisition of the adjacent Pagliarese estate, Felsina has gradually increased production from 77 hectares of vineyards to 300,000–350,000 bottles a year, dominated by a fine regular Chianti. A sister estate, Castello di Farnetella at Sinalunga, makes Chianti Colli Senesi, Sauvignon, a Pinot Noir (Nero di Nubi) and the excellent Poggio Granoni (Sangiovese with Cabernet and Syrah).

Tuscany

Grapes
Sangiovese 100%, hand picked in early October.

Vineyards
Grapes are selected in 3 plots covering 12 hectares on slopes facing southwest at 380–410 meters of altitude at Podere di Rancia in the commune of Castelnuovo Berardenga in southern Chianti Classico. Soils are mixed: sandstone and sandy quartz to the east, scaly clays with sand and limestone at the center, sand and alluvial pebbles to the west. Vines range in age from 8–31 years, older plantings at densities of 3,200 per hectare trained in a double arched cordon and newer plantings at 5,200–5,500 per hectare in the Guyot method.

Vinification and aging
Grapes are soft crushed and the must fermented in stainless steel vats at 28–30°C for 16 days on the skins. Malolactic fermentation is boosted by the *governo* in December, after which the wine is matured for 14–16 months in wood (part in new or once-used barriques and part in casks). The wine, of 13.5% alcohol, is bottled and cellared for 6–12 months before release.

Style and maturity
Chianti Classico Riserva Rancia has rich ruby-red color taking on garnet-orange tones on the rim over time. The bouquet is ample and harmonious with scents of ripe cherries and blackberries, spices and tobacco. On the palate it shows robust structure with full fruit sensations balanced by well-rounded wood tannins in flavors that become smooth and warm after about 5 years and attain peaks of depth and complexity between 10 and 15 years.

Serving
🌡 16–17°C, opening bottle 2 hours ahead of time.
🍷 Ample crystal glass (Bordeaux type).
🍽 Roast and grilled red meats and game, roast kid and spit-roasted pigeon.

Fontodi

Vigna del Sorbo
Chianti Classico Riserva
DOCG ♉

Producer
Azienda Agricola
Fontodi
di Domiziano e Dino
Manetti
Via San Leolino 89
50020 Panzano in
Chianti (Firenze)
Tel. 055 852005
Fax 055 852537

Owners
Domiziano and Dino
Manetti

Founded
1968

Winemaker
Franco Bernabei

Vineyard manager
Giovanni Manetti

Production
About 35,000 bottles
from choice years

Vintages
1999 1998 1997 1995
1994 1990 1988 1985

Price
● ●

If a photographer wished to capture the image of the new Chianti, he might portray Giovanni Manetti smiling brightly amid rows of new barriques in the lower level of Fontodi's ultramodern cellars. Or he might catch the impeccably dressed young man stepping from his four-wheel-drive vehicle into a vineyard replanted with select clones of Sangiovese. If the pictures came with an interview, readers would learn that Giovanni, who looks younger than 38, has a doctorate in economics and has devoted more than half of his life to building Fontodi into a model of modern winemaking in Tuscany.

Giovanni was 16 when he and older brother Marco took charge of the farm on the edge of the town of Panzano, while father Dino and uncle Domiziano ran their prestigious terracotta factory in another part of Chianti. They set about renewing Fontodi's rundown vineyards sloping into the vaunted vale known as the Conca d'Oro. But they realized that they needed expert advice to improve the wines, so they hired an enologist on the rise named Franco Bernabei.

The Chianti improved rapidly, but the first Fontodi wine to make an impact was Flaccianello della Pieve, a pure Sangiovese Super-Tuscan from 1981. The brothers kept the faith in Chianti, planting a plot called Vigna del Sorbo with Sangiovese and 10 percent Cabernet Sauvignon. From the great 1985 vintage they made their first Chianti Classico Riserva Vigna del Sorbo, a wine that came to rival Flaccianello and, from some vintages, to surpass it in class.

Critics may still be divided in preference between the two top wines, though even the regular Classico is so consistently good that James Suckling of *The Wine Spectator* in 1999 wrote that Fontodi "is clearly Italy's best producer of Chianti." Marco now runs the terracotta business, leaving Giovanni fully in charge of Fontodi. Fom 64 hectares of vines, he produces about 300,000 bottles of wine a year, including IGT Case Via Syrah and Pinot Nero and a white Pinot Bianco called Meriggio.

Tuscany

Grapes
Sangiovese 90%,
Cabernet Sauvignon
10%, hand picked in late
September–early
October.

Vineyard
Vigna del Sorbo, a plot of
7.5 hectares in schistous
galestro soils on slopes
facing southwest at
380–400 meters of
altitude at Panzano in the
commune of Greve at the
heart of Chianti Classico.
The vines, of an average
age of 28 years, are
planted at a density of
3,500 per hectare and
trained in the Guyot
cordon method.

Vinification and aging
Grapes are stemmed and
soft crushed and the
must fermented at
22–30°C for 18–20 days
on the skins in stainless
steel vats in which the
liquid is automatically
pumped over the cap.
After malolactic
fermentation, the wine,
of about 13% alcohol, is
matured for 20 months
in new barriques of
French oak from Allier
and Tronçais and bottled
and cellared for 8–10
months before release.

Style and maturity
Chianti Classico Riserva Vigna del Sorbo has an elegant ruby color with garnet highlights on the rim. The bouquet is rich and complex with scents reminiscent of cherries, blackberries and vanilla. On the palate it is full and round with firm structure bolstered by wood tannins that give it impressive depth and harmony with expansive fruit flavors that linger on the tongue. Already appealing at 4–5 years, the wine reaches a splendid prime between 8 and 12 years.

Serving
🍷 18°C.
🍷 Tall, ample glass (Bordeaux type).
🍴 Red meats, such as the thick slab of charcoal-grilled Chianina beef served rare in slices as *tagliata*, saddle of lamb, and poultry, such as free-range chicken roasted with herbs.

288

Frescobaldi

Montesodi
Chianti Rufina DOCG 🍷

Producer
Marchesi de'
Frescobaldi
Via Santo Spirito 11
50125 Firenze
Tel. 055 271 41
Fax 055 211 527
info@frescobaldi.it

Owner
Frescobaldi family

Founded
1300

Chief winemaker
Niccolò D'Afflitto

Vineyard manager
Lamberto Frescobaldi

Production
About 30,000 bottles
from choice years

Vintages
1999 1997 1996 1995
1993 1990 1988 1985

Price
●●

The Old World of wine embraced the New in 1995 when Marchesi de' Frescobaldi, vintners active in Florence since 1300, announced a joint venture with the Robert Mondavi Winery of California. The much-publicized product of that union is Luce, a blend of Sangiovese and Merlot from the Frescobaldi Castelgiocondo estate at Montalcino. The wine, first produced in 1993 by the team of Lamberto Frescobaldi, Niccolò D'Afflitto and Tim Mondavi, shows indubitable promise. An independent winery is being prepared for its production, though in the meantime tastings suggest that Luce is still in its trial phases, awaiting release of the great vintages of 1997 and 1999.

Connoisseurs won't need to wait to taste the prime of Montesodi, the Chianti Rufina that experts have rated as Frescobaldi's finest wine for years (although Brunello di Montalcino and the Merlot called Lamaione from Castelgiocondo also win high praise). Montesodi is a *podere*, one of the farms of Castello di Nipozzano, the historic core of the Frescobaldi dynasty that takes in eight estates in Tuscany with some 800 hectares of vineyards. Sangiovese grown in hard, arid soils there proves that vines that struggle produce wines of character, for Montesodi has an aristocratic aura that distinguishes it from all other Chianti, whether from Rufina or Classico or the six less illustrious zones that carry the appellation.

In all, Marchesi de' Frescobaldi, run by brothers Vittorio, Leonardo and Ferdinando Frescobaldi and their sons and daughters, produces about 6 million bottles of wine a year. Principal types are Chianti Rufina Castello di Nipozzano and the IGT red Mormoreto (from Cabernet), as well as Pomino DOC Bianco, Rosso and Vin Santo from the estate of Pomino. From Castelgiocondo come Brunello and Rosso di Montalcino along with the IGT Luce and Lucente (Sangiovese with Merlot).

Tuscany

Grapes
Sangiovese prevalently, hand picked in mid-October.

Vineyard
Montesodi, 20 hectares in stony, arid, lean calcareous clay soils on slopes facing south at 350 meters of altitude at Castello di Nipozzano in the commune of Pelago in the southern part of Chianti Rufina 20 kilometers east of Florence. The vines, of an average age of 26 years, are planted at a density of 3,000 per hectare and trained in the spurred cordon method.

Vinification and aging
Grapes are stemmed and soft crushed and the must fermented at no more than 30°C for 10 days on the skins in stainless steel vats with frequent pumping over the cap. After malolactic fermentation, partly in barriques, the wine, of about 13% alcohol, is matured for 12 months in small barrels of French oak (one third new annually), then bottled and cellared for 12 months before release.

Style and maturity
Chianti Rufina Montesodi has intense ruby color with garnet highlights on the rim. The bouquet is concentrated with ripe fruit sensations mingling with scents reminiscent of violets and vanilla. On the palate it has firm structure and impressive weight with fine balance between acids, tannins and ripe fruit flavors that gain in depth and length with time. The wine can be impressive after 4 or 5 years, though it tends to reach an elegant prime at about a decade.

Serving
🍷 18°C.
🍷 Tall, ample glass (Bordeaux type).
🍽 Roast and grilled beef and pork, spit-roasted game birds, duck and goose cooked in a wood-burning oven, aged Pecorino cheese from the nearby Mugello.

Isole e Olena

Producer
Isole e Olena
Località Isole 1
50021 Barberino Val
d'Elsa (Firenze)
Tel. 055 807 2763
Fax 055 807 2236

Owner
De Marchi family

Founded
1952

Winemaker
Paolo De Marchi

Vineyard manager
Paolo De Marchi

Production
About 35,000 bottles
from choice years

Vintages
2000 1999 1997 1993
1990 1988 1986 1983
1982

Price
● ●

Note
The American journal
The Wine Spectator
ranked Cepparello 1997
third among the top 100
wines of the world in
1999

Cepparello
Toscana IGT

The renaissance in Tuscan wine gained momentum when money, talent and ideas flowed into the region from outside. The ranks of itinerant winemakers, vine specialists and investors continue to grow, though perhaps no outsider has contributed more to the spirit of the revival than Paolo De Marchi from Piedmont, who has made Isole e Olena a landmark of modern Chianti Classico.

Paolo's father, a lawyer with a wine estate at Lessona in Piedmont, bought the adjacent Isole and Olena farms in 1952 and put the properties together. At first, the wine was sold in bulk to merchant houses, but in 1976 Paolo took over after earning a doctorate in enology and Isole e Olena has been on the rise ever since.

Paolo has always put prime emphasis on his vineyards, planting and grafting with select clones of Sangiovese for Chianti Classico. His faith in Sangiovese is summed up in Cepparello, the Super-Tuscan created in 1980 and named after a stream that runs through the property. Paolo also works successfully with Cabernet Sauvignon, Chardonnay and Syrah for wines that have come under the Collezione De Marchi label.

Visitors to Isole e Olena have sometimes been surprised to learn that wines of such style could issue from the hodgepodge of makeshift spaces that Paolo called his cellars. For years he assured doubters that the new *cantina* was imminent and, at last, his dream has materialized.

Paolo is convinced that the spacious new quarters will enable him to perform more efficiently and make his wines even better. That may be true, though Cepparello has long been ranked at the summit of pure Sangiovese, and the Collezione De Marchi Cabernet Sauvignon and Chardonnay merit similar esteem.

Paolo, who might be described as a youth approaching 50, keeps trim by manicuring his 45 hectares of vines, which produce about 200,000 bottles a year of wines that also include a revered Vin Santo.

Tuscany

Grapes
Sangiovese 100%, hand picked in mid-October.

Vineyards
Grapes are selected in the oldest and best positioned vineyards in soils that vary between schistous *galestro, alberese* limestone and calcareous clays on slopes oriented toward the southwest at 350–400 meters of altitude at Isole and Olena in the commune of Barberino Val d'Elsa on the western flank of Chianti Classico. The vines, aged between 13–36 years, are planted at densities ranging from 3,000–7,350 per hectare and trained in the arched *capovolto toscano* and Guyot cordon systems.

Vinification and aging
Grapes are stemmed and soft crushed and the must fermented in stainless steel tanks at 28–32°C for about 4 weeks on the skins with frequent pumping over the cap. After malolactic fermentation, the wine is matured for 15–18 months in small barrels of French (85%) and American oak – one third new annually. The wine, of 13–13.5% alcohol, is bottled and cellared for 8–12 months before release.

Style and maturity
Cepparello has unusually deep ruby color for Sangiovese, taking on garnet-orange tones on the rim over time. The bouquet is full and round with rich scents of ripe fruit and berries and a hint of vanilla. Robust structure gives the young wine a potent, compact feel with good acidity and attractive wood tannins in line with fruit flavors that become broader and longer on the palate with age. From great vintages, the wine can be attractive after 5 years, though it needs double that to show its true finesse.

Serving
🍷 16–18°C, decanting if young.
🍷 Tall, ample glass (Chianti type).
🍽 Roast and grilled beef and lamb, spit-roasted pigeon, wild boar braised in red wine, aged Pecorino cheeses.

Lungarotti

Rubesco Vigna Monticchio Torgiano Rosso Riserva DOCG ▮

Producer
Cantine Giorgio
Lungarotti
Via Mario Angeloni 16
06089 Torgiano
(Perugia)
Tel. 075 988 0348
Fax 075 988 0294
lungarotti@lungarotti.it
www.lungarotti.it

Owner
Lungarotti family

Founded
1962

Chief winemaker
Teresa Severini

Vineyard manager
Chiara Lungarotti

Production
50,000–70,000 bottles
from choice years

Vintages
1998 1997 1995 1992
1990 1988 1986 1983
1982 1981 1979 1977
1973 1971 1969 1966

Price
● ●

Note
Vintages of Rubesco
Monticchio dating back
to 1973 are available at
the cellars

Giorgio Lungarotti is remembered as the man who put Umbria on the world's wine map by proving that fine reds for aging could be produced at Torgiano in the hills along the Tiber river south of Perugia. He showed visionary zeal in creating the red and white wines that in 1968 earned Torgiano one of Italy's earliest DOCs. In 1990, Torgiano Rosso Riserva was elevated to DOCG, a personal tribute to Lungarotti's aristocratic Rubesco from the vineyard of Monticchio.

Today the winery is run by his stepdaughter Teresa and daughter Chiara, who direct winemaking and vineyard operations. Teresa points out that Rubesco Riserva, from Sangiovese and Canaiolo, is sold after aging for a short time in wood and many years in bottle. She lauds Giorgio Lungarotti's far-sightedness in keeping ample stocks from good vintages to sell later, "because he knew that the wine needed aging to reach complete harmony."

Rubesco Monticchio and the prestigious IGT known as San Giorgio (Cabernet with Sangiovese) rank among Italy's best values in aged wine. "It's curious how we've actually been criticized for our low prices by people who say they undermine prestige," says Teresa. "Well, we believe that wine should be affordable, whether it be a *novello* from the latest harvest or a great vintage red."

From 260 hectares of family vineyards and 40 hectares under supervision, Lungarotti makes about 2.5 million bottles of wine a year divided among 20 types, including a range of DOC Torgiano: non-reserve red Rubesco and white Torre di Giano Il Pino and varietal Cabernet Sauvignon and Chardonnay. The list of IGT takes in Il Vessillo, a blend of Pinot Noir and Cabernet Sauvignon, and Giubilante, a blend of Sangiovese, Canaiolo, Cabernets and Montepulciano.

Torgiano has become a tourist mecca with the museums created by Giorgio's wife Maria Grazia that house Italy's finest collections of the art and culture of wine and olive oil, and the Lungarotti hotel and restaurant Le Tre Vaselle.

Umbria

Grapes
Sangiovese 70% and Canaiolo, hand picked in late September and early October.

Vineyard
Monticchio covers about 20 hectares of medium-packed sandy clay soils on slopes facing southeast at 300 meters of altitude on the Brufa hill in the commune of Torgiano in the Tiber valley south of Perugia. Vines of 10–16 years of age are planted at a density of 4,000 per hectare and trained in a spurred cordon replacing the old double-arch Guyot.

Vinification and aging
Grapes are stemmed and soft crushed and the must fermented in stainless steel vats at 28°C for about two weeks on the skins. Malolactic fermentation occurs naturally in the following spring and the wine is matured for a year in 5,000-liter capacity casks of French oak. The wine, of about 12.5% alcohol, is bottled and cellared until release about 10 years after the harvest.

Style and maturity
Rubesco Monticchio on release after a decade shows a fine ruby-garnet color with tinges of orange on the rim. The bouquet is full and complex with scents reminiscent of cherries and blackberries and hints of underbrush and leather. On the palate, the wine is round and velvety with the warmly austere tones of age that linger elegantly on the palate. At a prime between 10 and 15 years, great vintages have kept impressively for 3 decades.

Serving
🍷 16–18°C, opening bottle several hours earlier or decanting.

♀ Ample crystal *ballon* (Burgundy type).

🍽 Roast and braised Chianina beef; rosettes of veal with Pecorino cheese and black truffles; duck braised in wine with honey.

Podere Il Bosco
Toscana IGT ❢

Producer
Tenimenti Luigi
d'Alessandro
Manzano
Via Manzano 15
52052 Cortona (Arezzo)
Tel. 0575 618 667
Fax 0575 618 411
tenimenti.dalessandro
@flashnet.it

Owner
D'Alessandro family

Founded
1967

Winemaker
Massimo d'Alessandro

Vineyard manager
Silvano Acquarelli

Production
35,000 bottles from
choice years

Vintages
1999 1998 1997 1996
1995 1992

Price
● ●

Note
With the 1999 vintage,
Podere Il Bosco,
previously Toscana IGT,
qualified under the new
Cortona DOC

Syrah had been slow in arriving in Italy, but if Podere Il Bosco indicates potential, it may be the next star among international varieties. Podere Il Bosco from the 1997 vintage won raves and high ratings from experts, who by consensus have designated it as Italy's finest Syrah.

Massimo d'Alessandro, a Roman architect who with brothers Francesco and Giulio owns and operates the Manzano estate near Cortona in eastern Tuscany, points out that conditions there provide an ideal habitat for Syrah. Yet they might not have considered planting it had Manzano not been located a short distance away from the Vino Nobile di Montepulciano and Chianti DOCG zones in a part of the Chiana Valley not considered prime vineyard territory, so the estate's wines could not qualify under either appellation.

The family acquired Manzano in 1967, though for years the brothers continued to make wines from local varieties for local consumption. Only as they acquired tastes for wines from France and other countries did they decide to try something new, calling in noted viticulturist Attilio Scienza for advice. Finding the calcareous clay soils and hot, dry climate similar to those of France's Rhône valley, Scienza suggested Syrah and Viognier, as well as Chardonnay and Sauvignon Blanc. In 1988, they began replanting vineyards under agronomist Silvano Acquarelli, increasing plant density from 2,000 to 7,000 vines per hectare.

Total production from 35 hectares has arrived at about 100,000 bottles a year, including a fine Chardonnay-Viognier blend called Podere Fontarca, a Sauvignon Blanc Le Terrazze and an unusually robust Gamay called Podere Il Vescovo. But the success of Syrah has encouraged the brothers to make that the premier wine, with production programmed to increase from 35,000 to 180,000 bottles a year. From the 1997 and 1998 vintages, Podere Il Bosco contains 10 percent of Sangiovese in the blend, a touch that Massimo assures admirers will make it even more distinguished in the future.

Tuscany

Grapes
Syrah 90%, Sangiovese 10%, hand picked in late September.

Vineyards
Grapes are selected in 4 plots (Vigna de Il Bosco, Vigna dei Cani, Vigneto di Migliara, Vigne delle Terrazze) covering 18 hectares of Syrah and 1.6 hectares of Sangiovese planted on medium-packed calcareous clay soils on slopes of various sun exposures at 270–290 meters of altitude at Manzano in the commune of Cortona in eastern Tuscany. Vines, planted from 1988 at a density of 7,000 per hectare, are trained in a spurred cordon.

Vinification and aging
Grapes are stemmed and soft crushed and the must fermented in stainless steel vats at a maximum of 32°C for no more than 10 days on the skins as the liquid is pumped over the cap 3 times daily. Malolactic fermentation occurs naturally and the wine is matured for 12–16 months in small barrels of French oak from Allier. The wine, of about 13% alcohol, is bottled and cellared for 6–8 months before release.

Style and maturity
Podere Il Bosco on release shows deep ruby-violet color, almost inky when young, with notes of ripe blackberries, pepper and spices on the nose. Though big and firm in structure and intense in flavor, textures are mellow and round, expanding with time to extraordinary opulence and length on the palate. Potential longevity isn't known, since the first vintage was 1992, but the wine seems to have the character to age in a similar way to a great Syrah from the Rhône.

Serving
🍷 17–18°C, opening bottle several hours earlier.
🍷 Ample crystal *ballon* (Burgundy type).
🍽 It excels with roast and grilled lamb, though it also goes surprisingly well with fish, such as salmon, swordfish and anchovies.

La Massa

Giorgio Primo
Chianti Classico DOCG ❦

Producer
Fattoria La Massa
Via Case Sparse 9
50020 Panzano in
Chianti (Firenze)
Tel. 055 852 722
Fax 055 852 722

Owner
Giampaolo Motta

Founded
1992

Winemaker
Carlo Ferrini

Vineyard manager
Carlo Ferrini

Production
20,000–40,000 bottles
a year

Vintages
2000 1999 1997 1996
1995

Price
●●

If some day Giampaolo Motta writes his memoirs, he might be tempted to start them with the words "Once upon a time…" For the story of how the boy from Naples realized his dreams in Chianti has the makings of a fable. Giampaolo had developed a powerful interest in wine by 1988, when he took leave of his family's leather works in Naples and came north to meet John Dunkley, the Englishman at Riecine (see page 316), where he acquired experience and motivation. After an interval at a large winery, Giampaolo moved on to new inspirations at Castello dei Rampolla (see page 270), where, in 1992, he learned that the next-door estate of La Massa was on the market due to a bankruptcy.

The neglected vineyards were more extensive than Giampaolo presumed to deal with, but scraping together funds, he managed to buy about half of those available and went to work with Carlo Ferrini in the rundown cellars. La Massa, in the vale known as the Conca d'Oro near the town of Panzano, occupies one of the most privileged sites of Chianti, where even the largely dreadful 1992 harvest yielded a small quantity of respectable wine.

Giampaolo decided to make only Chianti Classico in two versions, a top selection called Giorgio Primo (after his grandfather and his first vintage) and the second choice La Massa, which compares favorably with the top wines of many estates. No Super-Tuscans for Giampaolo, whose aim is to realize the maximum potential of Chianti at an estate that has been producing wine since about 1400.

As an admirer of Merlot, he blends some in with the prevalent Sangiovese, both picked at peaks of ripeness for wines that show Carlo Ferrini's master touch in their copious color and bouquet and marvelously mellow flavors. This style has made Giampaolo one of the most admired of the new generation of Chianti producers, though the boy from Naples seems to be having too much fun chasing his dreams to take seriously all the praise that's been coming his way.

Tuscany

Grapes
Sangiovese with 8–9%
Merlot, hand picked in
early October.

Vineyards
Giorgio Primo comes
from the estate's first
selection of grapes from
vines planted in schistous
galestro soils on slopes
oriented toward the south
and west at 350–420
meters of altitude 2
kilometers west of
Panzano in the heart of
Chianti Classico. Of 26
hectares of vines, 18 were
planted 25–30 years ago
at a density of 3,000 per
hectare and trained in an
arched *capovolto toscano*
system and 8 were
planted recently at 6,250
per hectare using a
spurred cordon system.

Vinification and aging
Grapes are stemmed and
soft crushed and the
must fermented in glass-
lined concrete vats at
30–35°C for 15–20 days
on the skins with
frequent pumping over
the cap. Malolactic
fermentation in
December is completed
in wood barrels before
the wine is matured for
18 months in 225-liter
and 500-liter capacity
barrels of French oak.
The wine, of about 14%
alcohol, is assembled a
month before bottling.

Style and maturity
Chianti Classico Giorgio
Primo has deep ruby-violet
color with rich bouquet that
suggests blackberries and ripe
cherries enhanced by bright
floral notes and hints of mint
and vanilla. Amply structured
and full on the palate, it has
rich, round fruit sensations
and soft tannins with mellow
flavors that gain in length and
complexity over time. Already
attractive at 2 years, it should
reach a prime at 5–7 years
and maintain class well over a
decade.

Serving
🍷 18°C.
🍷 Medium-sized glass (Chianti type).
🍽 Tuscan specialties, such as
pappardelle alla lepre
(noodles with hare sauce),
duck or goose or rack of
spring lamb with wild herbs
roasted in a wood-burning
oven.

Le Pergole Torte
Vino da Tavola di Toscana ❦

Producer
Fattoria di Montevertine
Località Montevertine
53017 Radda in
Chianti (Siena)
Tel. 0577 738 009
Fax 0577 738 265

Owner
Manetti family

Founded
1967

Winemaker
Giulio Gambelli

Vineyard manager
Bruno Bini

Production
About 18,000 bottles a
year, including magnums
and double magnums

Vintages
1999 1998 1997 1996
1995 1993 1992 1990
1988 1985 1981

Price
● ● ●

Note
Le Pergole Torte is prized
at auctions; in 1998, an
imperial of 1990 fetched
£1,078 and a double
magnum £682 at
Christie's in London

Sergio Manetti bought Montevertine in Chianti as a vacation retreat in 1967 and became so enamored of the farm that he sold his family steel business to finance the production of wine along with his numerous other diversions.

When his Chianti Classico began to win praise, Sergio decided to make an alternative wine that honored Tuscan tradition while appealing to what might be described as worldly tastes. With his winemaker friend Giulio Gambelli, possessor of an unerring palate, Sergio in 1977 created Le Pergole Torte, a pure Sangiovese aged in barrels of French oak. That wine, whose name refers to the twisted vines in a plot where old clones of Sangiovese prevailed, became the most admired pure native among the proudly individualistic reds known as Super-Tuscans.

Sergio continued to make Chianti Classico as a second red, but by 1985 he realized that the collective denomination did nothing for Montevertine's elite image, so he refused to use it thereafter. Instead, he fashioned "table wines" following the fortunes of the harvest and personal whims.

Sergio remained in patriarchal command of Montevertine until his death in 2000. The estate is now run by his son Martino, twin daughters Anna and Marta, and son-in-law Klaus Johann Reimitz, who work with vineyard specialist Bruno Bini. They make wine only from native varieties in 8.5 hectares of vines, where yields are held to minimal levels to produce about 60,000 bottles annually. These include three other reds—Montevertine, Il Sodaccio and Pian del Ciampolo (all from Sangiovese with Canaiolo), the dry white Bianco di Montevertine and the rich amber-colored "M" (both from Trebbiano and Malvasia).

Sergio pursued his eclectic interests up to the end, as an author of books and articles on wine and food, photographer and metal sculptor and compulsive collector of art, antiques and curios. "I'm a lucky man," he once confided. "I've been able to do pretty much everything I like to do in life."

Tuscany

LE PERGOLE TORTE

Grapes
Sangiovese 100%, hand picked in late October.

Vineyards
Le Pergole Torte covers 3.4 hectares of calcareous soils mixed with schistous *galestro* and *alberese* limestone on slopes oriented toward the southeast at about 430 meters of altitude in the upper Pesa valley at Montevertine in the commune of Radda in south-central Chianti Classico. The vines, of an average age of 26 years, are planted at a density of 2,700 per hectare and trained in the Guyot cordon method.

Vinification and aging
Grape bunches are individually selected before being stemmed and soft crushed and the must fermented on the skins for 25–30 days in glass-lined concrete tanks at 28–30°C, with pumping over the cap twice daily. Malolactic fermentation takes place naturally before maturation of about 2 years, first in barriques, then in casks of 1,600-liter capacity. The wine, of 13–13.5% alcohol, is bottled and cellared for 6 months before release.

Style and maturity
Le Pergole Torte has medium ruby color with scents reminiscent of violets, raspberries and herbal notes in the full, clean bouquet that deepens with time. Though not a big wine in a purely physical sense, it has uncommon elegance on the palate with vibrant fruit sensations counterpoised by soft tannins that give it unusual depth and length of flavors. The wine can be precociously attractive, though it reaches a prime between 6 and 7 years and retains finesse for at least a decade beyond.

Serving
🌡 18°C.
🍷 Tall, ample glass (Bordeaux type).
🍴 Homemade tagliatelle noodles with meat sauce, spit-roasted meats and poultry, Chianina beef braised in red wine, medium aged Tuscan Pecorino cheese.

Giovanna
Morganti

Le Trame
Chianti Classico DOCG ♥

Producer
Podere Le Boncie
Strada delle
Boncie 5
53019 Castelnuovo
Berardenga (Siena)
Tel. 0577 359 383
Fax 0577 359 383
gmorganti@nettuno.it

Owner
Giovanna Morganti

Founded
1990

Winemakers
Giovanna Morganti with
Maurizio Castelli

Vineyard manager
Giovanna Morganti

Production
13,000 bottles a year

Vintages
1999 1998 1997 1996
1995 1990

Price
●

If asked to describe the ideal Chianti, I would suggest a taste of Le Trame. The name translates as the schemes or plots or, poetically, as the whims of Giovanna Morganti, who explains: "It refers to a bet I made with myself, my dream to grow vines and make wine following my intuition and for my own pleasure."

Giovanna grew up amid the vineyards of Chianti. Her father Enzo managed the San Felice estate where, among other feats, he created Chianti Classico Riserva Poggio Rosso (see page 322). After graduating from the wine school in Siena, she began consulting with wineries in Chianti, while joining her father to develop their own small estate, Podere Le Boncie. When Enzo Morganti died in 1992, she was left alone to realize her dream.

Giovanna, now in her mid-thirties, continues consulting, but her heart obviously belongs to Le Trame. She has replanted parts of her two vineyards at high density in the low pruned *alberello* system rarely seen in Chianti. Besides Sangiovese, she grows the historical varieties of Canaiolo, Ciliegiolo, Colorino and Foglia Tonda for a rustic local touch. In the cellars, where Maurizio Castelli provides technical advice, she follows artisan methods, using open-topped oak vats for fermentation induced by natural yeasts and punching down the pomace cap with a wooden pole. In keeping with the whimsical theme, Le Trame's label depicts Giovanna and a vine as envisioned by a friend.

Production of Le Trame will grow slightly beyond the current 13,000 bottles a year when new plantings come to fruition, but Giovanna has no plans to create other wines. As she explains in her calm and cheerful manner, "I'm dedicated to making a wine that expresses my love of Chianti and the vines that have grown here for centuries."

Le Trame sums up the integrity, dignity and charm of Chianti. It also makes a perfect match with Tuscan country cooking in an era when some critics seem to have forgotten that the first purpose of wine is to be enjoyed with food.

Tuscany

Grapes
Sangiovese 90% with
Foglia Tonda, Colorino
and Ciliegiolo, hand
picked in early October.

Vineyards
Le Trame comes from
two plots—Le Boncie of
3.3 hectares and Poggio
of 1 hectare—on slopes
of *alberese* limestone soils
facing south-southeast at
360 meters of altitude at
the hamlets of San Felice
and Villa a Sesta in
southeastern Chianti
Classico. The vines, of an
average age of 11 years,
are planted at a density of
7,500 per hectare and
cultivated partly in a low,
spur-trained *alberello* and
partly in a Guyot cordon.

Vinification and aging
Grapes are stemmed and
soft crushed and the
must fermented in open-
topped oak vats at
25–28°C for 12–14 days
(the cap is broken by
hand 2 or 3 times daily),
remaining on the skins
for another 5 days.
Malolactic fermentation
takes place naturally
before maturing of at
least 14 months in 500-
liter and 700-liter barrels
of French oak. The wine,
of about 13% alcohol, is
bottled and cellared for at
least 6 months before
release.

Style and maturity
Chianti Classico Le Trame has
the brilliant ruby color of true
Sangiovese with bouquet that
is subdued when young but
opens with aeration as the
fragrance of pure, clean fruit
comes to the fore. The
structure is robust yet taut,
even sinewy when young, due
to ample tannins, though fruit
flavors triumph with time in a
wine of admirable balance and
long, smooth finish. The wine,
first made in 1990, has the
elements to gain in stature for
10–15 years.

Serving
- 18°C, after decanting the
  wine.
- Tall, ample glass (Bordeaux
  type).
- *Ribollita* (vegetable-bread
  soup), crostini (croutons)
  with chicken liver pâté,
  free-range chicken pan-
  roasted with rosemary,
  sage and garlic.

Moroder

Dorico
Rosso Conero Riserva
DOC ❢

Producer
Azienda Agricola
Alessandro Moroder
Frazione Montacuto 112
60029 Ancona
Tel. 071 898 232
Fax 071 280 0367
moroder@libero.it
www.members.
tripod.com/weinvino

Owner
Alessandro Moroder

Founded
1837

Winemaker
Franco Bernabei

Vineyard manager
Tarcisio Ricciotti

Production
About 30,000 bottles in
choice years

Vintages
1999 1998 1997 1995
1993 1990 1988

Price
● ●

The Marches, a blissful region between the Apennines and the Adriatic Sea, is a treasure trove of things to discover. One such delight is Rosso Conero, a wine of class and character whose virtues are scarcely recognized beyond the port city and capital of Ancona. That vigorous red comes chiefly from Montepulciano grapes (many producers avoid the optional Sangiovese at 15 percent) grown in calcareous soils on the slopes around Monte Conero, the massif dominating the Adriatic south of Ancona.

Rosso Conero is noted for rich fruit sensations, deep color, full body and supple roundness, traits that some tasters liken to Merlot, though others detect a peppery quality found in fine Syrah. To my taste, Rosso Conero stands proudly alone as a wine of winning personality that represents one of the best values among Italy's 300 or so DOCs.

Top producers have reduced grape yields and improved techniques, sometimes maturing the wine in small barrels of French oak. Alessandro Moroder has been a leader in the trend with the authoritative Rosso Conero Riserva known as Dorico (in reference to the Doric Greeks who settled Ancona).

The Moroder family bought the farm at Montacuto just south of Ancona in 1832 and built cellars in 1837. Yet the winery was leased for decades until Alessandro and his wife Serenella began bottling Rosso Conero from the 1984 vintage, following with Dorico from 1985. The arrival of Franco Bernabei as consulting enologist accounts for consistent class. From 20 hectares, Moroder makes about 100,000 bottles of wine a year, including regular Rosso Conero DOC, the IGT pink Rosa di Montacuto and the sweet white Oro.

Annual production of Rosso Conero rarely exceeds 2 million bottles, less than half of the potential of a wine that clearly merits greater renown. Other good producers are Conte Leopardi Dittajuti, Garofoli, Lanari, Marchetti, Enzo Mecella, Le Terrazze and Umani Ronchi (see page 332).

Marche

Grapes
Montepulciano 100%, hand picked in mid-October.

Vineyards
Grapes are selected from 18 hectares of vines in calcareous clay soils on slopes facing south and southeast at 200–250 meters of altitude at the village of Montacuto south of the city of Ancona on the northern edge of the Conero massif 1 kilometer from the Adriatic Sea. The vines, of an average age of 31 years, are planted at 2,300 per hectare and trained in traditional double-arched and spurred cordon methods.

Vinification and aging
Grapes are soft crushed and the musts fermented in stainless steel vats at 25–28°C for at least 15 days on the skins. Malolactic fermentation occurs naturally in wooden barrels, followed by maturation of at least 18 months, partly in casks of Slavonian oak and partly in barriques of French oak from Allier. The wine, of 12.5–13% alcohol, is bottled and cellared for 6 months before release.

Style and maturity
Dorico has a deep ruby color taking on tones of garnet and mahogany with age. The ample bouquet offers scents reminiscent of blackberries, wild cherries, spices, tobacco and vanilla. The wine is firm in structure, full, round and smooth on the palate with rich fruit sensations and fine balance and length of flavor. The wine rounds into form at about 5 years and from fine vintages maintains class well beyond a decade.

Serving
- 18–20°C, opening bottle at least an hour earlier.
- Ample glass (Syrah type).
- *Vincisgrassi* (lasagne with meats and cheeses topped with truffles), porchetta (roast suckling pig), chicken or rabbit *in potacchio* (braised with onion, tomato, rosemary).

Masseto
Toscana IGT 🍷

Producer
Tenuta dell'Ornellaia
Via Bolgherese 191
57020 Bolgheri
(Livorno)
Tel. 0565 762 140
Fax 0565 762 144
info@ornellaia.it
www.ornellaia.it

Owner
Marchese Lodovico
Antinori

Founded
1981

Winemaker
Andrea Giovannini

Production
About 30,000 bottles
a year

Vintages
1999 1998 1997 1996
1995 1994 1993 1992
1989

Price
● ● ● ●

Lodovico Antinori sold his shares in the ancestral Marchesi Antinori wine house in the early 1980s and set out on his own at Ornellaia to pursue a vision of winemaking that he describes as global. He acquired the upper part of the family's Belvedere estate at Bolgheri near Tuscany's Mediterranean coast and created an avant-garde winery next door to Tenuta San Guido, home of the legendary Sassicaia (see page 326). His mentor was André Tchelistcheff, the pioneer of premium California red wines, who designed state-of-the-art cellars that looked as if they had been lifted from the Napa Valley.

Lodovico, a free-spirited nobleman and world traveler, vowed that his aim was not to duplicate Sassicaia (a pure Cabernet), but to make modern red wines of great stature without the sharp edges of the classic reds of Tuscany or Bordeaux. On Tchelistcheff's advice, he planted Merlot to be blended at about 20 percent with Cabernet Sauvignon in the estate's top wine called Ornellaia. But Lodovico soon realized that the Merlot from the Masseto vineyard outshone the Cabernet. From the 1987 vintage he bottled it as a pure varietal called Masseto, creating a wine that has been described as the Tuscan answer to Pomerol.

Its success is due in part to the fact that he hired as special adviser Michel Rolland, Bordeaux's Merlot wizard, who had the vineyard grafted over with clones from Pomerol. But Lodovico, who insists that Masseto expresses the *genius loci* of Ornellaia, promises even better things as vines mature.

He continues to make Ornellaia (from Cabernet Sauvignon with Merlot) and a white wine from Sauvignon Blanc called Poggio alle Gazze. The estate, which has about 60 hectares of vineyards, produces about 500,000 bottles a year, including the red Le Volte (from Sangiovese with Cabernet and Merlot).

Lodovico Antinori recently renewed his California connections when he agreed to let the Robert Mondavi Winery acquire shares in Ornellaia and participate in its management.

Tuscany

Grapes
Merlot 100%, hand picked in mid-September.

Vineyards
The Masseto and Vigna Vecchia plots totaling 17 hectares in stony calcareous clay soils at 65–80 meters of altitude at Ornellaia in the Bolgheri sector of the commune of Castagneto Carducci. The vines were planted at intervals over 16 years at an average density of 3,700 per hectare (greater for recent plantings) and trained in a spurred cordon method.

Vinification and aging
Grapes are soft crushed and musts fermented in stainless steel vats at a maximum of 30°C for 18–20 days on the skins. After malolactic fermentation, the wine of 13–13.5% alcohol is aged for 2 years in small barrels of French oak before being bottled and cellared for a year until release.

Style and maturity
Masseto has deep ruby-mulberry color when young and opulent bouquet with scents of ripe fruit and hints of violets, vanilla, wild mint and cassis liqueur. Full and round on the palate, it has ripe, bold fruit flavors and creamy texture with soft wood tannins and hints of spices and bitter chocolate in its long finish. Though seductive in its youth, the wine has the stuff to become increasingly elegant for well over a decade.

Serving
🍶 18°C.
🍷 Tall, ample glass (Bordeaux type).
🍽 Rack of lamb roast with Mediterranean herbs, rabbit stewed with black olives, loin of the Tuscan *cinta senese* breed of pork roast with rosemary and wild fennel pollen.

Il Poggione

Brunello di Montalcino
DOCG 🍷

Producer
Tenuta Il Poggione
Sant'Angelo in Colle
53020 Montalcino
(Siena)
Tel. 0577 844 029
Fax 0577 844 165
ilpoggione@tin.it

Owners
Clemente, Leopoldo and
Livia Franceschi

Founded
1800

Winemaker
Fabrizio Bindocci

Vineyard manager
Fabrizio Bindocci

Production
An average of
140,000–150,000
bottles a year

Vintages
1999 1998 1997 1995
1994 1993 1991 1990
1988 1987 1985 1983
1982 1980 1979 1978
1977 1975 1970 1969
1967 1966 1965

Price
● ●

Mention of Il Poggione will always bring to mind Pierluigi Talenti, the manager who ran the estate with a feisty sense of purpose that resulted in the most consistent Brunello of all over the last three decades. It was Piero who convinced me that Brunello could be superb without being excessively priced, while supplying me with the estate's delicious young *rosso* in the days when aspiring authors were known to economize by buying wine in demijohns.

Piero died in 1999, leaving Il Poggione in the capable hands of his long-time associate Fabrizio Bindocci, who continues to make Brunello following traditional methods. The secret of Il Poggione's success is selection from vineyards of the vast estate owned by the Franceschi family since 1800. The sites around the hill village of Sant'Angelo in Colle lie on the southerly slopes of the commune of Montalcino in some of the most privileged positions for Brunello. The choice bunches from old vines go into Brunello and the remaining grapes into Rosso di Montalcino. Another selection in the cellars singles out Brunello Riserva from top vintages, but the main difference between that and the regular Brunello is an extra year in cask or bottle.

Piero Talenti once explained that from most vintages Il Poggione's grapes were so good that he largely let nature take its course in the cellars. His faith was confirmed in the "Taste of Tuscan History" event in Florence in 1996, when vintages of Il Poggione from the 1980s and 1970s clearly outshone Brunello from other estates.

From 100 hectares of vines (not all in production), Il Poggione makes about 400,000 bottles of wine a year, including the sweet white Moscadello di Montalcino DOC and an IGT called San Leopoldo (Sangiovese and Cabernet).

Pierluigi Talenti also established his own estate, known as Talenti-Pian del Conte, where in semi-retirement he made small quantities of Brunello and Rosso di Montalcino of exemplary quality. The estate is now run by his son Roberto.

Tuscany

Grapes
Sangiovese 100%, hand picked from late September to mid-October.

Vineyards
Grapes are selected from 48 hectares of vines on medium-packed stony soils on slopes facing south at 200–400 meters of altitude near Sant'Angelo in Colle in the southern part of the commune of Montalcino. The vines, ranging in age from 20–35 years, are planted at densities of 2,800–4,200 per hectare and trained in the Tuscan double-arched cordon method.

Vinification and aging
Grapes are stemmed and soft crushed and the must fermented in stainless steel and glass-lined concrete tanks at 28–30°C for 12 days on the skins. After malolactic fermentation, the wine, of 13.5–14% alcohol, is matured for at least 2 years in 10,000-liter casks of oak from Allier (France) and Slavonia, then settled in stainless steel tanks and bottled and cellared for at least 6 months before release.

Style and maturity
Brunello Il Poggione when released in the fifth year after the harvest has deep ruby-garnet color and rich bouquet that recalls blackberries, cherries and spices. The wine is full bodied with ripe fruit sensations well balanced by tannins in smooth flavors that have depth and length on the palate and an easygoing elegance. The wine is attractive from the start, though from great vintages it has been known to maintain vitality for well over 2 decades.

Serving
- 🍷 18°C in summer, 20°C in winter, decanting several hours earlier.
- 🍷 Ample crystal glass (Bordeaux type).
- 🍽 Guinea fowl with porcini mushrooms, woodcock roast with juniper berries, mature Pecorino cheese from nearby Pienza.

Poliziano

Producer
Azienda Agricola
Poliziano
Via Fontago 1
53040 Montepulciano
Stazione (Siena)
Tel. 0578 738 171
Fax 0578 738 752
az.agr.poliziano@iol.it

Owner
Federico Carletti

Founded
1961

Winemakers
Carlo Ferrini and
Federico Carletti

Vineyard manager
Federico Carletti

Production
From 30,000–60,000
in fine years

Vintages
1999 1998 1997 1996
1995 1993 1990 1988

Price
● ●

Asinone
Vino Nobile di Montepulciano
DOCG ▼

Vino Nobile di Montepulciano was called the king of all wines in the seventeenth century, long before its Tuscan rivals Chianti and Brunello di Montalcino rose to fame. But it must be admitted that the monarch hasn't always lived up to its name. Starting in the nineteenth century, Vino Nobile was upstaged by Chianti as it conquered the world in its straw-based flask, then by its neighbor Brunello whose legend of longevity was launched in the 1960s. When Vino Nobile was dutifully tapped for DOCG in 1981, critics considered it a faded aristocrat.

Since then winemaking in Montepulciano has undergone a transformation that has raised quality to unprecedented heights. No producer has been more enterprising than Federico Carletti in making Poliziano the leading name in Vino Nobile. The estate is named for Poliziano, or Politian, the Renaissance humanist poet from Montepulciano who was Lorenzo de' Medici's favorite companion. But Federico didn't feel the least bit intimidated by the past when he took command in the early 1980s. As he recalls: "In Tuscany, before we could learn how to make fine wines, we had to unlearn bad habits accumulated over centuries."

Working with enologist Carlo Ferrini, Federico revitalized his extensive vineyards and revised the style of his wines. That involved substituting ancient casks of chestnut and oak with smaller barrels, eventually including barriques from France. But the greatest gains came in the vineyards, with denser planting of select Sangiovese (known locally as Prugnolo Gentile), as well as Cabernet Sauvignon. Beyond regular Vino Nobile, Federico created the single-vineyard Asinone, which has turned out to be Montepulciano's model of modern nobility.

From 120 hectares of vines, Poliziano turns out 500,000–600,000 bottles a year, including DOC Rosso di Montepulciano, DOCG Chianti and two excellent IGT reds: Le Stanze (Cabernet Sauvignon) and Elegìa (late-harvested Sangiovese), though that was last produced in 1995.

Tuscany

Grapes
Sangiovese (called
Prugnolo Gentile locally)
100%, hand picked from
early to mid-October.

Vineyard
Asinone, 9 hectares in
stony soils of 15% clay
and 10% tufa on slopes
facing southwest at an
average of 350 meters of
altitude at Pietrose in the
Canneto area of the
commune of
Montepulciano. The
vines—6 hectares planted
31 years ago at a density
of 3,500 per hectare and
3 hectares planted
11 years ago at a density
of 5,000 per hectare   are
trained in a Guyot
cordon method.

Vinification and aging
Grapes are stemmed and
soft crushed and the
musts fermented on the
skins in stainless steel
tanks at 32°C for 5 days
and 28°C for 10 days
with frequent pumping
over the cap. Malolactic
fermentation occurs
naturally in barriques,
followed by 18 months of
maturation in 225-liter
and 500-liter barrels of
French oak. The wine, of
about 13% alcohol, is
bottled and cellared for a
year before release.

Style and maturity
Vino Nobile Asinone on
release in the third year after
the harvest has deep ruby-
violet color and ample
bouquet with scents that
recall black cherries, wild
berries, violets, spices and
vanilla. Full bodied and firmly
structured with concentrated
ripe fruit flavors underlined by
a youthful tannic grip, the wine
shows impressive harmony
and depth in its long, smooth
finish. After reaching a prime
between 6 and 10 years, wine
from top vintages will retain
nobility for 2 decades.

Serving
🍷 18–20°C, opening bottle an
hour or two earlier.
🍷 Ample crystal glass
(Bordeaux type).
🍴 Charcoal-grilled slabs of
Chianina beef; wood pigeon
braised with Vin Santo;
aged Pecorino cheese from
nearby Pienza.

Poggio Valente
Morellino di Scansano DOC ❢

Producer
Azienda Agricola
Fattoria Le Pupille
Località Piagge del
Maiano
58040 Istia d'Ombrone
(Grosseto)
Tel. 0564 409 518
Fax 0564 409 517
lepupille@tin.it
www.elisabettageppetti.
com

Owner
Elisabetta Geppetti

Founded
1978

Winemakers
Christian le Sommer
with Riccardo Cotarella

Vineyard manager
Marco Pierucci

Production
About 12,000 bottles in
choice years

Vintages
1999 1998 1997

Price
●

The new mecca of Tuscan wine is the Maremma, the hills inland from the Tyrrhenian Sea between Bolgheri and the border of Lazio. Wine producers from elsewhere in Tuscany and beyond have bought up vineyards there lately with a frenzy reminiscent of a gold rush. The focus of activity is the Scansano DOC zone southeast of the city of Grosseto, in arid hills that had been noted since the early nineteenth century as a modest source of red wine from Sangiovese, known locally as Morellino.

Production of Morellino in a modern context dates to 1978, when Alfredo Gentile began using French barriques to mature the wines of his family estate of Le Pupille. Counseled by the noted enologist Giacomo Tachis, Gentile also planted Cabernet Sauvignon, Merlot and Alicante as the base of Saffredi, a Super-Tuscan that has made a greater impact on the critics.

Today Le Pupille is owned by Gentile's daughter-in-law Elisabetta Geppetti, who works with her husband Stefano Rizzi and winemaker Christian Le Sommer with consultant Riccardo Cotarella. Elisabetta has continued to make Saffredi while renewing interest in Morellino, notably in the single-vineyard Poggio Valente from the 1997 vintage, a wine that may not show the international style of her Super-Tuscan but surpasses it in native integrity.

Growth in Scansano and nearby zones has brought new luster to the Maremma, where the Etruscans made wine three millennia ago. Many producers have been inspired by the success of Cabernet and Merlot at Bolgheri, exemplified by Sassicaia (see page 326) and Ornellaia's Masseto (see page 304). But wines like Le Pupille's Poggio Valente also herald a bright future for those who have kept the faith in Sangiovese.

From 29 hectares of vineyards (in constant expansion), Le Pupille also produces Morellino di Scansano in normal and *riserva* versions, along with the IGT Poggio Argentato and late-harvest Solalto from blends of white varieties.

Tuscany

Grapes
Sangiovese (Morellino) 85%, with Merlot, Alicante and Canaiolo, hand picked in late October.

Vineyard
A plot of 2.5 hectares in medium-textured stony clay soils on slopes at 200–250 meters of altitude at Poggio Valente in the commune of Magliano in Toscana. The vines, of 11–16 years of age, are planted at a density of 4,200 per hectare and trained in the Guyot and spurred cordon methods.

Vinification and aging
Grapes are stemmed and soft crushed and the must fermented in stainless steel tanks at 28–30°C for 20 days on the skins with frequent pumping over the cap. After malolactic fermentation in small barrels, the wine, of about 14% alcohol, is matured for a year in new barriques of French oak, then bottled and cellared for at least 9 months before release.

Style and maturity
Morellino Poggio Valente on release in the third year after the harvest has intense ruby-garnet color and pleasant bouquet with scents that recall morello cherries, ripe berries, wild herbs and vanilla. Solidly structured with ripe fruit flavors underlined by spicy wood tannins, the wine needs time to attain depth and length of flavors. First released from the 1997 vintage, Poggio Valente seems to have the stuff to shine for at least a decade.

Serving
🌡 18°C.
🍷 Ample glass (Bordeaux type).
🍴 Grilled and roast beef, pork and game, such as hare braised in Morellino and wild boar stewed with red wine and herbs.

Producer
Agricola Querciabella
Via Santa Lucia a
Barbiano 17
Località Ruffoli
50022 Greve in Chianti
(Firenze)
Tel. 02 8645 2793
Fax 02 8053 139
info@
querciabella.com
www.querciabella.com

Owners
Giuseppe Castiglioni and
family

Founded
1972

Winemakers
Guido De Santi with
consultant Giacomo
Tachis

Vineyard manager
Dales D'Alessandro with
consultant Carlo Modi

Production
About 18,000 bottles in
choice years

Vintages
1999 1997 1996 1995
1994 1990 1988 1985
1983

Price
●●

Querciabella

Camartina
Toscana IGT ♉

Giuseppe Castiglioni, a native of Milan, alternates interests between a steel business in Mexico and the Querciabella estate in Chianti Classico, which he bought in 1972. As a connoisseur of wines from around the world, Giuseppe Castiglioni has invested heavily and well in Querciabella, in new cellars and expanded vineyards that exemplify a perennial quest for perfection. He and son Sebastiano participate expertly in key steps of production while leaving the day-to-day operation in the hands of Guido De Santi, the resident winemaker whose credentials include a degree in law.

Their collaboration with consultant Giacomo Tachis seems to account for the impeccable class of Querciabella's elite production. From 26 hectares of vines come Chianti Classico and Chianti Classico Riserva DOCG, the Toscana IGT red Camartina (Sangiovese with Cabernet Sauvignon) and white Batàr (oak-fermented Chardonnay with Pinot Bianco – see page 362), as well as a sweet Vin Santo called Orlando.

As a devotee of pure Sangiovese, my sentimental favorite of Querciabella's reds would have to be the Chianti Classico Riserva, which stands with the exemplars of the denomination. But hedonistic instincts give the nod to Camartina, which to my taste over the years has come as close as any Super-Tuscan to expressing the perfect amalgam of Sangiovese and Cabernet in a style that somehow seems to bring out the best in both. The term Camartina is a fusion of Casaocci, as the hamlet of Querciabella was called in the eleventh century, and the name of Giuseppe Castiglioni's daughter Martina.

Beyond the Querciabella estate, where total production is about 195,000 bottles a year, the Castiglioni family is developing vineyards at Alberese in the Maremma near the coast of Tuscany and at Manzano in the Colli Orientali DOC zone of Friuli-Venezia Giulia.

Tuscany

Grapes
Sangiovese 75–80%, hand picked in early October, and Cabernet Sauvignon, picked a week later.

Vineyard
Plots called Faule, Montoro, Poggerina and Tinamicaio covering 6 hectares in stony soils of schistous *galestro* mixed with sand on slopes oriented south-southwest at about 400 meters of altitude at Ruffoli in the commune of Greve in the northeastern sector of the Chianti Classico zone. The vines, of an average age of 17 years, are planted at a density of 4,500–5,000 per hectare and trained in a spurred cordon method.

Vinification and aging
Grapes are stemmed and soft crushed and the must fermented separately in stainless steel tanks at 28–30°C, the Sangiovese for about 10 days on the skins, the Cabernet for 12–15 days. After malolactic fermentation, the wines are matured for 18–24 months in small barrels of French oak before being assembled. After blending, the wine, of about 13.5% alcohol, returns to barrels for 2 or 3 months. It remains at least 6 months in bottle before release.

Style and maturity
Camartina reaches a prime at 5–12 years, showing deep ruby color with a bright garnet cast on the rim. The bouquet is rich and penetrating with scents reminiscent of morello cherries, violets, tobacco and a vague suggestion of woodsmoke. The wine has full structure and great concentration with ripe fruit and spicy sensations set off by sweet tannins in long, smooth flavors. A wine of great depth and complexity, from top vintages it should retain class for a couple of decades.

Serving
🍾 18°C, opening bottle at least 2 hours earlier.
🍷 Ample glass (Bordeaux type).
🍽 Saddle of spring lamb roasted with wild herbs; goose roast in a wood-burning oven; aged Pecorino cheese from Pienza.

Castello di Brolio
Chianti Classico DOCG 🍷

Producer
Barone Ricasoli
Cantine del Castello
di Brolio
53013 Gaiole in Chianti
(Siena)
Tel. 0577/7301
Fax 0577/730225
barone@ricasoli.it

Owner
Company headed by
Francesco Ricasoli

Founded
1141

Chief winemaker
Carlo Ferrini

Vineyard manager
Massimiliano Biagi

Production
About 200,000 bottles
in choice years

Vintages
1999 1998 1997

Price
● ●

Amid the emanation of wine news from Tuscany in the 1990s, the top story had to be the return of Brolio to the front rank of Chianti Classico. Francesco Ricasoli, the 32nd Baron of Brolio, regained control of a winery that had stumbled through two decades of multinational ownership and in 1993 began restoring the domain to its former glory. His goal was achieved in the year 2000, when Castello di Brolio Chianti Classico from the 1997 vintage was launched as the premier wine of a domain that traces its history to 1141.

Many have heard the legend of Barone Bettino Ricasoli, who served as the second prime minister of a reunified Italy before retiring to Brolio, where in 1874 he devised the formula for Chianti based on the vigor of Sangiovese. Castello di Brolio symbolized Chianti Classico for a century. But under foreign ownership as the emphasis shifted to commercial wines the name Brolio lost much of its luster.

Francesco Ricasoli, working with general manager Filippo Mazzei and chief winemaker Carlo Ferrini, has put the accent decisively back on quality in wines from the Brolio estate, whose 227 hectares of vines are being steadily renewed, mainly with select clones of Sangiovese.

With the great 1997 vintage, the Ricasoli team selected its best Sangiovese for a wine of remarkable class of which they produced 204,000 bottles. The decision to call it Castello di Brolio Chianti Classico confirmed Francesco Ricasoli's commitment to the best known appellation in Italian wine and the estate that more than any other made it famous. Only that wine and the Chianti Classico called Brolio carry the name of the historic estate.

The firm, whose spacious cellars occupy a hollow beneath the castle, uses the trademark Barone Ricasoli for other wines, including Chianti Classico Riserva Rocca Guicciarda and IGT Casalferro (Sangiovese with Merlot), Formulae (Sangiovese), Torricella (Chardonnay) and Vin Santo. Wines from acquired grapes are also bottled under the Barone Ricasoli label.

Tuscany

Grapes
Sangiovese 100%, hand picked in late September–early October.

Vineyards
Grapes are selected from older vines among 227 hectares that range from 300–450 meters of altitude in sandy calcareous soils mixed with schistous *galestro* or, at lower points, reddish sands with alluvial stones on slopes facing south-southwest between Brolio and Monti in the commune of Gaiole in southeastern Chianti Classico. The vines, half 31 years old and the rest replanted at a density of 5,500–6,200 per hectare, are trained in spurred cordon.

Vinification and aging
Grapes are stemmed and soft crushed and the must fermented in stainless steel tanks at 31°C for 19 days on the skins. After malolactic fermentation, the wine, of about 13.5% alcohol, is matured for 18 months in barriques of French oak (65% new) and bottled and cellared for at least 8 months before release.

Style and maturity
Chianti Classico Castello di Brolio from the initial 1997 vintage has deep ruby-red color with bouquet that recalls ripe fruit and berries, morello cherries and vanilla. On the palate it shows firm structure with full fruit sensations set off by spicy wood tannins in smooth, long flavors that promise to gain greater depth and polish with time. The wine should approach a prime at 5–6 years and retain virtues for at least 15 years.

Serving
- 18°C.
- Tall, ample glass (Bordeaux type).
- Suckling pig roast in a wood-burning oven, spit-roasted pigeon and chicken, as well as aged Tuscan Pecorino cheese.

La Gioia
Vino da Tavola di Toscana ♀

Producer
Azienda Agricola Riecine
Località Riecine
53013 Gaiole in Chianti
(Siena)
Tel. 0577 749 098
Fax 0577 744 935
riecine@chiantinet.it
www.riecine.com

Owners
Gary Baumann and Sean
O'Callaghan

Founded
1972

**Winemaker and
vineyard manager**
Sean O'Callaghan

Production
8,000–12,000 bottles in
choice years

Vintages
1999 1998 1997 1996
1995 1994 1993 1991
1990

Price
● ●

Dunkley, O'Callaghan, Baumann—the names of the owners over the years—are clearly not Tuscan. Yet few wines have captured the essence of Chianti and its Sangiovese grape as faithfully as the reds of Riecine. This jewel of an estate overlooking Gaiole was acquired by John Dunkley in 1972 at the height of the English invasion of what some came to call Chiantishire. But John and his Neapolitan wife Palmina went native, making Chianti Classico with the help of young Carlo Ferrini that earned the hard-won praise of Tuscans.

A decade later, John and Palmina joined the Super-Tuscan parade with a pure Sangiovese called La Gioia di Riecine after the joy that their estate had brought them. In 1991, they were joined by Sean O'Callaghan, a young Englishman with a degree from Germany's Geisenheim wine institute. Although Riecine has always exemplified the Dunkleys' "small-is-beautiful" philosophy of winemaking, the laurels garnered over the years by the team of Ferrini-O'Callaghan have been entirely out of proportion to the estate's size.

Before his death in 1999, John had ceded his shares in the winery to Sean and an American, Gary Baumann, whose investment has enabled Riecine to expand vineyards (to 12 hectares) and build a new cellar. Total production will soon climb beyond the current 30,000 bottles a year.

Chianti Classico remains the base, though in good years about 25 percent becomes Riserva and in superior vintages the choicest Sangiovese is designated for La Gioia. Sean, who is now the sole winemaker, ages Chianti Classico in the traditional casks of French oak to maintain the original fruit characteristics of Sangiovese. La Gioia is a bigger, more complex wine with rounder, mellower flavors, which come from maturing in 225-liter barriques and 500-liter barrels of French oak. Sean describes its style as "international," but deep down La Gioia expresses all the joy of a special place in Chianti.

Tuscany

Grapes
Sangiovese 100%, hand
picked in late
September–early
October.

Vineyards
Grapes are selected from
9 hectares of vines in soils
of *alberese* limestone and
clay on slopes oriented
toward the south at about
450 meters of altitude at
Riecine overlooking the
town of Gaiole on the
eastern edge of Chianti
Classico. The vines, of an
average age of 26 years,
are planted at a density of
2,550 per hectare and
trained in the Guyot
cordon method.

Vinification and aging
Grapes are stemmed and
soft crushed and the
must fermented in
stainless steel vats at
20–33°C for 14–21 days
on the skins. After
malolactic fermentation,
mainly in wood, the wine
is matured for 18–24
months in small barrels
of French oak (45%
new). The wine, of
13–13.5% alcohol, is
bottled and cellared for
6 months to a year before
release.

Style and maturity
La Gioia has intense ruby-red
color with tinges of garnet on
the rim. The bouquet is rich
and ripe with scents of wild
berries, cherries, wood spice
and cacao. On the palate, it
shows ample structure with
full fruit sensations balanced
by soft wood tannins that give
it round, smooth flavors of

notable depth and complexity.
The wine seems to have the
constitution to last for
decades, but it may be at its
joyful best between 5 and 10
years.

Serving
🍷 18°C.
🍷 Tall, ample glass (Bordeaux
type).
🍽 Red meats, especially
charcoal-grilled Florentine
steak and rare roast beef
with Yorkshire pudding, as
well as aged English Stilton
cheese.

318

Ruffino

Romitorio di Santedame Toscana IGT ♀

Producer
Tenimenti Ruffino
Santedame
Via Santedame 23
53011 Castellina in
Chianti (Siena)
Tel. 0577 740 3758
Fax 0577 740 3758
ruffino@ruffino.it
www.ruffino.com

Owner
Ruffino

Founded
1877

Chief winemaker
Mauro Orsoni

Vineyard manager
Giovanni Folonari

Production
About 18,000 bottles a
year

Vintages
1999 1998 1997 1996
1995 1991

Price
● ●

The winery founded by Leopoldo Ruffino in 1877 was acquired by the Folonari family of Brescia in 1913 and developed into one of the largest and most reliable wineries of Tuscany. Ruffino was long noted as a prodigious producer of Chianti from its base at Pontassieve east of Florence, but in recent times the firm has developed properties in Chianti Classico, Montalcino and Montepulciano as sources of prestigious estate wines.

Ruffino's winemaking team, headed by Ambrogio, Marco and Giovanni Folonari and enologist Mauro Orsoni, provides several candidates for top honors among Italian reds. First comes Chianti Classico Riserva Ducale Oro, which has stood for decades as a model of how premium class can be achieved on a large scale. From the Nozzole estate comes Chianti Classico La Forra and the Super-Tuscan Il Pareto from Cabernet Sauvignon. Cabreo Il Borgo blends Sangiovese with Cabernet selected in vineyards in Chianti.

But to my taste the most captivating wine on Ruffino's formidable list is Romitorio di Santedame, conceived with the 1991 vintage from a unique combination of ancient Tuscan varieties: Colorino and Prugnolo Gentile. Colorino, whose name comes from coloring components in the skins, was historically used to darken Chianti, sometimes in the *governo* where dried grapes were added to the wine to induce a second fermentation. Prugnolo, a strain of Sangiovese, was found growing in the vineyards of Ruffino's Santedame estate near Castellina in Chianti. Being precocious, they were planted on cool slopes facing north to ripen slowly and favor the elements that account for extraordinary aromas. Together they make a wine that qualifies as the most original Super-Tuscan of the 1990s and decidedly one of the best, with an inimitable way of melding power with finesse.

Ruffino owns 14 properties in Tuscany with more than 700 hectares of vines, which account for a growing share of production of one of Italy's best known and most admired wine houses.

Tuscany

Grapes
Colorino 60%, Prugnolo
Gentile 40%, hand
picked between October
10 and 15.

Vineyards
Various plots covering
about 3 hectares in
medium-packed soils of
40% sand, 35% clay and
25% silt on a base of
schistous *galestro* on
slopes facing north-
northwest at 330–430
meters of altitude at
Santedame, Serelle and
Pianamici in the
communes of Castellina
and Barberino Val d'Elsa
in the southwestern part
of the Chianti Classico
zone. The vines, 25–30
years old, are planted at a
density of 3,000–5,000
per hectare and trained in
the spurred cordon and
espalier methods.
Another 3.5 hectares have
recently been planted.

Vinification and aging
Grapes are stemmed and
soft crushed and the
must fermented in
stainless steel tanks at no
more than 28°C for 8
days, remaining on the
skins for another 8 days.
After malolactic
fermentation at 22–23°C,
the wine, of about 13.5%
alcohol, is matured in
small barrels of French
oak for 15 months and
bottled and cellared for at
least 6 months before
release.

Style and maturity
Romitorio di Santedame on
release in the third year after
the harvest has deep mulberry
color with ruby highlights and
generous bouquet that recalls
violets and roses, ripe
cherries, wood spice and
vanilla. The structure is
immense yet accessible with
great concentration of fruit
and berry flavors rounded out
by wood tannins that give the
wine mellow complexity and
impressive length on the
palate. Though seductive from
the start, the wine seems to
have the constitution to
maintain style for 10–15 years.

Serving
🌡 18°C, opening bottle an
hour earlier.
🍷 Crystal glass (Bordeaux
type).
🍽 Traditional Tuscan dishes,
roast meats, *pollo alla
diavola* (spicy charcoal-
grilled chicken), *peposo*
(peppery beef stewed in
red wine).

Brunello di Montalcino
DOCG ☖

Producer
Cerbaiola di
Salvioni Giulio
Piazza Cavour 19
53024 Montalcino
(Siena)
Tel. 0577 848 499
Fax 0577 848 499

Owner
Giulio Salvioni

Founded
1985

Winemakers
Giulio Salvioni with
Attilio Pagli

Vineyard manager
Giulio Salvioni

Production
5,000–7,000 bottles
annually

Vintages
1999 1997 1995 1990
1989 1988 1987 1985

Price
● ●

Since the 1960s, when Brunello di Montalcino was the heritage of a handful of estates, production has proliferated to involve about 130 wineries with a potential output of more than 5 million bottles a year. The boom was bolstered by large companies that planted extensive vineyards, though it also opened the way for small-scale estates to surge to the forefront in prestige.

Gianfranco Soldera at Case Basse set an early example (see page 330), though perhaps the most respected artisan of recent years has been Giulio Salvioni, whose Brunello from the Cerbaiola estate is so precious that its devotees constitute little more than a cult.

Giulio Salvioni grew up on a farm, though he worked for years with the health board at Montalcino, leaving the vineyards of Cerbaiola to his father Umberto, who made a little wine for family and friends. Then, in the 1980s, Giulio and his wife Mirella decided to revive and expand the vineyards and to make a Brunello from the 1985 vintage that still wins superlatives from the privileged few who have tasted it of late. Wines from the outstanding 1990 and 1995 vintages were similarly impressive, expressing the old style of Brunello at its integral best. Yet Salvioni Brunello can be almost as good in off years, such as 1987, 1989, 1991 and 1992.

The explanation seems to lie in the vineyards of Cerbaiola, which Giulio and Mirella tend with excruciating patience, pruning and thinning to reduce grape yields to levels that would make no sense if they could not charge a small fortune for their Brunello. Giulio, who works with consulting enologist Attilio Pagli, follows traditional methods in his small cellars, fermenting wines at natural temperatures and aging them in Slavonian oak casks. The result is Brunello of such class that the limited production has to be rationed out to admirers, who seem more than willing to pay the price. Giulio and Mirella also make a bit of Rosso di Montalcino DOC from Sangiovese not considered worthy of Brunello.

Tuscany

Grapes
Sangiovese Grosso 100%, hand picked in early October.

Vineyard
A plot of 2.26 hectares in schistous *galestro* soils on a slope facing southeast at 420 meters of altitude at Cerbaiola about 2 kilometers southeast of the town of Montalcino. The vines, from 11–16 years of age, are planted at densities of 3,500–5,500 per hectare and trained in a spurred cordon method.

Vinification and aging
Grapes are stemmed and soft crushed and the musts fermented in stainless steel tanks at natural temperatures of 25–30°C for 25–30 days on the skins with frequent pumping over the cap. After natural malolactic fermentation, the wine is matured for at least 2 years (3 years prior to 1995) in 2,000-liter capacity casks of Slavonian oak. The wine, of 13–14% alcohol, is bottled without filtering and cellared until release in the fifth year after the harvest.

Style and maturity
Brunello Salvioni when released in the fifth year after the harvest has bright ruby-garnet color, showing orange tinges on the rim over time. The bouquet is elaborate with scents that recall cherries, violets, spices, herbs and, vaguely, tobacco. The structure is ample in great years, refined in others, though the wine invariably has rich and complex flavors of extraordinary finesse. It tends to reach a prime about a decade after the harvest, though the first vintage of 1985 should remain impressive for years to come.

Serving
🍷 18–20°C, after decanting.
🍷 Ample glass (Bordeaux type).
🍽 Spring lamb roast with aromatic herbs; pigeon baked in a crust, served with Tuscan beans; aged Pecorino cheeses from Pienza and Monte Amiata.

San Felice

Poggio Rosso
Chianti Classico Riserva
DOCG ❢

Producer
Agricola San Felice
Località San Felice
53019 Castelnuovo
Berardenga (Siena)
Tel. 0577 359 087
Fax 0577 359 223
sanfelice@agricolasan
felice.it
www.chianticlassico.com

Owner
Riunione Adriatica di
Sicurtà

Founded
1968

Winemaker
Leonardo Bellaccini

Vineyard manager
Carlo Salvinelli

Production
About 40,000 bottles
from choice vintages

Vintages
1999 1997 1995 1990
1988 1986 1985 1982

Price
●●

The ancient hamlet of San Felice was acquired in 1968 by the Riunione Adriatica di Sicurtà insurance group, whose investments transformed the Chianti Classico domain into a model of viticultural research and development. The estate was managed from the start by the late Enzo Morganti, a man of uncommon foresight who established a range of premium wines while planting 18 hectares of experimental vineyards, including a plot called the Vitiarium where more than 300 varieties grow, most of them native Tuscan.

In 1968, Enzo Morganti created Vigorello, the first modern wine to combine Sangiovese with Cabernet Sauvignon, anticipating Antinori's Tignanello (see page 252) and the flourish of Super-Tuscans to follow. In 1983, the firm acquired the Campogiovanni estate, source of impressive Brunello di Montalcino and Riserva Vigna del Quercione.

But Enzo's first love was Chianti, which San Felice produces in quantity from 200 hectares of vines. The bestsellers are a regular Chianti Classico and a reserve called Il Grigio, though the pride of San Felice is the single-vineyard reserve called Poggio Rosso. Enzo Morganti planted that plot with select clones of Sangiovese and the long-neglected Tuscan variety of Colorino, making the first wine from the 1978 vintage. Poggio Rosso has been praised as a prototype of modern Chianti, though Enzo himself liked to think of it as "elegantly rustic" like the land it comes from.

Winemaker Leonardo Bellaccini directs production of about 1.3 million bottles of wine a year, taking in Val d'Arbia DOC Belcaro and Vin Santo "In Pincis" and an IGT Chardonnay called Ancherona. From the Vitiarium, he has selected grapes from some vintages to make a unique wine called I Viziati, a name that reveals that vines are doted on like spoiled children. Old stone buildings on the estate have been restructured into the deluxe Borgo San Felice hotel and restaurant, part of the exclusive Relais et Châteaux group.

Tuscany

Grapes
Sangiovese 90% with Colorino Toscano, hand picked in late September–early October.

Vineyards
Poggio Rosso covers 10 hectares in calcareous soils of 40% clay, 30% sand and 30% silt on slopes facing southeast tapering into a plain at 390 meters of altitude at San Felice in the commune of Castelnuovo Berardenga in southeastern Chianti Classico. The vines, planted in 1974 (4 hectares) and 1978 (6 hectares) at a density of 3,000 per hectare, are trained in the spurred cordon and Guyot cordon methods.

Vinification and aging
Grapes are stemmed and soft crushed and the must reduced by 10% for greater concentration before fermenting in stainless steel vats at 30°C, remaining on the skins for 20–25 days. Malolactic fermentation takes place naturally in barriques before maturing for 18–20 months in 500-liter barrels of French oak. The wine, of 12.5–13% alcohol, is bottled and cellared for 10–12 months before release.

Style and maturity
Poggio Rosso when released in the fourth year after the harvest has intense ruby-red color, tending toward garnet with age. The ample bouquet recalls ripe plums, raspberries, blackberries and spices. On the palate, it combines firm structure and finesse, with rich fruit flavors balanced against tannins that soften over time as the wine takes on depth and complexity and a long, increasingly smooth finish. From great vintages, the wine is approachable after 5 years, reaching primes between 10 and 15.

Serving
- 18°C.
- Medium-sized glass (Bordeaux type).
- Tuscan meat dishes: grilled and roast beef, lamb and pork, braised pigeon and duck; well-aged local Pecorino cheeses.

San Giusto
a Rentennano

Percarlo
Toscana IGT ▮

Producer
Fattoria San Giusto a
Rentennano
Località Monti
53013 Gaiole in
Chianti (Siena)
Tel. 0577 747 121
Fax 0577 747 109
sangiustorentennano@
chiantinet.it
www.italywines.com

Owner
Martini di Cigala family

Founded
1905

Winemakers
Francesco Martini di
Cigala with Attilio Pagli

Vineyard manager
Luca Martini di Cigala

Production
About 18,000 bottles
from choice vintages

Vintages
1999 1997 1995 1993
1990 1988 1985

Price
● ●

The noble propensities of Sangiovese have been recognized for ages. Yet experts point out that systematic clonal selection of the vine is so recent that wines have reached only 70–80 percent of ultimate quality potential, as compared to 90 percent or better for those from the venerated French varieties of Cabernet Sauvignon and Merlot.

If there's that much room for improvement, brothers Francesco and Luca Martini di Cigala have reason to be inspired by the prospects for the Sangiovese which they fuss over endlessly in the vineyards of San Giusto a Rentennano. For Percarlo, their pure Sangiovese Super-Tuscan, has already rivaled the cream of Cabernet and Merlot.

In a well-publicized tasting in Germany a few years ago, Percarlo 1985 came in a close second to Château La Mission-Haut-Brion 1978 among 36 wines from vintages between 1970 and 1986 representing the top domains of Bordeaux, Tuscany and Piedmont. The surprising results were reached by a panel made up of respected German and Austrian journalists, sommeliers and connoisseurs.

If Percarlo is often the biggest and boldest Sangiovese of them all, it's because it comes from a special *terroir* and also because Francesco and Luca pick grapes very ripe to make a wine whose youthful power tends to overshadow the aristocratic attributes that emerge over time. From 30.5 hectares of vines, San Giusto a Rentennano produces about 75,000 bottles of wine a year, including DOCG Chianti Classico and a Riserva of uncommon size and durability. The estate also makes a superb Vin Santo (see page 366).

The brothers are convinced that Percarlo—named in memory of Carlo, a friend—will gain greater stature as they improve vineyards and perfect cellar techniques with consultant Attilio Pagli. As a sideline, they also produce La Ricolma, an IGT that has rapidly emerged as one of Tuscany's premier Merlots. Some critics consider La Ricolma a rival to Percarlo, but in the long run Francesco and Luca are placing their faith in Sangiovese.

Tuscany

Grapes
Sangiovese 100%, hand picked in late October.

Vineyards
Four plots (Sodone, Leccio, Corsignano, Galestrino) covering 5.5 hectares in prevalently tufaceous soils, in part gravel mixed with sand, light clay and marine fossils and in part *alberese* limestone mixed with sand or sandy clays, on slopes oriented toward the south at 250–280 meters of altitude at Monti in the commune of Gaiole in southern Chianti Classico. The vines, of an average age of 29 years, are planted at a density of 3,000 per hectare and trained in the Guyot spurred cordon method.

Vinification and aging
Grapes are stemmed and soft crushed and the must fermented in stainless steel vats at 31–33°C, remaining in contact with the skins for 15–20 days with frequent pumping over the cap. After malolactic fermentation, the wine, of 14–14.5% alcohol, is matured for 19–22 months in small barrels of French oak (50–60% new annually), bottled without filtering and cellared for 4–6 months before release.

Percarlo

SAN GIUSTO A RENTENNANO

MARTINI DI CIGALA

GAIOLE IN CHIANTI - SIENA - ITALIA

Style and maturity
Percarlo on release about 3 years after the harvest is invariably big and bold with deep ruby color and bouquet that recalls ripe cherries, violets and spices. Its powerful impact on the palate is underlined by firm tannins that take years to soften, as rich, ripe fruit flavors, notably bitter cherry, become broader and longer. From great vintages, the wine is approachable after 5–6 years, though it takes a decade or more to show its aristocratic depth and complexity.

Serving
- 17–19°C, decanting wine of more than 6 years.
- Tall, ample glass (Bordeaux type).
- Chianina (Tuscan) beef braised in red wine; roast pheasant with black truffles; wild boar stewed with wine, herbs and spices.

Tenuta San Guido

Sassicaia
Bolgheri Sassicaia DOC 🍷

Producer
Tenuta San Guido
Località Capanne 27
57020 Bolgheri
(Livorno)
Tel. 0565 762 003
Fax 0565 762 017
citaispa@infol.it

Owner
Marchesi Incisa della
Rocchetta

Founded
1940

Winemaker
Giacomo Tachis

Vineyard manager
Alessandro Petri

Production
About 150,000 bottles a
year

Vintages
1999 1998 1997 1996
1995 1993 1990 1988
1985 1979

Price
● ● ● ●

Note
1994 was the first
vintage labeled Bolgheri
Sassicaia DOC.
Previously Sassicaia was
labeled as Vino da
Tavola

S assicaia, once called Italy's greatest red wine by the eminent English author Hugh Johnson, was the harbinger of the modern vogue for Cabernet Sauvignon in Tuscany. Considered the original Super-Tuscan, and ranking for decades as the nation's most illustrious *vino da tavola*, Sassicaia became, in 1994, Italy's first wine from a single property to be awarded a DOC with a special zone of its own under the Bolgheri appellation.

The Sassicaia story began half a century earlier, when Marchese Mario Incisa della Rocchetta, a native of Piedmont, planted cuttings of Cabernet vines from Bordeaux's Château Lafite at his San Guido estate. That area, the Maremma, on the coast of Tuscany, was not considered suited to quality vines, and for years Mario Incisa made a little wine for family and friends while concentrating on his main occupation of raising thoroughbred racehorses.

Eventually, though, word of Sassicaia's undeniable signs of class spread, and from the 1968 vintage Incisa's nephew, Piero Antinori, of the prominent Florentine house, talked him into selling 3,000 bottles. Antinori winemaker Giacomo Tachis, assisted by the eminent Bordeaux enologist Emile Peynaud, gave Sassicaia a style that influenced a generation of Italian winemakers. The wine became a legend after a tasting sponsored by *Decanter* magazine in London in 1978 in which it triumphed over 34 select Cabernets from around the world.

Since Mario Incisa's death in 1983, the estate has been run by his son Nicolò, who has sagely expanded vineyards and built production to about 150,000 bottles annually. In keeping with the dignified estate image inspired by Bordeaux, the Incisa della Rocchetta family insists on making only one wine exclusively from its own vineyards.

Sassicaia, in great demand around the world, recently fetched $5,175 for six bottles of the 1985 vintage at a Christie's auction in New York. Some of its most ardent admirers in North America refer to the wine as simply "Sass."

Tuscany

Grapes

Cabernet Sauvignon 85%, Cabernet Franc 15%, hand picked in late September–early October. By law, no more than 2.7 kilograms of grapes per vine or 6 metric tons per hectare may be harvested.

Vineyards

Grapes come from 4 plots totaling 60 hectares—Sassicaia (12), Aia Nuova (20), Mandrioli (14), Castiglioncello (14)— ranging from 60–350 meters of altitude in the Bolgheri sector of the commune of Castagneto Carducci. The vines, of an average age of 27 years, are planted at a density of 3,500–5,000 per hectare in deep, stony, partially clay soils and trained in a spurred cordon on slopes with varied sun exposure.

Vinification and aging

Grapes are soft crushed and musts fermented in stainless steel vats at 28–31°C for 14–18 days on the skins. After malolactic fermentation is completed in oak barrels, the wine is aged for about 2 years in small barrels of French oak—half new and half used once. The wine, of 12–13% alcohol, is bottled without filtering and released in the third year after the harvest.

Style and maturity

Sassicaia has deep ruby-mulberry color when young, with scents that recall vanilla, ripe cherries, blackberries, cinnamon and other spices, and rich, deep, long flavors of notable *souplesse*. From great vintages, such as 1985 and 1988, it needs at least 5 years to show class, though true elegance arrives after a decade or more. From normal vintages, the wine can be attractive soon after release.

Serving

🌡 18°C.

🍷 Tall, ample glass (Bordeaux type).

🍽 Roast, grilled and braised meats and game, in particular beef, lamb and pheasant, as well as aged cheeses, such as Parmigiano Reggiano and Tuscan Pecorino.

Vigneto Bucerchiale Chianti Rufina Riserva DOCG 🍷

Producer
Fattoria Selvapiana
Località Selvapiana 43
50068 Rufina (Firenze)
Tel. 055 836 9848
Fax 055 831 6840

Owner
Francesco Giuntini
Antinori

Founded
1826

Winemaker
Franco Bernabei

Vineyard manager
Federico Giuntini
Massetti

Production
About 20,000 bottles
from choice years

Vintages
1999 1997 1996 1995
1994 1990 1985 1979

Price
● ●

Rufina, a zone east of Florence along the valley of the Sieve river in the foothills of the Apennines, was noted for red wines of power and durability long before they qualified as Chianti. Wines of the Frescobaldi Castello di Nipozzano (see page 288) and Pomino estates were admired in the nineteenth century. But, when the Chianti territory spread from the original zone between Florence and Siena to take in Rufina and much of central Tuscany, producers often filled flasks with local wines stretched with southern blends.

Francesco Giuntini, proprietor of the venerable Selvapiana estate in Rufina, is a soft-spoken nobleman whose lofty principles seem to account for his refreshing candor. At the "Taste of Tuscan History" event in Florence in 1996, his Selvapiana 1947 stole the show with its full ruby-garnet color, clean scents of ripe fruit and vital flavors of a wine that could have passed for 40 years its junior. Giuntini openly admitted that his family had "governed" the wine with concentrated musts from Puglia, as much Chianti had been bolstered for decades.

But, since he's been in charge, the wines of Selvapiana carry a Tuscan pedigree. The leading thoroughbred is the Chianti Rufina Riserva Vigneto Bucerchiale, from a place that was always known for superior Sangiovese. The first vintage was 1979 of a single-vineyard wine that upholds Rufina's age-old reputation for depth and staying power.

Giuntini and his adopted son Federico Massetti run the estate with 45 hectares of vines sprawled over a series of rises overlooking the Sieve north of the town of Pontassieve. They work with enologist Franco Bernabei to produce between 200,000 and 230,000 bottles a year, including regular Chianti Rufina of outstanding value, another Riserva called Fornace and a fine traditional Vin Santo. They also make a DOC Pomino red at the nearby Fattoria di Petrognano.

Tuscany

Grapes
Sangiovese 100%, hand picked in mid-October.

Vineyard
Bucerchiale, 9.95 hectares in calcareous clay soils on slopes facing southwest at 250–300 meters of altitude at Selvapiana in the southern part of the Chianti Rufina zone about 20 kilometers east of Florence. The vines—5.45 hectares planted in 1968 and 4.5 in 1993 at densities of 2,300 and 5,600 per hectare respectively—are trained in a spurred cordon method.

Vinification and aging
Grapes are stemmed and soft crushed and the must fermented without addition of yeasts in stainless steel vats at 30°C, remaining for about 20 days on the skins with frequent pumping over the cap. After natural malolactic fermentation, the wine, of about 13% alcohol, is matured for 12–15 months (20–30% in 2,500-liter casks of Slavonian oak, the rest in small French oak barrels), then bottled and cellared for at least 15 months before release.

Style and maturity
Vigneto Bucerchiale on release shows deep ruby-garnet color, taking on orange highlights with age. The bouquet is intense with ripe cherry and plum sensations mingling with subdued spice and floral scents. It shows firm structure and good weight with ample acidity and wood tannins underlying fruit flavors of impressive depth and length. The wine begins opening up after 5–6 years, though from great vintages it reaches an aristocratic peak at about 15 years.

Serving
🌡 18°C, opening the bottle an hour earlier.
🍷 Medium-sized glass (Chianti type).
🍽 Duck and goose roasted in a wood-burning oven, guinea fowl braised with rosemary and sage, wild boar stewed in red wine with juniper berries and herbs.

Brunello di Montalcino Riserva DOCG ▼

Producer
Azienda Agricola Case
Basse di Gianfranco
Soldera
Villa Santa Restituta
53024 Montalcino
(Siena)
Tel. 02 461 544
Fax 02 481 953 41
soldera@tin.it
www.soldera.it

Owner
Gianfranco Soldera

Founded
1972

Winemaker
Giulio Gambelli

Production
9,900 bottles of Brunello
Riserva from 1993

Vintages
1999 1997 1995 1994
1993 1991 1990 1988
1985 1983 1982

Price
● ● ● ●

Gianfranco Soldera is known around Montalcino as a haughty, impatient man with a mercurial temper, traits that seem incongruous with his apparently calm approach to the making of Brunello. In the vineyards of his Case Basse estate, he holds yields to the minimum, letting nature take its patient course in the cellars in elevating Brunello to maximum levels of quality and price.

Much credit for success goes to veteran winemaker Giulio Gambelli, who as a master taster rather than a technician upholds the theory that great wine comes from great grapes. But the dynamo at Case Basse is Soldera, a Milanese insurance broker who bought the small property in 1972 and has strived for perfection since with results that have generated envy in Montalcino's wine community but won him few friends.

Still, even detractors (including offended critics who no longer rate his wines) will admit that Soldera's Riserva from certain vintages has been the consummate Brunello di Montalcino. Prices are awesome, surpassing even those of the venerable Biondi Santi (see page 260) and even Angelo Gaja, whose Brunello from the adjacent Pieve Santa Restituta estate isn't nearly as expensive as his single-vineyard Barbarescos from Piedmont.

Case Basse's 8 hectares of vines, including 1.5 hectares recently planted, produce about 20,000 bottles of Brunello, divided in choice years between Riserva and two regular types that are confusingly labeled and decidedly overpriced. In some years, Soldera has made an unclassified wine called Intistieti, but the Sangiovese grapes used for that now usually go into Brunello.

At a Christie's auction in London in 1998, 12-bottle lots of Case Basse Brunello Riserva 1990 fetched £2,860 and the 1985 Riserva £2,530—among the most ever paid for relatively recent vintages of Italian wines.

Tuscany

Grapes
Sangiovese Grosso 100%, hand picked in September or October

Vineyards
Brunello Riserva comes from 2 plots: Intistieti of 4.6 hectares and Case Basse of 1.9 hectares in gravelly and schistous soils mixed with clay and sand on slopes facing southwest at 300 meters of altitude in the Santa Restituta area of the commune of Montalcino. The vines, planted in 1972–1973 at a density of 3,300 per hectare, are trained in a spurred cordon method.

Vinification and aging
Grapes are crushed and the musts fermented for 14–25 days in oak vars at natural temperatures as liquid is pumped over the cap three times daily. The wine is aged in Slavonian oak casks of at least 5,000-liter capacity for 66–70 months, as malolactic fermentation occurs naturally. The wine, of about 14% alcohol, is bottled without filtering and cellared for 10–12 months before release.

Style and maturity
Soldera Brunello Riserva on release about 7 years after the harvest has dark ruby color with purple tones tending toward garnet with age. The bouquet is intense with concentrated berry and fruit sensations and scents suggesting tobacco, roast chestnuts and tar. The impact on the palate reveals grandiose structure braced by ample acid and tannins offset by mellow fruit flavors with hints of bitter cherries and licorice at the finish. The wine, which normally starts rounding into form after a decade, has the elements to hold class for a further decade or 2.

Serving
- 18°C.
- Ample crystal glass (Bordeaux type).
- Roast and grilled meats and game dishes, such as boar stewed in sweet-sour wine sauce and pheasant braised in Brunello.

Umani Ronchi

Pelago
Marche Rosso IGT

Producer
Azienda Vinicola Umani
Ronchi
Strada Statale 16, Km
310+400
60027 Osimo (Ancona)
Tel. 071 710 8019
Fax 071 710 8859
wine@umanironchi.it
www.umanironchi.it

Owner
Bianchi Bernetti family

Founded
1955

Winemakers
Umberto Trombelli with
consultant Giacomo
Tachis

Vineyard manager
Luigi Piersanti

Production
About 24,000 bottles in
choice years

Vintages
2000 1999 1998 1997
1996 1995 1994

Price
● ● ●

Pelago, from its first vintage of 1994, triumphed in the 1997 International Wine Challenge in London as the top red wine among 6,750 entries from 37 countries. That feat seemed to have been greeted in Italy with more suspicion than celebration. Skeptics wondered how Umani Ronchi, a large winery known primarily for Verdicchio, had managed that miracle with a red wine. They had perhaps forgotten that the house's Rosso Conero DOC Cùmaro won the same award in 1988.

Massimo Bernetti, who heads the winery founded by Gino Umani Ronchi in 1955, admits that Pelago was conceived as an experiment to test how the estimable Montepulciano variety of the Adriatic region would fare in a blend with Cabernet and Merlot. There were certainly no tricks behind the sudden success, though a bit of wizardry was provided by consulting enologist Giacomo Tachis, master of Sassicaia, Tignanello and other Cabernet-based wines of renown.

It might be that Pelago 1994 benefited from the first flush of new vines, for the subsequently released 1995 and 1996 vintages haven't shown quite such splendor. Massimo Bernetti, who works with brother Stefano, son Michele and resident winemaker Umberto Trombelli, dismisses insinuations that the wine is an imitation Super-Tuscan. Rather, he points out that Pelago, whose name refers to deep seas, has a sunny Mediterranean disposition due to its origins in hills a short distance from the Adriatic. Montepulciano is at home there, but even Cabernet and Merlot develop special traits, according to Bernetti, who predicts that Pelago will have an even brighter future as vines mature.

From 150 hectares of vines and acquisitions, Umani Ronchi produces about 4.2 million bottles a year, including DOC Rosso Conero Cùmaro and San Lorenzo, Montepulciano d'Abruzzo Jorio, Verdicchio dei Castelli di Jesi Classico Casal di Serra (see page 374) and Plenio and Marche IGT Le Busche (Verdicchio and Chardonnay) and Maximo (sweet Sauvignon Blanc from botrytized grapes).

Marche

Grapes
Cabernet Sauvignon 50%, Montepulciano 40%, Merlot 10%, hand picked by variety between mid-September and mid-October.

Vineyards
Grapes are selected from separate plots (Montepulciano 15 hectares, Cabernet 5 hectares, Merlot 3 hectares) in loose calcareous soils on slopes facing southeast at 200 meters of altitude at a place called Sbrozzola in the commune of Osimo south of the port of Ancona. The vines, of an average age of 8 years, are planted at densities of 3,500 and 5,500 per hectare and trained in a spurred cordon.

Vinification and aging
Grapes are soft crushed and the musts fermented in stainless steel tanks at 28°C for 12 days on the skins with the cap submerged. After spontaneous malolactic fermentation, the wine, of about 13% alcohol, is matured for 12 months in barriques (90% of French oak from Allier, 10% American oak), then bottled and cellared for 20 months before release.

Style and maturity
Pelago on release in the 4th year after the harvest has deep ruby color with garnet highlights on the rim. The ample bouquet suggests blackcurrant typical of Cabernet with scents reminiscent of berries, spices, licorice and vanilla. The wine is amply structured, full, round and smooth on the palate with rich fruit and berry sensations and fine harmony and length of flavor. Though impressive young, it should reach a prime at 10–15 years.

Serving
🍷 18°C, opening bottle an hour earlier.
♀ Ample glass (Bordeaux type).
🍴 Charcoal-grilled lamb chops with thyme; rabbit braised in wine with wild fennel; spit-roasted wood pigeon, partridge and grouse.

Valentini

Montepulciano d'Abruzzo DOC

Producer
Azienda Agricola
Valentini
Via del Baio 2
65014 Loreto Aprutino
(Pescara)
Tel. 085 829 1138
Fax 085 829 1138

Owners
Edoardo and Francesco
Paolo Valentini

Founded
1650

**Winemakers and
vineyard managers**
Edoardo and Francesco
Paolo Valentini

Production
Varies according to
vintage

Vintages
1995 1994 1993 1992
1990 1988 1985 1977
1975 1973 1970 1968
1966 1961 1958 1957

Price
● ● ●

As the Italian wine industry rushes headlong into the future, Edoardo Valentini lives happily in the past on the estate in Abruzzo that has been in his family since the seventeenth century. From 64 hectares of vines around the lovely hill town of Loreto Aprutino, Edoardo could produce some 800,000 bottles of wine a year following the region's usual standards. But instead, the man with a law degree who describes himself as an artisan farmer limits production to a maximum of 50,000 bottles.

Edoardo is reluctant to discuss his techniques, other than to say that they were inspired by the ancient Romans. Yet this rugged individualist dutifully classifies his wines under the DOC of Montepulciano d'Abruzzo and Trebbiano d'Abruzzo. They are regularly ranked among the greatest reds and whites of Italy, not only by admirers of the rare and different but even by critics whose tastes run toward the conventional.

The Montepulciano vine carries the name of a Tuscan town, though it seems to be native to Abruzzo. In Edoardo's hands it becomes a red of monumental proportions that ages with a grace he attributes to its natural origins.

Edoardo and son Francesco Paolo, who has a degree in psychology, devote primary attention to their vineyards. They use a low-trellised *tendone* system to attain balanced components in grapes, a fraction of which are selected in choice years to be vinified and aged in well-seasoned oak casks. The others are sold off. If a vintage isn't up to par, they make wine anyway to keep the barrels from drying out and sell it in bulk later.

Edoardo notes that he has never used heating or cooling devices, containers in stainless steel or plastic or even so much as a filter. The Montepulciano goes into bottles of thick brown glass that protects it from the damaging effect of light during the years until Edoardo decides that it is ready. The wine may throw a bit of sediment, but Edoardo points out that the Romans used to meditate over dregs. (See also page 376.)

Abruzzo

Grapes
Montepulciano 100%,
hand picked between
October 5 and 20.

Vineyards
Grapes are selected from
40.5 hectares of vines in
separate areas
(Castelluccio 9,
Camposacro 25, Colle
Cavaliere 6.5) in
medium-packed
calcareous soils on slopes
between 300 and 350
meters of altitude with
various exposures in the
commune of Loreto
Aprutino west of the port
of Pescara. The vines,
between 23 and 35 years
of age, are planted at an
average density of 1,600
per hectare and trained in
a low-trellised *tendone*
system.

Vinification and aging
Grapes are crushed with
an antique roller device
and fermented at cellar
temperature in oak casks.
Malolactic fermentation
takes place naturally in
old oak casks of 3,500-
liter capacity during
aging, the duration of
which depends on the
vintage. The wine, of
13–14% alcohol, is
bottled without
clarification or filtering
and cellared for years
until the producer
considers it ready to
drink.

Style and maturity
Valentini Montepulciano
d'Abruzzo has dense purple
color with glints of ruby
visible if the glass is held up to
a light. The bouquet is a font
of sensations suggesting ripe
fruit and berries, blackberry
jam, old leather, coffee, pepper
and spices. Some of the same
are picked up on the palate of
a wine of massive structure
and great concentration of
flavors that become deeper,
smoother and longer with
time. Always impressive, prime
drinking seems to come
between 8 and 15 years,
though each vintage differs.

Serving
🍷 18°C, opening bottle an
hour earlier.
🍷 Ample glass (Bordeaux
type).
🍽 *Maccheroni alla chitarra*
(pasta of Abruzzo) with a
peppery meat sauce; roast
goose with oven-browned
potatoes; charcoal-grilled
pork and lamb.

Villa Cafaggio

Solatio Basilica
Chianti Classico Riserva
DOCG ♟

Producer
Villa Cafaggio
Via San Martino in
Cecione 5
50020 Panzano in
Chianti (Firenze)
Tel. 055 854 9094
Fax 055 854 9096
basilica.cafaggio@
tiscalinet.it

Owner
Basilica Cafaggio

Founded
1967

Winemakers
Stefano Farkas with
Stefano Chioccioli

Vineyard manager
Valerio Barbieri

Production
8,000–10,000 bottles in
top years

Vintages
1999 1997 1995 1993
1990 1988 1985

Price
●●

Note
The vineyard of Solatio
Basilica was replanted in
2000, so the wine will
not be produced for
several years

Villa Cafaggio lies west of the town of Panzano along the slopes of what has come to be called the Conca d'Oro, though Stefano Farkas started making Chianti in the valley well before the golden days. His father, an artist who had brought his family to Italy from their native Hungary, bought the estate in 1967 and put Stefano in charge of vineyards and cellars. Those were lean years in Chianti, and Stefano admits that he knew little about viticulture or enology then. But he struggled ahead with the determination that has carried his wines to the front ranks of Chianti Classico.

Success has not spoiled Stefano Farkas, who is convinced that the golden era of Chianti lies somewhere in the future. His view is backed by experience with Sangiovese, the main vine of Chianti, which he found in a state of neglect when he arrived. Since 1990, he has replanted more than half of his vineyards with a select clone of Sangiovese identified as F9A548. It yields small, thick-skinned grapes that result in wines of superior structure, concentration and finesse.

Stefano also grows Cabernet Sauvignon for use in two Super-Tuscans: Cortaccio, in which it dominates at 90 percent with Sangiovese, and San Martino, in which the proportions are reversed. Solatio Basilica was conceived in 1981 as a pure Sangiovese aged in barriques of French oak to qualify as a Super-Tuscan too. But when DOCG rules changed to allow pure Sangiovese wines into the fold, Solatio Basilica became a Chianti Classico Riserva of the new breed that is restoring luster to the denomination. Solatio refers to the sunny southern exposure of Basilica, a segment of the estate.

From 31 hectares of vineyards and 10 leased, Villa Cafaggio produces about 300,000 bottles annually of wines whose overall class seems to rise from vintage to vintage.

Tuscany

Grapes
Sangiovese 100%, hand picked in early October.

Vineyard
Solatio Basilica is a plot of 4 hectares in soils of schistous *galestro* and *alberese* limestone on slopes facing south at 388 meters of altitude at Villa Cafaggio west of the town of Panzano at the heart of Chianti Classico. The vines, of an average age of 31 years, were planted at a density of 2,800 per hectare and trained in an arched *capovolto toscano* cordon system.

Vinification and aging
Grapes are stemmed and soft crushed and the must fermented in stainless steel tanks at no more than 32°C for 7 days (remaining another 7–10 days on the skins) with frequent pumping over the cap. Malolactic fermentation at 20°C in wooden barrels is followed by 14 months of maturation in 225-liter barriques of French oak. The wine, of about 13% alcohol, is bottled and cellared for at least 6 months before release.

Style and maturity
Chianti Classico Riserva Solatio Basilica has bright ruby color with garnet highlights on the rim. The bouquet is full and balanced with scents reminiscent of violets and ripe cherries along with hints of spices and vanilla. Amply structured and harmonious on the palate, it has rich fruit sensations and soft tannins with warm flavors of impressive length and complexity. The wine approaches a prime at 5–7 years and will maintain style for well over a decade.

Serving
🌡 18–19°C.
🍷 Medium-sized glass (Chianti type).
🍴 Florentine beefsteak seared over wood embers; free-range chicken braised with garlic, sage and rosemary; aged Pecorino cheese from Pienza.

Bucci

Villa Bucci Riserva Verdicchio dei Castelli di Jesi Classico Riserva DOC ♀

Producer
Azienda Agricola Bucci
Via Cona 30
60010 Ostra Vetere
(Ancona)
Tel. 071/964179
Fax 071/964179
bucciwines@iol.it
www.villabucci.it

Owner
Bucci family

Founded
1982

Winemaker
Giorgio Grai

Vineyard managers
Giovanni Cerretelli and
Gabriele Tanfani

Production
15,000–20,000 bottles
in favorable years

Vintages
1998 1997 1995 1994
1992 1990 1988 1987
1983

Price
● ●

Verdicchio may be one of Italy's oldest vines. Some say it was a wild variety, *Vitis vinifera silvestris,* cultivated by the Piceni people, who inhabited Marche in the Iron Age. Others say it was part of the Greco-Trebbiano family introduced by the Greeks, who founded the port of Ancona. It was probably grown by the Romans, who spread viticulture through Marche, though the first written record of the name Verdicchio (which refers to the green color of its grapes and its young wines) was in 1569.

Yet only in the last couple of decades has Verdicchio been recognized as one of Italy's finest white wine varieties. A share of the credit for that is due to Ampelio Bucci, who in 1982 began to produce a serious Verdicchio from vines on the vast estate at Montecarotto that had been in his family since the eighteenth century. Ampelio, a management consultant in Milan, linked up with Giorgio Grai, a noted winemaker from Alto Adige, who gave the Villa Bucci Riserva his ingenious touches.

They kept things admirably pure, fermenting the wine in the natural cool of underground cellars and maturing it in traditional large casks of Slavonian oak. In those days, most Verdicchio was sold in the kitschy amphora bottle as a crisply fresh fish wine to drink in the flower of its youth. So the Bucci wood-aged reserve was considered an anachronism, but its round and mellow qualities and depth and length of flavors steadily won admirers while demonstrating Verdicchio's long-neglected noble nature.

Villa Bucci Riserva has grown in stature since, thanks to Ampelio's practice of selecting superior clones of Verdicchio and diffusing them through vineyards cultivated following organic methods. Even the younger, fresher Bucci Verdicchio Castelli di Jesi Classico shows exemplary style. From 26 hectares of vines, the estate produces 90,000–100,000 bottles a year, including the fine Tenuta di Pongelli Rosso Piceno DOC.

Marche

Grapes
Verdicchio 100%, hand picked in early October.

Vineyards
Grapes are selected from the Villa Bucci estate at Montecarotto, as well as plots at Serra dei Conti and Barbara, a total of 21 hectares in medium-packed calcareous soils on slopes facing east and west at 200–350 meters of altitude in the western part of the Castelli di Jesi Classico zone. The vines, of an average age of 26 years, are planted at a density of 2,200 per hectare and trained in the *doppio capovolto* arched cordon system.

Vinification and aging
Grapes from each vineyard are vinified separately, soft crushed and the free-run musts fermented in stainless steel tanks at natural cellar temperatures (20–23°C) for as long as possible. Malolactic fermentation occurs naturally during 18 months of maturing in casks of Slavonian oak of 5,000–7,500-liter capacity. The batches are assembled before bottling to enhance the complexity of a wine of about 12.5% alcohol that is cellared for at least another year before release.

Style and maturity
Villa Bucci Verdicchio Riserva on release in the third year after the harvest has bright straw color with green-gold highlights and full, complex aroma with scents reminiscent of hazelnuts, herbs, spices, honey and gunflint. Flavors are full and round in a wine of ample body and smooth texture with sensations of fruit and toasted nuts evident in a smooth finish. At a prime at about 5 years, the wine can gain mellow complexity for over a decade.

Serving
- 14–15°C, opening bottle an hour earlier.
- Tulip-shaped glass (Chardonnay type).
- Seafood, especially oysters and lobster; roast rabbit or chicken; medium-textured cheeses, such as the local Pecorino.

Castel de Paolis

Vigna Adriana
Frascati Superiore DOC ♀

Producer
Azienda Agricola Castel
de Paolis
Via Val de Paolis
00046 Grottaferrata
(Roma)
Tel. 06/9413648
Fax 06/94316025
info@casteldepaolis.it
www.casteldepaolis.it

Owner
Adriana Croce Santarelli

Founded
1992

Winemaker
Franco Bernabei

Production
About 19,000 bottles a
year

Vintages
1999 1997 1995 1993

Price
● ●

Frascati was, in a sense, the wine of Rome even before the Eternal City existed. Vineyards graced the same lovely hills around ancient Tusculum before it was conquered by the neighboring Romans. The town of Frascati got its name in the Middle Ages from the *frasca* or branch of brush that signaled wine available at inns, which in 1450 reportedly numbered 1,022. But in the 1970s, after centuries of glory as the golden nectar of Rome, Frascati lost its glitter when it was modernized, mass produced and widely exported.

A mild comeback began in the 1980s with Fontana Candida's Vigneto Santa Teresa (see page 352), followed with growing inspiration at a number of estates. An example is Castel de Paolis, where Giulio and Adriana Santarelli have shown how rapidly smart investments can yield splendid results. In the mid-1980s, when he was still Italy's Undersecretary of Agriculture, Giulio Santarelli, with the aid of specialist Attilio Scienza, began experimental planting of 12 hectares of vineyards with 18 different varieties, both native and international.

They formally founded the estate in 1992 and their Frascati Superiore Vigna Adriana won praise from the 1993 vintage. Since then, with the arrival of winemaker Franco Bernabei, all of the estate's eight wines have earned high ratings. Vigna Adriana illustrates how Frascati based on the softly aromatic grapes of tradition can be ennobled with a touch of the exotic, represented by Viognier. Equally impressive is the softly sweet version of Frascati called Cannellino.

Castel de Paolis produces about 110,000 bottles a year, including Frascati Superiore DOC Campo Vecchio and a range of IGT that takes in Selve Vecchie (Chardonnay and Sauvignon), Muffa Nobile (botrytized Sauvignon and Sémillon), Campo Vecchio (Syrah, Merlot, Cesanese, Sangiovese, Montepulciano), I Quattro Mori (Syrah, Merlot, Cabernet Sauvignon, Petit Verdot) and sweet Rosathea (Moscato Rosa).

Lazio

CASTEL DE PAOLIS

Vigna Adriana

Grapes
Malvasia del Lazio,
Bellone, Cacchione,
Trebbiano Giallo,
Bonvino, Grechetto,
Romanesca, Pecorino and
Viognier, hand picked in
October.

Vineyard
Vigna Adriana, a plot of
3 hectares in loose
volcanic soils of granular
tufa on slopes undulating
from north to south at
270 meters of altitude at
Castel de Paolis in the
commune of
Grottaferrata in the
southern part of the
Frascati DOC zone. The
vines, of an average age of
11 years, are planted at a
density of 5,500 per
hectare and trained in the
spurred cordon method.

Vinification and aging
Grapes are picked in 3
stages to assure that all
are fully ripe and each
batch is soft crushed and
the musts fermented
slowly in stainless steel
tanks, starting at 12°C
and gradually building to
18°C. The wine, of about
13.5% alcohol, is bottled
in stainless steel tanks
without undergoing
malolactic fermentation
and is bottled and
cellared for at least 6
months before release.

Style and maturity
Frascati Vigna Adriana on
release about a year after the
harvest has bright straw
yellow color with pale gold
highlights and fresh, flowery
aroma with scents reminiscent
of tropical fruit, peaches, citrus
and lavender. Full and round
on the palate, the zesty flavors
of fresh fruit come to the fore
in a wine of fine balance with
hints of toasted nuts and
herbs evident in a smooth,
refreshing finish. It reaches a
prime in about 2 years but can
hold style longer.

Serving
🍷 10–12°C.
🍷 Tulip-shaped glass.
🍽 *Fettuccine* noodles with
porcini mushrooms; *bucatini
all'amatriciana* (slender
pasta tubes with tomato,
onion, salt pork and grated
Pecorino Romano); grilled
and roast seafood.

**Castello
della Sala**

Cervaro della Sala
Umbria IGT ♀

Producer
Tenuta Castello della
Sala
Località Sala
05016 Ficulle (Terni)
Tel. 0763/86051
Fax 0763/86491
antinori@antinori.it
www.antinori.it

Owner
Marchesi Antinori

Founded
1940

Chief winemaker
Maurizio Angeletti

Vineyard manager
Claudio Pontremolesi

Production
About 156,000 bottles a
year

Vintages
1999 1998 1997 1996
1995 1994 1993 1992
1990 1989 1988 1987

Price
● ● ●

Marchesi Antinori, the Florentine house that inspired the Super-Tuscan phenomenon (see page 252), set a similar precedent in Umbria with the creation in 1985 of a barrel-fermented white based on Chardonnay, called Cervaro della Sala. It comes from Castello della Sala, the Antinori estate surrounding a magnificent fortress near Orvieto, the town renowned since the Middle Ages for golden, softly sweet wine from Procanico and other native varieties.

Niccolò Antinori acquired Castello della Sala in 1940 as a base for Orvieto Classico, which is still the mainstay of production in a regular version and the select Campogrande. Niccolò's son Piero, who has headed the firm since 1968, turned part of the estate into a proving ground for other varieties, ranging from Chardonnay and Pinot Noir to Sauvignon Blanc, Riesling and Traminer. The winemaking team of Giacomo Tachis and Renzo Cotarella applied the techniques of fermenting Chardonnay in new barrels of French oak. But Piero insisted that Cervaro della Sala express a distinctive Umbrian touch, which they realized with Grechetto, an ancient variety whose lively acidity and hearty flavors turned out to be an ideal complement for Chardonnay. Cervaro ranks as one of Italy's most distinguished and durable modern whites with a style closer to fine Burgundy than New World Chardonnay.

The name, which translates as "Stag of the Hall," refers to two branches of the powerful Monaldeschi family, which built the castle in the fourteenth century. Today its imposing round tower dominates the landscape over the Paglia river valley north of Orvieto, including 140 hectares of vineyards where Antinori produces about 600,000 bottles a year. Beyond Orvieto Classico Superiore DOC, other wines carry Umbria IGT, including varietal Chardonnay, Sauvignon and Pinot Nero and the sumptuously sweet Muffato della Sala, from botrytized Sauvignon, Grechetto, Traminer and Riesling.

Umbria

Grapes
Chardonnay 80%, Grechetto 20%, hand picked in early September and transported to the cellars in a refrigerated conveyer.

Vineyards
Grapes are selected in various plots totaling about 40 hectares in calcareous clay soils rich in fossils and volcanic deposits on slopes of varying sun exposure at 200–400 meters of altitude at Castello della Sala near Ficulle in the northern part of the Orvieto Classico zone. The vines, of an average age of 17 years, are planted at a density of 2,500–4,000 per hectare and trained in the spurred cordon method.

Vinification and aging
Grapes are stemmed and soft crushed and the musts remain in contact with the skins for about 8 hours at 10°C. The varieties are fermented separately in new barrels of French oak (Allier and Tronçais) for about 15 days, after which the wine on the lees undergoes malolactic fermentation during about 5 months in wood. The batches are blended and the wine, of about 13% alcohol, is bottled and cellared for at least 10 months before release.

Style and maturity
Cervaro della Sala on release in the 2nd year after the harvest has bright straw gold color and rich yet refined aromas with scents reminiscent of pineapple, apricot, spices and the buttery-toasty qualities typical of oak-fermented Chardonnay. Well structured, full and round on the palate, it shows fine balance and smooth, elegant fruit and vanilla flavors that gain in complexity and length for a decade or more.

Serving
- 9–10°C.
- Tulip-shaped glass (Chardonnay type).
- Freshwater crayfish with broccoli; bream baked with porcini mushrooms; veal scallops braised in white wine with sage.

Gaiospino
Verdicchio dei Castelli di Jesi
Classico Superiore DOC ♀

Producer
Fattoria Coroncino
Contrada Coroncino 7
60039 Staffolo (Ancona)
Tel. 0731/779494
Fax 0731/770205
coroncino@libero.it

Owners
Lucio Canestrari and
Fiorella De Nardo

Founded
1981

Winemaker
Lucio Canestrari

Vineyard manager
Lucio Canestrari

Production
9,000–10,000 bottles a
year

Vintages
1999 1998 1997 1996
1994 1993 1992 1990

Price
● ●

Lucio Canestrari planted a vineyard at his Fattoria Coroncino in 1982 and produced his first Verdicchio dei Castelli di Jesi Classico DOC three years later. In 1988, he acquired a steep, partly terraced hillside vineyard called Spescia and using a new soft crusher and a refrigeration system was able to produce a total of 16,000 bottles. Lucio and his wife Fiorella, who works with him, didn't like the sound of Spescia, so they decided to call the wine Vigna Gaia after their first daughter Gaia.

The wine, after winning favorable reviews, came to the attention of lawyers for Angelo Gaja of Piedmont, whose Chardonnay called Gaia & Rey was also named in part for his first daughter Gaia (see page 108). Lucio, who had been unaware of the coincidence, reluctantly agreed to drop the name under threat of legal action.

The wine from 1992 was issued as Vigna——. But the next year Fiorella came up with another name: Gaiospino. *Gaio*, the male equivalent of Gaia, refers to the joyful views from the steep vineyards amid olive groves and oak woods, *spino* to the thorns that prevail around the perimeter. As a local saying has it, if you put your hand in the brush without looking, you're liable to get stung. "All things considered," says Lucio diplomatically, "the name Gaiospino may be better suited to the setting."

Gaiospino has steadily improved to stand in the front ranks of Verdicchio dei Castelli di Jesi. Lucio, who makes the wine only from the Spescia vineyard, has reduced yields and introduced selective late harvesting, fermenting part of the wine in barrels of French oak.

From 6.7 hectares of estate vines and 1 hectare leased, Coroncino produces about 40,000 bottles of wine a year, mainly Verdicchio Classico Superiore, which also comes in versions called Il Coroncino, Il Bacco and Staffilo, as well as a Marche Bianco IGT called Le Lame, from Trebbiano and Biancame.

Marche

Grapes
Verdicchio 100%, hand picked when very ripe in October.

Vineyard
Spescia, a plot of 2.7 hectares in calcareous marls on steep, partly terraced slopes facing southeast at 320–400 meters of altitude in the commune of Cupramontana in the southern part of the Castelli di Jesi Classico zone. The vines, planted between the early 1980s and mid-1990s at densities of 1,660–5,000 per hectare, are trained in the Guyot cordon system.

Vinification and aging
Grapes are soft crushed and the juice is settled to separate solid matter. Fermentation of 70–80% of the must takes place in stainless steel tanks for 2–4 weeks at up to 20°C after which malolactic fermentation is induced. The rest is fermented in 500-liter capacity barrels of French oak, half new and half used once, where it stays on the lees until blending with the main batch about a year after the harvest. The wine, of 13.5–14% alcohol, is bottled and cellared until release.

Style and maturity
Gaiospino on release in the 2nd year after the harvest has luminous straw yellow color and rich, flowery aroma with scents reminiscent of peaches, elderberries and fruit blossoms. Flavors are full and round in a wine of ample structure and mellow texture with sensations of ripe fruit and wild herbs evident in an opulent finish. At a prime in 2–5 years, the wine can gain depth with further aging.

Serving
- 12–14°C.
- Tulip-shaped glass (Chardonnay type).
- Potato gnocchi with Pecorino cheese and black truffles; scampi with puréed lentils; mixed fry of Adriatic seafood.

Falchini

Ab Vinea Doni
Vernaccia di San Gimignano
DOCG ♀

Producer
Azienda Agricola Casale
di Riccardo Falchini
Via di Casale 40
53037 San Gimignano
(Siena)
Tel. 0577/941305
Fax 0577/940819
casale-falchini@tin.it
www.falchini.com

Owner
Riccardo Falchini

Founded
1964

Winemakers
Riccardo Falchini with
Giacomo Tachis

Vineyard manager
Riccardo Falchini

Production
About 14,000 bottles
a year

Vintages
1999 1998 1997 1995

Price
●

The Vernaccia vine has grown around Tuscany's multi-towered hill town of San Gimignano for nearly a millennium, though little is known about its origins or how it got its name. (It is not related to vines called Vernaccia of Sardinia, Marche or Liguria.) In ancient times, its wines were probably sweet and undoubtedly special. Among kudos, Michelangelo Buonarroti the Younger wrote in 1643 that Vernaccia "kisses, licks, bites, slaps and stings." Alas, when I came across it more than three centuries later, Vernaccia reminded me of watery Sherry reeking of bitter almonds.

Then, in the 1970s, Riccardo Falchini at his Casale estate introduced the cool fermentation that rendered Vernaccia fresh, clean, bright and fruity. Local farmers, who first criticized his radical methods, eventually adopted them as Vernaccia evolved from tediously traditional to monotonously modern, stripped of its former flaws as well as its age-old character.

Riccardo, who comes from a long line of Tuscan vintners, realized that Vernaccia had its limits as a vine. But by selecting clones and limiting yields he brought out unexpected personality. He had advantages over the competition in that he was aided by Giacomo Tachis, dean of Tuscan winemakers, and he had developed a worldly approach to wine, influenced by his American wife Lena.

His Vigna a Solatio was an early example of a successful oak-fermented Vernaccia. Riccardo followed up in 1994 with Ab Vinea Doni (Latin for "gifts from the vineyard") enhanced by a kiss of oak that lends elegance to a Vernaccia styled for the twenty-first century.

From about 35 hectares of vines, Riccardo, aided by his son Michael, makes about 350,000 bottles of wine a year, including regular Vernaccia, DOCG Chianti Colli Senesi, Vin Santo, fine bottle-fermented sparkling Falchini Brut (from Vernaccia with Pinot Bianco) and highly rated IGT reds Campora (Cabernet Sauvignon with Sangiovese) and Paretaio (Sangiovese).

Tuscany

Grapes
Vernaccia 90% with Chardonnay, part picked in late August and part 18–20 days later in September.

Vineyards
Plots of about 2 hectares in sandy clay soils with abundant marine fossils on slopes facing south-southwest at about 300 meters of altitude at Casale and Colombaia in the commune of San Gimignano. The vines, of an average age of 16–21 years, are planted at a density of about 3,500 per hectare and trained in a spurred cordon method.

Vinification and aging
Grapes are stemmed, soft crushed and separated from the skins and the clean musts are fermented in 225-liter barrels of French oak at 18°C for 20–25 days. Part of the wine is matured in barriques for 3–4 months and part in stainless steel without undergoing malolactic fermentation. The wine, of about 12% alcohol, is bottled and cellared for 3–6 months before release.

Style and maturity
Ab Vinea Doni on release about a year after the harvest has sunny straw yellow color with golden highlights and refined aromas with scents reminiscent of green apples, pineapple and vanilla. On the palate, it is round and smooth with fine balance between ripe fruit and a citrus-like acidity that evolves into a mellow, refined finish. Attractive after a year, it can hold style for a couple of years beyond.

Serving
🌡 12–14°C.
🍷 Tulip-shaped glass (Sauvignon type).
🍽 *Panzanella* (salad of crumbled bread with tomatoes, onion and basil); risotto with saffron and Parmigiano; grilled scampi.

Poggio dei Gelsi Vendemmia Tardiva Est! Est!! Est!!! di Montefiascone DOC ♀

Producer
Azienda Vinicola
Falesco
Località Le Guardie
01027 Montefiascone
(Viterbo)
Tel. 0761/825669
Fax 0761/825803
falesco@leonet.it

Owners
Riccardo and Renzo
Cotarella

Founded
1979

Winemaker
Riccardo Cotarella

Vineyard manager
Franco Feliciotti

Production
About 15,000 half
bottles a year

Vintages
1999 1998 1997 1995
1993 1991

Price
●

The triple endorsement chalked on the wall of a tavern at Montefiascone in 1111 by a tippling bishop's servant has probably engendered more jests than any of the many legends about Italian wine. Most modern Est! Est!! Est!!! di Montefiascone had been dry and insipid, making exclamations seem all the more absurd. But since Riccardo and Renzo Cotarella created their sweet Poggio dei Gelsi, the jokes have decidedly diminished.

The Cotarella brothers, who founded the Falesco winery in 1979, are noted for other accomplishments. Riccardo has piled up credits as one of the nation's busiest and best consulting winemakers, earning frequent mention elsewhere in this volume. Renzo, after running the Castello della Sala estate (see page 342), is now director of Marchesi Antinori.

How they find time to keep up with Falesco and its 65 hectares of vines is beyond the comprehension of ordinary mortals. But they do, and they manage to turn out 1,300,000 bottles a year, always of exemplary quality. The top wine by acclaim is Montiano, a Merlot that explains why Riccardo has been hailed as Italy's answer to Michel Rolland (the celebrated Bordeaux consultant) by no less a critic than Robert M. Parker, Jr. Riccardo also excels with Vitiano (Merlot, Cabernet and Sangiovese) and Ferentano (a white from Roscetto).

But to me Falesco's most praiseworthy achievement is the late-harvest Est! Est!! Est!!! from the vineyard of Poggio dei Gelsi, a splendid modern wine that remains loyal to a millennial tradition. Riccardo uses Trebbiano and Roscetto, varieties grown in Lazio since the Middle Ages. The original wine of Montefiascone was undoubtedly sweet, exquisitely so if the grapes developed *Botrytis cinerea* or "noble rot" as they do now in vineyards facing the crater lake of Bolsena.

Riccardo's main concession to modernity is his use of new barrels of oak instead of medieval casks of chestnut. Still, there seems little doubt that Poggio dei Gelsi would have left the bishop dazzled.

Lazio

Grapes
Trebbiano 55%, Roscetto 30% and other local varieties, hand picked when very ripe in the first half of October. Some 35–40% of the grapes are infected with *Botrytis cinerea*.

Vineyard
A plot of 2 hectares in crumbly, stony volcanic soils on a slope at about 400 meters of altitude facing west toward Lake Bolsena at Poggio dei Gelsi about 2 kilometers west of Montefiascone in northwestern Lazio. The vines, of an average age of 26 years, are planted at a density of 2,800 per hectare and trained in the spurred cordon method.

Vinification and aging
Grapes are soft crushed and the musts fermented for 30–40 days at 17°C in 225-liter barrels of French oak (Allier), where partial malolactic fermentation occurs during 8 months of maturing on the lees. The wine, of about 12% alcohol with 12% residual sugar, is bottled and cellared for 2 years before release.

1997

POGGIO DEI GELSI

vendemmia tardiva

EST! EST!! EST!!! DI MONTEFIASCONE
DENOMINAZIONE DI ORIGINE CONTROLLATA

375 mle   12% vol

FALESCO

IMBOTTIGLIATO DA AZIENDA FALESCO s.r.l.
MONTEFIASCONE (VT) ITALIA

È UTILE DISPERDERE IL VETRO NELL'AMBIENTE

Style and maturity
Poggio dei Gelsi Est! Est!! Est!!! Vendemmia Tardiva on release in the third year after the harvest has bright golden color with amber highlights and full aroma with scents reminiscent of mango, pineapple, candied fruit and vanilla. Full and round on the palate, its mellifluous fruit flavors are deftly amalgamated with the vanilla sensations of oak that amplify the complexity of the long, smooth, sweet finish. Impressive from the start, it seems to have the attributes to retain finesse for 8–12 years.

Serving
- 10–12°C.
- Tulip-shaped glass (Chardonnay type).
- Caciotta and Caprino (sheep and goat milk cheese) from Lazio; pastries called *pasticcetti di gnocchi*; *pizza dolce* with candied fruit and cinnamon.

Fazi Battaglia

San Sisto
Verdicchio dei Castelli di Jesi
Classico Riserva DOC ♀

Producer
Fazi Battaglia
Via Roma 117
60032 Castelplanio
Stazione (Ancona)
Tel. 0731/813444
Fax 0731/814149
info@fazibattaglia.it
www.fazibattaglia.com

Owner
Corporation President
Maria Luisa Sparaco

Founded
1949

Winemakers
Dino Porfiri with
consultant Franco
Bernabei

Vineyard managers
Antonio Verdolini and
Mirco Pompili

Production
About 15,000 bottles in
favorable years

Vintages
1998 1997 1995 1993

Price
●●

Fazi Battaglia launched Verdicchio to world popularity in the green amphora bottle that became almost as familiar a symbol of Italy as the Chianti flask. The bottle, designed in 1954 by Antonio Maiocchi, was inspired by the terracotta vases used by the ancient Greeks to transport wine from the Adriatic port of Ancona. The company, founded in 1949 by partners named Fazi, Battaglia and Federici, expanded vineyards to meet growing demand, building new cellars in 1956 at Castelplanio in the heart of the Verdicchio dei Castelli di Jesi Classico zone. Other wineries followed the lead with similar versions of the amphora that became fixtures in Italian restaurants everywhere. But as production was stretched beyond reasonable limits, Verdicchio gained a reputation as a lightweight. Fazi Battaglia maintained honest quality in the amphora wine identified as Titulus with an informative scroll around the neck of the bottle.

In 1969, Fazi Battaglia expanded its interests, acquiring Fassati, an estate known for Vino Nobile di Montepulciano in Tuscany. But before long, after decades of success, Verdicchio, like flask Chianti, began to lose popularity. By the 1980s, other Marche producers came to the fore with Verdicchio of unprecedented class, leaving Fazi Battaglia in the background.

In the 1990s, the corporation under Maria Luisa Sparaco moved smartly to re-establish leadership. The first step was the creation of Le Moie, a single-vineyard Verdicchio. That was followed in 1993 by San Sisto, a reserve Verdicchio from one of the most prized terrains of the Jesi zone. A wine of opulent style, San Sisto represents an outstanding value among Italy's oak-fermented whites.

Fazi Battaglia owns 300 hectares of vineyards as the main source of production of about 3,500,000 bottles a year. These include Rosso Conero DOC Passo del Lupo, Marche Sangiovese IGT Rutilus and sweet Arkezia Muffo di San Sisto from Verdicchio grapes infected with "noble rot."

Marche

Grapes
Verdicchio 100%, hand picked in mid-October.

Vineyard
Grapes are selected from 12 hectares of the 27-hectare San Sisto plot in medium-textured calcareous soils on slopes facing southwest at about 300 meters of altitude in the commune of Maiolati Spontini in the southern part of the Castelli di Jesi Classico zone. The vines, of an average age of 11 years, are planted at densities of 3,000 per hectare in an espalier system with cordon training.

Vinification and aging
Grapes are soft crushed and the juice is chilled for about 12 hours to separate solid matter. The clear musts are inoculated with select yeast cultures and fermented in small barrels of French oak, where malolactic fermentation occurs naturally during 8–10 months of maturation with periodic stirring of the lees in a process known as *bâtonnage*. The wine, of about 13% alcohol, is bottled and cellared until release.

Style and maturity
San Sisto on release 2–3 years after the harvest has bright straw yellow color with golden highlights and rich aromas of ripe fruit with hints of butter, vanilla and toasted nuts. Flavors are full and round in a wine of ample structure and smooth texture with sensations of fruit and nuts evident in a long finish. At a prime after 3–4 years, the wine gains mellow complexity with further aging.

Serving
- 12–15°C.
- Tulip-shaped glass (Chardonnay type).
- Tagliatelle with seafood sauce; roasted sea bass or gilthead bream; braised rabbit with tomatoes and olives.

Fontana Candida

Vigneto Santa Teresa
Frascati Superiore DOC ♀

Producer
Fontana Candida
Via di Fontana
Candida 11
00040 Monteporzio
Catone (Roma)
Tel. 06/9420066
Fax 06/9448591
giv@giv.it
www.giv.it

Owner
Gruppo Italiano Vini

Founded
1958

Chief winemaker
Francesco Bardi

Production
About 140,000 bottles a
year

Vintages
1999 1998 1997

Price
●

Roman *osterie* and *trattorie* in the 1960s served wine in flare-topped decanters with lead signets to certify liter, half-liter and quarter-liter measures drawn from ponderous glass containers atop refrigerated units. Wines from the nearby hills were noted for their deep yellow to golden colors and mellow, mouth-filling flavors. Hosts were known for little ploys, such as adding water to stretch supplies and swearing that wine of any provenance was "Frascati," then as now the prime white of the Castelli Romani.

Those open wines were fragile and prone to oxidation, so Romans tended to blend them with a lemony soft drink called *gassosa*—or, though this was an extravagance that drew disapproving glances, order a bottle of Frascati Superiore DOC. The likely choice was Fontana Candida in a squat bottle with gold-colored mesh around its base. Even then, Fontana Candida was the largest producer of Frascati, which, like other whites of the day, tended to be pale and crisp with fresh, clean flavors but scarcely a hint of the old-time personality.

In 1980, Francesco Bardi, who is still Fontana Candida's winemaker, selected Malvasia, Trebbiano and Greco grapes from a vineyard called Santa Teresa and made a wine of undeniable character that became the model for the modern revival of Frascati. The concept was that of a small estate, since Santa Teresa's 12 hectares produce about 140,000 bottles a year. But Bardi in his low-key manner is accustomed to thinking big, as director of a winery in the Gruppo Italiano Vini network that turns out some 8 million bottles a year, of which 6.5 million are exported.

Fontana Candida, whose cellars were built on the site of an ancient Roman villa, owns 25 hectares of vines and leases or supervises production of 72 hectares, acquiring grapes to complete a range that includes regular Frascati Superiore and sweet Cannellino and the Terre dei Grifi line, comprising a Malvasia del Lazio IGT of authentic personality.

Lazio

Grapes
Malvasia Bianca di Candida 30%, Malvasia del Lazio 30%, Trebbiano Toscano 30%, Greco 10%, harvested in early October.

Vineyard
A plot of 12 hectares in loose, well-drained volcanic soils known locally as *terrinelle* (rich in potassium and phosphorous) on slopes facing south-southwest at 300 meters of altitude at a place called Santa Teresa in the northeastern part of the Frascati DOC zone within the city limits of Rome. The vines, of an average age of 16 years, are planted at a density of 3,700–4,000 per hectare and trained in the Guyot and spurred cordon methods.

Vinification and aging
Grapes are soft crushed and the juice of Malvasia Bianca di Candida is macerated with the skins for 10–12 hours at 10°C. All musts are cold stabilized, inoculated with yeast cultures selected locally and fermented slowly at 15–17°C in stainless steel tanks. The wine, of about 12.5% alcohol, is settled in stainless steel tanks until bottling in March.

Style and maturity
Frascati Vigneto Santa Teresa on release in the spring after the harvest has bright straw yellow color with golden highlights and fresh, delicate aromas with scents reminiscent of honeysuckle, hawthorn, sage and ripe apples. Flavors are softly dry and finely balanced with sensations of ripe fruit and almonds in a refreshingly smooth finish. The wine reaches peaks between 1 and 2 years.

Serving
🌡 10–12°C.
🍷 Medium tulip-shaped glass.
🍽 Frittata with spring onions; fettuccine noodles with butter and Parmigiano; *cozze alla marinara* (mussels stewed with tomato, garlic, parsley).

Garofoli

Podium
Verdicchio dei Castelli di Jesi
Classico Superiore DOC ♀

Producer
Casa Vinicola
Gioacchino Garofoli
Via Arno 9
60025 Loreto (Ancona)
Tel. 071/7820162
Fax 071/7821437
mail@garofolivini.it
www.garofolivini.it

Owner
Garofoli family

Founded
1901

Chief winemaker
Carlo Garofoli

Vineyard manager
Carlo Garofoli

Production
About 40,000 bottles
a year

Vintages
1999 1998 1997 1996
1995

Price
●

No other producer has contributed so emphatically to the recent revival of Verdicchio as Casa Vinicola Gioacchino Garofoli of Loreto. The Garofoli family, active in the wine business since 1871, joined the trend of selling lighthearted Verdicchio in green amphora bottles. But in the early 1980s, as popularity ebbed, Garofoli came out with Macrina, a Verdicchio of depth and style issued in a serious Bordeaux-type bottle.

"We realized that Verdicchio's potential was largely untapped," says Carlo Garofoli, the soft-spoken dynamo who runs the vineyards and cellars. "By selecting clones and reducing grape yields, we were convinced that we could make Verdicchio that would hold its quality for a decade."

They planted new vineyards on choice sites around the town of Montecarotto and in 1984 created Serra Fiorese, the first commercial Verdicchio to be matured in small barrels of French oak. Although controversial at first—as any white aged in barriques was in Italy then—Serra Fiorese has stood the test of time. Yet, in tasting Serra Fiorese with Carlo and his brother Gianfranco, the firm's commercial director, I always had the impression that they consider the oak an extra, a bonus for those who might be drinking Verdicchio but thinking of Chardonnay.

Their alternative is Podium, first produced from the 1992 vintage from grapes picked very ripe in late October and processed in stainless steel with a long fining period on the lees. Podium is Verdicchio at its genuine best, full of flavor and vitality with a capacity to gain elegance with age in a way that is reserved only for noble varieties. What's more, it's one of the best values among Italy's premium white wines.

From 40 hectares of vines and grapes acquired from trusted growers, Garofoli produces about 2 million bottles a year. The range covers sparkling Verdicchio in both classic and tank-fermented versions and DOC Rosso Piceno and Rosso Conero, including the fine Riserva Grosso Agontano.

Marche

Grapes
Verdicchio 100%, hand picked in late October.

Vineyard
A plot of 10 hectares in medium-textured calcareous soils on slopes facing southeast at about 350 meters of altitude at the locality of Cupo delle Lame in the commune of Montecarotto in the western part of the Castelli di Jesi Classico zone. The vines, of an average age of 31 years, are planted at a density of 1,660 per hectare and trained in the espalier or double-arched cordon systems.

Vinification and aging
Grapes are soft crushed and the free-run must chilled to separate solid matter before fermenting for 12–18 days at 18°C in stainless steel tanks. After malolactic fermentation, the wine, of about 13.5% alcohol, is kept in contact with the lees for about 15 months at low temperature before bottling and cellaring for at least 4 months until release.

Style and maturity
Podium on release in the second year after the harvest has bright straw color with green-gold highlights and full, blossomy aroma with scents reminiscent of citrus fruit, sage and ripe apples. Flavors are full and round in a wine of ample structure and mellow texture with sensations of fruit and toasted nuts evident in a long, smooth finish. At a prime at 3 years, the wine gains complexity and elegance with further aging.

Serving
🍷 12–14°C.
♀ Tulip-shaped glass (Chardonnay type).
🍽 Ravioli with filets of sole; mixed grill of Adriatic seafood; rabbit *in porchetta* (roast with wild fennel, garlic, rosemary).

Marina Cvetić Colline Teatine IGT Chardonnay ♀

Producer
Azienda Agricola
Masciarelli di
Masciarelli G & C.
Via Gamberale 1
66010 San Martino sulla
Marrucina (Chieti)
Tel. 0871/85241
Fax 0871/85330
info@masciarelli.it
www.masciarelli.it

Owner
Gianni Masciarelli

Founded
1981

Winemakers
Romeo Taraborrelli and
Gianni Masciarelli

Vineyard manager
Giovanni Pirozzi

Production
About 13,000 bottles in
favorable years

Vintages
1999 1998 1997 1996
1992

Price
● ● ●

After decades of flooding markets with bargain bottles and bulk wines for blending, the bountiful vineyards of Abruzzo are beginning to live up to their long neglected potential. The new spirit in the mountainous Adriatic region is exemplified by Gianni Masciarelli, whose rise from the regiments of quantity to the regime of quality has made him one of the most admired winemakers of central Italy.

His grandfather planted vineyards in the 1930s at San Martino sulla Marrucina in the sun-drenched hills south of Chieti, but Gianni bottled the first wines from Cantina Masciarelli in 1981. His Montepulciano and Trebbiano d'Abruzzo DOC and a pink wine called Rosa found welcome markets in the Caribbean and Denmark due to decent quality and attractive prices. But Gianni, perhaps influenced by the achievements of his artisan friend Edoardo Valentini (see page 376), aspired to greater things.

He began by replanting at greater density, training vines in low cordon methods rather than the high canopy *tendone* method that had given Abruzzo the dubious distinction of realizing the most prolific yields of Italy's 20 regions. Along with select clones of Montepulciano and Trebbiano, Gianni introduced Cabernet Sauvignon and Chardonnay, while acquiring French barriques to make the wines of contemporary style.

The Masciarelli estate has expanded vineyards to 66 hectares, but production has leveled off at about 650,000 bottles a year divided into two lines: Villa Gemma, after the estate's manor, and Marina Cvetić, after Gianni's Yugoslavian-born wife, who works with him in the winery with the same tireless drive and enthusiasm.

Villa Gemma Montepulciano d'Abruzzo reached new heights from 1994 but I tasted it too late to give it a deserved place in this book. Trebbiano d'Abruzzo has also reached admirable levels. I have been even more impressed by recent vintages of Marina Cvetić Chardonnay, a wine of innate stature ennobled by a year of maturing in oak.

Grapes
Chardonnay 100%, hand picked in mid-September.

Vineyards
Plots totaling 1.9 hectares in calcareous clay soils on slopes facing various directions at about 300 meters of altitude in hills along the Foro river valley in the communes of Vacri and Bucchianico south of the city of Chieti. The vines, of an average age of 17 years, are planted at a density of 6,000 per hectare and trained in the Guyot cordon method.

Vinification and aging
Grapes are soft crushed and the musts fermented for 15–30 days at 18–20°C in small barrels of French oak (about 70% new annually), in which malolactic fermentation occurs spontaneously during a year of maturing on the lees. The wine, of about 14% alcohol, is bottled and cellared for 5 months before release.

Style and maturity
Chardonnay Marina Cvetić on release in the second year after the harvest has bright straw yellow color with golden highlights and ample aromas in scents that recall tropical fruits and peaches mingling with hints of honey, caramel and vanilla. Full bodied with richly complex flavors, mellow fruit sensations are deftly fused with oak in a long, elegant finish. A wine of uncommon depth, it should reach a prime in 5–8 years and hold style for a decade or more.

Serving
🌡 12–13°C, opening bottle an hour earlier.
🍷 Tulip-shaped glass (Chardonnay type).
🍽 Gnocchi with scampi; *scrippelle 'mbusse* (crepes with Pecorino in chicken broth); monkfish *alla cacciatora* (with chili peppers and tomato).

Fattoria la Monacesca

Producer
Azienda Agricola Fattoria
la Monacesca
Contrada Monacesca
62024 Matelica
(Macerata)
Tel. 0733/812602
Fax 0733/810593

Owner
Casimiro Cifola

Founded
1966

Winemaker
Roberto Potentini

Vineyard manager
Aldo Cifola

Production
About 50,000 bottles
and 3,000 magnums
a year

Vintages
1999 1998 1997

Price
●

La Monacesca
Verdicchio di Matelica DOC ♀

Matelica, a peaceful town in the Apennines, is sometimes called the second home of Verdicchio because production of its DOC wine is only a fraction of that of the larger Castelli di Jesi zone. Advocates, who consider Verdicchio di Matelica to be second to none, have been known to describe it as a red wine dressed in white. They explain that vines acclimatized to rigid mountain conditions make wines of greater strength and concentration, while sharp day–night temperature variations during the season account for pronounced aromas and flavors.

I realized that there was something to that when I tasted the monumental Verdicchio di Matelica of Fratelli Bisci from the 1982 vintage, early evidence that central Italy had a noble native white wine variety after all. Near the Bisci farm is Fattoria la Monacesca, acquired by Casimiro Cifola in 1966 and now run by his son Aldo, who has steadily improved the vineyards and cellars. La Monacesca, which once supplied wine to a Benedictine monastic order, has become the modern leader in Matelica under Aldo's guidance.

He works with Roberto Potentini to produce about 110,000 bottles a year from 27 hectares of vines. These include regular Verdicchio and single-vineyard la Monacesca, as well as Marche IGT Mirum (late-harvested Verdicchio with hints of Chardonnay and Sauvignon), Ecclesia (Chardonnay) and Camerte (Sangiovese and Merlot).

It would be romantic fancy to pretend that the Verdicchios of Matelica and Jesi are radically different or that experts could invariably tell them apart in blind tastings. The zones are separated by a scant 10 kilometers of rocky rises along the Esino river and the heights of Jesi can equal the altitudes of Matelica. Yet, as Aldo points out, certain vineyards of Matelica seem to transmit mineral elements of the soil into Verdicchio, tending to heighten acidic zest while adding fascinating nuances to aromas and flavors. The Verdicchio most clearly endowed with this *goût de terroir* is la Monacesca.

Marche

Grapes
Verdicchio 100%, hand picked in early October.

Vineyard
A plot of 9 hectares in calcareous sandy clay soils on slopes undulating from north to south at about 400 meters of altitude at Contrada Monacesca 4 kilometers north of the town of Matelica. The vines, of an average age of 31 years, are planted at a density of 1,700 per hectare and trained in the double-arched *controspalliera* and *capovolto* cordon systems.

Vinification and aging
Grapes are soft crushed and the musts chilled to separate solid matter and inoculated with Bayanus yeast cultures (without addition of sulfites) before fermenting for 15–20 days at about 20°C in stainless steel tanks. Malolactic fermentation occurs naturally in May during 6 months of maturing on the lees in tanks. The wine, of about 13.5% alcohol, is bottled and cellared for at least 3 months before release.

Style and maturity
Verdicchio la Monacesca on release about a year after the harvest has bright straw yellow color with green-gold highlights and refined aroma with scents reminiscent of quince and anise, taking on hints of citron and toasted nuts with time. Flavors are full and round in a wine of ample structure and mellow texture with sensations of fruit and mineral elements evident in a long, smooth finish. At a prime at 2 years, wine from top vintages can maintain style up to a decade.

Serving
🌡 12°C.
🍷 Tulip-shaped glass (Chardonnay type).
🍽 Maccheroni with zucchini and scampi; *orata all'anconetana* (gilt-head bream in a light tomato and herb sauce); Caprini (goat's milk cheeses).

Producer
Azienda Agricola
Palazzone
Località Rocca Ripesena
68
05019 Orvieto (Terni)
Tel. 0763/344921
Fax 0763/344921
palazzon@palazzone.com
www.palazzone.com

Owners
Giovanni and Lodovico
Dubini Locatelli

Founded
1969

Winemakers
Giovanni Dubini with
Riccardo Cotarella

Vineyard manager
Giovanni Dubini

Production
2,500–3,000 half bottles
(0.375-liter) in favorable
years

Vintages
1999 1998 1997 1996
1995

Price
● ●

Palazzone | # Muffa Nobile
Umbria IGT ♀

Palazzone was the name of an inn near Orvieto in the Middle Ages, when the town was renowned for sweet wines. The surrounding farm at Rocca Ripesena had been largely abandoned by 1969, when it was acquired by the Dubini Locatelli family, who restored buildings and replanted vineyards to realize their first vintage of Orvieto Classico DOC in 1982.

Young Giovanni Dubini had just begun to make his mark as a winemaker when he was named director of the Orvieto producers' consortium, a responsibility that left little time for the estate. Although wine production wasn't profitable then, Giovanni soon decided to devote himself totally to Palazzone. New cellars were built in 1988 and vineyards expanded to cover 24 hectares. Giovanni, expertly advised by Riccardo Cotarella, produces about 120,000 bottles of wine a year, divided between Orvieto Classico and creations from foreign varieties that have made an even greater impact.

Orvieto is one of the few places in Italy where *Botrytis cinerea*, noble rot, develops naturally in grapes left on the vine until late autumn, when damp mists envelope the Tiber and Paglia river valleys. Giovanni makes Orvieto Classico Vendemmia Tardiva from botrytized Procanico and Malvasia grapes, but their fragility creates a challenge.

In 1992, he planted Sauvignon Blanc, which is often blended with Sémillon in Sauternes and other sweet wines of Bordeaux, and by 1994, *voilà*, noble rot galore. *Muffa nobile* (as the fabled fungus is known in Italian) began to live up to its name in 1995 and seems to have gained in stature with each vintage to take its place among the most elegant sweet wines of central Italy.

Palazzone's total production includes dignified Orvieto Classico Superiore DOC Campo del Guardiano and Terre Vineate, along with Umbria IGT white Grechetto and Viognier known as L'Ultima Spiaggia (The Last Beach) and reds called Rubbio (based on Sangiovese) and often superb Armaleo (Cabernet Sauvignon and Cabernet Franc).

Grapes
Sauvignon Blanc 100%, hand picked in phases between late October and mid-November as bunches infected with *Botrytis cinerea* are individually selected.

Vineyard
A plot of 0.6 hectare in sedimentary clay soils on slopes facing north-northwest at 220 meters of altitude at Rocca Ripesena 3 kilometers west of the town of Orvieto. Vines were planted in 1992 at a density of 3,400 per hectare and trained in a spurred cordon method.

Vinification and aging
Whole grape bunches are soft crushed and the dense musts are fermented for 30–35 days at natural temperatures in new barrels of French oak (Allier), where malolactic fermentation also occurs during maturation that lasts until April. The wine, of 14–14.5% developed alcohol with 9–10% of residual sugar, is stabilized at cold temperatures in tanks before bottling and cellaring of 8 months until release.

Style and maturity
Muffa Nobile on release in the second year after the harvest has brilliant golden color and luxurious aromas with scents reminiscent of tropical fruit, candied orange peels, honey, vanilla and spices. On the palate, it is rich in texture and opulent in flavor with exquisite harmony in vivacious ripe fruit sensations that mellow into a honey-like sweetness on the finish. Though attractive from the start, the wine promises to retain class for a decade or more.

Serving
- 10–12°C.
- Tulip-shaped glass with long stem.
- *Foie gras*; *torcolo* (sponge cake with raisins and candied fruit); almond biscuits; after-dinner sipping.

Batàr
Toscana IGT ♀

Producer
Agricola Querciabella
Via Santa Lucia a
Barbiano 17
Località Ruffoli
50022 Greve in Chianti
(Firenze)
Tel. 02/86452793
Fax 02/8053139
info@querciabella.com
www.querciabella.com

Owners
Giuseppe Castiglioni and
family

Founded
1972

Winemakers
Guido De Santi with
consultant Giacomo
Tachis

Vineyard managers
Dales D'Alessandro with
consultant Carlo Modi

Production
About 20,000 bottles a
year

Vintages
1999 1998 1997 1995
1991 1990 1989 1988

Price
● ● ●

Giuseppe Castiglioni, who founded the Querciabella estate in Chianti Classico in 1972, is an admirer of white Burgundy with a particular fondness for certain crus of Montrachet. After putting the early emphasis on red wines, in the mid-1980s he planted Pinots to see how they would do on the sunny slopes of Tuscany, a region that had never been distinguished by its dry whites.

The first vintage was 1988, a blend of Pinot Blanc (Bianco) with Pinot Gris (Grigio) at 20 percent, fermented and matured in barrels of French oak. Pleasantly surprised, he decided to call the wine Bâtard-Pinot. That remained until 1992, when Chardonnay replaced Pinot Grigio and the name was shortened to Bâtard.

The wine, fashioned by the crack cellar team of Guido De Santi and consultant Giacomo Tachis, was drawing closer to Burgundy in style, though some observers found the name too close for comfort to Bâtard-Montrachet, Criots-Bâtard-Montrachet and Bienvenues-Bâtard-Montrachet. To avoid confusion and possible conflicts with the French, Giuseppe and his son Sebastiano decided to make it Batàr, altering the spelling if not the pronunciation.

Early vintages of the wine were rich and concentrated in flavor, though sometimes a touch too fat and oaky for my taste. Chardonnay and Pinot Bianco complement each other in a 50–50 blend that showed auspicious class in the 1995 and 1997 vintages. The decision to use less new oak with the 1998 vintage seems to account for the elegance that confirms Batàr as one of the finest Burgundy-style whites of Italy.

From 26 hectares of vines, Querciabella produces about 195,000 bottles of wine a year in newly expanded cellars. These include fine Chianti Classico and the Super-Tuscan Camartina discussed on page 312, as well as an excellent Vin Santo called Orlando. The Castiglioni family also has new vineyards in the Maremma near the coast of Tuscany and a small estate at Manzano in the Colli Orientali del Friuli zone.

Tuscany

Grapes
Chardonnay and Pinot Bianco, 50% each, hand picked between late August and early September.

Vineyards
Plots called Pallonaio, La Lama and Ruffoli covering 4.5 hectares in soils of sandstone with schistous *galestro* on slopes oriented south-southwest at about 400 meters of altitude at Ruffoli in the commune of Greve in the Chianti Classico zone. The vines, of an average age of 17 years, are planted at a density of 4,500–5,000 per hectare and trained in a spurred cordon method.

Vinification and aging
Grape bunches with stems are crushed very gently in pneumatic presses without mashing skins or seeds and the musts with selected yeast cultures ferment in small oak barrels for about 10 days at about 18°C after an initial peak. Malolactic fermentation occurs during 9–12 months of maturing in barriques of French oak (Allier), 80% new, 20% used once. The wine, of about 13% alcohol, is settled in stainless steel tanks for 3 months before being bottled and cellared for at least 4 months until release.

Style and maturity
Batàr on release about 2 years after the harvest has a deep straw yellow color with golden highlights and complex yet refined bouquet with scents reminiscent of pears, bananas, mango, citron and hints of saffron, oriental spices and vanilla. Flavors are rich and round with sensations of fruit, nuts and spices braced by a vein of acidity that adds a note of freshness to the long, smooth finish. The wine approaches peaks in about 5 years, though it seems to have the elements to improve for a further decade.

Serving
🌡 8–10°C.
🍷 Tulip-shaped glass (white Burgundy type).
🍽 *Pappa al pomodoro* (Tuscan bread, tomato and basil pap); chickpea purée with cuttlefish; sea bass roast with thin-sliced porcini mushrooms.

Tenuta Le Quinte

Virtù Romane Montecompatri Superiore DOC ♀

Producer
Tenuta Le Quinte di
Papi E. & C.
Via delle Marmorelle 91
00040 Montecompatri
(Roma)
Tel. 06/9438756
Fax 06/9438694
lequinte@tiscalinet.it
www.lequinte.it

Owner
Francesco Papi

Founded
1985

Winemaker
Pietro Zitoli

Production
About 30,000 bottles a
year

Vintages
1999 1998 1997

Price
●

Some of my fondest memories of wine date to my youthful days in Rome when I escaped frequently to the Castelli Romani, the hills southeast of the capital, and the towns of Frascati, Marino, Grottaferrata, Montecompatri and Rocca di Papa. Some cellars there had been hollowed into the tufaceous earth, cool grottoes where casks of chestnut wood held wine from the latest vintage, served in carafes with *porchetta*, slices of suckling pig roast with garlic and herbs, wedged between crusty slabs of country bread.

Those free-flowing wines of golden hue could be marvelous on a spring day, mellow and round with grapy fragrance and a mouth-filling goodness described as *abboccato*—not quite sweet but not dry either. The tastiest types, as I learned, came from varieties of Malvasia that had been grown in the hills for ages and not the Trebbiano that had gained the upper hand because of prolific yields and the steely dry flavors it gave to wines for shipping.

Recently, in Rome, I tasted a range of wines from the Castelli Romani, a series of clean, fresh, balanced whites that one could sip without really noticing. Except for one, Virtù Romane, from Tenuta Le Quinte in the neglected DOC zone of Montecompatri. If not a grand or glorious wine, it was a sheer delight to drink, with those scents and flavors that carried me back to those carefree days in the grottoes.

Le Quinte is owned by Francesco Papi, whose family has made wine there for four generations. He named the wine "Roman Virtues" because it comes from Malvasia and other varieties that express the "enormous potential of Rome's native vines."

From 10 hectares of vines, Le Quinte produces about 100,000 bottles of wine a year, including a tasty IGT Lazio red called Rasa di Marmorata (Cesanese and Montepulciano) and the sweet Dulcis Vitis (late-harvested Malvasia Bianca). The farmhouse was rebuilt in the seventeenth century on the foundations of the villa of Caligula, the Roman emperor who no doubt enjoyed the wine's virtues himself.

Lazio

Grapes
Malvasia Bianca del Lazio 60%, Grechetto del Lazio 25%, Bonvino and Bellone 15%, harvested in late October.

Vineyards
Plots covering about 5 hectares in loose, well-drained volcanic soils on slopes facing mainly southward at 300 meters of altitude in the communes of Montecompatri and Colonna in the Montecompatri DOC zone at the northeastern corner of the Castelli Romani. The vines, of an average age of 11 years, are planted at a density of 4,000 per hectare and trained in the Guyot and spurred cordon methods.

Vinification and aging
Grapes are soft crushed and the musts macerated with the skins for 6–8 hours before being clarified through an enzymatic process and fermented at 15–18°C for 15–20 days in stainless steel tanks. Malolactic fermentation is avoided, though recent vintages have been matured for 6 months in small barrels of French oak on an experimental basis. After bottling, the wine, of about 12.5% alcohol, is cellared for 3 months before release.

Style and maturity
Montecompatri Superiore Virtù Romane on release about a year after the harvest has bright golden color and full aromas with scents reminiscent of blossoms, peaches, pears, sweet spices and, vaguely, mint. Flavors are softly dry and round with mellow sensations of ripe fruit and spices in a refreshingly mouth-filling finish. The wine reaches a prime inside 2 years but can maintain goodness for a bit beyond that.

Serving
🍷 10–12°C.
♀ Medium, tulip-shaped glass.
🍴 Frittata with spring onions, potatoes and mint; grilled jumbo shrimp; turbot roasted with new potatoes and artichokes.

366

San Giusto
a Rentennano

Vin Santo
Vino da Tavola ♀

Producer
Fattoria San Giusto a
Rentennano
Località Monti
53013 Gaiole in
Chianti (Siena)
Tel. 0577/747121
Fax 0577/747109
sangiustorentennano
@chiantinet.it
www.italywines.com

Owner
Martini di Cigala family

Founded
1905

Winemakers
Francesco Martini di
Cigala with Attilio Pagli

Vineyard manager
Luca Martini di Cigala

Production
About 2,700 half-liter
bottles in favorable years

Vintages
1997 1996 1995 1993
1990 1988 1986 1985

Price
● ●

Note
Vintages from 1996 on
may qualify as Vin Santo
del Chianti Classico
Riserva DOC

The wines of San Giusto a Rentennano are as big and generous as their producers, brothers Francesco and Luca Martini di Cigala. (Percarlo, their pure Sangiovese Super-Tuscan, is described on page 324.) The brothers are just as devoted to Vin Santo, though that "holy wine" made in minute quantities following intricate procedures invariably challenges their patience and skills.

Vin Santo comes from an old Tuscan variety of Malvasia with a little Trebbiano dried for months after the harvest. Luca, who oversees the vineyards while Francesco runs the cellars, explains that infinite variables are involved in growing, harvesting and drying the grapes. "With a little help from nature we can more or less control those results," says Luca. "But when the musts go into barrels sealed for six years, well, then the fates take over."

"A lot depends on the mother," explains Francesco, referring to the residue in each barrel from previous batches. That matrix contains yeasts and other elements that guide the mysterious process of fermentation that recurs with heat and abates with cold. "In the end, though, the wine from each barrel has its own peculiarities," says Franceso. "When the blend is finally bottled, each vintage has unique character."

San Giusto is considered the closest rival to Avignonesi (see page 256) in the field of Vin Santo, which is crowded with contenders since nearly every farm in Tuscany makes a version of the wine. Francesco attributes the power of San Giusto's wines to the vigor of its soils, pointing out that grapes attain sugar levels unmatched even in hotter places in the south.

Developed alcohol in Vin Santo runs from 13–15 percent with residual sugars at 20–25 percent, sweeter even than Sicily's Moscato di Pantelleria. Yet the wine retains wood tannins and moderate acidity that keep it from being cloying. Technically analyzed, it's a bit of a monster; critically appraised, it's a magnificent mouthful.

Tuscany

Grapes
Malvasia 85–90% and Trebbiano 10–15%, hand picked in late September. Bunches are arrayed on cane mats or draped from rafters in a well-ventilated loft to dry for 100–150 days.

Vineyards
Two plots (Pancate and Corsignano) covering 1.7 hectares in tufaceous soils of gravel mixed with sand, clay and marine fossils on slopes facing south-southwest at 260–280 meters of altitude at Monti in southern Chianti Classico. The vines were planted 27 years ago at a density of 3,500 per hectare and trained in Guyot and spurred cordon methods.

Vinification and aging
Shriveled grapes are crushed and the musts go into *carati*, old chestnut barrels of 40–200 liters, and oak barrels of 75 and 100 liters, sealed with cement for 6 years as intermittent alcoholic and malolactic fermentations occur at natural temperatures fed by yeasts in the matrix that remains in each. Evaporation reduces volume by 45–50% of a wine of 13–15% alcohol with 20–25% residual sugars that is bottled and cellared for 6 months until release.

Style and maturity
San Giusto a Rentennano Vin Santo on release about 7 years after the harvest has deep golden color tending toward amber and elaborate bouquet with scents reminiscent of raisins, green walnut husks, toasted almonds and hints of coffee, spices and cocoa. Dense and rich in body and texture, the sumptuous sweetness recalls honey and figs, though mellow wood tannins and a hint of acidity add to the extraordinary depth of flavors and length on the palate. Excellent after 8–10 years, the wine reaches peaks at 15–20 years and should retain elegance for 3 decades or more.

Serving
- 12–15°C.
- Glass with ample bowl and narrow top.
- Aged and ripe cheeses; biscuits, pastries and tarts based on fruit and nuts; perhaps most impressive alone as a wine of meditation.

Le Vaglie
Verdicchio dei Castelli di Jesi
Classico DOC ♀

Producer
Casa Vinicola Santa
Barbara di Antonucci
Stefano & C.
Borgo Mazzini 35
60010 Barbara (Ancona)
Tel. 071/9674249
Fax 071/9674263
info@vinisantabarbara.it
www.vinisantabarbara.it

Owner
Stefano Antonucci

Founded
1987

Winemaker
Pierluigi Lorenzetti

Vineyard manager
Pierluigi Lorenzetti

Production
About 35,000 bottles
a year

Vintages
1999 1998 1997 1995
1993

Price
●

When Le Vaglie began to attract notice as a Verdicchio on the rise in 1994, its producer, Stefano Antonucci, was still working in a bank to finance his conversion of the family farm into a wine estate. After buying the full share of the property from the rest of the family in 1987, he piled up debts modernizing the cellars and acquiring vineyards. But finally, in 1995, the cellars generated enough of a turnover for Stefano to leave the bank and devote his time entirely to making wine.

Santa Barbara, as Stefano christened the estate after the small town of Barbara, makes a representative range of DOC and IGT wines of the Marches. But the main focus is on Verdicchio dei Castelli di Jesi Classico. The first to make an impact was Le Vaglie, conceived in 1992 from a vineyard of that name where grapes are picked very ripe (almost late harvest). The wine is partly matured in oak to give it mellow, complex qualities that exalt the inherent elegance of Verdicchio.

A recent creation is the Verdicchio called Stefano Antonucci Riserva, which is fermented and matured entirely in barrels. The wine is impressively big and bold, but to my taste lacks the fresh fruit qualities and overall finesse of Le Vaglie. Santa Barbara also produces Verdicchio in a regular version and the single-vineyard Pignocco Bianco vinified entirely in stainless steel.

Stefano works with Pierluigi Lorenzetti, who began in the vineyards and now also directs the cellars. From 15 hectares of estate vines and acquired grapes, Santa Barbara produces about 300,000 bottles of wine a year. These include a Rosso Piceno DOC and three types of Rosso delle Marche IGT: Stefano Antonucci (Merlot and Cabernet Sauvignon), Pignocco Rosso (Lacrima, Cabernet and Montepulciano) and Vigna San Bartolo (Montepulciano and Cabernet). Moscatell is a delicate sweet white from Moscato Bianco.

Marche

Grapes
Verdicchio 100%, hand picked in phases when very ripe in mid-October.

Vineyard
Grapes are selected in a plot of 4.4 hectares in medium-packed calcareous soils on a plain at 219 meters of altitude at Contrada Le Vaglie in the commune of Barbara in the northwestern part of the Castelli di Jesi Classico zone. The vines, of an average age of 31 years, are planted at a density of 2,500 per hectare and trained in the double-arched *doppio capovolto* cordon system.

Vinification and aging
Grapes are soft crushed and the musts clarified by an enzymatic process before fermenting in stainless steel tanks at 17–18°C for 15–18 days. Partial malolactic fermentation takes place during 8 months of maturation, mainly in tanks, though a third of the wine goes in to either 2,500-liter casks of Slavonian oak or 350-liter new barrels of French oak (Allier). The wine, of 13.5–14% alcohol, is bottled and released in June following the harvest.

Style and maturity
Verdicchio Le Vaglie on release about 9 months after the harvest has bright straw yellow color with green-gold highlights and graceful aromas with scents reminiscent of ripe apricots and peaches, acacia blossoms and spices. Flavors are full and round in a wine of ample dimensions and rich texture with sensations of ripe fruit and herbs evident in a clean, smooth finish. At a prime in 2–3 years, the wine can show depth with further aging.

Serving
🌡 12–14°C.
🍷 Tulip-shaped glass (Chardonnay type).
🍴 Ravioli of sea bass with shrimp and tomato sauce; turbot roasted with potatoes and artichokes; monkfish with puréed fava beans.

Balciana
Verdicchio dei Castelli di Jesi
Classico Superiore DOC ♀

Producer
Azienda Agricola
Sartarelli
Via Coste del Molino 24
60030 Poggio San
Marcello (Ancona)
Tel. 0731/89732
Fax 0731/89732
tralivio@sintech.net
www. sartarelli.it

Owners
Donatella Sartarelli and
Claudia Pozzi

Founded
1973 as Sartarelli-Conti
Vandi

Winemaker
Alberto Mazzoni

Vineyard manager
Franco Catalani

Production
About 11,000 bottles in
favorable years

Vintages
1999 1998 1997 1994

Price
● ● ●

Any lingering doubts that Verdicchio ranks with the noblest of Italian vines were largely laid to rest by the triumph of Balciana in the 1999 International Wine Challenge in London. That late-harvest Verdicchio dei Castelli di Jesi Classico Superiore from the 1997 vintage was judged the absolute top white wine among 8,500 entries from 34 countries.

Balciana had already won acclaim in Italy, though I must admit that my tastings of the early vintages, 1994 and 1995, left me with reservations. The wine was immense, fundamentally dry but with a curious mellifluous quality from the noble rot that develops on grapes picked in November. It was certainly not a typical Verdicchio.

After the victory, I ordered Balciana 1997 in a restaurant to try with fish. It overwhelmed seafood hors d'oeuvre and a pasta with crustaceans, so I tried it with lobster in the sauce the French call *Américaine* (with butter, tomato, garlic, Cognac and cayenne pepper). A better match, but not perfect. The next trial was with quintessential dishes of Marche: spicy fish soup called *brodetto all'Anconetana* and *pollo in potacchio* (chicken braised with onion, tomato, white wine and herbs), followed by the pungent cheese called *formaggio di fossa* buried in pits to ripen with mold. Balciana was clearly in its element.

This extraordinary Verdicchio comes from the Sartarelli estate, owned by Donatella Sartarelli and Claudia Pozzi. Production is the domain of Donatella's husband Patrizio Chiacchiarini and enologist Alberto Mazzoni, who also make a Verdicchio called Tralivio from a selection of normally ripe grapes. Both wines combine whopping dimensions with astonishing finesse and complexity in aromas and flavors. Since they are vinified in stainless steel without a trace of oak, those qualities must derive from the generous nature of the soils at Poggio San Marcello.

From 26 hectares of estate vineyards and 25 hectares leased, Sartarelli makes about 140,000 bottles a year.

Marche

Grapes
Verdicchio 100%, hand picked in phases as bunches develop *Botrytis cinerea* in early to mid-November.

Vineyard
Grapes are selected in a plot of 9 hectares in medium-packed calcareous soils on slopes facing northeast at 300–350 meters of altitude at Contrada Balciana in the commune of Poggio San Marcello in the west-central part of the Castelli di Jesi Classico zone. The vines, of an average age of 11 years, are planted at densities of 2,500–3,000 per hectare and trained in the Guyot cordon system.

Vinification and aging
Grape bunches with stems are crushed gently (0.5 atmosphere) in a lateral membrane press and the free-run must goes into stainless steel and glass-lined cement vats for 2 days at 5–7°C to precipitate 95% of the lees. Musts are heated to 17–18°C, setting off fermentation of 20–30 days at 18–20°C. The wine, of 14% alcohol, remains at 18°C in stainless steel tanks, clarified by periodic racking until September, when it is bottled and cellared at 16°C until release.

Style and maturity
Verdicchio Balciana on release in the second year after the harvest has brilliant yellow color with greenish highlights and soaring aromas with scents reminiscent of ripe apples, cantaloupe melon, acacia blossoms and spices. Flavors are basically dry but rich, round and warmly alcoholic in a wine of immense dimensions with ripe fruit sensations and a hint of toasted nuts in a long, smooth finish. Aging capacity isn't yet known in a wine conceived in 1994 that seems to have the elements that favor long life.

Serving
🍴 12–15°C, opening bottle an hour earlier.
🍷 Tulip-shaped glass (Chardonnay type).
🍽 *Stoccafisso all'anconetana* (dried cod with a spicy tomato-herb sauce); *coniglio in porchetta* (rabbit roast with wild fennel, rosemary and garlic); ripe cheeses.

Terre di tufi
Bianco di Toscana IGT ♀

Producer
Teruzzi E. & Puthod C.
Ponte a Rondolino
Località Casale 19
53037 San Gimignano
(Siena)
Tel. 0577/940143
Fax 0577/942016

Owners
Enrico Teruzzi and
Carmen Puthod

Founded
1974

Winemakers
Pierluca Freddi and
Alberto Bramini

Vineyard manager
Valerio Zorzi

Production
350,000–400,000
bottles a year

Vintages
1999 1998 1997 1995
1993 1990

Price
● ●

San Gimignano was a vinous backwater in 1974, when Enrico Teruzzi and Carmen Puthod from Milan bought Ponte a Rondolino with the idea of making wine. Their credentials were clearly not suitable. Enrico came from a family that could support his exploits as a jockey, skier, motorcyclist and yachtsman, and the French-born Carmen had been the prima ballerina at La Scala. But between them they possessed the energy, savvy and flair to run (or dance) circles around their tradition-minded neighbors.

After the first vintage, carried out in a revamped stable, Enrico shifted operations to cellars that have regularly expanded and always remained a technological step or two ahead of the competition. The early Vernaccia di San Gimignano was admirably fresh and fruity, a shock to Tuscans who had always believed that the wine by nature reeked of bitter almonds.

Enrico, never satisfied, charged ahead with innovations, installing a refrigeration plant that was soon computerized and devising new twists on fermentation and aging to make a Vernaccia of international style. He found the perfect tool in the 1980s: French barriques to mature the Vernaccia, which he called Terre di Tufo after the estate's tufaceous earth.

The wine with a label the size of a postage stamp made an immediate impact. But producers of Campania's Greco di Tufo insisted that "Tufo" was their name, so Enrico made it Terre di tufi (plural) and continued to build volume of what became Italy's most popular oak-matured white. Although it qualified for a time as Vernaccia di San Gimignano, Enrico finally conceded that Terre di tufi was special enough to rate the meaningless Toscana IGT.

From 180 hectares of vineyards, Teruzzi & Puthod produce about 1,100,000 bottles a year, including Vernaccia DOCG Vigna Rondolino and IGT Galestro (Trebbiano and Vernaccia), Carmen Puthod (Sangiovese vinified as a white variety) and Peperino (red Sangiovese). More than 80 percent of production is exported.

Tuscany

Grapes
Vernaccia 80% with Vermentino, Chardonnay and Malvasia, hand picked in September.

Vineyards
Grapes are selected from 71 hectares in tufaceous soils of yellow sand and clays on slopes facing south and southeast at an average of 300 meters of altitude at Ponte a Rondolino and other parts of the commune of San Gimignano. The vines, of an average age of 25 years, are planted at densities of 2,000–2,500 per hectare and trained in a spurred cordon method.

Vinification and aging
Grapes are soft crushed and the musts saturated with oxygen (hyperoxygenation) and cooled to 2–4°C to be statically decanted and clarified following analyses of oxidizable polyphenols and colloids. Fermentation with select yeast cultures lasts from 15–20 days at 17°C in stainless steel tanks and 225-liter barrels of French oak. The wine, of about 12.5% alcohol, undergoes malolactic fermentation during 4–6 months of maturing on the lees in barriques before being bottled and released in the spring.

Style and maturity
Terre di tufi on release in the spring after the harvest has a brilliant straw yellow color and graceful aromas with scents reminiscent of apricots, acacia blossoms and vanilla. On the palate, it is round and mellow with fresh fruit flavors well melded with lively acidity and hints of toasty oak in a smooth, lingering finish. After reaching a prime in 2–3 years, the wine can retain class for a few years longer.

Serving
- 10–15°C, opening bottle an hour earlier.
- Tulip-shaped glass (Alsatian type).
- *Carpaccio* of raw tuna; lightly smoked wild salmon; risotto with scampi; *vitello tonnato* (veal with tuna sauce).

Umani Ronchi

Casal di Serra
Verdicchio dei Castelli di Jesi
Classico Superiore DOC ♀

Producer
Azienda Agricola Umani
Ronchi
Strada Statale 16, Km
310+400
60027 Osimo (Ancona)
Tel. 071/7108019
Fax 071/7108859
wine@umanironchi.it
www.umanironchi.it

Owner
Bianchi Bernetti family

Founded
1955

Winemakers
Umberto Trombelli with
consultant Giacomo
Tachis

Vineyard managers
Luigi Piersanti with
consultant Carlo Modi

Production
About 120,000 bottles
a year

Vintages
1999 1998 1997 1995
1993

Price
●

As a long-time believer in Verdicchio, I've noted with pleasure that more and more experts rate it among the elite white wine varieties—and not only of Italy. Even when Verdicchio came mainly in kitschy amphora bottles, quality standards seemed to surpass those of other popular whites, a factor that I attributed to the intrinsic virtue of the grape.

Over the last two decades, Verdicchio has risen rapidly in the ranks of premium whites with wines from dozens of admirable producers, including small-scale estates. But the main messengers of the gospel of Verdicchio have been the relatively large wineries of Garofoli, Fazi Battaglia and Umani Ronchi by making estate wines of enviable class available in significant quantities.

Umani Ronchi produces single-vineyard Verdicchio dei Castelli di Jesi Classico Superiore Casal di Serra and Villa Bianchi at the rate of more than 250,000 bottles a year, complemented by an oak-fermented Riserva called Plenio. The winery founded by Gino Umani Ronchi in 1955 has been shaped by the Bianchi Bernetti family into a force in the Marches, not only with Verdicchio but with fine Rosso Conero and the blend called Pelago, which triumphed as the top red in the 1997 International Wine Challenge in London (see page 332).

Director Massimo Bernetti works with brother Stefano, son Michele and resident winemaker Umberto Trombelli at Umani Ronchi's new cellars. They benefit from the consultancy of Giacomo Tachis, whose master touches with oak give Plenio extra dimensions. But with a lunch of Adriatic seafood, I prefer Casal di Serra, whose fresh fruit sensations sum up the pure pleasure of Verdicchio.

From 150 hectares of vines and acquisitions, Umani Ronchi produces about 4.2 million bottles a year, including DOC Rosso Conero Cùmaro and San Lorenzo, Montepulciano d'Abruzzo Jorio, Marche IGT Le Busche (Verdicchio and Chardonnay) and Maximo (sweet Sauvignon Blanc from botrytized grapes).

Marche

Grapes
Verdicchio 100%, hand picked when very ripe in early October.

Vineyard
Casal di Serra, a plot of 15 hectares in medium-textured calcareous clay soils on slopes at about 350 meters of altitude in the commune of Montecarotto in the western part of the Castelli di Jesi Classico zone. The vines, of an average age of 21 years, are planted at a density of 3,000 per hectare and trained in a spurred cordon method.

Vinification and aging
Grapes are soft crushed and the free-run must chilled to separate solid matter statically before fermenting for about 30 days at a maximum of 15°C in stainless steel tanks. Malolactic fermentation occurs during 5 months on the lees in tanks, though 3–4% of the volume is matured in barriques and blended in at the end. The bottled wine, of about 13% alcohol, is cellared for at least 4 months until release.

Style and maturity
Verdicchio Casal di Serra on release in the summer after the harvest has bright straw color with green-gold highlights and vibrantly fresh aroma with scents reminiscent of ripe peaches and apples and hints of citrus and sage. Flavors are full and round in a wine of ample body and smooth texture with fruit sensations mingling with an almond undertone in a long, mellow finish. At a prime after a year or 2, the wine gains complexity and elegance for another 4 or 5 years.

Serving
🍷 12–13°C.
🍷 Tulip-shaped glass (Alsatian type).
🍽 Ravioli with scallops; scampi with puréed lentils from Castelluccio; jumbo shrimp with roast sliced potatoes and black truffles.

Valentini

Trebbiano d'Abruzzo DOC ♀

Producer
Azienda Agricola
Valentini
Via del Baio 2
Loreto Aprutino
(Pescara)
Tel. 085/8291138
Fax 085/8291138

Owners
Edoardo and Francesco
Paolo Valentini

Founded
1650

Winemakers
Edoardo and Francesco
Paolo Valentini

Vineyard managers
Edoardo and Francesco
Paolo Valentini

Production
Varies according to
vintage

Vintages
1997 1996 1995 1993
1992 1990 1988 1986
1985 1983 1982

Price
● ● ● ●

Trebbiano is Italy's most diffused and prolific white wine variety, as well as its most maligned, due to the generally insipid quality it renders. The name applies to what has been described as an ancient family of vines, though evidence suggests that not all cultivars are related. The strongest case for individuality is provided by Edoardo Valentini, whose Trebbiano d'Abruzzo stands supremely above the crowd.

Edoardo, whose grandiose Montepulciano d'Abruzzo is described on page 334, considers Trebbiano the most truly autochthonous of the region's vines. Not just because it has been there since Roman times, but because it conveys the essence of soil and climate and culture of Abruzzo, he explains. "Trebbiano tells the story of this place."

The man known as "lord of the vines" cultivates 64 hectares around the hill town of Loreto Aprutino, working with his son Francesco Paolo to produce a maximum of 50,000 bottles between Trebbiano, Montepulciano and the pink Cerasuolo, all covered by the DOC of Abruzzo.

They select a fraction of available grapes to be vinified and aged in oak casks following antique artisan methods. If a vintage isn't up to par, they make wine anyway to keep the barrels from drying out, selling it in bulk later. Select wines go unfiltered into bottles of thick brown glass that protects them from the damaging effect of light during the years until Edoardo decides that they are ready.

I first tasted the Valentini Trebbiano in 1968. The wine from the 1962 vintage showed its age in deep color and a layer of sediment at the base of the bottle. But it was magnificent: rich and ripe yet fresh and vital with the elaborate aromas and flavors that reminded me of a rustic version of a great white Burgundy. More than three decades of tastings have proved instead that this wine is not to be likened to any other from any variety, least of all Trebbiano.

Abruzzo

Grapes
Trebbiano 100%, hand picked between late September and mid-October.

Vineyards
Grapes are selected from 23.5 hectares of vines in separate areas (Castelluccio 4, Camposacro 14, Colle Cavaliere 5.5) in medium-packed calcareous soils on slopes between 300–350 meters of altitude with various exposures in the commune of Loreto Aprutino west of the port of Pescara. The vines, between 4 and 35 years of age, are planted at densities of 1,400–1,600 per hectare and trained in a low trellised *tendone* system.

Vinification and aging
Grapes are crushed with an antique roller device and fermented at cellar temperature in oak casks. Malolactic fermentation may occur naturally in oak casks of 5,000–6,000-liter capacity during aging, the duration of which depends on the vintage. The wine, of about 12.5% alcohol, is bottled without clarification or filtering and cellared for years until the producer considers it ready to drink.

Style and maturity
Valentini Trebbiano d'Abruzzo on release when the producers consider it ready (usually after 4–5 years) shows a lustrous gold-green color (not always perfectly lucid) with uncommon depth and vitality of scents and flavors, recalling flowers, herbs and fruits that range to the exotic.

With age (10 years or more), it achieves a lingering opulence on the palate that is singular among Italian whites.

Serving
🍷 10–12°C.
🍸 Ample, tulip-shaped glass.
🍴 Seafood, especially shellfish *antipasti* and the chowder called *brodetto*; *maccheroni alla chitarra* pasta with eggplant, tomato and chili pepper; chicken, rabbit or veal dishes.

The South

Campania, Puglia, Basilicata, Calabria

The four regions of Italy's southern peninsula take in the sunwashed vineyards that inspired the ancient Greeks to refer to their colonies there as Oenotria, the land of wine. The Greeks brought with them vines still grown today, among them Aglianico, Greco, Malvasia, Falanghina and Gaglioppo.

After a lapse of decades—or, in some places, centuries—as the south became a source of bulk wines for blending, each of the four regions has shown signs of a revival in the premium field. Leading the surge is Naples' region of Campania, where the antique Fiano, Greco and Falanghina make remarkable modern whites and Aglianico stands out in red Taurasi, the first DOCG of Italy's south.

Basilicata's Vulture zone is the other major source of Aglianico. Calabria, the mountainous toe of the Italian boot, is noted for red Cirò from Gaglioppo, though the recently rediscovered Magliocco is equally promising.

A southern giant is Puglia, long noted as a top source of wines for blending. That pattern is changing, with new emphasis on Negroamaro for premium red wines and rosé, as well as on Primitivo, a variety related to California's Zinfandel.

PRODUCERS

Campania 🍷 Feudi di San Gregorio 384, Mastroberardino 388; ♀ D'Ambra 396, Feudi di San Gregorio 398, Mastroberardino 400, Terredora Di Paolo 402, Villa Matilde 404 **Puglia** 🍷 Felline 382, Rosa del Golfo 392, Cosimo Taurino 394 **Basilicata** 🍷 D'Angelo 380, Paternoster 390 **Calabria** 🍷 Librandi 386

Cabernet Sauvignon grapes grown in Calabria

D'Angelo

Canneto
Basilicata Rosso IGT 🍷

Producer
Casa Vinicola
D'Angelo
Via Provinciale 8
85028 Rionero in
Vulture (Potenza)
Tel. 0972 721 517
Fax 0972 723 495

Owners
Donato and Lucio
D'Angelo

Founded
1944

Winemaker
Donato D'Angelo

Vineyard manager
Donato D'Angelo

Production
About 35,000 bottles in
choice years

Vintages
1998 1997 1995 1993
1990 1988 1985

Price
●

Donato D'Angelo, who studied at the Conegliano wine institute in the Veneto before taking charge of his family cellars, earned a reputation at an early age as the most talented winemaker of Basilicata. He brought new scope to Aglianico, a variety introduced nearly three millennia ago by the Greeks and revived three decades ago in a DOC red from a zone named for the volcanic massif of Vulture.

Some experts hailed Aglianico as the noblest variety of Italy's south and predicted a bright future. But Donato, like the few other producers who switched to selling wines in bottle rather than bulk, learned that building markets for Aglianico del Vulture was to be an uphill battle.

The problem was partly distance. Basilicata lies at the heart of the south, though its barren uplands are far from major markets. But the real dilemma was doubts among wine drinkers that southern reds could rival the established nobles of Piedmont, Veneto and Tuscany. Donato knew better, having watched tankers of Aglianico part for noted wine houses of the north since he was a youth. But he realized that to make an impression he would have to achieve new standards.

The answer was Canneto, created in 1985 from pure Aglianico selected in the best old vineyards of Rionero and matured in barrels of French oak. Canneto, named for the cane poles set in tripods that support the vines, could have qualified as DOC, but Donato kept it a proprietary wine as proudly independent as the rising stars of Tuscany that came to be known as Super-Tuscans.

Donato and brother Lucio have recently developed an estate where they make an IGT white from Chardonnay, Pinot Bianco and Incrocio Manzoni called Vigna dei Pini. For finesse it can rival renowned whites from Italy's Alpine regions, though again recognition has been slow in coming.

From 12 hectares of vineyards and acquired grapes, the D'Angelos produce about 250,000 bottles a year, including fine Aglianico del Vulture DOC Riserva Vigna Caselle.

Basilicata

Grapes
Aglianico 100%, hand picked in mid-October.

Vineyards
Canneto comes from the San Savino and Le Querce plots covering 5 hectares of medium-textured volcanic soils on slopes facing east and southeast at 450 meters of altitude in the commune of Rionero in the western part of the Aglianico del Vulture zone. The vines, of an average age of 26 years, are planted at a density of 5,000 per hectare and trained low onto cane poles in the form of a tripod, a method called *a capanno*.

Vinification and aging
Grapes are stemmed and soft crushed and the musts fermented for 10–12 days on the skins in stainless steel tanks at 28–30°C. After induced malolactic fermentation, the wine matures for 18–20 months in small barrels of French oak from Allier. Canneto, of about 13% alcohol, is bottled and cellared for at least 8 months before release.

Style and maturity
Canneto on release after about 3 years has deep ruby color that takes on garnet and brick red tones with age. The bouquet is clean and ample with hints of blackberries and vanilla, expanding over time to take on enticingly spicy nuances. On the palate, it shows full body with rich fruit offset by tannins that soften as flavors become warm and smooth with an elegantly long finish. The wine reaches a prime at 6–7 years and retains its class for at least a decade beyond.

Serving
🌡 16–18°C.
🍷 Ample glass (Bordeaux type).
🍽 Lamb roast or grilled or the innards stewed with ham, cheese and wine as *cazmarr*; richly flavored game dishes; aged cheeses such as Caciocavallo and Provolone.

Primitivo di Manduria DOC ▾

Producer
Azienda Agricola Felline
Via Santo Stasi Primo
Contrada Acuti
74024 Manduria
(Taranto)
Tel. 099 9711 660
Fax 099 9734 471
accademia@accademiadei
racemi.it

Owner
Perrucci family

Founded
1996

Winemaker
Roberto Cipresso

Vineyard manager
Salvatore Mero

Production
About 130,000 bottles a
year

Vintages
1999 1998 1997 1996

Price
●

It is no longer news that Puglia's Primitivo is related to California's Zinfandel. Yet, until very recently, most of the wine from that early ripening variety grown on the hot Salento peninsula was destined for blending vats of the north. The little Primitivo di Manduria DOC that did find its way into bottle packed the berry-like wallop that typifies Zinfandel, but it lacked the finesse of its California cousins. Primitive Port, as somebody put it.

Then, in 1996, the Perrucci family, whose Pervini cellars export large volumes of bulk wines, linked up with Roberto Cipresso, a spirited winemaker from the Veneto, to experiment with Primitivo from the vineyards of Felline. Cipresso even brought in barrels of North American oak in a successful effort to tame the Herculean Primitivo into a red of polish and poise. Wines from the 1997 and 1998 vintages have shown surprisingly well against noted California Zinfandels in blind tastings.

Felline's success inspired other wineries of Puglia to join the revival of Primitivo within a consortium known as Accademia de Racemi. The parent firm of Pervini came up with a series of single-vineyard Primitivo from growers in the zone. Other admirable efforts have been registered by Sinfarosa, Castel del Salve, Casale Bevagna and Masseria Pepe. Sinfarosa's Primitivo is actually called "Zinfandel" (though that term can't appear on bottles exported to the United States, where Californians have exclusive rights to the name).

From 33 hectares of vineyards, Felline makes about 250,000 bottles of wine a year. From 1977, Cipresso blended Primitivo with Montepulciano and small amounts of Cabernet and Merlot to create Vigna del Feudo, which has won glowing praise from critics. Also notable is a fine Salento Rosso IGT called Alberello.

Puglia

Grapes
Primitivo 100%, hand picked in early September.

Vineyards
Grapes are selected from plots of 15.5 hectares in stony red soils layered over calcareous rock on sloping plains at 85–90 meters of altitude at Bagnolo Vecchio in the commune of Manduria in the west central part of the Salento peninsula near the Gulf of Taranto. Vines ranging in age from 45–50 years are planted at a density of 5,000 per hectare and cultivated in the low, spur-trained *alberello*.

Vinification and aging
Most grapes are soft crushed but 25% are left whole for the first phase of fermentation in rotovinification tanks at no more than 32°C for 4–5 days on the skins. Alcoholic fermentation, continued in stainless steel tanks at a maximum of 24°C, is completed in small barrels of French and American oak, where malolactic fermentation follows naturally. After maturing for 9–12 months in barrels, the wine, of about 14% alcohol, is bottled and cellared for a time before release.

Style and maturity
Primitivo di Manduria has a deep purple color when young, tending toward ruby with age. The bouquet is redolent of berry-like fruit and cherries with what seems to be a whiff of eucalyptus. On the palate, it is rich and concentrated with soft, fairly sweet fruit sensations nicely balanced against wood tannins. The wine is ready to drink in 2 or 3 years, though it should hold for a decade, becoming smoother and longer in aftertaste.

Serving
🍷 15–16°C, preferably decanted.
🍷 Ample glass (Burgundy type).
🍽 Spicy pastas, such as shell-shaped *cavatieddi* with rocket and *orecchiette* with turnip greens, as well as chickpea soup, roast and grilled meats and game.

Feudi di San Gregorio

Taurasi DOCG 🍷

Producer
Feudi di San Gregorio
Aziende Agricole
Località Cerza Grossa
83050 Sorbo Serpico
(Avellino)
Tel. 0825 986 611
Fax 0825 986 230
feudi@feudi.it
www.feudi.com

Owners
Capaldo and Ercolino families

Founded
1986

Winemakers
Mario Ercolino and Riccardo Cotarella

Vineyard consultant
Attilio Scienza

Production
About 80,000 bottles a year

Vintages
2000 1999 1998 1997 1996 1995 1994 1991

Price
●●

Just a decade ago, in *The Wine Atlas of Italy*, I complained that achievements in Campania were so rare that commendable winemakers could be counted on one's fingers, scorning the field as "exasperatingly inert." I have since been forced to eat those words as the roll of commendable winemakers has grown beyond a couple of dozen.

Leading the field of newcomers is Feudi di San Gregorio, an extensive estate owned by the Capaldo and Ercolino families, whose enlightened approach to wine exemplifies the new enterprise in Campania. The winery, at Sorbo Serpico in the hills near Avellino, relies entirely on native grapes to produce what is without doubt one of the most impressive ranges of estate wines in Italy today.

The Capaldo and Ercolino families share credit for success with viticulturist Attilio Scienza and consulting enologist Riccardo Cotarella. With each vintage Feudi di San Gregorio gathers more praise and prizes for wines noted for weight, depth, polish and extraordinary concentration of fruit.

The fruit factor has given a new perspective to Taurasi, the aristocratic red from Aglianico that became the first DOCG of Italy's south. Traditional Taurasi required long aging in casks to reduce the tannic charge of Aglianico, though, as some lamented, the tough textures often outlasted the fruit. The Feudi team found that Taurasi when matured entirely in small, new oak barrels remains softer and rounder while retaining vital elements of color, aroma and fruit.

The estate's main Taurasi comes from two plots, though there is also a single-vineyard Piano di Montevergine of comparable class. Total production of about a million bottles of wine a year comes from 200 hectares of vines. Principal types are the superb IGT red Serpico (from Aglianico and Merlot) and an array of prize-winning whites: DOC Fiano di Avellino, described on page 398 (also the single-vineyard Pietracalda) and Greco di Tufo (also Cutizzi) and the IGT Campanaro (a sumptuous blend of Fiano and Greco).

Campania

Grapes
Aglianico 100%, hand picked in mid- to late October.

Vineyards
Grapes are selected from plots of 14.7 and 6.9 hectares in loose, fertile volcanic ash and stone soils on slopes facing south at 400–500 meters of altitude in the communes of Taurasi and Pietradefusi in the Irpinia hills northeast of Avellino. The vines, 11–13 years of age, are planted at a density of 5,000 per hectare and trained in the Guyot cordon method.

Vinification and aging
Grapes are stemmed and soft crushed and the musts fermented at 25–26°C for 24 days on the skins, partly in oak barrels and partly in stainless steel tanks. After malolactic fermentation, the wine, of about 13% alcohol, matures for 18 months in small, new oak barrels before being bottled and cellared for another 18 months until release.

Style and maturity
Taurasi has a rich ruby color with cherry-red tones on the rim. The bouquet is intense and ample with suggestions of ripe plums and berries and underlying hints of spices and vanilla. On the palate, it is rich and concentrated with good balance between fruit, acids and tannins and deep, long flavors that recall plums, black cherries and licorice. The wine approaches prime drinking after about 5 years and has the qualities to retain style for another decade or more.

Serving
- 18°C, preferably decanted several hours earlier.
- Ample *ballon* (Burgundy type).
- Roast and grilled lamb and beef; spit-roasted game birds; aged cheeses, such as Pecorino, Caciocavallo and Provolone from Campania.

Magno Megonio
Rosso Val di Neto IGT ❢

Producer
Casa Vinicola
Librandi
Strada Statale 106
Contrada San Gennaro
88811 Cirò Marina
(Crotone)
Tel. 0962 315 18
Fax 0962 370 542
librandi@librandi.it
www.librandi.it

Owners
Antonio Cataldo and
Nicodemo Librandi

Founded
1955

Winemaker
Donato Lanati

Vineyard managers
Antonio and Nicodemo
Librandi with Attilio
Scienza

Production
About 5,000 bottles
in choice years

Vintages
1999 1998 1995

Price
●●

Librandi, the extensive estate of brothers Antonio Cataldo and Nicodemo Librandi, has taken a commanding lead in Calabria with wines of class and character made in quantity and sold at irresistible prices.

The house specialty has always been Cirò, the classic red from the Gaglioppo variety grown in the area between the ancient cities of Sybaris and Kroton since Calabria was a garden of the Greeks. Librandi's Duca San Felice Riserva is an exemplary Cirò, occasionally rivaled by the single-vineyard Ronco dei Quattro Venti from Fattoria San Francesco.

Yet, Nicodemo Librandi will admit that Gaglioppo has its limitations and that Cirò could be a better wine if blended. To prove the point, former winemaker Severino Garofano created an alternative called Gravello (Gaglioppo with 40 percent Cabernet Sauvignon) that from 1988 on has been one of the most praised reds of Italy's south. Yet, as Nicodemo puts it, "We aren't going to bank our future on Cabernet." The answer, instead, might lie in another antique native vine, Magliocco.

Librandi's first wine from the variety was made in 1995, a red of such magnitude that they decided to bottle it only in magnums and to name it after Magno Megonio, the Roman centurion who left the first written document of viticulture in Calabria in the first century AD. Though only 2,000 magnums were made, more Magno Megonio will become available in regular bottles as the brothers continue their ambitious program of expansion under vineyard consultant Attilio Scienza and new winemaker Donato Lanati.

From 230 hectares of vines, Librandi produces about 2 million bottles a year, primarily Cirò DOC, which also applies to tasty rosé and white versions. They also make fine IGT white Critone (from Chardonnay with 10 percent Sauvignon), pink Terre Lontane (Gaglioppo with Cabernet) and sweet Le Passule (from Mantonico).

Calabria

Grapes
Magliocco 100%, hand picked when very ripe in early October.

Vineyard
A plot of 5 hectares in clay soils of the Neto river valley at about 30 meters of altitude on the Rosaneti estate in the Rocca di Neto-Casabona area near Calabria's Ionian coast between Cirò and Crotone. The vines, of an average age of 11 years, are planted at a density of 5,000 per hectare and cultivated in the traditional low *alberello* spur-trained method.

Vinification and aging
Grapes are stemmed and soft crushed and the musts fermented for about 15 days on the skins in 225-liter oak barrels at 28°C. After induced malolactic fermentation, the wine, of about 13.5% alcohol, matures for at least 3 years in small barrels of French oak, followed by 6 months in bottle before release.

Style and maturity
Magno Megonio from the original 1995 vintage showed a deep ruby-violet color and generous bouquet with ripe fruit sensations combined with notes of spice and vanilla. A wine of impressive structure and rich, round fruit sensations, it has a mellow, even sweet quality in smooth flavors gradually developing depth and complexity. Aging potential remains to be seen, but signs point to a decade or more for a wine that seems designed for modern sybarites.

Serving
🌡 18°C, opening the bottle an hour ahead of time.
🍷 Ample *ballon* (Burgundy type).
🍽 Spicy beef, lamb and game; *carne 'ncartarata* (pork cured with salt, peppers and wild fennel stewed with tomato and chicory); sharp southern cheeses.

Mastroberardino

Radici
Taurasi DOCG ▮

Producer
Mastroberardino
Via Manfredi 75/81
83042 Atripalda
(Avellino)
Tel. 0825 614 111
Fax 0825 614 231
mastro@mastro.it
www.mastro.it or
www.mastroberardino.
com

Owners
Antonio
Mastroberardino and
family

Founded
1878

Winemaker
Antonio
Mastroberardino

Vineyard manager
Antonio
Mastroberardino

Production
About 70,000 bottles in
choice years

Vintages
1997 1995 1993 1990
1988

Price
●●

Mastroberardino is a legendary name in Campania, due to the perennial feats of the family that in 1878 began to show that distinguished wines could be made from what are sometimes known as "archaeological vines": Aglianico, Fiano and Greco. Aglianico, whose name derives from *Vitis Hellenica,* in reference to its Greek origins, is the base of Taurasi, the red wine that in 1993 became the first DOCG of Italy's south. That promotion was considered a tribute to winemaker Antonio Mastroberardino, Tonino to his friends.

Taurasi comes from a zone lying to the east and north of the city of Avellino in the hills known in antiquity as the *campi taurasini,* whose abundant vineyards were described by the Roman historian Livy. Admirers of Taurasi will never forget Mastroberardino's Riserva from the 1968 vintage. Nor will they forget the earthquake of 1980 that devastated the family home and cellars.

Tonino and brother Walter responded with customary dignity, building a new winery that became a point of reference for the revival of the wines of Campania over the last two decades. Tonino, who acknowledges that the change influenced his style of winemaking, describes the Taurasi known as Radici as a symbol of the rebirth of his winery. Radici, first produced in 1986 from grapes selected in three different areas of the DOCG zone, is a model of contemporary style.

Since then, Walter and family have founded their own Terredora Di Paolo estate (see page 402), splitting the patrimony of vineyards and leaving Tonino and sons Carlo and Piero in command of the ancestral winery.

From 60 hectares of its own vines and 240 hectares under winery control, Mastroberardino produces about 2 million bottles a year, including Campania's classic whites Fiano d'Avellino (Radici, Vignadora, More Maiorum) and Greco di Tufo (Novaserra, Vignadangelo), along with Vesuvio Lacryma Christi DOC Bianco and Rosso and a range of IGT wines.

Campania

Grapes
Aglianico 100%, hand picked in late October.

Vineyards
Grapes are selected from 3 distinct plots of a total of about 20 hectares in calcareous clay soils at 450–600 meters of altitude in the communes of Montemarano, Lapio and Pietradefusi in the Irpinia hills east and northeast of Avellino. The vines, 11–26 years of age, are planted at a density of 2,500–3,000 per hectare and trained in the Guyot or *spalliera avellinese* cordon methods.

Vinification and aging
Grapes are stemmed and soft crushed and the musts fermented at 28°C for 10 days on the skins in oak barrels, in which malolactic fermentation follows. The wine, of about 13% alcohol, matures for at least 2 years in medium-sized oak barrels and barriques before being bottled and cellared for another year until release.

Style and maturity
Taurasi Radici has fine ruby-garnet color, evolving toward warm brick red with age. The bouquet recalls maraschino cherries, ripe berries, cedar and spices. On the palate it is full and round with soft tannins from a knowing touch of wood and attractive fruit sensations in a long, smooth finish. The wine approaches a prime at 7–10 years, though from great vintages it can maintain qualities for 2 decades or more.

Serving
🍷 18°C, opening bottle beforehand.
🍷 Ample *ballon* (Burgundy type).
🍽 Roast or braised lamb, beef and game birds, such as partridge or pheasant; spicy meat stews; mature cheeses.

Don Anselmo
Riserva del Fondatore
Aglianico del Vulture DOC

Producer
Azienda Vinicola
Paternoster
Via Nazionale 23
85022 Barile (Potenza)
Tel. 0972 770 224
Fax 0972 770 658

Owners
Giuseppe Paternoster
and sons

Founded
1925

Winemaker
Leonardo Palumbo

Vineyard manager
Giuseppe Paternoster

Production
12,000–13,000 bottles
and 400–500 magnums
in choice years

Vintages
1998 1997 1995 1994
1993 1992 1990 1988
1985

Price
● ●

The town of Barile, whose crest depicts a boy with a bunch of grapes and a barrel, traces its history of wine to the Greeks, who apparently introduced the Aglianico vine to the volcanic massif of Vulture. Yet it might be that winemaking began even earlier, when Basilicata was inhabited by the Lyki or Lucani people, who gave the region its alternative name of Lucania. Compelling evidence of Barile's vinous past can be witnessed in the area called the Scescio, where over the ages grottoes were hollowed into tufaceous cliffs as wine cellars.

In this classic setting, it may seem curious that the oldest existing winery was founded in 1925 by Anselmo Paternoster. Don Anselmo, as the venerated *vignaiolo* was known around Barile, has had an Aglianico del Vulture dedicated to him since 1985. Don Anselmo Riserva del Fondatore is rich and concentrated with the decisive fruit and tannic flavors that characterize the finest Aglianico.

Giuseppe Paternoster, who runs the winery with sons Vito, Sergio and Anselmo, points out that grapes come only from small plots of old vines of Barile. But, then, in the original part of the vast Vulture DOC zone, there is little else but small plots of old vines, since most recent planting has been concentrated on the lower, easier slopes to the east around the town of Venosa.

Vineyards of Barile have always shared space with olive and fruit trees on the dusky soils of the steep hillsides, where vines are trained low and supported by cane poles set in tripods in an antique method called *a capanno*. Most of the strong, dark Aglianico is still shipped away to be blended anonymously into wines of other places. But they say that the winemakers of Barile are planning a revival. If so, they have their model in Don Anselmo.

The Paternoster family owns 6.5 hectares of vineyards and manages another 10 hectares to produce 100,000–120,000 bottles a year of Aglianico and Basilicata IGT Bianco di Corte (from Fiano) and sweet Clivus (from Moscato).

Basilicata

Grapes
Aglianico 100%, hand picked between late October and early November.

Vineyards
Three plots—Cerro, Rotondo, Pian di Carro—covering about 3 hectares of medium-textured volcanic soils on slopes facing southeast at 600 meters of altitude in the commune of Barile in the western part of the Aglianico del Vulture zone. The vines, of an average age of 41 years, are planted at a density of 6,000–7,000 per hectare and cultivated in the low, spur-trained *alberello* method.

Vinification and aging
Grapes are stemmed and soft crushed and the musts fermented for 15–20 days on the skins in stainless steel tanks at 25–28°C. After malolactic fermentation, the wine matures for 22 months, half in 600-liter barrels of French oak (Allier) and half in 2,500-liter casks of Slavonian oak. The wine, of about 13% alcohol, is bottled and cellared for at least a year before release.

Style and maturity
Don Anselmo on release 5 years after the harvest has deep ruby-garnet color taking on brick red tones with age. The bouquet is generous, with scents reminiscent of violets, blackberries and spices. On the palate, it shows full body with ripe fruit sensations offset by tannins that soften as flavors become warm and velvety with a long finish. After reaching a prime at 7–8 years, the wine can show style well beyond that time span.

Serving
🌡 18–20°C, decanting an hour earlier.
🍷 Ample glass (Bordeaux type).
🍴 *Cuturieddu* (lamb stewed with vegetables and herbs); chicken braised with tomato, peppers and olives; aged cheese such as Caciocavallo Podolico.

Rosa del Golfo
Rosato del Salento IGT ♟

Producer
Rosa del Golfo
Via Garibaldi 56
73011 Alezio (Lecce)
Tel. 0833 281 045
Fax 0833 281 045

Owners
Lina and Damiano Calò

Founded
1939

Winemaker
Angelo Solci

Vineyard manager
Saverio Gabellone

Production
About 130,000 bottles
a year

Vintages
1999 1998 1997

Price
●

M ino Calò introduced me to Rosa del Golfo in the 1970s, when I still thought that the only pink wine worth knowing was the French Tavel. I quickly became an admirer of the wine and of the genial Mino, who was known around Italy as the prince—or, sometimes, king—of *rosato*.

Mino's grandfather Damiano made wine a century ago at his farm at Alezio on Puglia's Salento peninsula. His son Giuseppe, who moved to Albizzate, near Milan, to sell the family wines in northern Italy, returned to Alezio in 1958 and bought a cellar of his own. Mino arrived on the scene in 1963 and introduced cold fermentation methods to prove that Salento, which was noted for heavy reds from Negroamaro and Malvasia Nera, could use the same varieties for exquisitely fresh and fruity rosé. Yet, as Mino insisted, the wine was not strictly speaking a creature of modern technology, since it employs the ancient system of maceration with the grape skins to render free-run juice in such limited quantity that they refer to it as *lacrima* or teardrop.

They called the wine Rosa del Golfo, after the flower it resembles and the nearby Gulf of Gallipoli. As demand grew, the Giuseppe Calò & Figlio cellars set up a network of growers in the area who agreed to let them supervise production from vines trained in the traditional *alberello* low bush system.

In 1988, Mino decided to call the winery Rosa del Golfo, though at the same time he began to develop a series of complementary wines with Angelo Solci, the enologist whose family owns Milan's foremost wine-shop. The wines, like Rosa del Golfo, qualify as Salento IGT: white Bolina (from Verdeca and Chardonnay) and red Portulano and Scaliere di Rosa del Golfo (both from Negroamaro and Malvasia Nera).

Mino died in 1999, leaving the winery to his wife Lina and son Damiano to carry on the family tradition.

Puglia

Grapes
Negroamaro with 10%
Malvasia Nera Leccese,
hand picked in early
September.

Vineyards
Grapes are selected from
60 hectares of vines
planted in sandy
calcareous clay soils on a
well-ventilated plateau at
50–100 meters of altitude
in the communes of
Alezio, Parabita,
Sannicola and Tuglie in
the southwestern part of
the Salento peninsula
overlooking the Gulf of
Gallipoli. Vines owned
by various growers are
cultivated in the low,
spur trained *alberello*.

Vinification and aging
Grapes are stemmed, very
gently crushed and left
for 24–36 hours in
contact with the skins to
impart components of
color, flavor and aroma
before the free-run must
(20–22% of the total) is
drawn off to be
fermented at 16–18°C
for about 2 weeks in
stainless steel tanks. The
wine, of 12.5–13%
alcohol, is settled in tanks
for 6 months to be lightly
fined and clarified and
released soon after
bottling.

Style and maturity
Rosa del Golfo has brilliant
rose-petal pink color with
coral highlights and scintillating
aromas of fresh fruit, berries
and flowers. It has rich texture
for a rosé with clean, well-
defined fruit sensations that fill
the mouth and linger on the
tongue. Though usually at its
zesty best within 18 months of
the harvest, some vintages
remain fresh and vital for 2 or
3 years beyond.

Serving
🍷 12°C.
🍷 Long-stemmed, tulip-
shaped glass.
🍽 Seafood *antipasti* and
salads; fish soups; roast sea
bass or grouper; poultry
and veal dishes; soft, fresh
cheeses, such as Puglia's
Burrata and Giuncata.

394

Cosimo Taurino

Patriglione
Rosso del Salento
Vino da Tavola ❢

Producer
Azienda Agricola
Taurino Cosimo
Strada Statale 605
73010 Guagnano
(Lecce)
Tel. 0832 706 490
Fax 0832 706 242
taurino@tin.it
www.taurino.it

Owner
Francesco Taurino

Founded
1972

Winemaker
Severino Garofano

Production
About 30,000 bottles in
choice years

Vintages
1995 1994 1993 1990
1985 1982 1981 1979
1975

Price
● ●

I first met Cosimo Taurino years ago at the Vinitaly fair in Verona, where he invited me to try his wines. Most reds of Puglia were better suited for blending than bottling then, so mindful of the many wines to taste from more glamorous regions at the fair, I tried to politely decline. But he insisted, addressing me as *dottore* with a knowing smile and a promise that I'd be pleasantly surprised.

He was right. They packed all the punch that the reds of the hot Salento peninsula are noted for, but Cosimo's heavyweights also showed style. They were named Patriglione and Notarpanaro after vineyards at Guagnano, where his father Francesco had established cellars noted for honest blending wines. But Cosimo, a pharmacist, had entered the business convinced that the reds of Salento could distinguish themselves in bottles.

The challenge was to harness the savage strength of Negroamaro (whose name "black-bitter" tells a lot about it) and tame it into something approaching a blue blood. Cosimo's scholarly winemaker Severino Garofano proved to be up to the task. They let the grapes for Patriglione ripen fully on the vine before harvesting and put the wine through a slow fermentation at low temperature on the skins for up to 50 days. Wood for aging has been modified over the years from large casks to small barrels of French oak.

Patriglione has extraordinary richness and depth, though even with the mellowness of age it tends to show more vigor than finesse. It was once classified as Brindisi DOC, but, like Notarpanaro, it qualifies as Rosso del Salento Vino da Tavola (recently IGT). All the Taurino wines carry extremely reasonable prices, which may explain why they are better known abroad than in Italy.

When Cosimo Taurino died in 1999, he left the winery in the capable hands of his son Francesco. From 140 hectares of vines, the estate produces about 1.5 million bottles a year, including fine DOC Salice Salentino Rosso Riserva and IGT Chardonnay del Salento.

Puglia

PATRIGLIONE
19.93.

ROSSO DEL SALENTO
VINO DA TAVOLA

Grapes
Negroamaro 90% and Malvasia Nera, hand picked when very ripe in early October.

Vineyard
Patriglione, a plot of 15 hectares in medium-textured calcareous clay soils on plains at 60 meters of altitude at Guagnano in the central part of the Salento peninsula about 20 kilometers west of Lecce. Vines, of an average age of 41 years, are planted at a density of 4,000 per hectare and cultivated in the low, spur-trained *alberello*.

Vinification and aging
Grapes are stemmed and soft crushed and the musts fermented at a maximum of 26°C in glass-lined cement tanks, remaining on the skins for about 50 days. After malolactic fermentation, the wine, of about 14% alcohol, matures for 12 months in 225-liter barrels of French oak (Allier and Tronçais) before being bottled and cellared for years before release.

Style and maturity
Patriglione on release about 6 years after the harvest has a deep ruby-purple color, tending toward garnet with greater age. The bouquet is rich and ripe with scents reminiscent of berries, raisins, spices and leather. On the palate, it is full and concentrated with ripe fruit sensations offset by mellow wood tannins and a hint of almond in its long finish. The wine reaches a prime at about a decade but will hold impressively for another.

Serving
- 20°C, after decanting.
- Ample glass (Burgundy type).
- Roast and grilled red meats and game; *gnumerieddi* (skewered lamb innards with pork and cheese grilled over wood coals); aged Canestrato Pugliese cheese.

Tenuta Frassitelli
Epomeo IGT Bianco ♀

Producer
D'Ambra Vini
d'Ischia
Via Mario D'Ambra 16
80070 Panza Forio
d'Ischia (Napoli)
Tel. 081/907210
Fax 081/908190
info@dambravini.com
www.dambravini.com

Owner
Andrea D'Ambra

Founded
1888

Winemaker
Andrea D'Ambra

Vineyard manager
Andrea D'Ambra

Production
About 28,000 bottles a
year

Vintages
1999 1998 1997

Price
● ●

Visitors to Ischia might find it hard to believe that wine represented the main source of income for centuries on an island that has become the popular beach resort of the Gulf of Naples. Ischia's once verdant coastline sprawls with hotels, restaurants, pizzerie, bars, villas and beach structures that have forced vineyards ever higher onto the slopes of the spent volcano of Monte Epomeo.

Francesco D'Ambra, who built a business selling Ischia's wines in Naples, founded a winery of his own on the island in 1888. Today his grandson Andrea is dedicated to making wines of modern appeal while striving to revive the island's heritage of vines. That is not an easy mission, considering that some vineyards are planted as high as 600 meters on slopes so steep that grapes are transported down by monorail.

Challenges are nothing new to the D'Ambra family, who have held out for decades as others abandoned vineyards to take advantage of the growing tourist trade. Andrea's uncle, popularly known as Don Mario, managed to buy back the family's stock in the winery after a partnership with a national group lowered quality to the point that it threatened to ruin the D'Ambra name.

Andrea remains loyal to Ischia's traditional varieties of Biancolella and Forastera for white wines and Per'e Palummo (or Piedirosso) for reds. His favorite is Biancolella, a vine that may have arrived from Corsica, where it was known as Petite Blanche. The high vineyards of Tenuta Frassitelli seem to account for the wine's exquisite fragrance and rich fruit sensations with vibrant acidity. Tenuta Frassitelli, like the other single-vineyard Biancolella of Vigne di Piellero, had been qualified as Epomeo IGT. But with the 2000 vintage Tenuta Frassitelli will be classified as Ischia Biancolella DOC.

D'Ambra owns 5 hectares of vines and controls another 7 hectares, relying on acquisitions to produce about 450,000 bottles of wine a year. These include Ischia DOC Forastera and Per'e Palummo from Tenuta Montecorvo.

Campania

Grapes
Biancolella 100%, hand picked in early October and conveyed downhill by monorail.

Vineyard
A plot known as Pietramartone e Tifeo of 4 hectares in tufaceous soils rich in silica, potassium and sodium on steep slopes facing south-southwest at 500–600 meters of altitude at Tenuta Frassitelli on Monte Epomeo in the commune of Serrara Fontana on the island of Ischia. The vines, of an average age of 21 years, are planted at a density of 6,000 per hectare and trained in the Guyot cordon method.

Vinification and aging
Grapes are stemmed and soft crushed and the musts separated from the skins at cold temperature before fermenting at 20–22°C in stainless steel tanks for 8–12 days. The wine remains in tanks for a time with the lees, which are stirred in a process known as *bâtonnage*. After bottling, the wine, of about 12% alcohol, is cellared for 60 days before release.

Style and maturity
Tenuta Frassitelli when released in the year after the harvest has pale straw color with green-gold highlights and fresh, fruity aromas reminiscent of broom in blossom and bay with a hint of banana underneath. On the palate, it is softly dry and delicately fruity with round, fresh flavors balanced by bracing acidity and a hint of almond on the finish. The wine reaches a prime in about a year, though some prefer it after 3 years when it assumes a mellow complexity.

Serving
- 10–12°C.
- Medium-sized, tulip-shaped glass.
- Seafood *antipasti*; spaghetti with *vongole veraci* (small clams); *cuoccio in acqua pazza* (tub gurnard in a flavored fish stock).

Feudi di San Gregorio

Campanaro
Fiano di Avellino DOC ♀

Producer
Feudi di San Gregorio
Aziende Agricole
Località Cerza Grossa
83050 Sorbo Serpico
(Avellino)
Tel. 0825/986266
Fax 0825/986230
feudi@feudi.it
www.feudi.com

Owners
Capaldo and Ercolino
families

Founded
1986

Winemakers
Mario Ercolino and
Riccardo Cotarella

Vineyard consultant
Attilio Scienza

Production
About 20,000 bottles a
year

Vintages
1999 1998 1996

Price
● ● ●

F eudi di San Gregorio, whose Taurasi I described on page 384, exemplifies the new enterprise in the vineyards of Campania. The owners, the Capaldo and Ercolino families, rely entirely on native grapes to produce one of the most impressive ranges of estate wines in Italy today. Winemaker Mario Ercolino works with viticulturist Attilio Scienza and consulting enologist Riccardo Cotarella to create wines of weight, depth, polish and extraordinary concentration.

The estate's Fiano di Avellino DOC called Campanaro exemplifies the contemporary style of a white wine from a vine that may have been cultivated by Oscan tribes in the hills of Hirpinia as early as the third century BC. The Roman scholar Pliny the Elder called it *uva apiana* in reference to the way its sweet grapes attracted *api* (bees). Apianum, the Latin name for the vine that became known as Fiano in Italian, may still be used on labels.

Grapes for Campanaro are picked very ripe in late October and fermented in new oak barrels on the lees to develop depth and tone and a capacity to mature into a wine of uncommon complexity. The estate's other Fiano di Avellino DOC called Pietracalda can rival it in style, as can the two selections of Greco di Tufo DOC called Cutizzi and Camigliano.

From 80 hectares of vines, the estate produces about a million bottles of wine a year. Reds take in DOCG Taurasi, including Piano di Montevergine Riserva, and IGT Serpico (from Aglianico, Piedirosso and Sangiovese), as well as a stylish white Falanghina IGT. Fiano is also the source of a wine called Privilegio, made from grapes partly infected by "noble rot."

Feudi di San Gregorio was named after Gregory the Great, who was pope in the sixth century when the church owned feudal domains in the hills of Hirpinia. Brothers Enzo and Mario Ercolino run the estate with a respect for nature that they say was inspired by Saint Gregory.

Campania

CAMPANARO®

1998

Grapes
Fiano with about 10% Greco, hand picked when very ripe in late October.

Vineyards
Grapes are selected from 2 plots in the Irpinia hills to the north and east of Avellino: Campanaro in calcareous soils of stony marl and volcanic ash in the commune of Tufo and Valle dei Ruggi in calcareous soils of stony marl and sandstone in the commune of Sorbo Serpico. The vines, 11–13 years of age, are planted on slopes facing southeast at 400–500 meters of altitude at a density of 5,000 per hectare and trained in the Guyot cordon method.

Vinification and aging
Grapes are soft crushed and the free-run musts are chilled to precipitate solid matter before fermenting at 18°C in new oak barrels of 225-liter capacity. Malolactic fermentation occurs during 6 months of maturing on the lees in barrels. After bottling, the wine, of about 13.5% alcohol, is cellared for at least 4 months until release.

Style and maturity
Campanaro on release in the second year after the harvest has bright straw yellow color with golden highlights and deep aroma with scents reminiscent of pineapple, papaya and honey with notes of anise and vanilla. On the palate, it shows full structure and round, smooth texture with concentrated fruit sensations underlined by hints of almonds and spices in a long, smooth finish. The wine reaches a prime in about 3 years and can hold style for at least 3 years beyond.

Serving
🍷 12–14°C.
🍷 Tulip-shaped glass (Chardonnay type).
🍽 Pasta with creamed zucchini flowers and fried basil; rice mold with shellfish sauce; lightly smoked Provola cheese.

Mastroberardino

Vignadangelo
Greco di Tufo DOC ♀

Producer
Azienda Vinicola
Mastroberardino
Via Manfredi 75/81
83042 Atripalda
(Avellino)
Tel. 0825/614111
Fax 0825/614231
mastro@mastro.it
www.mastro.com or
www.mastroberardino.
com

Owners
Antonio
Mastroberardino and
family

Founded
1878

Winemaker
Antonio
Mastroberardino

Vineyard manager
Antonio
Mastroberardino

Production
About 100,000 bottles a
year

Vintages
1999 1997 1996 1993
1990

Price
●

On my first visit to the Mastroberardino family winery in the late 1970s, Antonio (Tonino), the winemaker, had me taste the white Greco di Tufo and Fiano di Avellino matured in casks. He explained that the wines tended to be a little hard and sharp when young and that a few months in wood gave them balance, depth and tone. They were indeed the most dignified whites of Italy's south.

Greco was evidently brought to Italy around 600 BC by Greeks from Thessalonica. Planted in the volcanic soils around the town of Tufo, the vine developed characteristics that set it apart from others of the name. The Mastroberardino family, led by Angelo, the older brother who died in 1978, led the drive to recognize Greco di Tufo as DOC. In 1980, an earthquake devastated their cellars. Tonino and brother Walter built a new winery with the latest in equipment, a twist of fate that influenced a change in winemaking styles. The Mastroberardino brothers, who had led the recovery of what they referred to as "archaeological vines," stepped to the forefront with the new technology that revolutionized the wines of Campania.

Greco di Tufo has become a modern white of vibrantly fresh fruit qualities that make it a delight to drink young, though it has the stuff to maintain style for years. It is made in a regular version and selections known as Novaserra and Vignadangelo (after Angelo).

Since then, Walter and family have founded their own Terredora Di Paolo estate (see page 402). Tonino and sons Carlo and Piero retain the ancestral Mastroberardino winery, whose distinctions include conducting research into the wines of ancient Pompeii.

From 60 hectares of family vines and 240 hectares under winery control, Mastroberardino makes about 2,500,000 bottles a year, including the Taurasi DOCG Radici described on page 388. Equally distinguished are selections of Fiano d'Avellino DOC (Radici, Vignadora, More Maiorum).

Campania

Grapes
Greco di Tufo 100%, hand picked in early October.

Vineyards
Grapes are selected from plots totaling about 15 hectares in calcareous clay soils at about 500 meters of altitude in the communes of Montefusco and Santa Paolina in the northeastern part of the Greco di Tufo DOC zone in the Irpinia hills north of Avellino. The vines, of an average age of 16 years, are planted at a density of 2,500–3,000 per hectare and trained in the Guyot cordon method.

Vinification and aging
Grapes are stemmed and soft crushed and the juice is macerated with the skins at cold temperatures for about 12 hours. After inoculation with selected yeast cultures, the musts ferment at 21°C in stainless steel tanks. Malolactic fermentation is induced in tanks during a 3-month maturation period before bottling of a wine of about 12% alcohol that is released soon after.

Style and maturity
Greco di Tufo Vignadangelo when released a few months after the harvest has bright straw yellow color and vital aromas with scents reminiscent of apricots, pears, apples and ferns. Fresh fruit sensations abound on the palate, offset by zesty acidity and a hint of bitter almond on the finish. The wine reaches a prime at about 2 years, though from top vintages it can maintain qualities for a decade.

Serving
🍶 10°C.
🍷 Tulip-shaped glass (Chardonnay type).
🍽 Mussels in a soup with tomato and hot peppers; spaghetti with small *vongole verace* clams and zucchini; turbot in *acqua pazza* (spicy fish stock).

Terredora
Di Paolo

Terre di Dora
Fiano di Avellino DOC 🍷

Producer
Terredora Di Paolo
Via Serra
83030 Montefusco
(Avellino)
Tel. 0825/968215
Fax 0825/963022

Owners
Walter, Paolo, Lucio and
Daniela Mastroberardino

Founded
1978

Winemakers
Paolo and Lucio
Mastroberardino

Vineyard managers
Paolo and Lucio
Mastroberardino

Production
About 120,000 bottles
a year

Vintages
1999 1998 1997 1996
1995 1994

Price
●

B rothers Antonio and Walter Mastroberardino in 1994 divided the wine dynasty that had reigned supreme in Campania for more than a century. Walter and his wife Dora Di Paolo established a new estate with their children, Paolo, Lucio and Daniela, claiming a major share of the company vineyards and leaving the ancestral winery, founded in 1878, in the hands of Antonio (see pages 388 and 400).

Walter and family, who called their new estate Vignadora, continued to work with the so-called "archaeological vines" (Aglianico, Fiano and Greco) that had made Mastroberardino a legend in Italy's south. But as their wines drew increasing attention, they also created confusion among consumers, because they used the names Vignadora for Fiano di Avellino and Vignadangelo for Greco di Tufo as did the parent firm.

In 1998, Walter and family changed the estate name to Terredora Di Paolo, in honour of Dora, who in 1978 had insisted on buying the winery that would now be considered avant-garde anywhere. The vineyard for Greco became Terre degli Angeli and for Fiano Terre di Dora.

Those sterling contemporary whites from vines that trace their origins to antiquity remain the most acclaimed of Terredora Di Paolo. Walter is still active, though he prefers to remain in the background of an estate whose motto, *Ex cinere resurgo* (I arise from the ashes), refers to the rebirth brought about by Paolo and Lucio, who head winemaking and vineyard operations, and Daniela, who handles administration and public relations.

Terredora boasts the greatest spread of vines for premium wines of Campania, with 120 hectares in 6 prime sites of the Irpinia hills, source of a formidable range of 600,000 bottles a year. These take in single-vineyard Fiano di Avellino Campo Re, Greco di Tufo Loggia delle Serre, Taurasi DOCG Fatica Contadina and Aglianico d'Irpinia IGT Il Principio. A second line of classic wines of Irpinia includes regular Fiano and Greco DOC and the Irpinia IGT Falanghina and a rosé called Rosænovæ.

Campania

Grapes
Fiano 100%, hand picked in early October.

Vineyard
Terre di Dora, a plot of 12 hectares in calcareous clay soils on slopes facing south and southwest at about 400 meters of altitude in the commune of Montefalcione in the Irpinia hills in the northeastern sector of the Fiano di Avellino DOC zone. The vines, of an average age of 16 years, are planted at a density of 2,500 per hectare and trained in the bilateral Guyot cordon method.

Vinification and aging
Grapes are stemmed and gently pressed and the juice macerated with the skins for 12 hours at 6°C, followed by gentle crushing and clarification by static decantation at low temperatures. After inoculation with selected yeast cultures, the musts ferment at 18°C for about 3 weeks in stainless steel tanks. Partial malolactic fermentation occurs in tanks during a 4 month maturation period for a wine of about 12% alcohol that is released about a month after bottling.

Style and maturity
Fiano di Avellino Terre di Dora on release in the spring after the harvest has bright straw yellow color with pale gold highlights and vital aromas with scents reminiscent of blossoms, ripe pears and apples with hints of honey and toasted nuts. Fresh and round on the palate, the mellow fruit sensations are balanced by zesty acidity with a suggestion of grapefruit and hazelnuts in a long, smooth finish. The wine reaches a prime at about 2 years, though from top vintages it can maintain style for a decade.

Serving
🍷 8–10°C.
🍷 Tulip-shaped glass (Chardonnay type).
🍴 Fried zucchini flowers stuffed with ricotta and shrimp; pasta with eggplant, tomato and squid; turbot roasted with potatoes and herbs.

404

Villa Matilde

Vigna Caracci
Falerno del Massico DOC ♀

Producer
Fattoria Villa Matilde
Strada Statale Domitiana
Km 4700
81030 Cellole (Caserta)
Tel. 0823/932088
Fax 0823/932134
info@fattoriavilla
matilde.com
www.fattoriavilla
matilde.com

Owners
Maria Ida and Salvatore
Avallone

Founded
1967

Winemaker
Riccardo Cotarella

Production
About 22,000 bottles in
favorable years

Vintages
1999 1997 1995 1993
1990

Price
● ●

The premier wine of ancient Rome was Falernian, from the hills of Campania overlooking the Tyrrhenian Sea near the fork of the Appian and Domitian Ways. Falernian, recognized as the first Grand Cru of Rome, was renowned for the so-called Opimian vintage of 121 BC, whose wines were admired a century later. Wines known as Falernum or Falerno were produced until the late nineteenth century, when they were prized by the Russian czars and Swedish royal court. Then phylloxera devastated the vineyards.

More than half a century later, Francesco Paolo Avallone, while studying Roman law in Naples, noted that classic texts frequently eulogized Falernian. Aided by scholars, he identified the ancient varieties as Aglianico, Piedirosso and Falanghina and revived them in the vineyards of his Villa Matilde at Cellole in the original Ager Falernum on the edge of the volcanic Massico massif.

When Falerno del Massico became DOC in 1989, Aglianico and Piedirosso were designated for the Rosso and Falanghina for the Bianco. The name Falanghina evidently derives from the Latin Phalernimum, indicating that it made the original wine of Falerno, which was probably white and sweet.

Today, Salvatore and Maria Ida Avallone carry on their father's work at Villa Matilde with similar scholarly passion. Working with noted enologist Riccardo Cotarella, they make DOC Falerno del Massico Rosso and Bianco. The latter comes in an elegantly dry version from the Vigna Caracci, fermented and matured in oak as a sterling modern replica of the venerable Falanghina.

Their Vigna Camarato, a pure Aglianico that doesn't qualify as Falerno DOC, is one of the most esteemed red wines of Italy's south. From 62.5 hectares of vines, Villa Matilde produces about 390,000 bottles a year, including varietal Aglianico, Falanghina and Piedirosso, white Pietre Bianche and rosé Terre Cerase. The ancient Roman Grand Cru of Cæcubum has been revived as Cecubo, a red from Abbuoto, Primitivo, Piedirosso and Coda di Volpe.

Campania

Grapes
Falanghina 100%, hand picked when very ripe in mid-September.

Vineyard
Vigna Caracci, a plot of 3.3 hectares in volcanic soils at 140 meters of altitude on the lower slopes of the spent volcano of Roccamontina at San Castrese in the commune of Sessa Aurunca in the Falerno del Massico DOC zone of northwestern Campania. The vines, of an average age of 26 years, are planted at a density of 5,800 per hectare and trained in the Guyot cordon method.

Vinification and aging
Grapes are soft crushed and the musts are macerated with the skins at low temperature before fermenting at 16–22°C in small barrels of French oak (Allier—a third new annually), where the wine undergoes partial malolactic fermentation during 6–8 months of maturing on the lees. The wine, of about 13.5% alcohol, is settled in stainless steel tanks before being bottled and cellared for at least 6 months until release.

Style and maturity
Vigna Caracci on release in the second year after the harvest has pale straw color with golden highlights and distinctive aromas with scents reminiscent of wild roses, banana, cocoa butter, toasted hazelnuts and vanilla. Full and round in body, it has mellow fruit and nut flavors of depth and complexity with good length on the palate. It reaches a prime in 2–4 years and maintains style for a few years beyond.

Serving
🌡 12°C.
🍷 Tulip-shaped glass (Sauvignon type).
🍽 Lightly smoked Scottish salmon; *crespelle ripiene* (crêpe envelopes with Mozzarella, tomato and Parmigiano stuffing); poached rock lobster.

The Islands

Sardinia, Sicily

The wines of Sardinia and Sicily express the individuality that sets the Mediterranean's two largest islands apart from one another and even more significantly from the regions of mainland Italy.

Historically both islands specialized in strong, often fortified wines that seemed to voice the natural accent of their hot maritime climates. Then came the revolution that modernized cellars and brought in new varieties from abroad for light, dry whites and reds to meet international tastes. Yet each island has retained a wealth of localized vines and traditional ways of winemaking.

Sardinia has elevated Vermentino di Gallura to DOCG status, while maintaining the antique splendor of Vernaccia di Oristano. But perhaps the most inspiring progress has been made with Cannonau and Carignano in red wines for aging.

In Sicily, the grand tradition of Marsala has been revived with a new sense of purpose among producers of that unique wine. The soaringly sweet Malvasia delle Lipari and Moscato di Pantelleria hold their own amid the rise of modern dry whites. Sicily's native Nero d'Avola has gained stature as one of the south's noblest red wine varieties.

PRODUCERS

Sardinia ♟ Argiolas 408, Santadi 412, Sella & Mosca 414, ♟ Argiolas 418, Capichera 420, Contini 422, Cantina Sociale Gallura 428 **Sicily** ♟ Duca di Salaparuta 410, Tasca d'Almerita 416; ♟ Marco De Bartoli 424, Florio 426, Hauner 430, Salvatore Murana 432, Pellegrino 434, Planeta 436, Tasca d'Almerita 438

Vineyards on the Regaleali estate of Tasca d'Almerita in Sicily

Turriga
Vino da Tavola di Sardegna 🍷

Producer
Argiolas
Via Roma 56/58
09040 Serdiana
(Cagliari)
Tel. 070 740 606
Fax 070 743 264
info@argiolas.it
www.cantine-argiolas.it

Owner
Antonio Argiolas

Founded
Early 1930s

Winemakers
Mariano Murru with
Giacomo Tachis

Vineyard manager
Giuseppe Argiolas

Production
About 50,000 bottles a
year

Vintages
1999 1998 1997 1995
1994 1993 1992 1991
1990 1989 1988

Price
● ●

The promise of Sardinia is epitomized in the wines of Argiolas, the name of the family which in the mid-1980s courageously transformed its extensive vineyards in a previously unheralded part of the island into proving grounds for the future. Antonio Argiolas, now in his eighties, and sons Franco and Giuseppe, kept the faith in varieties that were for the most part local classics. Rather than breaking with Sardinia's honorable vinous traditions, they revised them with a flair that has had a positive influence on others.

Their crowning achievement is Turriga, a red based on Cannonau, Sardinia's prime red variety related to the Grenache of France and Garnacha of Spain. Cannonau makes generally potent reds, usually dry though also sweet and fortified (see Anghelu Ruju, page 414). Turriga, which includes token amounts of other local varieties and doesn't qualify as DOC, shows how Cannonau's raw power can be tempered by deft wood aging to become a wine of velvety finesse. Resident winemaker Mariano Murru benefits from the experience of consultant Giacomo Tachis, though the Argiolas family is due most of the credit for a wine created in 1988 that has brought a new sense of style to the island's reds.

Sardinia's northern and eastern hills were long considered to be the promised land of Cannonau, but Argiolas has shown that the southern sector of the island can rival them. The estate has 220 hectares of vines around Serdiana and Siurgus Donigala in rolling hills north of Cagliari. They produce about 1.5 million bottles a year of wines that include the highly rated white *vini da tavola* called Argiolas (from Vermentino and Malvasia) and sweet Angialis (from Nasco and Malvasia), as well as fine DOC Vermentino di Sardegna Costamolino.

Grapes
Cannonau 85%, Carignano 5%, Malvasia Nera 5%, Bovale Sardo 5%, hand picked between mid-September and early October.

Vineyard
Turriga of about 15 hectares in stony calcareous marl on slopes facing northwest at 350 meters of altitude in the commune of Siurgus Donigala in the Turri hills about 40 kilometers north of Cagliari. The vines, of an average age of 26 years, are planted at a density of 6,000 per hectare and trained in part in a low bush *alberello* and in part in the Guyot cordon method.

Vinification and aging
Grapes are stemmed and soft crushed and the musts fermented in stainless steel tanks at 28–30°C for 16–18 days. After malolactic fermentation and stabilization in glass-lined cement tanks, maturation takes place in small barrels of French oak for 18–24 months. The wine, of 12.5% alcohol, is bottled and cellared for a year before release.

Style and maturity
Turriga's natural stature is signaled by dense red color with reflections of ruby on the edges, turning toward garnet with age. The bouquet is redolent of ripe fruit and berries with scents of Mediterranean herbs and wild flowers. The wine of ample dimensions shows depth of flavor even when young (4–5 years), becoming rounder and softer with age as tannins mellow, heightening sensations of fruit and spices. Ultimate aging potential isn't known, since all vintages to date are still impressive.

Serving
🌡 16–18°C.
🍷 Ample crystal glass (Burgundy type).
🍽 *Porceddu* (suckling pig), lamb or kid roasted Sardinian fashion at the open hearth; matured Sardinian Pecorino cheese.

Duca Enrico
Rosso – Vino da Tavola
di Sicilia

Producer
Casa Vinicola Duca di
Salaparuta
Via Nazionale 113
90014 Casteldaccia
(Palermo)
Tel. 091 945 111
Fax 091 953 227
vinicorvo@vinicorvo.it
www.vinicorvo.it

Owner
Ente Siciliano per la
Promozione Industriale

Founded
1824

Chief winemaker
Angelo Paternò

Production
130,000–140,000
bottles a year

Vintages
1999 1998 1997 1996
1995 1993 1990 1989
1988 1987 1986 1985
1984

Price
●●

Sicily's foremost winery was founded in 1824 by Edoardo Alliata di Villafranca, Duca di Salaparuta, who built cellars beside his castle at Casteldaccia east of Palermo and made wines that became the island's pride. His grandson Enrico enhanced the tradition in the first half of the twentieth century, importing equipment and knowhow from France to make dry red and white wines that conquered markets in Italy and abroad under the brand name Corvo (Italian for crow).

Duca Enrico, as he was known, personally ran the cellars until his passing in 1946. After a lapse, the house was acquired in 1961 by a Sicilian holding company that has gradually expanded production to the current rate of 9,200,000 bottles a year. Unlike so many large wineries of the south, Duca di Salaparuta set standards of unerring quality at various levels of price, even though the company owns no vineyards but acquires grapes from choice parts of the island. Since wines don't come exclusively from DOC zones, they qualify as Vino da Tavola di Sicilia.

Long-time chief winemaker Franco Giacosa, a perfectionist from Piedmont, experimented for years with Sicilian and foreign vines before deciding on Nero d'Avola for Duca Enrico from the 1984 vintage. That aristocratic red brought new luster to Duca di Salaparuta, as well as to Nero d'Avola, a Sicilian variety that had been known mainly for lending body, color and strength to blends.

Before his recent departure, Giacosa also introduced Bianca di Valguarnera, an oak-fermented white from Inzolia, a Sicilian alternative to Chardonnay. Noteworthy among the Duca di Salaparuta range are the always reliable Corvo Bianco and Rosso, the refined white Colomba Platino, the smooth red Terre D'Agala and the fortified red called Ala, whose unique flavor comes from aging in barrels of bitter cherry wood.

Sicily

Grapes
Nero d'Avola 100%, hand picked in late September and early October.

Vineyards
Grapes are acquired from vineyards in calcareous clay soils on slopes facing south at 50–150 meters of altitude in the Gela and Pachino areas of southeastern Sicily. The vines, ranging in age from 16–21 years, are planted at a density of 5,000–6,000 per hectare and cultivated in the low, spur-trained *alberello* system.

Vinification and aging
Grapes are stemmed and soft crushed and the musts fermented for 5–10 days on the skins in automated stainless steel vinification tanks at 28–30°C. After induced malolactic fermentation, the wine matures for 2 years partly in casks of 5,000–25,000 liter capacity and partly in small barrels of French oak. Duca Enrico, of about 13.5% alcohol, is bottled and cellared for at least a year before release.

Style and maturity
Duca Enrico begins to reveal style after about 5 years as its bright ruby color takes on garnet tones on the rim. The bouquet is intense, with scents reminiscent of berries, spices and nuts. On the palate, rich fruit flavors come forward to balance off soft wood tannins in a wine of full body with depth and complexity increasingly apparent over a span of 10–12 years.

Serving
🌡 16–18°C.
🍷 Ample glass (Bordeaux type).
🍽 Roast or grilled beef and lamb, *farsumagru* (veal braised with pork, eggs, cheese and herbs); Sicilian cheeses, such as Pecorino, Caciocavallo and Provola.

Santadi

Terre Brune
Carignano del Sulcis
Superiore DOC ▯

Producer
Cantina Sociale Santadi
Via Su Pranu 12
09010 Santadi (Cagliari)
Tel. 0781 950 127
Fax 0781 950 012

Owners
A cooperative of growers

Founded
1960

Winemakers
Piero Cella with
Giacomo Tachis

Production
About 6,000 bottles in
choice years

Vintages
1997 1996 1995 1994
1993 1990 1988 1986

Price
● ●

The vines of Sardinia arrived from various lands around the Mediterranean to make the island the most idiosyncratic wine region of Italy. Phoenicians, Carthaginians and Romans introduced varieties that are still grown today, though the majority of Sardinia's vines trace their roots to Spain, whose *conquistadores* arrived in the thirteenth century.

Carignano came from Aragon, where it is known as Cariñena, though it enjoys its greatest popularity in southern France as Carignan. Jancis Robinson, in *Vines, Grapes and Wines,* wrote that Carignan "probably produces more red wine than any other variety in the world," noting that it is extremely productive and makes wines of "low–mid quality."

Carignano proliferated in the arid coastal plains and islands of Sulcis in southwestern Sardinia, where it was long prized as a powerful blending wine. But when bulk wine markets dwindled in the 1980s, growers of the cooperative at Santadi reduced yields and refined cellar techniques to produce Carignano del Sulcis worthy of a DOC. Selections were bottled under the names Tre Torri and Rocca Rubbia Riserva.

With the 1984 vintage, Terre Brune was created by blending Carignano with a bit of the local Bovaleddu matured in small barrels of French oak. Terre Brune, named for the burnished color of the soils of Sulcis, has been further refined by winemaker Piero Cella and consultant Giacomo Tachis to bring Carignano to new heights of style, concentration, longevity and prestige.

The Cantina Sociale Santadi, led by progressive-minded President Antonello Pilloni, groups 250 growers with some 550 hectares of vines to produce about a million bottles a year of wines of admirable quality and reasonable price. Among them are DOC Vermentino di Sardegna Cala Silente and Nuragus di Cagliari Pedraia and the IGT white Villa di Chiesa (Vermentino and Chardonnay) and red Araja (Carignano and Cabernet). Carignano del Sulcis DOC Baie Rosse is made in collaboration with the nearby Cantina Sociale di Calasetta.

Sardinia

Grapes
Carignano 95% with
Bovaleddu, picked in
September.

Vineyards
Grapes are selected from
growers with vines in
prevalently clay soils
mixed with sand on
coastal plains and river
valleys on gradual slopes
at up to 70 meters above
sea level in the so-called
Basso Sulcis area around
the town of Santadi at
the southwestern corner
of Sardinia. The vines,
ranging in age from
26–36 years, are planted
at a density of
4,000–6,000 per hectare
and trained in a low bush
alberello system known
locally as *a sa sardisca*.

Vinification and aging
Grapes are stemmed and
soft crushed and the
musts fermented in
stainless steel tanks at
25–28°C for 12–14 days
on the skins. After
natural malolactic
fermentation, the wine,
of about 13% alcohol, is
matured in small barrels
of French oak (Allier and
Tronçais) for 15–18
months, then bottled and
cellared for 6 months
before release.

TERRE BRUNE®
1995

CARIGNANO DEL SULCIS
DENOMINAZIONE DI ORIGINE CONTROLLATA
SUPERIORE
IMBOTTIGLIATO ALL'ORIGINE DALLA C.S. SANTADI S.C.R.L.
SANTADI · SARDEGNA · ITALIA
750 ML ℮   ITALIA   13% VOL

Style and maturity
Terre Brune on release in the
3rd year after the harvest has
deep ruby color that takes on
garnet tinges with time. The
bouquet is enticingly full with
scents reminiscent of ripe fruit
and berries, spices and cacao.
On the palate, it is well
concentrated with richly
aromatic fruit and spice
sensations and soft, round,
warm flavors braced by wood
tannins. The wine approaches a
prime at 3–4 years after the
harvest, maintaining style for
about a decade.

Serving
🌡 18–20°C, preferably
decanted.
🍷 Ample *ballon* (Burgundy
type).
🍽 Stewed lamb and kid with
Mediterranean herbs; wild
boar braised in red wine;
aged Pecorino Sardo
cheese.

Anghelu Ruju
Vino Liquoroso Tradizionale di
Alghero Riserva ❦

Producer
Tenute Sella & Mosca
Località I Piani
07041 Alghero (Sassari)
Tel. 079/997700
Fax 079/951279
sella-mosca@
algheronet.it
www.sellaemosca.com

Owner
Corporation headed by
Bonomi family

Founded
1899

Chief winemaker
Mario Consorte

Vineyard manager
Stefano Biscaro

Production
About 24,000 bottles in
choice years

Vintages
1995 1991 1987 1979
1977 1975

Price
● ●

Note
Anghelu Ruju
from 1995 on qualifies
as Alghero Liquoroso
Riserva DOC

In 1899, the Sella and Mosca families from Piedmont bought a tract of land north of the Sardinian port of Alghero and began converting the marshy plains into vineyards. As the leading winery in Sardinia for decades, Sella & Mosca is one of Italy's largest estates with 500 hectares of vines for wines that introduced the concept of modern to the ancient island.

The emphasis is on premium dry wines under director Mario Consorte, who has been with the firm since 1961 and is also president of the Association of Italian Enologists. But to my taste the most captivating wine of the range is the opulently sweet Anghelu Ruju, a monument to Sella & Mosca's past.

It was conceived soon after World War I by Erminio Sella, a lover of Port, who planted cuttings of vines brought back from Portugal's Douro. When they proved disappointing, Sella turned to Cannonau, a variety of Spanish origin (Garnacha) that thrived in Sardinia. He dried the grapes in the sun to concentrate sugars and flavors and fortified the wine with alcohol, aging it for years in barrels like Port.

The wine was called Porto Conte, after the Sardinian town of that name. But, in 1936, the Portuguese claimed exclusive right to the terms Porto and Port. So it became Anghelu Ruju after the Stone Age necropolis discovered by accident on the Sella & Mosca estate. Today Anghelu Ruju, with its heady aromas and warm, lingering flavors, is qualified as *liquoroso* (fortified) and is described on the label as a "wine for meditation."

Sella & Mosca produces about 6 million bottles of wine a year, including the highly regarded DOC Alghero Rosso Marchese di Villamarina (Cabernet Sauvignon) and Tanca Farrà Riserva (Cannonau and Cabernet), white Torbato Terre Bianche and Sauvignon Le Arenarie, as well as DOCG Vermentino di Gallura Monte Oro and DOC Cannonau di Sardegna and Vermentino di Sardegna La Cala.

Sardinia

SELLA&MOSCA

ANGHELU RUJU

VINO LIQUOROSO
TRADIZIONALE DELL'ALGHERO
RISERVA
1988

PRODOTTO, INVECCHIATO E MESSO IN BOTTIGLIA DA
TENUTE SELLA & MOSCA S.p.A. - ALGHERO - ITALIA

750 ml e   Y I P I n° 5 - SS   18% vol

Grapes
Cannonau 100%, hand picked in late September and dried in the sun for 15 days on cane mats.

Vineyards
Grapes are meticulously selected from 30 hectares of vines in sandy clay soils of gradually undulating plains at about 40 meters above sea level at I Piani north of Alghero in northwestern Sardinia. Vines, of an average age of 21 years, are planted at a density of 2,600 per hectare and trained in the trellised pergola method.

Vinification and aging
The shriveled grapes are crushed and stemmed and musts fermented for 4–5 days on the skins with frequent pumping over and breaking of the cap. Solid matter is removed and fermentation continues at low temperature for 30–50 days or until natural alcohol reaches 12–13% with 8% residual sugars. Centrifuging, filtering and cooling arrest the fermentation and wine alcohol is added to bring the total to 18%. Aging of 8 years in 7,000-liter oak casks is followed by assemblage in stainless steel tanks before bottling.

Style and maturity
Anghelu Ruju on release after 8 years of wood aging has a violet-ruby color with tinges of crimson on the rim. The bouquet is rich and exotic with scents reminiscent of ripe berries and dried fruit, cinnamon and walnut husks. It is expansive on the palate with richly aromatic fruit and spice sensations, smooth texture and warm, authoritative flavors reminiscent of vintage Port. The wine has the constitution to maintain its attributes for decades.

Serving
🍷 16°C.
🍷 Small to medium tulip-shaped glass (Port type).
🍽 Desserts, especially if based on chocolate; aged cheeses, such as Pecorino Sardo, Gorgonzola and Stilton; after-dinner sipping.

Rosso del Conte
Sicilia IGT ❢

Producer
Conte Tasca
d'Almerita
Viale Regione Siciliana
399
90129 Palermo
Tel. 091 657 4642
Fax 091 657 2673
tascaspa@tin.it

Owner
Tasca d'Almerita family

Founded
1830

Winemakers
Tonino Guzzo and
Giuseppe Cavaleri

Vineyard manager
Giuseppe Tasca
d'Almerita

Production
About 90,000 bottles in
choice years

Vintages
1999 1998 1997 1995
1994 1993 1991 1990

Price
● ●

The summer sun parches Sicily's highlands to a Saharan pallor that accentuates the green of the orderly spread of vines of Regaleali. That name derives from "Rahl Ali" or "Racaliali" (Ali's hamlet), dating to the Middle Ages when Sicily was an adjunct of the Arab world. Vines may have been grown there as long ago as the fourth or fifth century BC, though it wasn't until 1830, when the vast feudal domain was acquired by the Tasca family, that Regaleali became an oasis of viticulture.

The estate's wines won recognition, though Regaleali's rise to the summit began in the late 1950s when Giuseppe Tasca d'Almerita took over. He believed that Sicily's potential for fine wine equaled that of northerly places, with the bonus of Mediterranean sunshine. Another advantage was ample water, thanks to a reservoir built by his father Lucio to irrigate vines during summer droughts.

In the 1960s, Regaleali Rosso and Bianco debuted as exemplary dry, fruity wines from Sicilian grapes. Conte Giuseppe, an authentic connoisseur, began work on a wine based on promising native varieties, Nero d'Avola and Perricone, aged in wood to develop the same sort of depth and complexity as the great reds of the world. To say that he succeeded might create a misconception, for Rosso del Conte has proved to be a wine of splendid individuality.

Giuseppe's son Lucio now runs Regaleali, working with his sons Giuseppe and Alberto and a vineyard-cellar team that continues to raise quality in wines from 350 hectares. Foreign varieties have arrived, notably Cabernet Sauvignon and Chardonnay for wines of exceptional weight and style that have upstaged the natives in critical acclaim and price.

But I continue to identify Regaleali with Rosso del Conte, even if it has undergone revisions of late to acquire rounder, softer flavors and superior weight and balance. It's more worldly now, but the wine, like the late Conte Giuseppe, still speaks from the heart of old Sicily in a way that is both eloquent and down to earth. (See also page 438.)

Sicily

Grapes
Nero d'Avola 90% and Perricone, hand picked in mid-October.

Vineyards
Plots called San Lucio (6.7 hectares), Sant'Anna e Ciminnita (7 hectares) and Case Vecchie (9 hectares) in medium to compact calcareous clay soils on slopes facing south and southeast at 400–600 meters of altitude at Regaleali in the commune of Vallelunga Pratemeno in the highlands of central Sicily. The vines, planted between 1959 and 1976 at an average density of 4,000 per hectare, are cultivated in the spur-trained *alberello* and espalier systems.

Vinification and aging
Grapes are stemmed and soft crushed and the musts fermented for 10 days on the skins in stainless steel tanks at 26–28°C. After malolactic fermentation, the wine of about 14% alcohol matures for 10 months in 350-liter barrels of French oak (Allier and Tronçais) before being bottled and cellared for at least 10 months until release.

ROSSO
DEL CONTE

1997

Style and maturity
Rosso del Conte on release about 2 years after the harvest has deep ruby-violet color, taking on garnet tinges on the rim over time. The bouquet is generous, with scents reminiscent of cherry liqueur, wild herbs, spices and nuts. On the palate, rich cherry and plum flavors underlined by a hint of bitter chocolate are well sustained by wood tannins in a wine of full structure that gains depth and complexity over a span of 10–15 years.

Serving
🍷 18°C, opening the bottle at least an hour earlier.
🍷 Ample *ballon* (Burgundy type).
🍴 Spit-roasted leg of lamb with Mediterranean herbs; Sicilian meatloaf with *caponata* (eggplant stew); aged Caciocavallo cheese.

Producer
Argiolas
Via Roma 56/58
09040 Serdiana
(Cagliari)
Tel. 070/740606
Fax 070/743264
franargi@tin.it

Owner
Antonio Argiolas

Founded
Early 1930s

Winemakers
Mariano Murru with
Giacomo Tachis

Vineyard manager
Giuseppe Argiolas

Production
7,000–8,000 bottles
a year

Vintages
1999 1997 1995 1993

Price
● ●

Argiolas

Angialis
Isola dei Nuraghi IGT ♀

Nasco is one of those enigmatic grape varieties that give the wines of Sardinia their uniqueness and mystique. Since there is no evidence that it arrived with Spaniards (who brought other vines to the island) or with earlier settlers, such as the Romans and Phoenicians, Nasco is considered splendidly indigenous. The variety was noted in the mid-nineteenth century as the source of softly sweet to off-dry wines of inimitable character. But its vines yield modestly, and though it qualifies as a wine under the DOC of Nasco di Cagliari, production has faded on the rolling Campidano plains northwest of the island's capital.

The variety has shown style in the Nasco di Ortueri from Cantina Sociale Samugheo and as a sweet fortified wine made by Sella & Mosca as Monteluce, which qualifies under the DOC of Alghero Passito. The strongest argument for a comeback of Nasco is Angialis, the seductive sweet wine of Argiolas, the family estate that has been revising Sardinian traditions with a flair that has had a positive influence on others.

Antonio Argiolas and sons Franco and Giuseppe courageously transformed their extensive vineyards north of Cagliari into proving grounds for the future with a red wine called Turriga (see page 408). In 1989, they revived Nasco (with a trace of Malvasia di Cagliari) in Angialis, which conveys the warm vigor of Sardinian sunshine into a dessert wine of exquisite harmony. Angialis qualifies under the IGT Isola dei Nuraghi, in reference to the curious stone towers of prehistoric origin found around the island.

Resident winemaker Mariano Murru works with consultant Giacomo Tachis to produce about 1.5 million bottles of wine a year. Reds take in IGT Turriga and Korem (both from blends based on Cannonau) and DOC Cannonau di Sardegna (Costera) and Monica di Sardegna (Perdera). Whites include fine DOC Vermentino di Sardegna (Costamolino) and IGT Argiolas (from Vermentino, Chardonnay and Sauvignon).

Sardinia

Grapes
Nasco 95% and Malvasia di Cagliari, hand picked in October when they start to shrivel on the vine.

Vineyard
Selegas–Vigne Vecchie of about 5 hectares in stony calcareous marl on slopes facing southeast at 250 meters of altitude in the commune of Selegas in the Trexenta area about 40 kilometers north of Cagliari. The vines, of an average age of 21 years, are planted at a density of 5,500 per hectare and trained in part in a low bush *alberello* and in part in the Guyot cordon method.

Vinification and aging
The shriveled grapes are stemmed and soft crushed and the musts macerated for a time with the skins at cold temperatures before fermenting in stainless steel tanks at 18–20°C for 25–30 days. Malolactic fermentation occurs naturally during 15–16 months of maturation in 225 liter barrels of French oak. The wine, of about 13.5% alcohol with 12.5% of residual sugar, is bottled and cellared for 6–8 months before release.

Style and maturity
Angialis on release in the third year after the harvest has bright yellow-gold color with brassy highlights and intense bouquet with scents reminiscent of dried fruit (figs, dates, apricots) and hints of pineapple, mango, vanilla and nutmeg. On the palate it has dense, smooth texture and mouth-filling flavors with concentrated fruit sensations braced by cleansing acidity in a long, velvety finish. At a vital prime after 4–5 years, it has the stuff to remain elegant for years beyond.

Serving
🍷 12–13°C.
🍸 Small tulip-shaped glass.
🍽 Mature Pecorino Sardo cheese; Sardinian sweets and biscuits based on almonds, such as *torta di mandorle*, *amarettus*, *croccante di mandorle* and *papassinus*.

Capichera
Vendemmia Tardiva
Vermentino di Gallura DOCG ♀

Producer
Capichera-Azienda
Agricola Ragnedda
Località Capichera
07021 Arzachena
(Sassari)
Tel. 0789/80654
Fax 0789/80612
capichera@tiscalinet.it

Owner
Ragnedda family

Founded
1980

Winemaker
Fabrizio Ragnedda

Vineyard manager
Fabrizio Ragnedda

Production
About 20,000 bottles
a year

Vintages
1999 1998 1997 1992
1991 1990

Price
● ●

Vermentino has rapidly emerged—or re-emerged—as one of Italy's foremost white wine varieties, supported by mounting evidence of class in Liguria, Tuscany and Sardinia. Origins of the vine are uncertain. Some say it arrived in Sardinia from Spain, others that it came from France via Corsica. Vine historian Mario Fregoni theorizes that it originated in the Middle East and was brought by the ancient Greeks to Liguria.

Whatever the origins, Vermentino seems most thoroughly at home on Sardinia's northern promontory of Gallura, where it attained DOCG status in 1996. Since it tends to make strong, full-bodied wines, producers often harnessed its vigor by picking grapes early to attain a fresh, fruity style to appeal to visitors to the Costa Smeralda and other resorts.

Brothers Fabrizio and Mario Ragnedda bucked that trend at their Tenute di Capichera in 1990, when they began picking very ripe grapes for Vendemmia Tardiva, the first Vermentino di Gallura to be fermented in small oak barrels. That wine has come to be regarded as the giant of the appellation, appropriately enough, since Capichera is known for its prehistoric stone "Tomb of the Giants," called Coddu Vecchju in Sardinian.

The brothers are descendants of the Ragnedda and De Muro families that arrived from Spain and established farms around Arzachena, in hills overlooking the Costa Smeralda. In recent times, as neighbors left to get involved in tourism, the Ragnedda family has expanded vineyards and cellars to make Capichera the leading estate of Gallura. Fabrizio and Mario have been joined by brothers Giorgio and Alberto and sisters Caterina and Giovannella in running the estate.

From 50 hectares of vines, they produce about 200,000 bottles of wine a year, including two other versions of Vermentino di Gallura: Capichera, whose rich, round qualities are enhanced by a light touch of oak, and the lighter, fresher Vigna 'Ngena. A promising red is the Isola dei Nuraghi IGT Assajè from Carignano grapes.

Sardinia

Grapes
Vermentino 100%, harvested by hand in late September or October.

Vineyard
Capichera Coddu Vecchju, a plot of 8 hectares in sandy, stony granite soils on slopes oriented east and west at 120 meters of altitude on the Capichera estate in the commune of Arzachena in Sardinia's northern Gallura promontory. The vines, ranging in age from 17–27 years, are planted at a density of 3,000 per hectare and trained in the espalier system.

Vinification and aging
Grapes are soft crushed and separated from the skins before fermenting for 10–20 days at 20–23°C in 225-liter barrels of French oak (Allier), where malolactic fermentation may occur naturally during 3–4 months of maturation on the lees in barriques (half new, half used once). The wine, of about 14% alcohol, is bottled and cellared for 2–3 months until release.

Style and maturity
Vermentino Capichera Vendemmia Tardiva on release in the year after the harvest has bright straw yellow color with golden highlights and full aromas with scents reminiscent of apricot, mandarin orange, spices and vanilla. Amply structured, it has dry but deep and round fruit flavors that linger on the palate through a long, smooth finish underlined by hints of nuts and toasty oak. The wine reaches a prime in 2 or 3 years, but some vintages can show mellow complexity for up to a decade.

Serving
🍶 12°C.
🍷 Medium to ample, tulip-shaped glass.
🍽 *Burrida* (spicy fish stew); pan-roasted Sardinian rock lobster; *porceddu* (spit-roasted suckling pig).

Contini

Antico Gregori
Vernaccia di Oristano Riserva
DOC

Producer
Azienda Vinicola
Attilio Contini
Via Genova 48/50
09072 Cabras (Oristano)
Tel. 0783/290806
Fax 0783/290182
vinicontini@tiscalinet.it
www.tiscalinet.it/contini

Owners
Contini family

Founded
1898

Winemaker
Antonio Contini

Vineyard manager
Antonio Contini

Production
Each selection consists of
about 4,000 half-liter
bottles

Vintages
Blend of top vintages
dating back a century

Price
● ● ●

Sardinia's Vernaccia di Oristano is reputed to have Sherry-like character. Antonio Contini, whose family has produced Vernaccia for over a century, wouldn't deny a connection, since Spaniards introduced winemaking techniques to the island during their long dominion. But, he insists, Vernaccia has distinct personality that accounts for its reputation as the most Sardinian of wines.

The Vernaccia vine seems to have been grown in the arid sand flats of the Tirso river basin near the town of Oristano since the Middle Ages. Though origins are uncertain, it is not related to other Italian varieties of the name. Grapes are picked very ripe to make wine with the sustenance to undergo long aging in barrels of Sardinian oak and chestnut in an environment that feels winter's cold and summer's heat.

Barrels are never full, so a veil of yeast known as flor forms over the wine in a gradual oxidation process similar to that of Sherry. Yet most Vernaccia does not undergo the solera method that is normal in Sherry of fractional blending of young wines with older ones aged in wood for decades.

Contini makes a regular Vernaccia di Oristano DOC aged 5 years in barrels and a Riserva aged for 8–10 years. The first, dry and toasty, is a fine *aperitivo* and makes a superb match with the local fish soup called *burrida* and the dried mullet roe called *bottarga*. The Riserva is opulent enough to go with pastries and desserts.

A special selection of Vernaccia is called Antico Gregori, as the old vineyard terrains are known, in which top vintages are blended and aged using the solera method in small barrels that contain old wines, some dating back a century. Antico Gregori might be compared to a fine Amontillado Sherry, but it deserves to be contemplated on its own as a wine that is splendidly Sardinian.

Contini also produces Sardegna DOC Cannonau and Vermentino, as well as the IGT red Nieddera and white Karmis, a light, dry wine made from Vernaccia grapes.

Sardinia

Grapes
Vernaccia 100%, hand picked when very ripe between late September and mid-October.

Vineyards
Grapes are selected from 20 hectares in Gregori, lean, sandy soils mixed with clay and pebbles on flatlands at about 20 meters of altitude north of the Tirso river in the communes of Cabras, Baratili San Pietro, Zeddiani, Riola, Nurachi and Solarussa near Oristano. Vines, of an average age of 16–21 years, are planted at a density of about 6,000 per hectare and trained in the low bush *alberello* method.

Vinification and aging
Grapes are soft crushed and the musts separated from the skins ferment in stainless steel vats at 20–22°C for about 20 days. The wine is aged in casks of Sardinian oak and chestnut varying in capacity from 600–2,000 liters, though filled to about 80%, leaving a void where a veil of yeast known as flor forms. Antico Gregori, of about 17% alcohol, is a selection of vintages aged for decades by the solera method of blending younger wines with older.

Style and maturity
Antico Gregori, a blend of Vernaccia from top vintages, shows deep amber color with old gold highlights. The bouquet is rich and complex with scents reminiscent of sun-dried apricots, almonds, toasted hazelnuts and rarefied notes suggesting dried rose petals and sandalwood. Flavors are opulent yet smoothly dry and warm with hints of caramel and burnished wood in a long, luxuriant finish. At a prime on release, this wine will hold its tone for decades.

Serving
🍷 16–18°C, opening the bottle 30 minutes earlier.
🍷 Tulip-shaped glass of medium size.
🍽 Sharp cheeses, notably aged Pecorino Sardo; lightly sweet pastries or tarts based on almonds; after-dinner sipping.

Vecchio Samperi
Riserva 30 Anni Solera
Vino Liquoroso ♀

Producer
Marco De Bartoli & C
Contrada Fornara
Samperi 292
91025 Marsala (Trapani)
Tel. 0923/962093
Fax 0923/962910
Marcodebartoli@tin.it

Owner
Marco De Bartoli

Founded
1978

Winemakers
Renato, Sebastiano and
Marco De Bartoli

Vineyard manager
Marco De Bartoli

Production
About 5,000 half-liter
bottles a year

Vintages
Non-vintage wine of
aged blends

Price
● ● ● ●

Marco De Bartoli might be regarded as a living symbol of Marsala and Sicilian wine in general, with his respect for the past and faith in the future burdened by doubts over perennial contradictions.

In the 1970s, he took over Baglio Samperi from his mother Josephine. The estate had grown grapes for Marsala for two centuries, but Marco, with a doctorate in agronomy and an admirable record as race car driver, had no intention of coasting along with an industry in decline. He converted sun-baked farm buildings into cellars where he pursued his personal visions of Marsala, while gracing available spaces with a collection of vintage automobiles.

So deftly did he blend young vintages with old in the perpetual process known as solera that his Vecchio Samperi of 20 and 30 years was recognized as the *ne plus ultra* of Marsala. But Marco pointedly avoided the appellation for his special blends, as he barreled around Italy in revamped sports cars, relying on his gift of the gab and ironic sense of humor to sell wines that were decidedly out of vogue.

The Vecchio Samperi blends could qualify as Marsala Vergine Stravecchio DOC, which may be fortified with wine alcohol. But Marco keeps them truly virgin, even if natural alcohol levels are so high that they must be labeled as *liquoroso* (fortified). From 25 hectares of vines, Marco and sons Renato and Sebastiano make about 100,000 bottles a year, including Marsala Superiore DOC Riserva and sweet Vigna La Miccia and the unclassified sweet Inzolia di Samperi. They also produce Bukkuram, a Moscato di Pantelleria Passito that reinforced the renewed status of that sweet wine.

Marco served for a time as president of the Regional Institute of Wines and Vines, a role which forced him into the uncomfortable position of trying to be conventional and diplomatic. He didn't always succeed and that may explain why dubious legal action was brought against him that blocked part of his production for years until he was recently absolved of the charges.

Grapes
Grillo with Inzolia, hand picked in late September.

Vineyards
Grapes are selected from about 20 hectares of vines in medium-textured sandy calcareous soils on plains a few meters above the level of the nearby sea at Samperi southeast of the city of Marsala at the western tip of Sicily. The vines, of an average age of 16 years, are planted at a density of 7,000 per hectare and trained in the low bush *alberello* and *controspalliera* espalier methods.

Vinification and aging
Grapes are crushed and the musts fermented at 30°C for about 30 days in traditional chestnut casks. The wine remains in casks for about a year before it is introduced into 225-liter oak barrels containing blends of earlier vintages, from which a portion has been transferred to other barrels in the perpetual solera process. Each year about 20% of the blend of old vintages is drawn off and bottled as a wine of 17.5% alcohol.

Style and maturity
Vecchio Samperi Riserva 30 Anni Solera has deep amber color with tarnished gold highlights and extraordinarily elaborate bouquet with scents reminiscent of toasted nuts, raisins, caramel, fine old brandy and burnished wood. Rich and concentrated on the palate, its decidedly dry flavors repeat the sensations on the nose in a wine of great depth and complexity with a long, warmly alcoholic finish. At a prime on release, the wine will remain elegant for many years to come.

Serving
- 🍷 16–18°C.
- ♀ Ample glass.
- 🍴 Sicilian pastries and tarts based on vegetables, fruit or nuts; sharp or ripe cheeses, such as Pecorino Siciliano and Gorgonzola; perfect for after-dinner sipping.

Florio

Vecchioflorio Riserva
Vino Marsala Superiore Riserva
Ambra Semisecco DOC ♀

Producer
Società per Azioni
Vinicola Italiana S.A.V.I.
Florio
Via Vincenzo Florio 1
91025 Marsala (Trapani)
Tel. 0923/781111
Fax 0923/982380
marsala@cantineflorio.it
www.cantineflorio.com

Owner
ILLVA Saronno group

Founded
1833

Chief winemaker
Marco Rabino

Production
About 45,000 bottles
a year

Vintages
1993 1991 1989 1988

Price
● ●

The creation of Marsala is attributed to John Woodhouse, a merchant from Liverpool who settled in the Sicilian port city and in 1773 shipped barrels of the local wine fortified with alcohol to better withstand the voyage to England. His success, including the supplying of Lord Nelson's fleet, inspired an industry that remained largely in English hands until 1833, when Vincenzo Florio built a spacious winery, or *baglio,* facing the port of Marsala.

Florio, who became known as the king of Marsala, lived through the golden era when the wine, aged and blended in barrels to develop luxuriant burnished wood and caramel flavors, was as admired in Victorian England as Sherry, Port and Madeira. Thriving exports brought the number of producers to 45 by the turn of the century. But, after World War I, demand declined and before long concoctions of Marsala flavored with egg, cream, coffee and other syrups appeared on the market. Real Marsala came to be regarded more as a cooking wine than an aperitif or after-dinner drink and its reputation suffered.

In 1986, after decades of slumping fortunes, a new law took effect redefining Marsala DOC in traditional styles, led by the Superiore and Vergine, both with Riserva versions that stand with the finest aged wines of their type. Florio has taken the lead in the revival, with about 3 million bottles of Marsala DOC a year to account for 30 percent of total production, dominating the premium field with the trio of Vecchioflorio (the toasty dry Superiore and Vergine and the exquisitely sweet Riserva). Other types of Marsala produced are Vergine Terre Arse and Baglio Florio and Targa Riserva 1840, along with sweet wine called Morsi di Luce from Zibibbo grapes from the island of Pantelleria.

Società per Azioni Vinicola Italiana Florio, as the company has been called since 1929 when it was bought by Cinzano of Turin, is now owned by the ILLVA Saronno group.

Sicily

Grapes
Grillo and Catarratto, hand picked from mid- to late September.

Vineyards
Grapes are selected from 300 hectares of vines dispersed through coastal plains and low hills at 2–80 meters above sea level in lean, red clay soils between the towns of Birgi and Petrosino and centered in the port of Marsala at the western tip of Sicily. The vines, 36–41 years of age, are planted at a density of 6,000–8,000 per hectare and trained in the low bush *alberello marsalese* method.

Vinification and aging
Grapes are soft crushed and the musts fermented at 16–20°C for 8–10 days in stainless steel vats. The base wine, of about 13% alcohol, is blended following the Florio formula with *mistella* (sweet wine and wine alcohol) and *cotto* (cooked-down must) and aged in oak casks for 36–40 months, followed by a fining period of 32–36 months in barrels of 300-liter capacity. The wine, of 19% alcohol, is bottled and cellared for 2 months before release.

Style and maturity
Vecchioflorio Riserva on release about 8 years after the vintage has an old gold color with amber highlights and refined bouquet with scents reminiscent of toasted nuts, raisins, spices and vanilla. Full and concentrated on the palate, it has rich, warm, softly sweet flavors with hints of caramel, bitter almond and burnished wood in a long, luxuriant finish. At a prime on release, the wine will hold its tone for decades.

Serving
🌡 15–16°C.
🍷 Tall tulip-shaped glass.
🍽 Sicilian sweets, such as *cannoli* (crisp pastry tubes with ricotta-candied fruit filling) and *cassata* (sponge cake with almond paste and candied fruit).

Cantina Sociale Gallura

Producer
Cantina Sociale Gallura
Via Val di Cossu 9
07029 Tempio Pausania
(Sassari)
Tel. 079/631241
Fax 079/671257
www.cantinaga
lluratempio.it

Owner
Cooperative winery

Founded
1956

Chief winemaker
Dino Addis

Vineyard supervisor
Dino Addis

Production
About 120,000 bottles a
year

Vintages
1999 1998 1997 1996

Price
●

Canayli
Vermentino di Gallura Superiore
DOCG ♀

Tempio Pausania is the main town of Gallura, the wooded upland of northern Sardinia noted historically for its mild hill climate, salubrious mineral waters, cork oaks and strong white wine from the Vermentino grape. The Cantina Sociale Gallura, founded at Tempio in 1956, is the most prominent source of Vermentino di Gallura and one of three cooperatives—along with Cantina Sociale Giogantinu at Berchidda and Cantina Sociale Vermentino at Monti— that led the drive to elevate the wine to DOCG in 1996.

Vines may be grown all over the island for Vermentino di Sardegna DOC, whose fruity, fresh qualities have made it increasingly popular with the seaside crowds. But few would argue that Vermentino reaches heights of class and character in Gallura. Dino Addis, director and chief winemaker of the Gallura cooperative, explains that vineyards there are planted on relatively cool rises amid woods that help maintain the humidity that accounts for the zesty acidity and flowery fragrance of Vermentino.

The cooperative groups 160 growers with 325 hectares of vineyards, of which 176 hectares are in Vermentino. So Addis selects to make three distinct types of Vermentino di Gallura DOCG. Mavriana is the lightest and freshest, designed to drink fairly young. Piras is richer with round, smooth qualities that shine over a year or two. Canayli comes from grapes harvested late when rich in sugar and extract to make a white of uncommon fruit concentration and decisive personality, yet with a freshness that makes it a delight to drink young. Canayli is named for a *cussorgia* or hamlet settled in antiquity by shepherds in the Gallura hills.

Total production of about a million bottles a year includes wines classified under the IGT of Colli del Limbara, notably white Balajana, a Vermentino matured in small oak barrels, and two types of Nebbiolo: Karana and the oak-aged Dolmen. Also of excellent value—as are all the wines of this cellar—is the Campos rosé and the sweet Moscato di Tempio DOC *spumante*.

Sardinia

Grapes
Vermentino 100%, hand picked when fully ripe in late September.

Vineyards
Grapes are selected from various plots totaling 73 hectares in lean, gravelly granite and sandy soils on slopes at 250–300 meters of altitude in a valley named for the hamlet of Canayli between the towns of Luras and Calangianus in Sardinia's northern Gallura hills. The vines, of an average age of 16 years, are planted at a density of 3,500–3,800 per hectare and trained in the *controspalliera* variation of the espalier system.

Vinification and aging
Grapes are soft crushed and separated from the skins before fermenting for about 8 days at 22°C in stainless steel tanks. The wine, of 13.5% alcohol, is left on the lees in tanks for a few months without undergoing malolactic fermentation before being bottled and cellared for 4–6 months until release.

Style and maturity
Vermentino di Gallura Canayli on release in the year after the harvest has bright straw yellow color with emerald green highlights and ample aroma with scents reminiscent of freshly squeezed grapes, oranges, magnolia blossoms and green peppers. Well structured and round on the palate, its rich fruit flavors are underlined by zesty acidity in a dry, balanced, smooth finish. The wine reaches a peak in about 2 years but will hold its style longer.

Serving
🍾 10°C.
🍷 Medium tulip-shaped glass.
🍽 *Culingiones* (ravioli) with ricotta-chard filling and tomato sauce; *cassòla*, a piquant fish soup; fresh Pecorino Sardo cheese.

Malvasia delle Lipari Passito DOC ♀

Producer
Carlo Hauner
Azienda Agricola
Via Umberto 1
Località Lingua
98050 Santa Maria
Salina (Messina)
Tel. 090/9843141
Fax 090/9222665

Owners
Carlo Hauner's heirs

Founded
1968

Winemaker
Cesare Ferrari

Vineyard manager
Pierluigi Donna

Production
About 20,000 bottles
and half bottles a year

Vintages
1999 1998 1997 1996
1995 1994 1993 1992
1991 1987

Price
● ● ●

Malvasia was probably brought by the ancient Greeks to Sicily's Aeolian Islands, whose volcanic soils rendered a sweet wine described as the "ambrosia of the gods." Cultivation thrived for millennia on what came to be known as the Lipari isles, though after phylloxera decimated vineyards a century ago, production sadly declined. When Carlo Hauner, a designer and painter from Milan, arrived for a vacation on the isle of Salina in 1963, Malvasia was little more than a local curiosity.

"The wine wasn't very good," Hauner recalled, "but I could sense the potential." Enamored of Salina, he settled there in 1973 and began clearing land overgrown with brush and brambles and planting vineyards. "At first people thought I was another speculator who would turn the land into a tourist development," Hauner once related. "Then, when they realized that I was serious about making wine, I guess they figured I was crazy."

He started out using traditional methods to make a little wine for family and friends. But the Malvasia from some vintages was too good to escape the attention of connoisseurs and critics. In the 1980s he expanded production, building a modern cellar that blended in perfectly with the Mediterranean landscape to make a wine of unique splendor.

Malvasia delle Lipari DOC comes in Naturale and Passito versions. The Naturale shows the inherent elegance of Malvasia, especially in the Riserva made in exceptional years. The Passito, from grapes dried after the harvest on cane mats, has an intensity of color, bouquet and flavor that seems to sum up the essence of the ancient Mediterranean.

After Hauner's death in 1996, his daughter Alda and family have continued to cultivate 18 hectares of vines to make about 60,000 bottles of wine a year, including dry IGT Salina Bianco and Rosso and Agave Bianco and Rosso. The estate also produces the renowned capers of Salina preserved in sea salt.

Sicily

malvasia delle lipari
denominazione di origine controllata
PASSITO 1998

*imbottigliato da:
Hauner Carlo az. agr. s.r.l.
in Salina, Italia*

℮ 750 ml
alc. eff. 12,5% vol

Hauner

Grapes
Malvasia delle Lipari 95% and Corinto Nero, hand picked in late September when they start to shrivel, then placed on cane mats in sheds for 10–15 days to concentrate further.

Vineyards
Grapes are selected in 3 plots—Capo Faro of 8.4 hectares and Malfa of 5.8 hectares in the commune of Malfa and Lingua of 5.8 hectares in the commune of Santa Maria Salina—in soils of volcanic magma rich in potassium and magnesium on slopes at 70–120 meters of altitude on the island of Salina. The vines, of an average age of 16 years, are planted at a density of 4,000 per hectare and trained individually either in the low bush *alberello* or espalier method.

Vinification and aging
The shriveled grapes are soft crushed and the musts cooled to 1°C for a day and fermented for 10–12 days in stainless steel tanks at 13°C before chilling to 3°C to arrest the process. The wine, with about 13% of developed alcohol and 12–14% residual sugar, is kept in refrigerated tanks for at least 6 months before bottling.

Style and maturity
Hauner Malvasia delle Lipari Passito on release about 2 years after the harvest has bright amber color with orange highlights and beguiling bouquet with scents reminiscent of dried apricots, raisins, citrus fruit, spices and Mediterranean herbs. On the palate, it is full and concentrated with rich, warm, softly sweet flavors that suggest dried apricots, orange marmalade and almonds in a smooth, opulent finish. The wine seems to reach a prime of vitality inside 5 years, though it will last longer.

Serving
🍾 8–10°C.
🍷 Medium tulip-shaped glass.
🍽 Sicilian sweets: *crispeddi* (fried rice balls), *mustazzole* (almond biscuits), candied orange peel, watermelon and peach sorbet.

Martingana
Moscato Passito di Pantelleria
DOC ♀

Producer
Azienda Agricola
Salvatore Murana
Contrada Kamma 276
91017 Pantelleria
(Trapani)
Tel. 0923/915231
Fax 03923/915541

Owner
Salvatore Murana

Founded
1984

Winemakers
Salvatore Murana and
Antonio D'Aietti

Vineyard manager
Salvatore Murana

Production
About 8,000 bottles and
half bottles (0.375-liter)
in favorable years.

Vintages
1998 1997 1996 1994
1993 1991 1989 1988

Price
● ● ●

Pantelleria was called the isle of the winds by the Phoenicians, who introduced the Moscato di Alessandria variety, known locally as Zibibbo. Vines then as now were planted on terraces in shallow craters in the volcanic soils to protect them from winds that whip across the sea from the nearby Sahara. Zibibbo was mainly a source of raisins until the nineteenth century, when its plump grapes began to be used for Moscato of unequalled strength and sweetness.

DOC was introduced in 1971 for Moscato di Pantelleria and the more opulent Passito from grapes dried in the sun, but trade in the wine remained largely in the hands of outsiders and the local cooperative. Salvatore Murana was among the first to break the pattern when he founded his own estate in 1984. His early wines were promisingly rustic, but the tireless Salvatore, a warm and witty winemaker who works as a fireman, has steadily polished skills to become the undisputed leader on Pantelleria.

He makes Moscato di Pantelleria from the Mueggen and Turbè vineyards, and two versions of Passito. Khamma comes from a plot near his home and cellars, Martingana from terraces at the sunniest point of the island, where grapes develop exceptionally concentrated sugars. For Martingana, Salvatore picks part of the crop in early August and extends bunches on wood-framed mats to dry in the sun for about three weeks; grapes are rotated to prevent mold. Then the rest of the crop is picked and crushed and united with the sun-dried batch to be aged in barrels and turned into a golden-amber wine of antique Mediterranean splendor.

From 9 hectares of vines and 3 rented, Salvatore makes about 50,000 bottles of wine a year, including IGT Sicilia La Serra, a dry white from Catarratto, and aromatic Gadì from Moscato.

In 1999, Martingana won the Oscar as Italy's best sweet wine from the *Gambero Rosso* guide. Salvatore, who drinks it rather warm, recommends Martingana with chocolate; my preference is at cellar temperature and splendidly alone.

Sicily

Grapes
Zibibbo (Moscato di Alessandria) 100%, hand picked in August in 2 phases, the first batch dried in the sun on mats called *stenditoi* for 20–22 days and the second picked very ripe on the vine.

Vineyards
A plot of about 3 hectares in soils of sandy, gravelly pumice on terraced slopes facing south at 50–150 meters above the sea at Cala Martingana at the southeastern part of the isle of Pantelleria. The vines were planted between 1929 and 1931 at a density of 2,500 per hectare and trained in a low spur-trained method known as *alberello greco*.

Vinification and aging
The partly dried grapes are soft crushed and the musts combined with those from the freshly picked grapes crushed previously. Fermentation at 25°C in stainless steel tanks lasts for 40–50 days until it arrests naturally in a wine of about 15% developed alcohol with up to 14% of residual sugar. The wine matures for 12–18 months in small oak barrels and is settled for 4–6 months in tanks before bottling.

Style and maturity
Moscato Passito di Pantelleria Martingana on release about 3 years after the harvest has dense old gold color with amber highlights. Aromas are deep and elaborate with scents reminiscent of dried and candied fruit, citrus blossoms, spices, vanilla and Mediterranean herbs. On the palate, it is rich and concentrated with sweetness that builds to a voluptuous crescendo without becoming cloying, thanks to fine fruit acid balance and lingering undertones of herbs, vanilla and licorice. At a prime in about 5 years, the wine seems to have the constitution to shine for decades.

Serving
🍷 20–23°C (Murana), 13–16°C (the author).
🥂 Tall tulip-shaped glass.
🍽 Aged cheeses, such as Ragusano, Piacintinu and Pecorino Siciliano; pastries with almonds and figs; after-dinner sipping.

Producer
Carlo Pellegrino
& C.
Via del Fante 39
91025 Marsala (Trapani)
Tel. 0923/719911
Fax 0923/953542
info@carlopellegrino.it
www.carlopellegrino.it

Owners
Pellegrino family heirs

Founded
1880

Winemakers
Enrico Stella and
Gaspare Catalano

Vineyard manager
Vincenzo Corazzina

Production
About 20,000 bottles
annually

Vintages
Non-vintage wine of
aged blends

Price
●

Pellegrino

Marsala Vergine Soleras Secco DOC ♀

After the advent of the English in Marsala, as related in the entry on Vecchioflorio (page 426), production of Sicily's famous fortified wine came into Italian hands. Paolo Pellegrino founded the winery in 1880 that his son Carlo expanded into one of the largest and most reliable producers of Marsala and Sicilian wines in general.

Pellegrino followed the trends through Marsala's historical ups and downs, including production of the so-called *speciali* types flavored with eggs, cream and other sweet concoctions. But lately the firm has been among the leaders of the revival of Marsala with the emphasis once again on dignified reserves realized through long barrel aging and masterful blending. Exemplary are the Marsala Superiore Secco, Oro and Garibaldi Dolce, though the version that best illustrates why the pride of Sicily deserves to stand with the world's great fortified wines is Vergine Soleras.

Marsala producers learned the solera system of fractional blending in Spain in the nineteenth century, though over time the leading houses developed their own versions of the method. Pellegrino follows a "perpetual" process of introducing the new wine, fortified with alcohol, into casks that contain blends of earlier vintages, from which a portion (10–20 percent) has been transferred to another cask. The locally coopered oak casks come in capacities of 5,000, 10,000 and 20,000 liters. They are placed in rows stacked upon one another with the smallest at the top, where the new wine is introduced, and the largest at the bottom, where the finished blend of vintages 10–15 years old is drawn off and bottled as Marsala Vergine Soleras.

Pellegrino has 189 hectares of vineyards and produces about 4 million bottles a year of DOC and IGT wines from various parts of Sicily, including a fine Moscato di Pantelleria. Only rarely is a wine from a great year aged alone to be issued as Marsala Vergine with the vintage, which in modern times have been 1962 and 1980.

Sicily

Grapes
Grillo 50%, Inzolia 30%, Catarratto 20%, hand picked in late September when very ripe and beginning to shrivel on the vine.

Vineyards
Grapes are selected from about 66 hectares of vines in medium-textured clay soils on tapering coastal plains at 8–15 meters above sea level in the commune of Marsala at the western tip of Sicily. The vines, of an average age of 21 years, are planted at a density of 4,500 per hectare and trained in the low bush *alberello marsalese* method.

Vinification and aging
Grapes are soft crushed and the musts fermented at 18–20°C for 10–15 days in stainless steel vats. The new wine is fortified with neutral wine alcohol when it begins the solera or soleras process of fractional blending in oak casks as described on the opposite page. The wine, a blend of aged vintages, contains 19% alcohol when it is bottled and released.

Style and maturity
Pellegrino Marsala Vergine Soleras has deep amber color with old gold highlights and refined bouquet with scents reminiscent of toasted nuts, raisins, spices, vanilla and rarefied hints of dried roses and burnished wood. Full and concentrated on the palate, it combines rich, warm textures and cleanly dry flavors with hints of dried fruit, caramel and bitter almond in a long finish. At a prime on release, the wine will hold its style for decades.

Serving
🍴 15–16°C with food, 10°C as aperitif.
🍷 Tall tulip-shaped glass.
🍴 Pastries and tarts based on vegetables, fruit or nuts; sharp or ripe cheeses, such as Pecorino Siciliano and Gorgonzola; an excellent aperitif.

Producer
Planeta
Contrada Dispensa
Interno 1
92013 Menfi
(Agrigento)
Tel. 091/327965
Fax 091/327965
planeta@tin.it
www.planeta.it

Owner
Planeta family

Founded
1995

Winemaker
Carlo Corino

Vineyard manager
Fabrizio Moltard

Production
About 70,000 bottles in
favorable years

Vintages
1999 1998 1996 1994

Price
● ●

Planeta

Chardonnay
Sicilia IGT ♀

Planeta is a shining example of why Italy's wine establishment is focusing ever greater attention on Sicily these days. The vast estate in the southeastern part of the island has been owned by the Planeta family since the sixteenth century. Diego Planeta presides over the immense Settesoli cooperative at Menfi and has headed Sicily's regional wine board. But he let the younger generation—led by nephew Alessio and daughter Francesca—determine the new directions of a winery that became a leading name in Sicily virtually overnight.

Planting of the 260 hectares of vineyards actually began years before the founding in 1995, which explains why Chardonnay, Cabernet Sauvignon, Merlot and other wines from that vintage emerged to immediate acclaim. More have come to the fore in the meantime, including impressive blends based on native varieties. But the wine that has made the most resounding impact is the gargantuan Chardonnay.

The avowed aim of the Planeta family is to make a Sicilian Chardonnay, though I'm not sure that they've entirely succeeded. The estimable Steven Spurrier, in the British magazine *Decanter,* described it as "a very successful New World style version of an Old World Chardonnay"—the New World link no doubt strengthened by winemaker Carlo Corino, a Piedmontese who spent much time in Australia.

Up to now, I've found the Planeta Chardonnay to be a bit too rich in alcohol and heavy on oak to fully please my palate, but the wine has been praised to the skies by other critics in Italy and abroad. What strikes me is its promise, the great depth and length of flavors that bespeak the generosity of Sicilian sunshine.

Recent production of about 750,000 bottles a year is destined to grow. Cabernet Sauvignon and Merlot are rich and ripe, though two blended reds are more intriguing: Santa Cecilia (Nero d'Avola and Syrah) and La Segreta Rosso (Nero d'Avola and Merlot). Alastro and La Segreta Bianco blend Grecanico and Chardonnay.

Sicily

Grapes

Chardonnay 100%, hand picked in the first half of August.

Vineyards

Two plots—14.5 hectares on slopes facing southwest in the 51-hectare Ulmo vineyard and 7 hectares on slopes facing northeast in the 52-hectare Dispensa vineyard—in stony calcareous soils at about 200 meters of altitude beside Lago Arancio, a reservoir between the towns of Menfi and Sambuca di Sicilia in southwestern Sicily. The vines, planted at Ulmo 17 years ago and at Dispensa 6 years ago at densities of 3,800 and 4,200 per hectare, are trained in the *controspalliera* and Guyot cordon systems.

Vinification and aging

Grapes are soft crushed and the musts macerated with the skins at 7–8°C before being separated and fermented at 20°C for about 15 days in 225-liter barrels of French oak (Allier). Malolactic fermentation occurs during 10 months on the lees in barriques, half new and half used once. The wine, of about 14.5% alcohol, is bottled and cellared for 6 months until release.

Style and maturity

Planeta Chardonnay on release in the second year after the harvest has deep straw yellow color with golden highlights and full aromas with scents reminiscent of pineapple, grapefruit, honey, vanilla and toasty oak. Immensely structured with plush texture, it has warm, concentrated fruit sensations and great depth and length of flavors. At a prime at about 3 years, the wine should have the stuff to hold its own for a decade.

Serving

- 14°C, preferably decanted.
- Ample glass (Montrachet type).
- Pasta *con le sarde* (with sardines, saffron and wild fennel); grilled swordfish steaks; veal scallops cooked with Marsala.

Nozze d'Oro
Bianco Sicilia IGT ♀

Producer
Conte Tasca
d'Almerita
Viale Regione
Siciliana 399
90129 Palermo
Tel. 091/6574642
Fax 091/6572673
info@tascadalmerita.it

Owner
Tasca d'Almerita family

Founded
1830

Winemakers
Tonino Guzzo and
Giuseppe Cavaleri

Vineyard manager
Tommaso Morana

Production
About 100,000 bottles a
year

Vintages
1999 1998 1997 1996
1995 1994 1993

Price
● ●

Nozze d'Oro was conceived in 1985 by Giuseppe Tasca d'Almerita to honor the golden anniversary of his wedding with Franca, to whom the wine was dedicated "with immense love." Conte Giuseppe, as he was known, decided on an original blend of the native Inzolia grape with what was then described as a localized species of Sauvignon grown at his Regaleali estate in the highlands of central Sicily. Enough Nozze d'Oro was made to permit a bit of commerce, proving such a hit that production was increased.

The localized Sauvignon has been verified as an indigenous variety now called Tasca. In some years, its grapes have been attacked by *Botrytis cinerea*, the noble rot that confers a mellifluous savor to a basically dry white, while adding glints of amber-gold to the color. Thanks to the success of Nozze d'Oro, Inzolia has grown in estimation to become a preferred source of Sicilian whites.

Giuseppe's son Lucio has run Regaleali for years, working with his sons Giuseppe and Alberto and a vineyard-cellar team that continues to elevate quality in wines from 350 hectares of high-altitude vines. Foreign varieties have arrived, notably Cabernet Sauvignon and Chardonnay, for wines of exceptional weight and style that have upstaged the natives in critical acclaim.

Chardonnay is the base of Almerita Brut, Italy's finest classic method sparkling wine made south of Lombardy, and is blended with Inzolia in the recently conceived Leone d'Almerita. It was blended with Moscato in Nozze di Diamante, the diamond anniversary sweet wine issued in 1995 to raves from the fortunate few who tasted it. But that was not repeated.

Nozze d'Oro has come to be considered the blond equivalent of Rosso del Conte, whose virtues are described, along with notes on the long history of Regaleali, on page 416. Those wines have an Old World gentility about them with a warmth and generosity that sums up the nature of the late Conte Giuseppe.

Sicily

Grapes
Inzolia and Tasca in equal parts, hand picked in early October.

Vineyards
Plots called Barbabietole (8.4 hectares), Regina (4.5 hectares), Stazione (2.6 hectares) and San Vincenzo (7.2 hectares) in medium to compact calcareous clay soils on slopes oriented toward the south at 450–600 meters of altitude at Regaleali in the commune of Vallelunga Pratemeno in the highlands of central Sicily. The vines, planted between 1972 and 1986 at an average density of 3,500 per hectare, are trained in the Guyot cordon system.

Vinification and aging
Grapes are stemmed and soft crushed and the musts are settled for a few hours before fermenting for 15 days in stainless steel tanks at 16–18°C. Malolactic fermentation is avoided during 6 months of maturing on the lees in tanks. The wine, of about 12.5% alcohol, is bottled and cellared for 8 months until release.

Style and maturity
Nozze d'Oro on release in the second year after the harvest has deep straw yellow color with amber-gold highlights and ample aromas with scents reminiscent of ripe figs and apricots, wild herbs, elderberries and pistachio. Those same sensations carry over to the palate in full, round flavors with a mellowness that conveys the sweetness of fruit ripened in Sicilian sunshine. At a prime in 2 or 3 years, the wine develops notable complexity with a few years of further aging.

Serving
🍷 12°C.
🍸 Tulip-shaped glass (Chardonnay type).
🍴 *Perciatelli* (noodles) with wild greens and ricotta; rice salad with tuna, tomatoes and capers; eggplant *caponata* with baby octopus.

440

Index of selected wines

Index of selected wines by classification

Index of other wines mentioned

Acknowledgements
Photographs of bottles of wine: Filippo Gambarotto and Pietro Grandese.
Photographs on pages 2, 28-29, 128-129, 248-249, 378-379, 406-407: Mick Rock, supplied by Cephas Picture Library.
Illustrations: Trevor Lawrence. Glasses from the Riedel series of specialized wine glasses.